BEAUTIFUL BABIES,
FABULOUS FAMILIES,
WONDERFUL WORLD

This book is dedicated to my three wonderful children, without whom this book would never have happened.

BEAUTIFUL BABIES, FABULOUS FAMILIES, WONDERFUL WORLD

by

Mrs Belinda 'NIM' Barnes

Published by

FORESIGHT

The Association for the Promotion of Pre-Conceptional Care

© 2009 Foresight

Published by
The Association for the Promotion of Pre-Conceptional Care
178 Hawthorn Road,
Bognor Regis,
West Sussex PO21 2UY

www.foresight-preconception.org.uk

Registered Charity No. 279160

ISBN 978-0-9545933-6-0

Production by
Print Rite,
Freeland,
Witney,
Oxon OX29 8HX
for the publishers

Origination and printing by
Artisan Litho,
Kingston Business Park,
Kingston Bagpuize
Oxon OX13 5FB

Typeset by Juliet Loudon

The information provided in this book is intended for general information and guidance only, and this should not be used as a substitute for consulting a qualified health practitioner. Neither the author nor publishers can accept any responsibility for your health or any side-effects of any treatment described in this book.

CONTENTS

INTRODUCTION

by Professor John Dickerson

O ne of my main scientific interests, throughout my academic career, has been in the effects of nutrition on growth and development. Studies in experimental animals, as well as observations and studies in children, have clearly shown that deficiencies or excesses of energy, protein and a variety of minerals and vitamins, can have important effects on these processes. Human beings are very special 'animals', and a successful marriage can depend to a large extent on the partners being able to produce normal, healthy children. The 'National Health Service' cannot provide the support and detailed investigations of both partners which may be necessary to identify and deal with nutritional and other problems which may be the cause of family disappointments and distress.

I count it a great privilege to have known Belinda Barnes, and in a very small way to have been associated with the growth of 'Foresight', which came into being in 1978, to help childless couples. It was designed to help such couples to identify the causes of their problems and to provide the necessary advice and help to deal with them.

This book, written by Belinda Barnes, radiates the knowledge and enthusiasm for her subject which she has accumulated over the years. Her writing style is inimitable and an expression of her own commitment and personality. The book is illustrated throughout with real 'case histories'. It is more than an account or 'biography' of 'Foresight', and can be warmly recommended as a textbook for all those interested or concerned with helping hitherto disappointed couples to realise their ambitions, or longings, to have a family.

Professor John W. T. Dickerson PhD, Hon. D. Sc, R.Nutr.
Emeritus Professor of Human Nutrition
University of Surrey
Guildford
Surrey

FOREWORD

By Dr. Patrick Kingsley, M.B., B.S., M.R.C.S., L.R.C.P., F.A.A.E.M., D.A., D.Obst. R.C.O.G.

My father was in General Practice for about four decades in the middle of last century, and I remember discussing with him the subject of miscarriages at a time when I was studying for an Obstetrics and Gynaecology Post Graduate examination. He had practised in a small town where the GP knew everything about his patients. He was so respected by everyone that he was often consulted about non-medical things such as whether to buy a house or not or whether such and such a job was right for a person. The church was packed to the rafters when we finally said goodbye to him.

He told me that a miscarriage was a rare event in his early practice years, but that it was becoming more common as he was getting closer to retirement. He had always found it hard to console a couple that had suffered a miscarriage, and he had found it so much harder when a woman had her second. He was always aware that the husband often suffered as much as his wife, something that is not always appreciated nowadays.

Not so long ago I heard that a woman is not referred for specialist investigation until she has had her third miscarriage. Just how desperate she would be by then is hard to imagine. The only way I was able to help at the time was to say that perhaps the physical body of the child was not ready for this world but its spirit was, and that it would find its way into the world in due course. Such a thought often helped a bit at a time of great mourning, but I would also say that perhaps her body was not quite in the perfect condition to receive the baby. After all, the onset of a period has been described as the 'weeping of the disappointed womb'. How much more might that be so with a miscarriage?

If miscarriages are becoming more frequent as the facts would suggest they are, and a full term pregnancy must surely be considered to be the normal outcome expected of a pregnancy, what on earth is going on? Why is it happening, for there must be a reason? It would seem that many other medical conditions are becoming more common at the same time. I remember reading an article that was reprinted from a medical journal of sometime around 1900. It described a famous Consultant Physician with a group of medical students and young doctors round the bed of a patient in a hospital ward. The Consultant told them to study the case carefully because it was very rare and such a case was not likely to be seen again. He declared the patient had had a heart attack!

When I was a medical student I knew I had to learn anatomy and physiology but found it a bit boring. My student colleagues and I desperately wanted to be in the hospital wards dealing with sick people — patients. We were sure that was where our talents lay. When we did reach that stage, we were shown how to make a diagnosis and apply the correct treatment, usually a surgical operation or a prescription drug. Basically we were shown how to 'correct' the abnormality. What was rarely ever discussed was why the problem had developed. Nor were we shown how to try to return the abnormality back to the normal. That just wasn't anywhere in our teaching.

Most of my medical practice has been investigating the 'why', by taking a detailed history and asking questions not normally asked, certainly not in the five or seven minutes a GP may be allocated with each patient. Yes it took a long time, but then it was worth it and my patients certainly appreciated my approach. So many of them kept saying that they wanted to know why their condition had developed and were not interested in merely taking a drug to suppress the symptoms, with all the risks of adverse effects that so many drugs have. I found it unnecessary to prescribe drugs although I was aware they were sometimes of value.

This approach of mine was why Nim Barnes asked me to become her first Medical Adviser all those years ago. I had always wanted to specialise in Obstetrics and Gynaecology, and to be involved in guiding prospective parents to achieve a successful pregnancy and a healthy beautiful child was a real honour. I felt that when I delivered a baby I was helping the fruits of other people's labours!

Nim Barnes' Foresight has undoubtedly helped very many parents. I don't think it is ethical to do double-blind studies on such an issue, but you can compare Foresight's results with the rest of the country, in which case they stand out as highly successful, especially when you consider that couples that try a Foresight programme have nearly always already had a sad outcome, so to begin with they are 'worse' than an average group with which a comparison is being made.

The Foresight programme looks at the whole body and tries to identify any problems the mother and the father may have, looking at their life styles in particular. When you read through this wonderful book you will see the approach Nim has worked on. Over the years she has identified what has prevented some women from getting pregnant in the first place or failing to hold on to their pregnancy or not producing a full-term healthy infant. We should all apply that approach in our daily lives to be more healthy.

Nature endowed all animals and man with the ability to reproduce their species. When habitats are destroyed by man's activities, species die out because their environment is no longer conducive to their survival. Television programmes remind us of this all the time. Why should man be any different?

Unfortunately people still go to their doctor and say, "Doctor! I have a problem. Will you fix it for me please!" Anyone who follows the Foresight programme will have to take charge of their life, will have to think what they are doing, think what they are putting into their mouths and consider what they may be doing wrong. By writing this wonderful book, Nim has started this whole process by pointing out what someone can do. All her experience is here for everyone to read. It is a treasure trove of information. It is what I have practised for over thirty years. I know it works because my patients tell me it does.

CHAPTER 1

HOW FORESIGHT CAME INTO BEING, AND WHERE WE HAVE GOT TO!

SO you want to have a baby? It is the most important and happy-making idea you have ever had. You feel you have secretly loved and waited for him all your life. And you can't wait to see him – or her, as the case may be.

Yet..... he doesn't seem to be coming along? Well, hopefully we can help. We usually can. We do a lot of this, and we have done it for nearly 30 years as I write these words.

I adore babies. I can't bear things going wrong with babies. This is why I founded Foresight in the first place. It was not *originally* to help with infertility, it was to try and ensure that *all* babies were born healthy and normal, able to realise their full potential, physically and mentally, and therefore able to have a wonderful, happy and productive life. However, along the way, we discovered that our programme also solved infertility in about 78% of cases.

How Foresight Evolved

Before my marriage, I had been a Nursery Nurse in a Day Nursery for some years, so babies were already a large part of my life. (Those beloved little characters I looked after in the 1950s must be nearing retirement age by now! I hope they have all had really happy lives.)

However, for a whole variety of reasons, my own babies did not have such a good start. This was all around 50 years ago, and we did not have much information available regarding deficiencies, heavy metals, allergies, toxins - whatever. We were pretty clueless about how to set about perfecting things. Consequently, my sons had lots of allergies – coeliac condition, hyperactivity, dyslexia in one; and a tendency to asthma and eczema, if given the wrong foods, in the other. My baby daughter had tumours on the spinal cord. You could get really desperate at these times. It all had to be solved. I read everything that I could lay my hands on.

All *was* thankfully resolved and I will not burden you here with all the traumas along the way. Enough to say that I came out of the experience

1

determined to spend the rest of my life finding out (and spreading around) *what parents needed to know* to prevent disaster from afflicting their beloved babies. Then giving them this information, in time. For this reason I founded Foresight. It has been quite a mental and logistical marathon, but now, *here we are*!

To fill in a bit of the background, we need to leap backwards to the late 1960s, when my youngest started school. I had some time and space and I started on my mission. There had been plenty of straws in the wind, in the intervening years. I find life arrives in a series of "signalling straws" which lead on to the future missions.

Straw number one blew in, in 1973 when I read an article by Roger McDougall, the play-write, in the Friday Telegraph Magazine. He told us how he had overcome his Multiple Sclerosis (MS) by going on a gluten free, milk free diet and taking supplements. My elder son was a coeliac, but in those days the gluten free diet was very little heard of, almost nothing was available ready-made, and the taking of supplements was regarded as strictly for the "cranks".

Nevertheless, this sounded too momentous to be ignored, and I felt I could help. At the time, we were living next door to a Cheshire Home where there were 11 people suffering from MS. I knew the cook there quite well, as I used to go round with superfluous vegetables from our garden. I was/am an enthusiastic but rather disorganised gardener, and we often had gluts of tomatoes, marrows or whatever. The next time I went round, I took the cutting from the Telegraph with me and showed it to John, the cook. He was a diabetic so the fact that modifying the diet could help an illness was not a mystery to him. "I can help with gluten free recipes," I said, "I am used to it."

"We could really help them; I would love to do that." he said.

We went to see the Warden. My first rude awakening to the frequently encountered opposition to health improvement was in his immediate reaction: *"It is all very fine, but what will happen to my wheelchair allowances if they can all get out and walk about?"* We assured him that, *when inspectors were scented*, they would all rush back to their wheelchairs and jump in!

We were allowed, for a while, to help them. All bar one patient made huge improvements. Three, who had homes to go to, went home. Then the policy was reversed, as "it was not scientifically proven", and patients relapsed.

Meanwhile, my friend Gilly Gibbons and I copied out four pages of diet and recipes (on a very old Gestetner printer which showered us with purple ink), and sent them round to all the other Cheshire Homes. One, to our knowledge, took it up and had great success. Eventually, the local neurologist took up the idea, as did several private physicians, and I believe now the regime is used with a great many MS patients.

However, it took years of delay for "research", to emerge – sadly too late for many. All this made us realise the tragedies that stemmed from the problems of the huge, financially involved and hierarchical nature of the health care machine. It was a structure not well suited to the sensitive, individual and immediate needs of people with health problems. It was inhibited by possessiveness and power structures, statutes and pecking orders. These could produce total intellectual constipation. This was 30 years ago. Slowly, things have advanced.

I am telling you all of this, so you may better understand all the complications of founding an organisation for achieving perfect health in preparation for a perfect pregnancy! Nowadays, this is almost always possible, but your babies still have to rely on *your* individual effort, willingness and free thinking, so that you may achieve it.

Times have moved on quite a lot since then, and things are getting easier. There are now wonderful people all over the country who have become involved in many different aspects of natural health care. This has brought forth Colleges of Nutrition, Osteopathy, Homeopathy, Reflexology, Acupuncture, Naturopathy etc. From these, every year in June, there emerges a whole new army of people, mostly women, very well informed on all aspects of natural health enhancement.

Back to our narrative: Straw number 2 blew by because I was also lucky enough to have moved close to the sister and the wife of Professor Humphrey Osmond. Humphrey, at that time, was pioneering nutritional approaches to mental illness. Initially he worked in Canada with Dr Abe Hoffer, and later in Alabama. At that time he was mainly giving Vitamins B6, B3, and Vitamin C. His sister, Dorothy, still one of my greatest friends, told me about this. She felt it would help regarding my elder, hyperactive, dyslexic, coeliac son. She was right. The difference it made to him was life-changing for the whole family. It opened all our eyes to the interdependence of nutrients and brain function. (More anon.)

Straw number 3 came along when I met the irreplaceable Father Dunstan of Barrow Hills in Witley, a Roman Catholic priest who was trying to help priests suffering from alcoholism. A great character, highly intelligent, compassionate and with a great sense of humour, he was anxious to try anything new that would help. I was able to introduce him to Humphrey Osmond and Abe Hoffer, and their work with nutritional support for mental illness and addictions. Dunstan started giving vitamins and minerals as well as emotional support to the priests, and found it made the world of difference. Later, he went on to establish WACA, the Westminster Advisory Centre on Alcoholism, which flourishes today, although sadly Father Dunstan has passed on.

Straw number 4 landed when Jane, Humphrey's wife, and I went up to Surrey University to talk to Professor Parke about Humphrey's work. In the course of the meeting he said to us, *"Never underestimate your own power.*

Never give up. If you write one letter a day for a year, if one person in 100 is interested, by the end of the year you will have 3 or even 4 people on your side. Take it from there." He also introduced us to Professor John Dickerson, Professor of Human Nutrition, who was a wonderful support and ally. He became our first advisor and encourager when the Foresight organisation was formed, and, although now retired is still a source of knowledge and encouragement. At this time he gave me access to the wonderful library of Surrey University. I remember the light pouring in down the stairs when I first walked up them, and praying so hard I would find what I needed to help the babies. Down the years, what I read there has been endlessly useful.

Straw number 5 was when Humphrey Osmond suggested the "Journal of Orthomolecular Psychiatry". From these pages I found another great friend and guiding light, the paediatrician Dr Elizabeth Lodge-Rees of California. She had written an article on allergy, coeliac condition and hyperactivity which rang so many bells with me, I asked her over to stay with us for a holiday in England. To my joy, she said "Yes! Never been to England. Sounds like fun!" A few weeks later I was picking her up at Heathrow!

She brought a whole bale of further straws! She was pioneering nutrition and allergy work with hyperactive children. Her hand luggage was so heavy with books, she claimed her arms had grown as long as an orang-utan carrying them for us! Poor Beth, but it was worth it!

Some years prior to this in the UK, Vicky Colquhourn and Sally Bunday had formed the *"Hyperactive Children's Support Group"*. Gwyneth Hemmings had formed *"The Schizophrenia Association of Great Britain"* and Margery Hall had founded *"Sanity"*. Dr Jean Munro, later a household name for her work with allergic illness, was part of this scene, and all were pressing ahead with finding out more about the deleterious effects of food additives, lead, chemical pollutants and allergenic foods on brain function. That most manifestations of mental aberration are biochemical in origin is now generally accepted in the 2000s, but this was rejected by the establishment in those days. It was a long search to find doctors who were interested. If these findings had been examined/accepted at that time by the establishment, millions of families could have been happier and years of acute personal suffering by the children and parents could have been avoided.

Those who were lucky enough to come across a doctor who understood nutrition and allergy pulled through.

I belonged to all these organisations and we had superb help from a small cohort of doctors who were pioneering the work and were sympathetic to our aims, and generous with their time and knowledge. We are forever in their debt. At the outset as well as Dr Jean Munro, we knew particularly well Dr Patrick Kingsley, Dr Damien Downing, Dr Pam Tatham, Dr Stephen Davies, Dr Alan Stewart, Dr Lambert Mount, Dr David Owen, and Dr Mark Payne.

There was also the superb Latto family –four enormously enlightened Doctors who were part of the core who created the resurgence of Sir Robert McCarrison's work in the "McCarrison Society".

Sir Robert was an army doctor in India at the beginning of the last century. He noticed how in certain areas in India there were diseases peculiar to that area. In other areas there were different diseases, or much less disease. He was intelligent enough to link the bodily breakdowns to the paucities in the diets eaten in the different locations. This led him to study, with the analytical methods available to him at that time, what vitamins and minerals were present in which foods, and exactly what they did for the people who ate them. His book is a mine of glorious information and often comes up for sale on eBay! Alternatively, you can read much of his work on the website, www.mccarrisonsociety.org.uk. It is as relevant today as it was in his own time. Well worth reading.

Back in the 1970s we knew **Dr Damien Downing** who now runs the York Laboratories and has been a leading light in the allergy field. Dr Patrick Kingsley from Leicestershire was wonderful to us, and also understood and did significant work in the whole area of allergic illness.

At an early stage in the existence of Foresight, Dr Kingsley and I went to see them at the "Department of Health". We hoped to interest them in the idea of Preconceptual Care. We sat in a small, windowless, dark brown room, where representatives of the DoH sat and drank coffee and ate sugar coated biscuits..... I had sent them our then current booklet "Guidelines for Future Parents" ahead of the visit. A representative of the DoH, who could not have weighed less than 20 stone, waved it at us angrily and said, *"This strikes me as a very elitist little book"*. *"No, indeed,"* I said. *"Foresight is for everybody. I just want to help all babies to be born normal and well."*

"Well, why do you mention quail's eggs?" she said. I was mystified. *"Quail's eggs are very cheap,"* I assured her. In those days they were 1½ pence each! *"Never mind that,"* she said, *"****our**** sort of people don't eat quails' eggs. They wouldn't know how to cook them."* *"You just boil them for 1½ minutes. It couldn't be easier, I promise you."* I replied. *"It's written on the box".*

"Nevertheless," she continued, *"This sort of thing will just make the difference between ****your**** sort of children and ****ours**** all the greater."* I felt totally non-plussed.

"Madam," said Dr Kingsley, *"You surely cannot be suggesting that all the children in the country should be kept disadvantaged simply to lessen social divisions? Surely this objective would be far better served by a strategy to improve the health and ability of one and all?"*

The other side of the table swigged their sugared coffee, munched on their biscuits and despite all we put before them, remained un-persuaded of any advantages in the health improvement of prospective parents. 30 years on there have not been any huge advances! (But fortunately the recent financial aspects are now inducing a few stray sparks of interest in beneficial policies. And so is Jamie Oliver, God bless him!)

However, this encounter convinced Dr Kingsley and myself that we needed to do a major research project to demonstrate the effectiveness of normalising mineral status and optimising health prior to pregnancy.

It only took three months for them to decide they wanted to start a family. So when Lisa miscarried early on in the pregnancy they were devastated. Changes in lifestyle were made and they tried again six months later. Nothing. One year later, a laparoscopy revealed that Lisa had a blocked Fallopian tube but was assured that this was not a problem, so they carried on trying, unsuccessfully, for a baby for another year.

Thumbing through a magazine, Lisa read that Nutrition can play a big part in fertility. She found a Nutritional Therapist that just happened to be a Foresight Practitioner. Lisa also took reflexology sessions before trying for conception and throughout the pregnancy.

Both went onto the Foresight programme; what little alcohol they drank was stopped. They ate organic foods, used a water filter and took all their supplements. It took a year to get his very high lead and copper levels down, and Lisa's age was against her. As soon as their levels were optimised, it was decided that it was now or never and "bingo"! Lisa became pregnant at their first attempt.

Their Foresight baby daughter was born after a lengthy labour weighing 6lbs 3oz. Six months later they decided that their daughter needed a sibling. Straight back onto the Foresight programme in preparation for conception. Four months later, Lisa was ready once again and conceived straight away. Foresight Baby Daughter no. 2 was safely delivered after a short labour weighing 7lbs 3oz.

"I had very healthy pregnancies. The girls are very bright, so aware of their surroundings and so astute! Having been told that there was "no reason" for infertility, we felt left in the dark and really crest-fallen. Foresight was fantastic in being proactive. They were a real boost, and we felt that we were once again doing something. 'Thumbs-up' to Foresight and we recommend Foresight to everybody. It's a fantastic thing to do, any child deserves such a good start."

We were ruminating about this when another bale of straw rolled by! To help repay Surrey University for their kindness, I volunteered to collect a huge parcel of frozen placentas from St George's, Tooting, and bring them down to the University as they needed them for a Study. Suffice to say that by the time we arrived at the University forecourt, the parcel had fallen apart... it was a hot day... *don't even think about it*! 'Security' found me freaking out in Reception.

Dr Neil Ward arrived to my rescue with a small army of quite saintly young students who produced gratitude, commiseration, disinfectant, soapy water and determined elbow grease in equal amounts, and in due course my car was driveable again. This resulted in a long and cheerful association with Surrey University which gave us the excellent study, which is reproduced on our website, and in Appendix 6.

As you will see for yourselves, this research makes it quite clear how relevant mineral metabolism is to fertility, reproductive health and indeed health generally.

To return to our narrative:

This is just a *tiny fraction* of the luck, generosity and help I had on the way through to founding and developing Foresight. I could in fact, write an entire book on this alone, but that is *not* what you bought this book *for*, so we must pass on to our main theme without further ado!

We all need to pioneer our own way through to normal fertility, and birth of normal, healthy babies, by achieving the nutritional and mineral status in our own body, that will build a healthy body and brain in the foetus. We need to give the sperm and the ova the nutrients they need; eliminate a load of unnecessary and potentially damaging toxins; get rid of any bugs; suss out any allergies or parasites that may be impairing either parents' absorption; and eliminate any electromagnetic pollution. (This too can impair fertility and also can cause malformations, leukaemia and cancer. It has also been implicated in chromosomal disorders like Down's Syndrome.) We also need to go over the home for any toxic chemicals and eliminate them.

So what do we do to get it right? Read on.

In the course of this book, we will devote a chapter to going into each aspect of the environment that can be problematic, *why* they could be damaging, *why* they reduce fertility, and above all, *what to do about it*. I will introduce work by co-authors who are more authoritative in their writing than I am. I will also tell you my own take on everything – the point of view of the ordinary woman and mother.

The Plan of Campaign is 7-fold. All of the pieces of the health jigsaw that we have found important to make the *whole* picture are here. I have written a chapter on each of them, to include references to the science that lies behind the programme. Not all the aspects apply to everybody, as you are all individuals. You are all as different as your faces! This is what makes helping you such a complex business – and so interesting. That is what makes having babies so fascinating too – they always arrive so different to each other!

I would read it all through. You will find what particularly applies to you – and if you don't, you can ring us up and tell us why not, and exactly what your individual problems are, and we can discuss it, and hopefully help to find a solution!

However, although every couple is different, these are the basic thoughts worth taking on board:

MAIN AREAS OF CONCERN

You need to be eating well. Good food that suits you. Good food that will nourish your baby. No harmful additives. No pesticides – so everything organic. No genetically modified 'weirdo' stuff. No excess sugar. Clean water.

You need *not* to be taking in a lot of "voluntary social poisons" that clobber you and will seriously harm the baby, like tobacco, alcohol, street drugs, caffeine, or over-the-counter medical drugs.

You need to avoid use of the contraceptive pill and/or the copper coil. If they have been used in the past, you need to specifically address the deficiencies that this will have created. Whatever you do, learn Natural Family Planning. That way, *you* are in control in the future, your fertility and health are left intact.

You need to be free from bugs, such as genito-urinary infections, candida and parasites. You also need to recognise and eliminate any allergens.

You need to have a hair analysis and supplemental and cleansing programme to ensure you have plenty of all the essential trace minerals the baby needs to make himself, and as little as possible of the toxic metals that could harm him.

You need to be free from electromagnetic pollution from underground rivers, cracks in the substrata or from the many man-made sources (such as mobile phones etc.)

You need to recognise the plethora of toxic substances in cosmetics and every day household goods, and learn how to avoid them.

Foresight now works with nutritional therapists, homeopaths, herbalists, reflexologists, naturopaths, and others. There is a huge surge forward of knowledge in the alternative field, and if mothers and fathers join in with this, we can all forge ahead. See Chapter 11 on how they can help your specific problems.

On many occasions we find this programme will sort out polycystic ovaries. They are often due to low zinc, B6 and essential oils. Low sperm counts may be due to nutritional factors, but also to genitourinary infections (GUI), allergies, electromagnetism (especially mobile phones) etc. Sometimes blocked fallopian tubes respond to the programme, plus reflexology or acupuncture. Homeopathy will often manage to combat hidden infections. As the health problems in the parent generation are coped with, any health problems in the future babies are pre-empted or at least minimised as we go along.

They had it planned nicely. Four years after the wedding they had a lovely daughter. It was straight forward with "no problems". Two years later, after conceiving again, Julie felt so nauseous and so very ill, she miscarried at eleven weeks due to "blighted ovum".

Devastated, she took a long time to get over the miscarriage, both mentally and physically.

A year passed and Julie felt ready to try again. Once again, debilitating tiredness and that terrible nausea. An 8 week scan at the Early Pregnancy Unit showed that there was something very wrong. A week later every thing was removed from the womb, and tests and treatments were performed until her hormone levels returned to normal.

Julie's Mum got in touch with Foresight after seeing an advert, and shortly after this, the information pack arrived with "loads of literature". From then on, both Julie and her husband focused on health, diet, and had regular reflexology. They had their hair analysed, and both took all their supplements.

Once she was signed off from the Charing Cross Hospital in April, Julie conceived at the first attempt! Although there was some nausea and sickness, it was nothing like that which she endured prior to her miscarriages. The six week scan showed a healthy heart beat. "We were so elated. Really elated seeing that little heart beat"! In the fullness of time, a 9lb 9oz baby boy was safely delivered to overjoyed parents.

"He is totally different from my daughter; he is so calm, so much more content. Now we have one of each. I keep pinching myself, it's so wonderful, he's such a joy!

My prayer is that if Preconceptual care becomes the norm, reproductive tragedy, child ill-health, and indeed ill-health generally, can gradually become largely a thing of the past.

The 2007 ONS (Office of National Statistics) figures of 45,000 premature babies, 4,500 left with a lifelong disability, is not a situation that should be allowed to continue. The ONS states that one baby in 84 is born malformed, but this is accompanied by a helpful letter pointing out that the Government has ordered a change in the categories, and doctors are told NOT to report a whole long list of sadnesses such as "spina bifida occulta" and so on. The true figure for anomalies of any kind is nearer to one in 17, we gather. Where no action is taken preconceptually, about one family in nine is likely to have a little person starting life with a problem they will have to overcome.

Mostly, they do so magnificently. However, *how much happier it would all be* if these agonies could be avoided in the first place.

With the full Foresight "works", pregnancies can take place more naturally. Babies need *not* be so frequently miscarried (our statistic was 3.5% at our last count up, as against 25% nationally), nor born prematurely, brain damaged, nor with allergies or other ongoing problems.

As I am sure you will know, the last 50 years has seen a regression in human intellectual ability, as well as in health. Dr Bernard Rimland, whose position was to test the intake to the American Army for their intelligence, found the average IQ dropped one point every year.... Over 30 years this gets worrying. Quite simply, this has been because, if the unborn baby's body is badly affected by deficiencies, toxins, exogenous hormones, bugs and radiation, this will also affect his or her brain cells.

Children's little bodies are often badly affected by crucial deficiencies which lead to allergic reactions. These cause them ongoing miseries such as asthma, eczema, epilepsy, irritable bowel syndrome, and migraine. (Later in life this general level of poor health can lead to more obesity, diabetes, heart disease, cancer, auto-immune diseases such as poor thyroid function, arthritis, MS and ME etc.)

Children's little brains are affected similarly by the same toxins and deficiencies. This can lead to hyperactivity, dyslexia, Attention Deficit Hyperactivity Disorder (ADHD), Asperger's and autism. (Later in life this can also lead to severe forms of mental illness and criminal behaviour.)

At a national level, a general intellectual deterioration manifests as less ability in writing (books, plays, TV programmes); composition (music); art (pictures, sculpture); sport and so on. In the end, if we don't do something about it, among all the other disappointments, we will end up watching and listening to nothing but rubbish on the media and everywhere else! This whole feebleness of intellect could lead to the deterioration of the human soul, and the inability of mankind to progress.

We need to take stock.

It would be magical to arrive at the dawn of an era where ordinary people all support each other, where love becomes easier, and where common sense breaks through. Where people take their lives back into their own hands and realise they don't *have* to be ill, tired, dependant, nervous or "below-par" in any way.

Women need to find quiet times to be themselves again, and to tap into the Soul of Womanhood. The love of your mother, grandmothers, and all the women who helped to create *you* down the centuries will be supporting you and spurring you on, as you make the efforts needed to turn things around. They all took the trouble to keep themselves well and therefore fertile – or you would not be here! They all love you, and they don't want it to come to an end here!

After suffering 3 miscarriages, Michelle read an article in the national press about the work of Foresight. However, it wasn't until she became pregnant again, which sadly ended in a still birth, that she decided she must do something that would ensure the best for her own health as well as that of any future baby.

continued on next page

Michelle contacted Foresight and so began the Foresight Preconception Programme. Although there was no heavy metal toxicity reflected in her hair mineral analysis, both her calcium and magnesium levels showed up as being very low, but not as low as her selenium and zinc levels. Three lots of Hair Mineral Analysis later, the levels of these minerals had improved enough for a pregnancy to occur.

This time the pregnancy held, and an 8lb 1oz baby boy was safely delivered after spontaneous labour. "He is feeding well, and is a really happy, smiley, and very contented baby and so strong"! Says mummy!

"The changes to my diet were not difficult - the most difficult thing was to remember to take all the supplements" said Michelle, "I think that people should follow the Foresight Programme to ensure optimum health for both the parents and ultimately their child. For me it was not a sacrifice to give up certain things from my diet and to take all those pills but an honour, so that I could give the best start in life to my baby."

Mothers have always been the ones to carry evolution forward. If there needs to be a huge effort to make the Next Step, then this is where we are going, and they will be backing you all the way.

Fertility is natural. Being healthy and happy is natural. Every little female mouse in the cornfield, every singing bird in the trees, every bison grazing on the prairie, every lioness striding the savannah, even the *father* penguin shuffling around on the ice, keeping the egg warm *against all the odds*, they all know how you feel too. They also feel with you. Tap into this enormous *planetary* emotion too, and let them all carry you forward. You are not alone. The world turns on the strength of this special love and universal effort.

This knowledge will give you the patience and the strength to succeed. From the Big Bang (when ever that was?), until now, this is what has carried the world forward. Some of the book, (my bits!) are written from the soul to celebrate, and some of it (the science bits) is written with the help of more erudite beings, using the intellect to cerebrate. Go with the bits of the jigsaw which best suit your style – but don't discard the rest of it! If you put all the bits in place, there is your Plan of Campaign for your future family.

I feel the human racc needs to get back to How We Were Meant To Be. Do you agree? Let's get together, get well-fed, and get rid of all the "Drugs, Bugs, Plugs and Fugs" as I term all our bug-bears, and make a start on it!

Onward!

CHAPTER 2

NUTRITION

WHAT YOU NEED TO EAT – WHY YOU NEED TO EAT IT – WHAT TO AVOID – AND HOW TO AVOID IT TO ACHIEVE A HEALTHY PREGNANCY

If all prospective human mothers could be fed as expertly as prospective animal mothers in the laboratory, most sterility, spontaneous abortions, stillbirths, and premature births would disappear; the birth of deformed and mentally retarded babies would be largely a thing of the past.[1]

So said Roger Williams in the 1970s, pondering the very question I had posed to John Dickerson at about the same time. "Why did we not take as much trouble with our human prospective mothers as they do with the laboratory rats?" I remember shrieking with joy when I saw that paragraph in Roger Williams' book. (He was Professor of human nutrition at Texas University at the time). The two of his books I love the most are "Nutrition Against Disease" and "The Wonderful World Within You".

He is a pithy and witty writer, and the books are still available on eBay and really rewarding reading. I feel everyone who reads him will not only have a fabulous family, but will also live to a ripe old age![2,3]

Gail Bradley put it so well in the last book she and I wrote together:

Good nutrition is the foundation of the Foresight approach to preconception care. It is vital for health, proper development and successful reproduction at all stages of life, from cells in the embryo to old age. It can help to clear the body of poisons, such as lead.[4,5,6,7] *It can help to protect against infection by building a healthy immune system.*[2,8,9] *It is important for mental well-being.*[1,2,10,11,12,13,14,15]

Nutritional research

It is not always easy to do nutritional research for ethical and scientific reasons. Animal studies can provide valuable data to help understand the human situation[1,16,17,18,19] but it is not always possible to extrapolate the findings to humans. However, it has been found that in all types of animal life, from insect to mammal, a diet which supports normal adult life is not necessarily sufficient to support reproduction. There is no evidence that human beings are different.[1,7,20] (ie. To be a Mum, you need a bit more of everything. As you are making another person, as well as keeping yourself going, this is not really surprising). Examples of the truth of this philosophy are apparent in the work of three pioneers in nutrition.

Three pioneers in nutrition

Some of the most remarkable research into the effects of nutrition on health was done in the 1930s by Drs Weston Price[2], Francis Pottenger[21] and Sir Robert McCarrison.[22] (See the bibliography – all are available on eBay). Although working independently, their main conclusions were the same: good health depends on good nutrition. Their research findings have never been disproved, though they were for a long time ignored by the medical profession, the food industry, dieticians and governments. For many years, those who accepted them were labelled 'cranks'. Only for the last few decades or so has poor nutrition being recognised as a factor in ill health. NACNE[23], COMA[24], the BMA[25] and the Health Education Council[26] all issued reports in the 1980s and 1990s which advocated some changes in the national diet, though each fell well short of the recommendations of our three pioneers. (However, thank God for Jamie Oliver and some of the TV chefs for waking the country up a little bit!)

Dr Weston A. Price was an American dentist who was distressed by his profession's inability to find the *cause* of dental caries and peridontal disease.[2] He discovered that people who did not live in industrialised parts of the world had good teeth, so he took time off from his practice and travelled for ten years collecting evidence from all the races of the world. His subsequent book covered many aspects of nutrition, including the vitamin and mineral content of food; soil fertility; nutrition and pregnancy; vegetarianism; the effects of processing food; and the inadequate foods which produced severe degeneration. His book is not just about nutrition – it is a history of various tribes; it is an anthropological study; it is a book on agriculture, covering work that has never been written about since. Understandably he is known as 'The Darwin of Nutrition'.

His findings are all the more significant considering they apply regardless of the native diet he was studying. No matter who the people were, he found that as soon as they started to eat white flour and white sugar and other processed products such as tinned foodstuffs, they began to suffer ill health and there were increasing dental and skeletal changes and other problems, including mental problems, in the children. The actual contents of the original diets varied considerably, from the fish and seal eaten by the Eskimos, the oatmeal porridge, oatcakes and seafood of the Gaelics to the rye and milk products diet of the Loentschental Swiss. However, whatever the constituents of the original diet, when a modern diet was adopted, the number of health and fertility problems increased dramatically. Why? Because our refined, packaged, processed "dead" food does not have the vitamins, minerals and therefore enzymes that we need to "run a body".

Dr Francis Pottenger[21] was an American physician whose work with cats confirmed Price's findings. He observed that cats fed on scraps of raw meat were healthier than those fed on cooked meat. This led him to some remarkable research over ten years, spanning many cat generations and involving hundreds of cats. Basically, he compared the effects of feeding one group on cooked meats, pasteurised milk and cod liver oil, and another group on raw meat, raw milk and cod liver oil. The latter group were healthier, had good skeletal structure, and reproduced healthy offspring. The former group had a high level of sickness, including allergies, birth defects and poor skeletal structure such as misshapen skull, narrow palate and jaw. They also exhibited serious behavioural problems, such as poor mothering and feeding. With each succeeding generation these problems increased. Even when placed on a raw meat diet, it took four generations of breeding before the inherited damage triggered by the cooked meat and pasteurised milk was corrected. (NB: So we had better buck up!)

Following these discoveries Pottenger turned to the study of human nutrition. He was particularly concerned with the effects of chemical fertilisers and processed foods, including cooked foods. He knew from his earlier work that a healthy soil was important and that this was dependent on good manure. The growth of weeds in the runs of the cats fed on raw meat, after the cats had vacated them, was luxuriant. Little growth was seen in the runs of those fed on cooked meats. Clearly, the quality of excrement, reflecting that of the diet, was an important factor in the difference. Pottenger became renowned for his work with patients, advocating the benefits of raw food in the diet.

Sir Robert McCarrison[22] was a British doctor who served in the Indian Army, during which time he conducted many experiments in nutrition, showing how human health is dependent on the wholeness of food. Having noticed that most Sikhs, Pathans and Humzas were healthy and well-developed, while the Bengalis and Indians in the south were disease-ridden and underdeveloped, he investigated the possible reasons using colonies of rats. Feeding them the equivalent diet of the various Indian groups, he found that each rat colony replicated the health status of the group whose diet it had been fed. He kept meticulous notes on diets, weights, health and condition at death. Those who were given a diet which deviated from the principle of eating healthy food grown on healthy soil, in as near its natural state as possible, suffered ill health. These were the rats that had numerous diseases, reproductive failures, and behavioural problems, in one instance resorting to cannibalism. He concluded:

I know of nothing so potent in maintaining good health in laboratory animals as perfectly constituted food; I know of nothing so potent in producing ill-health as improperly constituted food. This, too, is the experience of stockbreeders. Is man an exception to the rule so universally applicable to the higher animals?[22]

Thus we have three men whose research findings all concluded that the quality of food was vitally important in good health, and for whom quality

15

meant wholeness. If the food was treated in such a way that it lost something, by refining, tinning, or heating, health would be affected. They also understood the importance of a healthy soil in providing good food.

It is interesting to digress here for a moment, and ponder on the findings – until so recently studiously ignored by most of the establishment - that the quality of the food had a bearing on the quality of the *behaviour*.

The quality of the food eaten by many people in the western world has altered enormously over the last 40 to 50 years. More food is tinned, bottled, packeted, precooked and frozen than ever before. Much has travelled thousands of miles from where it was produced. On the way over, it will have lost valuable vitamins and enzymes. It will, in fact, be dead. (This is why many people dislike vegetables, when stale they taste so bitter.) Fruit will be picked unripe, so it will travel better, but as a result it will taste sour, so children may refuse to eat it.

Before I dive off into the joys and complications of growing some of our own, let's just go back to the observation of Robert McCarrison that rats, who lacked essential nutrients resorted to violence and even cannibalism (which is not normal "rat culture".)

However, no doubt there is a deep physical/mental/emotional instinct, where the basic and primitive part of the brain says, "*We do not have enough food – fight for yourself – get out there and grab*". As our vitamin and mineral status is reduced do we see more of this: "me *first, out of my way*" mentality emerging? Is there more "*elbowing in*", and more "*passing by on the other side*" than they're used to be?

We are hearing all the time about mayhem in some of the schools, gun battles and knife attacks in the streets. People are nervous to leave their homes at night in some areas. Occasionally, there is a horrible series of sadistic murders, even, in more than one case, cannibalism.

Where food does not provide well for basic mental and physical energy, do we turn to alcohol, coffee, cigarettes, Mars bars, leading on, as sometimes it can, to cravings and the use of street drugs? These give a brief boost of energy, which is followed by precipitous fall, as we run out of endorphins... Feelings of exhaustion, lead to irritability, inefficiency, paranoia, or gross acts of cruelty. Relationships fail, jobs are lost, things take a turn for the worse...

We got married in 2001, and by early 2002 we started trying for a baby. Conception was swift but so was miscarriage. After the second miscarriage, my sister mentioned Foresight which we dismissed as nonsense.

After yet another miscarriage, we felt that there was a problem and perhaps IVF would diminish the chances of another lost pregnancy? Sadly, after both IVF and ICSI, I miscarried yet again. It was at this point that we were reminded of Foresight. However, undeterred we attended a meeting at a

continued on next page

fertility clinic to seek further advice and we were told that we would "not have children naturally" and that we should consider other options like egg donation, adoption etc. We asked about Foresight. The advisor told us that it was "a mad idea, but if we wanted to waste £300 on overpriced minerals then we could do!"

We left the clinic with our world having fallen apart. Next day I called Foresight, spoke to both Nim and Tanya in floods of tears, but after two hours felt hope yet again.

That evening we sent off our hair samples and embarked 100% on the Foresight Programme with gusto. We had a geo survey, turned organic, grew our own vegetables and really took it to the extreme.

The hair analysis results were shocking, showing very low levels of Zinc which Nim explained was probably the main problem. We set about correcting these. We also sought fertility advice from a fertility consultant.

Within a very short time I found that I was pregnant again. I wasn't excited; I just didn't believe anything could come of it. Throughout the pregnancy I was as sick as anything and loved every minute of it! It was an anxious time and I didn't truly believe I was having baby until our son was delivered by caesarean section.

It only took 48 hours for me to start panicking that our son would be an only child! Six weeks later I conceived again, sadly I miscarried. Was it because I hadn't followed up with the Foresight programme and had let myself go so much? Calling Nim once again, I was put back on the Foresight Programme with even more tablets than before, and a short time later became pregnant once again and in due course our daughter was safely delivered.

We know what we did worked. We feel better for the lifestyle changes we made thanks to Foresight and we still follow a healthy organic diet — and I have just extended our veggie patch!

This will then be described as "depression", and, if this leads, via the GP, to Seroxat, Prozac and the like, we are on the rocky road to mental illness and even, possibly, suicide.

However, how to prevent all of this was all there and demonstrated for our benefit in the rat world nearly 100 years ago.[1,2,11,15] So let's take it all on board, once and for all, and create a well-nourished, strong and sane new generation without any of these problems. *It is all up to us!*

The concept of biochemical individuality

Another important name in the history of nutrition is Dr Roger Williams, the American biochemist referred to at the start of this chapter. In his research he found that we are all biochemically different.[27] This means that everyone has needs for levels of nutrients that are individual to them alone, especially in respect of vitamins and minerals and amino acids. It is an important principle often overlooked in medical studies and dietary advice. Research has shown, for example, that some individuals may need many times the Recommended Daily Allowance (RDA) of a vitamin or mineral if they are to remain healthy.[15,27,28,29] Also, importantly, in certain conditions, such as pregnancy, requirements will alter.

The importance of food before pregnancy

It is essential to eat properly during pregnancy, but it is better to start, if possible, before conception. Good nutrition in the man helps to ensure healthy sperm and optimum sexual activity.[1,2,4,14,15,17,30,31,32] Poor nutritional status in the woman can cause ovulation failure and other problems with fertility, as birth-rate studies during famines have shown.[33,34,35] The woman will need to have her body packed with all the nutrients the embryo will require to develop into a healthy foetus. Ideally she should be neither very overweight, nor underweight, since both can have adverse effects on pregnancy outcome.[33,36,37,38,39,40,41,42,43,44] (However, as some of us are greyhounds and some of us are St Bernard's, we should not be too harassed about our weight by officious officialdom!)

The importance of food during pregnancy

The work of our three pioneers has shown how important the right food is in pregnancy. Subsequent studies have confirmed this. Women on good diets have better pregnancy outcomes than those on poor diets. Women who have acted upon the dietary advice they have been given also have better pregnancy outcomes. Better maternal nutrition can lower infant mortality rates. Most important of all, the size, and the function of the child's brain is dependent on good maternal nutrition.[45,46,47,48,49,50,51]

Lawrence Study

174 women who had previously given birth to an infant with spina bifida were recruited and were followed up through their subsequent 186 pregnancies. They were divided up as to those on a "Good Diet", those on a "Fair Diet" and those on a "Poor Diet". Outcomes were as follows:

	Good Diet (no. 53)	Fair Diet (no. 88)	Poor Diet (no. 45)
Miscarriages	0 (0%)	3 (3.5%)	15 (33%)
Spina Bifida (terminated)	0 (0%)	0 (0%)	8 (18%)
TOTAL:	0 (0%)	3 (3.5%)	23 (51%)

Of those on a "Good" or "Fair" diet, only 3 babies were miscarried out of 141 - making 1 pregnancy in 47. This compares well with the UK average of 1 in 4. Of those on the "Poor" diet, 23 out of 45, or just over half the babies were lost.[40] This work should be more widely known than it is. The message is that this tragic deformity is entirely preventable. Why is it that what is basically *good news* is so often buried or ignored?

Canadian Study

This is the Birth Record of a poor mother in Montreal. The birth outcomes were recorded before and after a nutritional programme provided by the Alice Higgins Foundation. This consisted of dietary advice, and the provision of a pint of milk, an egg and an orange per day.

Of the first eight children she gave birth to, before dietary advice and food allowances were given, 6 were below 2,500 gms, none were above 2,750 gms, two were below 1,750 gms and one of these died.

All eight were neurologically damaged and the seven survivors had to be institutionalised.

After the Alice Higgins programme, however, the next 3 births were much happier. The weights ranged between 3,500 gms, and 3,750 gms, and all three children were mentally sound.

The supplement programme cost $125 per child. Up to the 1980s, the institutionalising of the seven handicapped children had cost the State $300,000 - and counting.[52]

This is an extreme case, but it is not atypical of what is going on worldwide. So many children are being born subtly or overtly handicapped and the family grief is total, and the tax-payer's impoverishment is spread over lifetimes. This is likely to escalate unless we make a concerted effort to take things in hand.

Regarding weight gain in pregnancy, in this situation, small is NOT beautiful! Research has shown that the old idea that a woman should not put on much weight was wrong. In a London study, mothers in Hampstead who had higher calorie intakes than mothers in Hackney, had babies who were in some cases 2lb heavier.[52,54,55] Dr. Ebrahim, Institute of Child Health, London, found that mothers who gained more than 30 lb had the best birth outcomes.[53] Other research which has given food supplements to women has found that those who took them had bigger babies.[2,9,46] Women who are underweight at conception, and who gain less than 11 kg, or 24 lb, during pregnancy, often have babies who are small-for-dates or growth retarded. (NB: If you have been anorexic, when you come to Foresight, tell us this. We need to know).

Janet married at 23 and never imagined she would be unable to conceive. So when she and her husband decided to try for a family, and it didn't happen, she was devastated. She began to panic.

continued on next page

Two years later they began all the usual investigations which reveal "unexplained infertility". A "satisfactory sperm count" did nothing to start bells ringing. Having decided to go down the IVF route in 1997, the first IVF failed, due to hyper-stimulation and Janet was admitted as an emergency to hospital. She decided *"I am never going down that route again".*

"We then decided to adopt, and adopted our little boy at 6 months old". Whilst going through the process, Janet fell pregnant but suffered a miscarriage at 12 weeks. A second conception took place 18 months later which was tragically terminated as the scan showed the baby had died.

A few months later Janet read about Foresight, and although her husband was concerned that Janet had been through so much already, they decided to do the Foresight Programme.

Although both were eating a very similar diet, their individual nutritional status was radically different.

Nim advised them to use Natural Family Planning (NFP) until both their mineral levels were improved. They both followed the Foresight Programme "to the T".

Janet soon found that she had conceived. A beautiful baby girl, weighing 8lbs 6oz was born after trying for a family for 10 years. Two years later, Foresight Baby no.2 arrived, she weighed 8lbs 4oz and "is doing really well".

"I felt that I had Foresight on my side, so a big thanks to you all for everything over the last few years". Janet, Newcastle.

Clearly, if you eat a great deal more, without exercising more, you will put on weight. But it is important to eat the right foods. Besides taking in extra calories for growth and energy, you need extra vitamins, minerals, essential fatty acids, and amino acids. Moreover, if you eat the right foods, you will have less of a problem in losing the weight after birth, while breast-feeding, without a special slimming programme. It is therefore a good idea to eat the most nutritious food you can.

A healthy diet

There are many misconceptions about a healthy diet, which have arisen mainly because we have strayed from the teachings of our three pioneers. In reviewing the importance of nutrition to preconception, Foresight originally drew from their work,[2,21,22] and also that of Roger Williams,[1] Carl Pfeiffer,[15] Adelle Davis,[9] Isobel Jennings,[16] Eric Underwood,[30] Lucille Hurley,[56,57,58] Donald Caldwell and Donald Oberleas. Since then, we have continued to revise our recommendations as appropriate.

It is really quite simple to eat properly as any wholefood cookery book shows. (We recommend *The Foresight Wholefood Cookbook*,[59] which gives good basic guidance on diet and an excellent selection of recipes.)

A good diet comprises carbohydrates, fats, proteins and clean water. Within these groups are found the various vitamins and minerals that are essential for well-being. There has been so much research done on the various components that we are restricting the information in this chapter considerably, though the papers mentioned give further guidance.

CARBOHYDRATES should be unrefined, 'with nothing added and nothing taken away' – ie. Brown! They include starches, sugars and fibres. They provide energy, B complex vitamins and many of the essential minerals.[60] Contrary to popular belief, they are not fattening if they are eaten in the form of complex carbohydrates.[22] This is good news, as they are also cheap!

However there is a horrible substance called phytate, which lurks in raw grains, and unless dealt with in a pre-emptive way, can prevent the uptake of the zinc, calcium etc by the gut.[59]

The way to deal with phytate is (a) by soaking muesli overnight in the fridge. Just put your portion into a bowl and add as much milk as it can soak up by the morning. This has the added advantage that it is a bit quicker to eat in the morning – not quite such a laborious chew! (b) when using flour to make bread, this will respond to "proving" with the yeast. This is probably why bread has been traditionally made with yeast for hundreds of years - or maybe it was just a happy accident! Either way, if you make your own bread, make it with yeast or with sourdough, now thought to be more effective against phytate.[59]

A word of warning, if you put your dough in the airing cupboard to rise, stand the bowl on a tray. Take it from one who knows, if it rises over the top of the bowl, it takes wash after wash to get the yeasty smell out of towels and bed linen, if it goes over them!

Good sources: Complex carbohydrates, including whole grains (wholemeal flour, millet, wholemeal bread, oatmeal, buckwheat, brown rice, maize meal), fresh vegetables and fresh fruit.

Bad sources: Simple carbohydrates, including sugars, white flour, white bread, white pasta, sweets. These are all poor in fibre, vitamins and minerals.

PROTEINS are sometimes called 'building blocks', as they are used to build or repair enzymes, muscles, organs, tissues and hair. Proteins are made of amino acids which are broken down in the body to form other amino acids. We are only just beginning to realise the potential of amino acids in health. Two amino acids, spermadine and aspermine, play a major role in the synthesis of semen.[61] Their levels have been found to be low in men who have low sperm counts. Fortunately, with the right foods and supplements, it is usually possible to raise the levels and help improve sperm count quite quickly. (Many other factors are also involved in the production of healthy sperm[62]; as explained in the following chapters).

Amino acids are especially important in digestion as they form the enzymes necessary for the digestive processes. Thus if they are in short supply, digestion may be affected and this may result in malabsorption, causing shortages of other nutrients in the body. Such shortages can interfere with fertility and pregnancy.[61] Animal products and fish contain all the amino acids. However, to get the full range from vegetable sources you need to combine nuts with pulses, or nuts with seeds, or pulses with seeds. Combining is an excellent way to improve the quality of protein eaten.[59,63]

Good sources: Fresh meat, poultry, offal, fish, shellfish, milk, eggs, cheese, nuts, pulses and seeds (including whole grains).

Poor sources: Bought pies, TV meals, sausages and hamburgers, salamis, pates and other processed meats. Twice-cooked meat, as this is not fresh.

FATS provide energy and build the cell walls. Although animal fats are sometimes linked with illnesses such as arteriosclerosis, heart disease and some cancers, we need both animal and vegetable fats as part of a healthy diet. Eaten in the correct proportion and as part of a wholefood diet, there is no need to eliminate animal fats, such as butter, unless there is a specific reason, like cow's milk allergy. Polyunsaturated fats which occur in vegetables, nuts, unheated vegetable oils and fish oils, should all be included in the diet. (See essential fatty acids below.) Olive oil is best for heating. You do not, therefore, generally need to eat margarines high in polyunsaturates and often highly processed! (For those who do need alternatives to butter and cream, The Foresight Wholefood Cookbook is a useful source.)[59]

WATER, if it is clean, contains useful trace elements. Sadly, much of our water is less than ideal, often having high levels of nitrates, nitrites, chemicals, copper, lead, aluminium, pesticides, fluoride and other toxins.[64]

When we have done a hair analysis, we usually have clues about the tap water being drunk. Over-high copper, usually with some lead, is the most common bugbear. High copper and lead, found together, can almost always be traced back to a corroding pipe. Sometimes we see high levels of aluminium in a hair sample. Generally this is due to aluminium flocculants used to clear peaty particles from the water, although it may be from a deodorant.

When we come across these problems in the hair, we suggest a tap-water test at our laboratory, also in some cases, a dust test, or a test of cosmetics or other commonly used or ingested substances. Almost always, this way, we can track down the source.

It is now possible to obtain ABS plastic pipes, said to be safe for potable water, and more recently, I have heard they are making glass ones. It is possible to get fibre glass and stainless steel tanks. Hopefully things are advancing. There are many types of water filter now available – see the web. A lot more attention needs to be paid to the plumbing. The relevance of water quality to people's health appears to be much under estimated.

VITAMINS AND MINERALS

We make no apology for what may seem to some readers a disproportionate coverage of vitamins and minerals. This is deliberate. The importance of these vital substances, though admitted, generally tends to be underestimated by the medical profession *and dieticians.*

As long ago as 1916, a doctor wrote in the Lancet:

"Whatever the nature and whatever the mode of action of these puzzling substances, it is beyond question that their absence from the food does profoundly affect not only the physical health, but the mental health also."[65]

How much attention has been paid, in nearly 100 years of escalating levels of illness and insanity, and of declining fertility, to this profoundly important finding?

In experiments with various species, if a specific vitamin or mineral was totally omitted from the diet during the first three months of pregnancy it was found that a particular defect appeared in most of the litters, regardless of the species.[1,2,16,18,19,20,45] Deficiencies can also affect fertility.

I believe Nature is a lot brighter than we are. If a woman's body has insufficient nutrients the future foetus is going to need, the ovaries say, *"No, not this month"* and just switch off. The sperm beds evidently do likewise. Thirty years of Foresight work has shown us that more often than not they will "switch on" again when the nutrients arrive. It is humbling to realise that something as small as a sperm can be a whole lot brighter than we are. Remember, you can get 9,000 onto a full stop if you have the patience! These little fellows are bright enough to know when the going is too tough, and often to save us from the tragic outcome of a damaged or non-viable baby.

Although some doctors and dieticians do not admit the necessity of vitamin and mineral supplements, there is abundant evidence on their value before and during pregnancy and during lactation.[46,54] The stores of trace elements built up by the foetus have a strong influence on the infant's copper, iron and zinc status. However, the liver does not accumulate manganese so the infant may be at risk of deficiency. The nutritional requirements of the new-born are strongly influenced by the foetal stores.[47] Any level of deficiency can be serious for the infant, since the brain continues to grow and develop very rapidly for at least two years after birth. Under-nourishment, especially under four years of age, alters the brain development and activity and, if prolonged, can cause irreversible damage.[2,9,48] Many research papers in the literature demonstrate the above. So voluminous is the research done on this that we can only concentrate below on a small proportion. So many of you ask me every day on the telephone: *"What do they all <u>do</u>?" "Are they really necessary?" "Do they really make a difference to fertility?"* and so on.

So, I am printing for you here everything in the way of research that Gail

Bradley and I have put together that answers all the questions.

If you find this section too academic, turn over the yellow pages. By the end of the book you may want to return to read this section as it does contain useful information. Happy reading!

VITAMINS

Foresight recommends all prospective parents and lactating mothers to have a hair analysis and to supplement with the Foresight vitamins and minerals, which have been specially formulated by the Foresight medical advisers and are made by G & G to provide a balance of essential nutrients. The only "packers" used are organic vegetable powders. With the "key" ingredient i.e. Zinc, we always provide the "companion nutrients" that are used in its metabolism, ie manganese, B6, folate and vitamin A. In this way the absorption/utilisation of the key ingredient is enhanced, and it does not deplete the body of other nutrients as it is utilised. Foresight does not recommend exceeding the doses suggested, or taking any mega-doses, especially of individual substances, unless advised to do so by a person who is experienced in nutritional medicine, after appropriate tests. All the ingredients in the Foresight capsules are given on the label.

FAT-SOLUBLE VITAMINS. These include Vitamins A, D, E, K and the essential fatty acids, sometimes called Vitamin F. Because they are fat soluble, the body can accumulate stores of them against shortages. However, in pregnancy especially, these stores may need supplementing.

Vitamin A can be obtained direct from animal products in the form of retinol, or from vegetables in the form of carotene. Carotene is then changed in the body, with the help of zinc, to proplasma Vitamin A, the form the body can use, when it is needed. If sufficient zinc is not available to complete this step, it is possible to become Vitamin A deficient.[66,67]

Vitiman A is essential for healthy eyes, hair, skin, teeth, the mucus membranes, such as the lining of the mouth and good bone structure. It plays a part in good appetite, normal digestion, the making of red and white blood cells, and helps to make the male hormones concerned with reproduction.[16]

Deficiency problems in animals include increased susceptibility to infections, kidney stones, and reproductive system problems in both males and females.[68] In humans, the eyes and also the hearing are most affected,[2,69] though there are numerous reports of other conditions being helped by Vitamin A supplementation, e.g. mental illness, skin problems and sexual problems. In the animal foetus, **too little** Vitamin A can result in eye defects, hydrocephalus, diaphragmatic hernia, cleft palate and cleft lip, undescended testicles, and heart defects. It is associated with neural tube defects and stillbirths.[52,16,55,71,72]

Women with diabetes mellitus tend to have more malformed babies. Problems include microcephaly, hydrocephalus, cardiac defects, and cleft palate. Vitamin A deficiency may be involved.[2,16] Vitamin A deficiency has been associated with nutritional anaemia. One study reported that 'Improvement in Vitamin A status may contribute to the control of anaemia in pregnant women.'[55] Another study has advocated supplementing staple foods with Vitamin A.[16]

According to Professor John Dickerson, nobody can measure a unit as small as 1mcg. His conversion is 1iu=0.3ug of retinol.

From our leaflet "Vitamin A in Pregnancy"

The measurement of Vitamin A has recently been changed from the old "iu" (international units), with which we were all familiar, to the new "European Correctness" of "mcg" or micro-grams, sometimes written as µg.

These two measurements do not reflect exactly the same thing. The international units were used to give the potency of the source (which can vary with the oil soluble vitamins). The mcg only gives the weight. However, the powers-that-be have ruled that to convert iu of Vitamin A to mcg, we divide by 3.33, and so, for all practical purposes, this will now have to serve us. To avoid confusion we will give both measurements, as you may find either in papers, or on tubs of supplements.

For pregnancy, Foresight advises 2,500iu (750mcg) - 5,000iu (1,500mcg).

Vitamin A excess can be dangerous in pregnancy, but so can Vitamin A deficiency. *The dangers of Vitamin A deficiency have been too little understood or published over the last decade.*

Scientific advice on what constitutes excess Vitamin A in pregnancy is very variable. The Denner Report quoted 10,000iu (3,000mcg). Professor Merlyn Werbach of the University of California (arguably the world authority on foetal nutrition) says 40,000iu (12,000mcg). An Australian source gives 25,000iu (7,500mcg).

Foresight programmes are always very conservative, as the obvious approach is to give <u>enough</u> to avoid any danger of deficiency, while giving very little more than this, to be sure of staying within the safe limit.

Even our most generous programmes give less than half the most conservative upper limits, which was the Denner Report's 10,000iu (3,000mcg). France and Canada give 5000iu (1,500 mcg) as supplementation to all pregnant women.

It is interesting to note in this context that during the war (when, despite rationing, most people's diet was more nutritious than that of today), the Government decreed all pregnant women should have "a teaspoonful of cod liver oil" daily. It is hard to assess the amount of Vitamin A, as a lot would have depended on the size of the teaspoon, but it is likely to have been in the region of 5,000iu (1,500mcg). At the present time, in the USA, pregnant women are given 5,000iu (1,500mcg) Vitamin A daily. In some areas of Australia, they are given 10,000iu (3,000mcg). UNESCO campaigns for funding to give Vitamin A to pregnant mothers in the Third World to stop babies from being born blind.

Both vitamin A excess and deficiency deformities in experimental animals have been recorded by Dr Isobel Jennings of Cambridge, and by Dr Weston Price of California.

Isobel Jennings. MRCVS, Cambridge - Foetal animal studies by a veterinary pathologist.

Vitamin A – Excess and Deficiency

Excess	Deficiency
Cranial anomalies	No eyes
Cleft Palate	Micropthalmias
Hare Lip.	Blindness
Eye defects	Hydrocephalus
Hydrocephalus	Cardiovascular Anomalies
Spina Bifida	Urogenital Anomalies
Exencephalus	Diaphragmatic Hernia
	Hydrospadias
	Cryptorchidism

Dr Weston Price, of California, lists Vitamin A deficiency as causing problems with the development of the eyes, ranging from impaired sight, to blindness, to being born with no eyes (anopthalmia). Dr Price also reported damage to the nerves leading to the ears, and therefore impaired hearing, ranging to total deafness. Prolongation of the gestation period and long and difficult labour were reported in rats. Calves were reported as being born small and less likely to survive. Farm animals generally were reported to have had less successful reproduction and lactation, and less resistance to infection, where Vitamin A levels were less than optimum.

Lack of Vitamin A in the diet of pigs resulted in "extreme incoordination and spasms", and a tendency to abortion and farrowing dead piglets. Another researcher quoted by Price showed that lack of Vitamin A produced disturbances in "oestrus and ovulation", leading to sterility.

Professor Hale of the Texas Agricultural Experimental Station, found that as well as piglets being born blind, "depriving pigs of Vitamin A for a sufficient period produced severe nerve involvements, including paralysis and spasms so the animals could not rise to their feet." (NB: Would this be relevant to cerebral palsy in the human infant?)

Professor Hale also found that if the sire of any species was deprived of Vitamin A, he would become sterile.

Disturbances of the development of the upper and lower jaw and tooth decay were also reported in humans whose diets lacked Vitamin A. Further information can be found on the web at: wwwpricepottenger.org/ Articles /NoEyes.html and also at www. westonaprice.org/ vitamins /vitaminsaga.html

In 30 years of running Foresight we have not seen any of the deformities listed above in "our" babies. I would not therefore be tempted to supplement above 5,000iu (1,501 mcg), (although you could probably take up to 10,000iui (3,000mcg) without harm.) However, I think there could be a case made out for a little more with the multiple births, especially triplets.

I would also not be confused or bullied into taking less than 2,500iu (750mcg) as this could lead to the risk of serious malformations. 45,000 babies (1 baby in 16) are now born in Britain with malformations annually. The largest groups include those with malformations listed on the last page (research by Isobel Jennings) which are proven by scientific research to be due to Vitamin A deficiency. This is a tragedy probably greater than the thalidomide debacle, and it should be more easily preventable, as all the research is out there, and has been for many years.

At the present time, The Department of Health (DoH), say they "*have no position on Vitamin A in pregnancy*". They passed me on to the Food Standards Agency who passed me back to the DoH. At present (Summer 2008) the FSA are advising not more than 2,100iu daily, but in this they are at odds with every other country in Europe, the USA, Canada and Australia. Our level of premature birth and disability is also higher than that of these other countries.

We continue to advise you to take between 2,500iu (750mcg) and 4,232iu (1,270mcg) daily, before and throughout pregnancy.

You are welcome to take this information to your GP, midwife or health visitor if this would be helpful. If they (or you) have any scientific papers that contradicts what I am saying, or supports it, I would be particularly grateful to be sent a copy, as I would be very interested to study them.

References:
The Denner Report, London, HMSO (c1990)
Werbach, M., "Nutritional Influences on Illness", Third Line Press, California. USA (1988)
Naish, F., and Roberts, J., "Better Babies", Random House, Austraila. P57., (1996)
Jennings, I.W., "Vitamins in Endocrine Metabolism",
William Heinemann Medical Press, pp 130-131 (1972)
Price, W.A., "Nutrition and Physical Degeneration",
The Price Pottenger Nutrition Foundation, La Mesa, California, USA. (1945)
Hale, F., "Pigs born without eyeballs", J. Hered. 24, pp 105-106. (1935)

Do note that both Australia and the USA advocate 8,000iu (2,400mcg) per day for pregnant women. Most European countries advocate at least 5,000iu (1,500mcg) per day. This safeguards the sight and hearing, prevents undescended testicles and other anomalies of the genitalia in little boys and makes other problems as listed previously less likely.[2,16]

It is possible to go to the website of the EVM, the Government "Expert Group on Vitamins and Minerals", and study the research they have based their decisions on.

As you will be able to see for yourselves, there is no study showing problems with taking supplementation of less than 10,000iu. In fact, most of the studies quoted as showing harm were based on self-medicating women who were taking incredibly "over the top." doses, with levels such as 150,000iu a day etc. This was in the USA. I do not think supplements with levels in this area are even available in Europe. A lot of the studies were unscientific and sloppy, talking about "high levels" and "low doses" etc without giving any indication of what these represented!

We do not want any Foresight baby ever to be less than perfect as a result of all this Establishment muddle. We suggest sticking with supplementation between 2,500iu and 5,000iu. This way, you are safe from both deficiency and overdose.

Good sources: Vitamin A – fish oils, especially cod liver, fatty fish, egg yolk, organ meat, whole milk, butter, cream, cheese, yoghurt. Carotene – spinach, carrots, red pepper, broccoli, kale, chard, tomato, apricot, marrow, butter, cream.

It is best taken with full B-Complex Vitamins C, D, E, essential fatty acids, calcium, phosphorus and zinc.[73]

Liquid paraffin prevents the absorption of Vitamin A, so should never be used. Long, slow cooking of vegetables can destroy carotene.

Vitamin D is necessary for the growth and maintenance of bones and teeth. It also aids calcium and phosphorus absorption.[74]

Lack of Vitamin D in adults may lead to hot flushes, high sweats, leg cramps, irritability, nervousness and depression.[9,10,70] Other signs include osteoporosis, osteomalacia, pains in the hips and joints, and dental caries.[1,2,9,10] In children, rickets and tooth decay may be present. There may be other signs of bone deformities. Poor skull development can lead to impairment of brain development. See Dr June Sharpe's Study of the High Raised Palates on the next page. Poor jaw development may give buck or snaggle teeth. It may also inhibit the function of the eustacian tubes leading to constant middle ear infection. There may be receding chins or foreheads, or large bossing foreheads with deep-set eyes. The middle face may be cramped or narrowed, pushing the palate upwards and/or forwards.[1,2,9,10] Price found that most retarded children and those with learning difficulties had high raised palates.[2] Asymmetrical development of the skull may distort the membrane carrying the blood supply to the brain cells, and inlets for the blood supply may be occluded by deformed platelets. This can affect the supply of nutrients, oxygen and glucose to the brain. Girls with insufficient Vitamin D during childhood may have narrow pelvic development[75] which may later in life make childbirth difficult.

Good sources: Vitamin D can be obtained in the food or through the action of the sun on oils in the skin. This latter method is important, since food sources tend to be poor. Hence, it is wise to build up stores during the summer months, by allowing the action of the sun on the skin. However, since the destruction of the ozone layer, we have to be more careful, but perhaps work is now underway to help to reduce this hazard.

Food sources include fish oil and fatty fish. There are small quantities in whole milk, free range eggs and butter.

It is best taken with Vitamins A and C, choline, essential fatty acids, calcium and phosphorus.[73]

Liquid paraffin can prevent its absorption so should not be used.

Excess Vitamin D can lead to a range of unpleasant symptoms.[9,10]

Vitamin E prevents the oxidation (destruction by oxygen) of Vitamin A and is needed for the utilisation of essential fatty acids and selenium. It can protect from scarring after burns, surgery and injury and is important in wound healing, such as the healing of abrasions after birth.[9,10,73] Davies claims that some congenital heart defects will disappear if it is given from early babyhood.[9,10] It has also been suggested that it has a protective effect against some haemorrhage in premature babies. Researchers at the University of Edinburgh have suggested it may be another factor that can be useful in the treatment of infertility in the male, since it is necessary for flexibility in the cell walls of the sperm – abnormal sperm are less flexible.[75]

Without it, people can develop anaemia, and enlarged prostate glands. Premature aging can take place with liver and kidney damage, varicose veins and heart attacks. Phlebitis, strokes, protruding eyes, muscle degeneration and muscular dystrophy can occur.[1,9,10]

Deficiencies in animals have caused muscular dystrophy, central nervous system disorders such as encephalopathy, vascular system defects, and foetal reabsorption.[75] In rats, deficiencies lead to abnormalities including exencephaly, hydrocephalus, joined fingers and toes and oedema.[16] In human babies, they lead to anaemia, jaundice, weak muscles, retarded heart development and squint.[2,9,10,16]

Vitamin E may prevent miscarriage and help to ease labour by strengthening the abdominal muscles. Prolonged labour, because of weak muscles, can lead to problems for the baby as it becomes starved of oxygen during the birth process.[9,10,73]

Good sources: Unrefined (cold pressed) oils, whole grains, wheat germ, nut, whole milk, egg yolk, green leafy vegetables, avocado. It is best taken with Vitamins A, full B-Complex, C, essential fatty acids, manganese, selenium.[73]

Essential Fatty Acids or EFAs are fatty acids that cannot be made by, or in, the body. They therefore need to come from the diet. EFAs are involved in many metabolic processes, as opposed to fatty acids, of which there are many, and which play a lesser role. There are only two families of EFAs - the omega 6 Linoleic acid or LA; and omega 3 a-Linolenic acid ALA.

EFAs are important because they form a large part of the membranes of all cells and they give rise to hormone type substances called prostaglandins. These are used to make sex and adrenal hormones, anti inflammatory responses, they can affect all systems of the body. They help in the absorption of nutrients and activate many enzymes.[73,76]

Because of the wide role of these substances in the cells, deficiencies can give rise to a large number of disorders, including allergies, gallstones, diarrhoea, varicose veins, skin problems, and heart and circulatory conditions.[77]

In reproduction, EFA deficiency may be a factor in pre-elampsia.[78] There may be infertility, especially in the male. In rats with deficiency, the pups were of lower birth weight than was expected.[16]

Deficiencies have also been reported in hyperactive children, alcoholics and drug addicts.[76,79]

Recently, (in the 2000s), work on the omega-3 fatty acid has been centred on behaviour and intelligence in schoolchildren, and in juvenile delinquents. Huge improvements have been seen in youngsters who previously were failing in learning situations and behaving badly.

If only they could all be given everything they need from the moment that the sperm and the ova start to form – maybe could we have a problem free world? Why not?

Good sources: Nuts, unrefined oils, nut butters, cold pressed oils, green leafy vegetables, seeds and fatty fish.

They are best taken with Vitamins A, C, D, E and phosphorus.[73]

Vitamin K is generally made in the healthy intestine. It is essential for blood clotting, which explains why it has sometimes been given to women in injection form at the time of birth. It was felt that if the baby was short of this vitamin at birth, there could be a risk of bleeding. Later it was given to the newly born baby, since even small haemorrhages of the brain could be serious.[75]

More recently, however, there has been some controversy over this. Some studies have linked Vitamin K injections to later development of leukaemia in the child.[80] Be sure to make your own decisions over this. If you have been short of Vitamins A and E during the pregnancy, (which could reduce the strength of the blood vessel walls) or have been taking aspirin or heparin, (given to thin the blood and therefore to reduce the clotting) the risk of haemorrhage may be increased. (Be sure to read the Foresight booklet on aspirin in pregnancy.) If this has not been the case, the risk will be commensurately less. However, if a woman is healthy and eats plenty of green leafy vegetables, she should have a good store of the vitamin and will have a baby who has adequate stores. Also, Vitamin K is included in the Foresight Vitamin Supplement, so deficiency will be less likely.

WATER–SOLUBLE VITAMINS include the B-Complex and C. Since these are readily absorbed in water, they are easily lost to the body through urine (except B12). However, the body does have very limited stores, though any shortage is serious.

B-Complex – B vitamins should never be taken on their own, but always in conjunction with other B vitamins because they are linked in function. Dosing with one alone may lead to a greater need for usage of others, thereby creating a deficiency. In nature, no B vitamin is found on its own. However, it is possible for a person to have a greater than usual need of any one, since we are all biochemically different.[1,14,16] (see above.)

"He is Lovely!" says Tracy when referring to her 3 month old son. "He was 8lbs 13oz at birth, long and big and strong, and has been gaining weight steadily since birth. He is feeding well and I feel so blessed."

Before coming to Foresight, Tracy became pregnant naturally. Unfortunately pressure from a fibroid caused her waters to break which lead to a termination at 23 weeks. During the next 6 years no further conception took place, so Tracy and her husband went to seek medical advice. The IUI specialist informed them that Tracy was fertile and that she was producing many eggs, but unfortunately the IUI failed.

A homeopath by profession, Tracy attended a Foresight Practitioners Training Day which she found very interesting. So much so that she decided that both she and her husband would go onto the Foresight Programme themselves. The first Hair Mineral Analysis results showed that her husband had high levels of Lead and even higher levels of Copper in his system which could account for the specialist saying that her husband's sperm, although high in quantity, had very low motility.

Their supplement programme began just after Christmas and by the following April, Tracy knew she was pregnant!

"It's so simple when you compare it to IUI and IVF" says Tracy who is still on the programme. "I am also healthier and have more energy, and I would recommend it to anybody, far better than bombarding the body with drugs and compromising the body systems. If more people knew about it, it would be fantastic. I am 40 years old, and if I decided to have another baby, I would certainly do the Foresight Programme again."

During stress, infection, pregnancy, lactation and childhood, there is an increased need. Lack of almost any B vitamin can lead to blood sugar problems causing reactive hypoglycaemia.[75]

Some of the B vitamins can be made in a healthy intestine or liver, though it is not certain how much of that synthesised can be used in the body.[16,15,73] This does not happen where the gut is not healthy, as for example where there is undiagnosed condition, use of alcohol or candidiasis or where certain drugs (antibiotics and sulphonamides) are given. These circumstances can exacerbate any shortfall in the diet.[1,9,10,73]

B-Complex is best taken with Vitamins C, E, calcium and phosphorus.[73]

Vitamin B1 (thiamine) is needed to break down carbohydrate into glucose.

Deficiencies lead to mental symptoms such as depression, irritability, temper tantrums, failure to concentrate and poor memory. There may be fatigue, feeling listless, muscle weakness, aches and pains, anorexia, neuritis, digestive problems, heart problems and shortage of breath.[14,17,73,75]

Deficiency in animals has been linked with sterility, relative infertility,[2,16] low birth weight and stillbirth.[14,15,56,78] In pregnancy, a shortage can lead indirectly to loss of appetite and vomiting, in the mother, which may cause the baby to be born with a low birth weight.[75]

Good sources: Wheat germ, rice polish, whole grains, brewer's yeast, nuts, dry beans, peas, lentils, seeds, rice, heart, kidneys.

It is best taken with full B-Complex, Vitamins C, E manganese and suphur.[73]

Vitamin B2 (riboflavin) assists in the breakdown and utilisation of carbohydrates, fats and proteins. It is essential for healthy eyes, mouth, skin, nails and hair. It works with enzymes in cell respiration.[16]

Signs of deficiency are sensitivity to light, sore and bloodshot eyes, broken capillaries in cheeks and nose, wrinkled or peeling lips and dry upper lips. There may be cracks at the corners of the mouth and dermatitis.[9,14,73] Experimental animals have developed cataracts, possibly because without Vitamin B2 they could not use their Vitamin A.[16,73] Since it works in conjunction with other nutrients and enzymes, deficiency symptoms may not disappear on straight supplementation. It should be given in conjunction with other B-Complex vitamins.[73,75]

In animal reproduction, deficiency has been found to cause sterility, stillbirths, small misshapen foetuses, reduced oxygen consumption in the liver and reduced enzyme activity. Rats have been born with blood disorders, misshapen jaws, cleft palates, joined claws, oedema, anaemia and degeneration of the kidneys.[16] In humans, Vitamin B2 deficiency is considered to be one of the worst in pregnancy,[80] with cleft palate and shortening of limbs as risks.[81] These are both seen in smokers' children, especially the shortening of limbs. *(NB: If you are a smoker's child like me, you can't purchase a garment without having to take up the sleeves. Maddening!)*

Good sources: Brewer's yeast, kidney, tongue, leafy green vegetables, whole milk, fish, butter, egg yolks, nuts.

It is best taken with full B-Complex and Vitamin C.

Vitamin B2 is sensitive to light, so it is destroyed if milk in glass bottles left on the doorstep. Avoid this if possible. *However, this is usually no longer a problem, as most milk is now sold in supermarkets in opaque cardboard containers. Progress!*

Niacin or nicotinamide – sometimes known as B3 – aids in the utilisation of energy. It is important for a healthy skin, digestive system, and the normal functioning of the gastrointestinal tract. It is also needed for proper nerve function, as a co-enzyme[14,15,16] and for the synthesis of sex hormones.[73]

Deficiencies have often been linked with the three 'D's' – dermatitis, diarrhoea and dementia. There can also be a coated tongue, mouth ulcers, anorexia, dyspepsia or intermittent constipation. Mental symptoms include depression, confusion, hostility, suspicion and irrational fears. Sufferers become tense, nervous, miserable, subject to dizziness, insomnia, recurring headaches and impaired memory.[1,9,10,14,15,73,75]

Nicotinamide deficiency in rats has been found to produce young with cleft palate and/or hare lip and hind limb defects.[16]

One of those things that puzzled me for many years – I knew that cleft palate was more commonly seen in agricultural workers' and market gardeners' children. Why should this be? Then I read a paper by M. K. Johnson, of the Medical Research Council[82] (no less), which told us that nicotinamide was the only nutrient that would take the organophosphate pesticides out through the liver. Then I realised that people using organophosphate regularly would be using up their nicotinamide on liver function, and this could be starving the sperm of this essential nutrient.

It is awe-inspiring to realise, so exact is the work of nature, that somebody as small as a sperm can have a deficiency! I am told that you could get 9,000 sperm onto a full stop! (Mark you, if you tried, one of them would be bound to jump off and spoil it all!) But, the dears can still be deficient if not serviced with enough care.

How meticulous is Nature, that when a man produces 100 million sperm, each one will be perfect, if the environment is uncontaminated. Yet still how primitive are we that we splash pesticide and industrial chemicals around, we swallow drugs, additives, alcohol and inhale smoke, inhalants - God knows what - and we never even pause to wonder what it all does.

What a *work of art* a sperm must be. And so full of spirit. We should be much more thoughtful on their behalf than we are.

Good sources: Brewer's yeast, lean meats (not pork), liver, poultry, fish, wheat germ, whole grains, nuts, especially peanuts, whole milk and whole milk products.

Nicotinamide is best taken with full B-Complex and Vitamin C.[73]

Pantothenic acid is needed for every cell in the body as, without it, sugar and fat cannot be changed into energy. It is important for a healthy digestive tract, and essential for the synthesis of cholesterol, steroids and fatty acids and the utilisation of choline and PABA. It can help the body to withstand stress.[1,15,16,73]

Deficiency causes a wide variety of complaints. The adrenal glands do not function, leading to a paucity of adrenal hormones which regulate balances in the body. This may cause low blood sugar and low blood pressure. There will be a shortage of digestive enzymes, slow peristaltic action (movement along the digestive tract), indigestion and constipation following as a result. Too little is also linked with food allergies.[1,9,10,16]

As with all the B vitamins, the mental symptoms of deficiency are many, including depression, causing the sufferer to be upset, discontented and quarrelsome.[1,14,15] There may be headaches and dizziness. These symptoms are common with low blood sugar.

In animals, deficiencies have given rise to a variety of foetal abnormalities, which mainly affect the nervous system.[16] Also, cleft palate, heart defects, club foot, lack of myelination, and miscarriage have been noted.[1,9,10,16,75] Sterility is also mentioned.[9,10,16,73] Similar problems in humans are suspected.[9,10,16] (Damage to the myelin sheath, which protects the nerves is present in multiple sclerosis, (M.S.). Maybe making sure people have enough before birth and throughout their lives, could give some protection against this terrible condition?)

Good sources: Organ meats, brewer's yeast, egg yolks, legumes, whole grains, wheat germ, salmon, human milk, green vegetables.

It is best taken with full B-Complex, Vitamin C and suphur.[73]

Vitamin B6 – pyridoxine – is needed to make use of the essential fatty acids and many of the amino acids. It is essential for growth and the synthesis of RNA and DNA. It helps maintain the balance of sodium and potassium in the body and is necessary for nerve and muscle function. It helps to prevent tooth decay, kidney stones, atherosclerosis and heart disease, if it is present in abundance.[1,9,10,14,15]

Lack of B6 can mean less use is made of minerals such as zinc, magnesium and manganese (see below). There may be headaches, halitosis, lethargy, pain and cramps in the abdomen, rash around the genitals, anaemia, anorexia, nausea, vomiting, diarrhoea, haemorrhoids, dandruff, dermatitis of the head, eyebrows and behind the ears, sore lips/tongue, and a rash round the base of the nose. Hands can become cracked and sore. Night-time problems include insomnia, twitching, tremors, leg and foot cramps and nervous lethargy, and inability to concentrate.[1,9,10,14,15] Premenstrual tension syndrome (P.M.T.) often responds to B6 supplementation, as do nausea, vomiting, oedema and the convulsions of eclampsia in pregnancy.[1]

Foetal abnormalities, including cleft palate, have been linked to B6 deficiency. Babies born with B6 deficiency have low scores on general condition ratings.[83] There may be seizures in the newborn.[15]

Unfortunately, once again, (as with vitamin A), inaccurate information has meant a panic in official circles about the safety of B6.

In huge doses, such as 250mg, given over some weeks, too much B6 can induce "neuresthesia" or lack of feeling in the fingers and toes. This problem disappears in a few days if the high doses are discontinued.

In any case, in practice, B6 is not used in this way. Women who suffer very bad PMT have sometimes taken doses of 250mg or more for a couple of days before their period was due and for the first day of their period. I am not aware of this ever causing any side-effects, and the PMT relief was found helpful. Researchers then tried giving these very high doses, 250mg – 500mg for weeks on end. This did prove problematic and based on the evidence of these studies, vitamin B6 preparations may be forbidden over 10mg. (This now appears to be the case, Summer 2008).

Motivation for these types of studies has to be considered. Possibly removing this simple solution will increase the sales of HRT, which fell, due to research revealing the links with cancer, thrombosis, migraine and osteoporosis.

When faced with an unaccountable situation, the French used to say, *"cherchez la femme"* – look for the woman involved... Now people say, *"follow the money"*. Yes, lots of scares regarding natural therapies and nutrients are much publicised because the natural therapies work! Lots of lucrative little illnesses disappear, which is hugely frustrating for those who make vast fortunes out of selling medicaments for these little illnesses!

Good sources: meats, whole grains, organ meats, brewer's yeast, blackstrap molasses, wheat germ, legumes, peanuts.

It is best taken with full B-Complex, Vitamin C, magnesium, potassium, linoleic acid and sodium.[73]

Para-amino benzoic acid (PABA) is unique in being a 'vitamin within a vitamin', occurring in combination with folic acid.[73] It stimulates the intestinal bacteria, so they make folic acid, which is then used in the production of pantothenic acid. It helps with protein breakdown and use, and the formation of red blood cells. It is important in skin and hair colouring. It can soothe burning, especially sunburn.[1,14]

Lack of PABA can cause "patchy" looking skin, as it is needed for smooth skin pigmentation. As it is also needed for hair colouring, shall we see if it can help us to avoid grey hairs naturally? *Because we're worth it!*

Good sources: brewer's yeast, wheat germ, whole grains, liver and yoghurt, organ meats, green leafy vegetables.

It is best taken with full B-Complex and Vitamin C.[73]

Biotin is necessary for the body's fatty acids and carbohydrates. It also helps in the utilisation of protein, folic acid, pantothenic acid and Vitamin B12.[73] It is useful in the treatment of candidiasis.[84]

Deficiency is linked with depression, panic attacks, extreme fatigue, muscle pain, nausea, pain around the heart, dry peeling skin, hair loss, conjunctivitis, loss of appetite, pallor of skin and mucus membranes and lower haemoglobin. In children there may be stunted growth, and adults may become thin to the point of emaciation.[1,9,14,15,]

In rats, biotin deficiency is linked with resorption of the foetus and death in the first few days after birth, due to damage to the liver, heart and blood vessels.[16]

Some autopsies were done on very young American soldiers who were tragically victims of the war in Vietnam. Many were found to have degeneration of the heart and blood vessels typical of biotin deficiency. This research was all out there then. All it takes is a B Vitamin tablet every day, to prevent so much tragedy. Why do people ignore all this superb work, done, no doubt, at huge expense, coming out of universities all over the world? Why do Governments pay for it to be done (with our money!), if they are not going to act on it, when it turns up enormously useful information? Why?

Good sources: Egg yolks, liver, unpolished rice, brewer's yeast, whole grains, sardines, legumes.

Raw egg white destroys biotin

It is best taken with full B–Complex, Vitamin C and linoleic acid.[73]

Inositol is needed by human liver cells and bone marrow cells. It is necessary for fat metabolism and transport, as well as healthy skin and hair. It combines with methionine and choline to make lecithin, a substance needed for the myelin sheath – the protective covering for the nerves. Lecithin also carries Vitamins A, D, E and K around in the blood.

Lack of inositol may cause falling hair, eczema, abnormalities of the eyes, constipation, irregular heart action and a slowing down of the digestive system.[9,10,73] *Again, could we pre-empt M.E.?*

Good sources: Whole grains, citrus fruits, brewer's yeast, molasses, meat, milk, nuts, vegetables and eggs.

It is best taken with full B-Complex and linoleic acid.[73]

Choline is needed for the formation of DNA and RNA and for making nucleic acid in the centre of the cell. It is used in normal muscle contraction. It is used to make lecithin (see above) and is involved in nerve functioning.

Lack of choline can lead to headaches, dizziness, strokes, haemorrhage in the eye, noises in the ear, high blood pressure, awareness of heart beat, oedema, insomnia, constipation, and visual disturbances.[9,10,73]

Because of its role in acetylcholine, a neurotransmitter, deficiency is linked with mental disorders. Animal experiments have shown a lack can cause fatty liver and haemorrhages in the heart muscle and adrenal gland.[1] And it is linked with the development of stomach ulcers, liver cancer and kidney damage in young animals.[75]

Organophosphate (OP) insecticides, which are in common use, inactivate choline-containing enzymes, which are necessary for manganese absorption. This prevents the uptake of manganese by the plants. This can lead to manganese deficiency in the food and thus in the human who eats it! "Rust" on lettuce stalks is a sign of a lack of manganese.[59]

Eating organic food, and thus avoiding much contact with/consuming of OP pesticides will make the absorption of Inositol and Choline easier. Lecithin granules available from health stores are a good way of boosting your intake, if you have been exposed to too much "pesticide drift" from neighbouring fields or gardens. At the same time, I would use Nicotinamide + to help cleanse the liver of organophosphates.

Although, I am told, the use of pesticides has fallen to about half what it was 20 years ago, the problems of drift remain with us. Lots of us buying organic food and/or growing our own will contribute to a further decline in pesticide use. This will help everybody.

Good sources: Egg yolks, organ meats, brewer's yeast, wheat germ, soya beans, fish, legumes, green vegetables.

It is best taken with Vitamins A, full B-Complex and linoleic acid.[73]

Vitamin B12 (cynocobalamin) is needed for the production and regeneration of red blood cells, and carbohydrate, protein and fat metabolism. It helps with iron function and is used with folic acid in the synthesis of choline.[73] It is involved in the synthesis of RNA and DNA.

Although it is often said to occur almost exclusively in animal products, this is not true. It also occurs in well-water which has been exposed to the soil. Dr John Douglass reports that, *'People who consume peanuts and sunflower seeds have adequate levels of B12. This indicates that the B12 is synthesised in the gut when the diet includes these foods. Eating seeds and sprouted seeds apparently provides the necessary nutrients to promote B12 synthesis.'*[78]

Unfortunately however, there has been "genetic modification" of peanuts, and for some people this appears to have made them into a very allergenic

37

substance. Tales of anaphylactic shock, a potentially lethal allergic reaction involving the heart, have become all too common. There has been a huge decline in the population of little song-birds such as blue tits. Has putting out peanuts for them contributed to this, by making them ill or sterile? Sadly, I think it may have.

We gather it is now proposed (2008) that GM foods can come over from the States and be sold in this country *without being labelled as such* – soya, peanuts and maize, we are told. (Presumably because we have not been buying the GM stuff – for very good reason!)

More recently, we are told that maize is being made into biofuel in the USA. So have there been some adverse reports on using it as a food? We are not going to be told, I guess. I would avoid peanuts, or try to track the origin. We may have to do the same with sweetcorn and soya. Adverse effects have been noted in experiments with animals, we have been told. We need to be very alert about this one.

 The Soil Association certified organic foods, are NOT GM. Look for their little "knickers in a twist" logo on produce. This may prove to be very important.

Deficiency of B12 causes pernicious anaemia, deterioration of nervous tissue, sore mouth and tongue, neuritis, strong body odour, back stiffness, pain and menstrual disturbances and a type of brain damage. A very severe deficiency leads to deterioration of the spinal cord, with paralysis finally appearing.[9,10,14,15,75]

In pregnancy the foetus does not seem to be affected by variations in the mother's level. However, it has been noted that if *several generations* of rats are kept deficient, the death rate in young animals rises sharply and their weight at four weeks old is reduced. The young of deficient mothers are often hydrocephalic and have eye problems.[75]

(NB: We do not know how many generations of our relatives have been deficient SO FAR! Let's stop the rot, before the situation gets any more hairy!)

Good sources: Organ meats, fish and pork, eggs, milk, cheese, yoghurt. For vegetarians, useful quantities can be found in soy sauce, tempeh, miso, dulse, kelp, spirulina, seeds, sprouted seeds. Some types of brewer's yeast also contain small amounts.

It is best taken with full B-Complex, Vitamin C, potassium and sodium.[73]

Folic acid is needed for the formation of red blood cells in the bone marrow, the making of antibodies and the utilisation of sugars and amino acids. It is also important for the formation of nucleic acids, substances essential for the growth and reproduction of all body cells, so it plays a crucial role in pregnancy.[73] It helps the digestive process. It works with B12 in making haemoglobin in the blood. It is essential for zinc metabolism.[70]

Deficiency in the adult can lead to pernicious and other types of anaemia,[1415] depression, dizziness, fatigue, pallor and susceptibility to infections. Anaemia in pregnancy can be a factor in smaller placentas, urinary tract infections and premature birth.[78]

Folic acid deficiency is common, and pregnancy exacerbates it. Foetal abnormalities in the young of deficient animals include cleft palate and hare lip, deformed limbs, malformations of the heart, diaphragm, urogenital system, blood vessels, adrenals, spina bifida, malformations of the eye, skeletal deformities, underdevelopment of the lung and kidney, cataracts, brain deformities, oedema and anaemia.[16] Foetal death and miscarriage or resorption may occur.

In litter animals, if folic acid is given at the time of resorption of some of the foetuses, others may survive to term but may have hydrocephalus.[85] If deficiency occurs during pregnancy, microcephaly can be seen in the new-born rats.[86]

In humans, folic acid has been the subject of much attention in pregnancy, especially in relation to neural tube defects, such as spina bifida. A number of studies have been done which suggest that women who are given supplements of folic acid in the month before conception and for the first 8-10 weeks afterwards, are less likely to have a malformed baby.[87,88]

Many of the research methods of these older studies were criticised as not proving the value of folic acid supplements. However, research has now lead the Government to recommend folic acid supplements for pregnant women.[89,90,91]

Taking all the research into account, there can be little doubt that folate deficiency in the mother, especially in the early stages of pregnancy, can be a major contributory factor in causing neural tube defects. But Foresight recommends that folic acid supplementation needs to be considered as part of a balanced supplementation programme. Professor Wald claimed that increasing intake by adding folate to flour used to make bread and cakes would not cause harm and would prevent 1500 of the 2000 spina bifida babies born each year.[92] However, Pfeiffer has shown that folic acid supplementation can have adverse effects on some schizophrenics.[14] Wholesale supplementation of the population is not advisable. Eating wholefoods, which contain a balance of vitamins is preferable with balanced supplementation as required. (See also manganese and zinc). 400mcg of folic acid daily has been part of the Foresight programme since 1979. However, it is always given in conjunction with other B Complex vitamins.

Good sources: Green leafy vegetables, brewer's yeast, organ meats, whole grains, wheat germ, milk, salmon, root vegetables, nuts.

It is best taken with full B-Complex and linoleic acid.[73]

NB: I am sure we have all seen the appeals in the newspapers for the poor little scraps with their hare lips and (probably) cleft palates. We are told these can be reversed for £150. Maybe, *and* they could have been prevented with a good multivitamin for about £11. No anguish, no pain or shock. It's a no brainer, really, isn't it?

Vitamin C keeps the collagen (connective tissue) healthy and resistant to penetration by viruses, poisons, toxins such as lead, dangerous drugs, allergens, and/or foreign materials. It promotes healing after surgery, infection or injury, including broken bones. It keeps the capillary walls intact. It helps the absorption of iron, preventing anaemia. It is important for mental health.[175,176,177]

Deficiency symptoms include scurvy, dandruff, and haemorrhages on the thighs, buttocks and abdomen, swollen and bleeding gums, leading to infection, ulceration and loss of teeth. There may be spontaneous bleeding. Children who are short of Vitamin C are prone to infections, have poor teeth and gums. Their bones break easily, they bruise easily and quickly tire and become irritable.[178] It has been linked with miscarriage.[179]

Good sources: Citrus fruit, rose hips, sprouted alfalfa seeds, tomatoes, green peppers, broccoli and other green vegetables, blackcurrants, strawberries and other soft fruits, bananas, apples, pears, carrot, cauliflower, new potatoes eaten with their skins and parsley.

Vitamin C is lost in storage. It is best taken with all vitamins and minerals, bioflavonoids, calcium and magnesium.

To tell you about the minerals, see Chapter 7 on Hair Mineral Analysis.

So what do we do?

Luckily, there is *plenty we can do.*

FOOD AND BEYOND

Food purchase and preparation

Knowing the contents of a healthy diet, you want to ensure that you do not spoil them by the wrong sort of preparation. Again a good wholefood cookery book will help, but here are some very basic guidelines:

1. Buy everything you can "organic". It has more nutrients in it, it is less toxic –ie it has less chemicals such as pesticides in it, and if it has the Soil Association logo it will not be GM contaminated. *These are three major benefits.*

2. Avoid much packet, tinned, precooked and generally stale food.

3. Buy everything you can fresh, keeping "sat on the shelf stuff" to a minimum. When you do have to buy manufactured stuff, use FIND OUT to check out the additives.

4. Buy carbohydrates whole where possible: Wholewheat flour bread, cakes and biscuits, brown rice etc. Sweeten with brown sugar, maple syrup, honey or molasses.

5. Eat as much food as you can in its raw state – most vegetables and fruit are delicious raw.

6.   *If you cook it:*

   • Steam rather than boil.

   • Stir fry rather than deep fry.

   • Grill, roast or stew rather than fry.

   • Prepare food as near to eating as possible.

   • The Foresight Wholefood Cookbook gives you lots of really good recipes.

Conclusion

It is often said that 'We are what we eat', and, like most clichés, there is an element of truth in it. If we want to be healthy, we must eat healthy food. If we want to have healthy children, we must recognise that this means providing the best ingredients – that is, the best food. This means food which is grown on good soil, or reared in healthy conditions, and eaten as near its natural state as possible. Fortunately, there is a rapidly increasing awareness that organic produce is superior and it is becoming much more available. Enjoy it, knowing that this was the type of food our three pioneers found to promote wellbeing and productive success! But also recognise that with modern life-styles, it is unlikely to give you all you need to prepare for pregnancy and lactation – you will need to supplement it.

Here are some bits and pieces of relevant research:

RUTGERS UNIVERSITY REPORT BY FIRMAN E BEAR, 1948

"Variation in Mineral Composition of Vegetables"

Percentage of Dry Weight/Quantities per 100 Grams Dry Weight Trace Elements/ppm Dry matter					
Veg:	**Snap Beans** *Organic* Non-org	**Cabbage** *Organic* Non-org	**Lettuce** *Organic* Non-org	**Tomato** *Organic* Non-org	**Spinach** *Organic* Non-org
Mineral Ash	*10.45* 4.04	*10.38* 6.12	*24.48* 7.01	*14.2* 6.07	*28.56* 12.38
Phosphorus	*0.36* 0.22	*0.38* 0.18	*0.43* 0.22	*0.35* 0.16	*0.52* 0.27
Calcium	*40.45* 15.5	*60* 17.5	*71* 16	*23* 4.5	*96* 47.5
Magnesium	*60* 14.8	*43.6* 13.6	*49.3* 13.1	*59.2* 4.5	*203.9* 46.9
Potassium	*99.7* 29.1	*148.3* 33.7	*176.5* 53.7	*148.3* 58.8	*237* 84.6
Sodium	*8.6* 0.9	*20.4* 0.8	*12.2* 0	*6.5* 0	*69.5* 0
Boron	*73* 10	*42* 7	*37* 6	*36* 3	*88* 12
Manganese	*60* 2	*13* 2	*169* 1	*68* 1	*117* 1
Iron	*227* 10	*94* 20	*516* 9	*1938* 1	*1584* 49
Copper	*69* 3	*48* 0.4	*60* 3	*53* 0	*32* 0.3
Cobalt	*0.26* 0	*0.15* 0	*0.19* 0	*0.63* 0	*0.25* 0.2

Henry Schroeder, Battleborough, Vermont

Refined Flour Contains:

(when compared with amounts found in wholewheat flour, taken as 100%)

Thiamine	23%	Chromium	13%
Riboflavin	20%	Manganese	9%
Nicotinamide	19%	Iron	19%
Pyridoxine	29%	Cobalt	13%
Pantothenate	50%	Copper	10-30%
Folic Acid	33%	Zinc	17%
Vitamin E	14%	Molybdenum	50%
		Magnesium	17%

Basis of Balanced Diet (take into account individual allergies)

<u>5 helpings per day of:</u>
Fruits and vegetables – organic, raw, cooked, dried and juiced.
Seeds, nuts and nut butters. (Soil Association label)

<u>2 helpings per day of:</u>
Meat, poultry, fish, game, shellfish, molluscs.

<u>4 helpings per day of:</u>
Grains – whole or crushed, raw or cooked. Cereals, bread, flour products, Rice Dream, Provomil. (If allergic to gluten, avoid wheat, oats, barley and rye.)

<u>3 helpings per day of:</u>
Dairy products – cow, goat and sheep; Milk, Yoghurt, Cheese, Butter, Crème Fraiche, Cream.
Eggs – hen, duck, goose and quail.
(If allergic to dairy, avoid as necessary. Substitute with "Rice Dream with Calcium". Some people who are allergic to cow's milk can manage goat's or sheep's milk, and products.)
Avoid White Flour and Sugar
Avoid Excess Tea, Coffee, Chocolate
Avoid Excess Canned and Packet Foods

The Three Golden Rules

1.   Organic. Whenever you can. *Think Green!*
2.   No refined carbohydrates. *Think Brown!*
3.   No hazardous additives. *Think Colour-free!*

FILTER DRINKING WATER (To Avoid Lead, Pesticides, Nitrates, Estrogens and Excess Chlorine and Copper)

<u>Suggestions to be considered for daily menus</u>: (just ideas to browse around and pick and choose)

<u>Breakfast</u>

Whole carbohydrates, bread, crisp-breads or muesli, porridge, cereals, fruit, fruit juice, yoghurts. Black molasses, honey, maple syrup.

Fresh, unsweetened juices.

If preferred, cooked breakfast*: fried wholewheat bread or potatoes/mushrooms, tomatoes, bananas, dates or prunes/bacon. Egg or fish, cooked as preferred. Fry fish in a small amount of oil or grill.

If allergic to milk, use milk alternatives, Oatley, Rice Dream, Provomil, almond milk (and hazelnut milk).

On bread or toast, butter, olive oil spread, nut butters, low sugar marmalade, jams, jelly or honey.

*beneficial if lunch is not a major meal.

Lunch (if main meal)

Meat, poultry, fish, offal, shellfish etc. Potatoes, rice, pollenta or pasta. 2 vegetables. Choose from: 1 bulb, (leeks or onions), 1 root, (beetroot, parsnip, carrot, swede), 1 legume, (runner & dwarf beans, peas, butter beans). 1 leaf or flower – (cabbage, spinach, greens, Khol Rabi, Broccoli, Cauliflower) Green salad, tomatoes, peppers, celery & apple, sultanas, other dried or fresh fruit.

Dessert: Dairy & fruit dessert. Dairy desserts include yoghurt, custard, junket, milk jelly, rice, semolina, sago, tapioca, cornflour, blancmange etc. Cheese and fruit. Sponge, crumble or pastry puddings or pancakes can be made with whole-grain flours.

Lunch (if secondary meal)

Whole-wheat bread protein sandwich: (ham, egg, sardine, salmon, prawn, pilchard, mackerel, trout, nut butter, cheese, tongue, beef, chicken etc) with a variety of salads. NB: Keep in a fridge if taken to work. Meat can "go off" if kept in a warm office. Soup can be taken in a vacuum flask. Raw fruit & yoghurt or cheese, with wholegrain biscuits. Simple fruit juice or smoothie.

Tea (if major meal)

Hot soup. Cold meats, fish or poultry and salad. Fish & chips. (Grilled tomatoes, baked beans. Peas, broccoli.) Wholegrain cakes, biscuits, bread, pancakes.

Dairy pudding and fruit, nuts, dried fruits. Sponge, crumble or pastry puddings made with whole-grain flours. Whole-wheat biscuits & cheese.

Herb tea, juice, milk or milk substitute. Marmite, Bovril or other beefy hot drink.

Tea (if snack meal)

Whole-wheat bread, cakes, scones, biscuits. Juice, herb tea, milk, Rice Dream or as above, or soup, or yoghurt. Dried or fresh fruits or nuts, or salad. Dollop of Greek yoghurt into hot soup.

Dinner/Supper (if main meal) see suggestions for Lunch given above.

Dinner/Supper (if snack meal) suggestions as sample menus given above.

*Alternate butter with oil-based spreads. Use nut butters, cream cheese, goat's cheese, honcy, sugar- free jams and jellies. Marmite and similar yeast spreads if yeast is not a problem.

Avoid, as far as possible, processed, tinned and packet foods, microwaved foods, excess tea and coffee and ersatz drinks with sugar substitutes and artificial colouring and flavourings, confectionery and white flour products. "Eat Organic" whenever possible. For more information and ideas, see the Foresight Wholefood Cookbook.

Ruth Jervis's Invaluable Practical Tips for the Kitchen[59]

1. Eat food fresh. Avoid storing fruit and vegetables wherever possible. Where inevitable, store in a cool place.
2. Avoid preparing in advance.
3. Use mineral water for boiling and use for soups or gravy.
4. Do not overcook. Heat destroys B complex vitamins and vitamin C.
5. Do not cook at all if it can be eaten raw! (You can *graze* mustard and cress!)
6. Make bread with yeast. Shop-bought bread made with bicarbonate of soda contains phytates which interfere with the absorption of zinc and calcium.
7. Soak muesli in the fridge overnight to destroy phytates. Phytates prevent the absorption of vital minerals such as calcium and zinc.
8. Boil the water first and add vegetables to minimise oxidation and loss of vitamin C, or preferably steam them. (Yes, they taste better steamed, too.)
9. Serve foods promptly after cooking.
10. Use stainless steel, enamelled or glass cookware. Aluminium is a toxic substance which accumulates in the body
11. Grill rather than fry food, if frying, use oil rather than hard fats. (Discard oil after use). Stir frying in a minimum of oil is the frying method of choice.
12. Many vegetables can be braised in the oven in a closed dish, moistened with stock.
13. Avoid microwaved foods, as this can destroy vitamins and enzymes in the food.
14. Filter all drinking water and cooking water, or use bottled water
15. Avoid hazardous colourings and other food chemicals.
16. Use eggs from free-range hens, preferably organically fed.
17. Peas, beans and lentils and the pectin from apples are natural ways of increasing the elimination of toxic metals.

Having bought all this Very Good Food, are you going to like it? Is the family going to like it? Will they eat it? *Or will they complain?* Well, firstly you have to explain to everybody, *"why"*. Explain that it will make them more good-looking, nicer, and much more clever – it will!

Secondly, I would say, if you are having to make big changes, make them gradually over a few weeks. Do not be too sudden! If you are changing over from white to brown flour for example, change a quarter of the recipe at a time.

Thirdly: Get them all to join in! If you are making homemade bread for example, involve them in it. Make it an "all hands on deck" situation! They will be keener on the loaf they kneaded for themselves!

GROWING OUR OWN

Fourthly, producing "own produce" can be hard work, but it can also give a great sense of achievement!

It is possible to buy organic rock dust (minerals!), organic manure, organic compost and organic water-on seaweed liquid manures. If you have stables near you, find out about horse-dung. If they ride near you in a rural situation, take a plastic bag and a trowel with you for a walk! This way you get it for free! If you have even a small amount of garden that is doing nothing, have a go! Why not?

I have found the easiest things to grow are runner beans, they are so prolific and go on and on for ages. You can buy little plants about 3 inches high in February or March. They need some sticks or netting to grow up. If they are in a prominent part of the garden, you can push in some climbing nasturtium pods here and there amongst them for visual effect! Or you could plant some sweet peas, and they will all look quite jolly and decorative together. Tomatoes can be put in a tub or growbags, along a sunny wall or fence. The growers are becoming quite innovative and you can now get climbing ones that have tiny little tomatoes, and keep on producing them, while growing up a rambler rose or similar.

If you can get four to six sweetcorn plants they can all stand together and will produce several cobs each. You can then pick them and sit in the garden and eat them raw which is lovely, much nicer than cooked. They even have their own little handle, so you don't have to bother with skewers!

The same goes for lettuce, it is a different taste when really fresh. So is baby spinach and beetroot leaves. Eat with chicory, nuts and pine kernals. Never let leaves be dreary. The bottom line is to make it all interesting and *delicious* and *fun*. Am I the only person who finds leaves pretty dull without dressing them up a bit? But hey, there are all the old sauces and garnishes. Red currant jelly on cabbage? Mint jelly on lots of things! Red onion garnish, apple sauce, - put sultanas in salads, and use nut butter with chopped apple in the salads too. Put marmalade on coleslaw (yes! It is lovely!) – watch Master-Chef etc, and pinch all their lovely ideas – even the ones John and Greg don't seem to go for! Chop up celery, lettuce, apple and plum and mix it with nuts and/or pine kernels, a 'dip' of cream cheese and onion. Have a go and let us know! Send all your ideas into the Newsletter, and we can spread them around!

Eat coleslaw with red currant jelly, sultanas, soaked prunes or apricots, a scoop of nut butter or a dollop of Greek yoghurt. Cut up celery and lettuce with grapes or pears and add nuts and pine kernels. Mix with cream cheese, or yoghurt, mayonnaise or honey, balsamic vinegar and oil. If you are more conventional, add herbs such as chervil.

Use maple syrup with avocados. Eat bland things with stuff with plenty of taste like sultanas, chopped apples, orange segments, grapefruit, cherries, plums?

Cooked plums are rather sour. Raw plums with avocado and lettuce are lovely, mixed with mayonnaise, yoghurt or cream cheese. Raw cabbage could be shredded up and mixed with red-currant jelly. Or sultanas and apple, or orange and grated carrot. If green leaves are a bit dull, mix them with something you do like. Grated cheese, if you are not milk allergic, tomato puree, chopped up apple, apricots, orange segments – bits of any fruit you like! Mix it all together, use a bit of honey, and a lot of imagination!

For savoury salads, prawns, sardines, crab, salmon, fried scallops are delicious, (and full of zinc!) For seafood sauce mix tomato ketchup, mayonnaise and cream in equal quantities.

Home grown lettuce is not bitter. If you need to pull it a while before you eat it – if you have an allotment a wee while away for example, - bring it in roots and all, and put the roots in water in a vase. Like a flower, it will go on living for a bit, and you can pull leaves off as you need them. If the garden is just outside the door, you can pull leaves off as you need them, as with everlasting spinach, baby beetroot plants and so on.

I find leeks and beetroots are very easy to grow. You buy little things about an inch high and put them in with a teaspoon. I like teaspoon gardening, it is not too onerous.

Peas, I find tend to be eaten by mice, but perhaps if you have a cat you will be luckier! We have tried brassicas, but if you are organic you have to try and cover them up with lots of muslin-like stuff, as otherwise you find you are running a white butterfly farm. Non-organic neighbours find this irritating, a bit like you are running a college of burglary.

I saw a TV programme about a Swedish girl (I think) who had a balcony to her town flat where she grew salad in large pots and sat amongst it all, eating freshly picked leaves. It looked great.

Gooseberry bushes don't take up too much space, neither do a few raspberry canes. You can get terracotta tenements for strawberries.

Just do what you can in the space you have. If you have space for a tree anywhere, even a little one, this is wonderful. The blossom is so pretty and picking your own fruit is one of the most cheerful occupations I know. I am sure many of you will be much more enterprising and innovative than I have been. Let us know, at Foresight, and we can put your ideas in the Newsletter.

47

Useful organisations are Garden Organic (www.gardenorganic.org.uk), The Soil Association (www.soilassociation.org), Good Gardener's Association (www.goodgardeners.org.uk). WORM (wessexorganic.org.uk)

If you are not allergic to gluten, there are wonderful brown breads, pitta breads, even, I see, whole-wheat organic pizzas! I can't eat flour myself, but looking along the shelves, I think you can have a Field Day, or 9 months of Field Days – or a lifetime of them come to that – on all the organic and wholegrain stuff there is out there!

With meat and poultry, remember to stick to organic. They have had a better life, and they will be much better for you too, not being laced with antibiotics, growth enhancers, extra hormones and so on, which can be a cause of feminisation of men, and infertility in women – quite apart from the cancer risk.

If you are going to try growing your own, try adding rock dust for minerals and liquid organic seaweed manure and compost and horse manure to your soil. Every positive move you make enhances your garden's basic fertility, and this will enhance your own as you eat the produce!

Get a few cookbooks – old and new – the Foresight one is good, (I can say this as I did not write it myself!) It was written for us by Norman and Ruth Jervis who were the daughter of the founder, and head chef of Enton Hall, the first of the "health hydros". Talk about relevant experience – they had a lifetime of it!

FOOD PREPARATION

Cooked or Raw food

Many famous doctors and naturopaths have advocated the benefits of raw foods, including Max Bircher-Benner, Max Gerson, Kristine Nolfi, John Douglas and more recently Gabriel Cousins. Most of them recommend a vegetarian diet comprising of 75 per cent raw food and 25 per cent cooked, though some of are not averse to between 75% and 100% raw, depending on the individual. Why do so many of them recommend that 'cooking may damage your health'? There are many reasons quoted, only some of which we can list:

- Cooking destroys vitamins. For example, if you cook fresh peas for five minutes, you destroy 20-40 per cent of Vitamin B1 and 30-40 per cent of Vitamin C. (Luckily peas are delicious raw!)

- Cooking destroys enzymes. These are essential for the efficient metabolism of food. For example, the phosphotases in milk, which break down the phosphorus-containing compounds as in lycene, are destroyed when milk is pasteurised. The result is that most of the calcium that milk contains becomes insoluble, making milk constipating.

- Other proteins are deformed, with some of the amino acids being destroyed, while others may be altered so they are useless.

- Fats heated to high temperatures change their structure from the 'cis' type, which the body needs and uses, to the 'trans' type, which the body cannot use, and which causes harm to health.

However, not all foods *can* be eaten raw: So, cooking does have some advantages:

- It destroys harmful organisms, especially in meat, poultry and some shellfish. It breaks down toxins in red and black beans. It changes the tough connective tissue in meat to gelatin, making eating easier.

- You can eat more cooked food than raw - maybe not an advantage if you are overweight!

Balance is the key, with plenty of raw food in a varied diet.

Microwave ovens

Microwave ovens 'cook' food not by the application of heat to it, but by generating heat from within it. There is no reliable work on how cooking in microwave ovens affects the nutritional value of the food. However, we do know some of the effects of microwave energy. Regulations about leakages are strict. You may buy a detector to check for leakages but there are no standards for such devices. Some work well, others do not. It is advisable to have a qualified repairman service your oven annually.

If you must use one, do not stand near it when it is on: do not cover food with plastic to cook. We know that microwaves affect cells inside the body but we do not know the 'safe' limit of microwave exposure. However, we do know that the official pronouncements on the 'safe' level have been dropping steadily over the last 20 years.

Me, I would get rid of it. A Danish study on mice showed after eating microwaved food, they got stomach cancer. Do we need this? Other studies have said microwaving destroys all vitamins and enzymes in the food. If this is true, it does us no good at all, and what is wrong with good old-fashioned cooking – especially if we are eating a lot of our food raw anyway?

To conclude:

What a Marathon of a chapter this has been! You and I both probably feel a bit exhausted!

However, hopefully Gail's academic tour de force will have given you pages where you can find the solution to many ills, not to mention those of friends and family, and let's hope you can find the vital spark to go a bit wild in the kitchen with the right ingredients!

49

Now we know *which* deficiencies cause *which* malformations and health problems in the babies, *now* we know why Nature will switch off the ovaries when you are not well enough nourished. The ovaries are just saying, "Here, hey, you can't get pregnant this month! You haven't enough zinc/selenium/manganese. It could mean disaster for the baby."

They then turn off. I suspect this is an age-old instinct. It happens in the wild, in times of famine, when another mouth to feed would be unwelcome. (This is also why farm livestock is so very well catered for. All the *vets* know "well-fed" means "fertile").

Two miscarriages and two ectopic pregnancies made a natural conception impossible when both severely damaged fallopian tubes were removed.

Helen knew that natural conception could never take place, so her only course of action was to take up the offer of three IVF attempts on the NHS. The first IVF attempt failed. The second embryo transfer was also rejected. After 4 years of infertility and with one more IVF attempt to go, Helen decided to seek help.

Following a car crash, Helen was trying acupuncture for her back and at the same time to find a remedy for infertility. Her acupuncturist suggested Foresight. After surfing through the Foresight website both Helen and her partner joined the Foresight Programme. Helen by now had stopped working full time.

It took six Hair Mineral Analyses and supplement adjustments before both partners felt that they were nutritionally and mentally ready, and attempting their third and final free IVF. Behold the pregnancy held! An 8lb 8oz baby girl was delivered by caesarean section. "We burst into tears and just couldn't take it all in. We had a wonderful baby. Today she is a very alert little girl, taking everything in around her, very content, thriving really well and sleeping through from 7pm to 7am from 16 weeks old! She is the first grandchild on my mother's side. She is cherished".

Once you get well, if the delay has not been too long, the ovaries will turn on again. In a few cases, they need to be reminded by a little reflexology or acupuncture, which can stimulate them by sending extra energy in their direction.

The same applies with the sperm. Zinc and selenium are particularly important. Once the sperm are all well fed, they become strong and purposeful. They remember what they are meant to be doing!

As your nutrition improves so do your looks. Your hair will become like the girls in the adverts for hair dye – without you having to bother to dye it! People have come to Foresight with hair problems, like big bald patches or receding hairlines (like Queen Elizabeth I) and in a few months it has all grown back in again. One lady was completely bald and came to us wearing a wig. After a few months on the Foresight programme, it came back so fast, it was reported to us: *"It is so thick, but so short, it looks like rabbit's fur!"* It had to go through that stage, of course, before it became longer, but she was absolutely delighted with it!

Nature is really brilliant. Lovely hair, smooth skin, bright eyes - and what happens? Men will fall in love with you, and you can take your pick – just as Nature intended!

The same with the chaps! A lot of Foresight fathers get promotion or do really well at what they are doing – as well as fatherhood! Strong and healthy means *efficient*, as well as virile!

It is a shame, and a huge waste of money, all the girls having Botox for shrivelled lips (lack of B2,) having "breast implants" for sagging bosoms, (too little food generally,) and paying huge sums of money to get the "surprised Chinese" look, due to tightening up all the wrinkles with a facelift.....(wrinkles due to a lack of Vitamin E, A and zinc).

Beauty glows through from the inside out, just get the diet into gear and watch it happen.

The food has been poor. The soil has been over worked and for this reason the food has been low in nutrients – even what we assume to be the "good" stuff. *But we can all make a brilliant recovery!*

It is important that we do ASAP! As a country, we cannot cope with any more years when the depression, excess drinking and drug taking (whether cannabis, Seroxat, heroin, ecstasy, Prozac, gin, whisky, cigarettes, or benzodiazepines, whatever) is the "norm"!

We are flagging in energy and breeding sick children. We are running the NHS ragged and it is running out of all of its (our!) funds, and we are also doing ghastly things to the wild-life.

Billions of pounds worth of foreign substances (as above) are being urinated into the drains and it is all going out to sea and killing off loads of fish, or affecting the soil, being picked up by the bees and the birds etc and causing ecological mayhem.

We must get back to natural food, clean water, brighter, better-looking, more productive people, happier children....

Well, there is a lot to be done. Onward!

References:

1.   Williams, R J (1973) Nutrition Against Disease, London, Bantam, page 51.
2.   Price, Weston A. Nutrition and Physical Degeneration. Le Mesa, CA, Price-Pottinger Foundation 1945
3.   Hoffer, A. 'Orthomolecular Nutrition at the Zoo'. Orthomolecular Psychiatry 1983, 12(2). 116-128

4.   Lodge-Rees, E (1983) Trace elements in pregnancy In: J Rose (Ed) Trace elements in health, London, Butterworths

5.   Lodge-Rees, E (1983) Prevention versus problems in pediatric science In: The Next Generation, Foresight

6.   Sohler, A et al (1977) Blood lead levels in Psychiatric Outpatients Reduced by Zinc and Vitamin C, J orthomolecular Psychiat 6(3): 272-276

7.   Ward, N. Durrant, S. Sankey, R J. Bound, J P. And Bryce-Smith, D.(1990) Elemental Factors in Human Foetal Development, J of Nutritional Medicine 1, 19-26

8.   Davis, A (1974) Let's Have Health children, Unwin paperbacks

9.   Davis, A (1954) Let's Eat Right to Keep Fit, New York, New American Library

10.   Tuormaa, T. The Adverse Effects of Zinc Deficiency, Foresight

11.   Bryce-Smith, D (1979) Environmental trace elements and their role in disorders of personality, intellect, behaviour and learning ability in children. Proceedings of the second new Zealand Seminar on Trace Elements and Health. University of Auckland, 22-26 January.

12.   Bryce-Smith, D and Hodgkinson, L (1986) The Zinc Solution, London, Century Arrow.

13.   Caldwell D F Oberleas, D (1969) Effects of Protein and Zinc Nutrition on Behaviour in the Rat Perinatal Factors Affecting Human Development 85:2-8

14.   Pfeiffer, Carl C (1975) Mental and elemental Nutrients, new Canaan, Keats

15.   Pfeiffer, Carl C (1978) 'Zinc and Other Micro-Nutrients', New Canaan, Keats

16.   Jennnings, I W (1970) Vitamins in Endocrine Metabolism, London

17.   Passwater, R and Cranton, E (1983) Trace Elements, Hair Analysis and Nutrition

18.   Vallee, B (1965) Zinc In: Comar, C L an dBronner, E S (eds) Mineral Metabolism, Vol II B, London, Academic Press

19.   Oberleas, D et al 91972) Trace Elements and Behaviour, Int Review Neurobiology Sup

20.   Ward, N et al (1987) Placental element levels in relation to foetal development for obstetrically "normal" births: A study of 37 elements, evidence for effects of cadmium, lead, and zinc on foetal growth and smoking as a source of cadmium. Int J Biosocial Res 9(1):63

21.   Pottenger, F M (1983) Pottenger's Cats, La Mesa, Price Pottenger Foundation

22.   Mc Carrison, Sir R (1984) Nutrition and Health, London, McCarrison Society

23.   Health Education Council. A discussion paper on proposals for nutritional guidelines for health education in Britain. Prepared for the National Advisory Committee on Nutrition Education by an ad hoc working party under the Chairmanship of Professor V.P.T. James. NACNE, September 1983.

24.   DHSS-COMA. 'Diet and cardiovascular disease', London, HMSO, 1984

25.   Report of the Board of Science and Education. 'Diet, Nutrition and Health', British Medical Association, March 1986

26.   The Health Education Council (now the Health Education Authority) has issued many booklets, as well as the NACNE report

27.   Williams, R J (1956) Biochemical Individuality: the basis for the genetotrophic concept, New York.

28. Kesserm Nucgaekm (1980) 'Nutrition and Vitamin Therapy', New York, Bantam, 1980

29. Hawkins, David, Pauling, Linus, 'Orthomolecular Psychiatry, Treatment of Schizophrenia', San Francisco, CA, W.H. Freeman and Company, 1973

30. Underwood, E J (1977) Trace Elements in Human and Animal Nutrition, new York, Academic Press

31. Jameson, S (1984) Zinc Status and Human Reproduction in : Zinc in Human Medicine proceedings of a Symposium on the role of zinc in health and disease, Isleworth

32. Ward, N I (1995) Preconceptual Care and Pregnancy Outcome, Journal of Nutritional and Environmental Medicine, 5, 205-8

33. Wynn, Arthur and Margaret, 'Prevention of Handicap of Early Pregnancy Origin'. Today – Building Tomorrow: International Conference on Physical Disabilities, Montreal June 4-6, 1986, First Session

34. Antonov A.N., 'Children born during the siege of Leningrad in 1952', J Pediatr, 1947, 30, 250-259

35. Smith, G.A., 'Effects of maternal undernutrition upon the newborn infant in Holland (1944-1945)', J Pediatr, 1947, 30, 250-259

36. Kamen, Betty and Si, 'The Damen Plan for Total Nutrition During Pregnancy', New York, Appleton-Century-Crofts 1981, 21-30. This gives a good overview of weight gain during pregnancy.

37. Montagu, Ashley, 'Life Before Birth', New York, New American Library 1961, 23

38. Doyle, W., Crawford, M.A. et al., 'The association of maternal diet and birth dimensions', J Nut Med, 1990, 1, 7-9

39. Reusens, B, et al., 'Controlling Factors of Foetal Nutrition', In: Carbohydrate Metabolism in Pregnancy, eds: Sutherland H.V., Stower, J.M., New York, Springer-Verlag, 1979, 209

40. Laurence, K.M. et al., 'Increased risk of recurrence of neural tube defects to mother on poor diets and the possible benefits of dietary counselling', Br Med J, 1980, 281, 1509-1511

41. Mortimer, G. Rosen, 'In The Beginning: Your Baby's Brain Before Birth', New York, New American Library, 1975, 25

42. Cannon, Geoffrey, 'Why Hampstead babies are 2lbs heavier', The Sunday Times, 28 March 1983

43. Ebrahim, G.J., 'The Problems of Undernutrition'. In: Nutrition and Disease, ed: Jarrett, R.J., Baltimore, University Park Press, 1979, 29

44. Rush, David, et al., 'Diet in Pregnancy: A Randomised Control Trial of Nutritional Supplements', Birth Defects Original Article Series, Vol 16, No 3, New York, Alan R. Liss Inc, 1980, 114

45. Hurley, Lucille, 'Developmental Nutrition', Englewood Cliffs, NJ, Prentice-Hall, 1980

46. Harrell, Ruth F. et al., 'The Influence of Vitamin Supplementation of the Diets of Pregnant and Lactating Women on the Intelligence of Their Offspring', Metabolism, 1956, 5, 555-562

47. Picciano, Mary Frances, 'Nutrient Needs of Infants', Nut Today, 1987, Feb, 8-13

48. Baird Cousins, 'Effects of Undernutrition on Central Nervous System Function', Nutr Reviews, 1965, 23, 65-68

49. Churchill, John A., et al. 'Birth Weight and Intelligence'. Obstet Gynecol, 1966, 28, 425-429

50. Seidmann, Daniel S., Laor, Arie, et al. 'Birth weight and intellectual performance in late adolescence.' Obstet and Gynecol. 1992, 79: 545-6
51. Holiverda-Kuipers, J., 'The cognitive development of low birthweight children', J Child psychology and Psychiat, 1987, 28, 321-328
52. Alice Higgins Foundation – Birth outcomes before and after a nutritional programme. Montreal.
53. Ebrahim, G J 91979) The Problems of Undernutrition In: Ed: R J Jarrett Nutrition and Disease, Baltimore, University Park Press
54. Peer, L.A,. et al., 'Effect of vitamins on human teratology', Plast Reconst Surg, 1964, 34, 358
55. Suharno, Djoko, West, Clive, E. et al., 'Improvement in the vitamin A status may contribute to the control of anaemic pregnant women', Lancet, 1993, 342, 1325
56. Hurley, L (1980) Developmental Nutrition, Englewood Cliffs, New Jersey
57. Hurley, L et al (1976) Teratogenic effects of magnesium deficiency, J Nut 106: 1254-1260
58. Hurley, L (1969) Zinc Deficiency in the Developing Rat, Am J Clin Nut 22: 1332-1339
59. Jervis, R and N (1984) The Foresight Wholefood Cookbook, London, Roberts Publications
60. Schroeder, H A (1973) The Trace Elements and Man, Old Greenwich, Devin-Adair
61. Erdmann, Robert, Meiron Jones, 'The Amino Revolution', London Century paperbacks, 1987, 82
62. Barnes, B. Male Infertility – Fighting Back (2003) Foresight
63. Moore Lappe, Francis, 'Diet for a Small Planet', New York, Ballentine, 1975
64. National Pure Water Association, York.
65. Mercier, Chas., 'Diet as a Factor in the Causation of Mental Disease', Lancet, 1916, i, 561
66. Smith, J.C. et al., 'Alterations in vitamin A metabolism during zinc deficiency and food and growth restriction', J Nut, 1976, 106, 569-574
67. Smith, J.C. et al., 'Zinc: a trace element essential in vitamin A metabolism', Science, 1973, 181, 954-955
68. Robson, John R.K., 'Malnutrition: its causation and control', New York, Gordon and Breach, 1972, 401
69. Hodges, Robert E., Adelman, Raymond D., 'Nutrition in Medical Practice', Philadelphia, W. B. Saunders, 1980, 43
70. Lesser, Michael, (1980) Nutrition and Vitamin Therapy
71. Hale, F., 'Pigs born without eye balls', J Hered, 1935, 24, 105-106
72. Gal, Isobel, et al., 'Vitamin A in relation to Human Congenital Malformation', 149
73. Nutrition Search Inc. 'Nutrition Almanac', New York, McGraw-Hill Book Company, 1979, 94
74. Marks, John, 'A Guide to the Vitamins', Lancaster Medical and Technical Publishing Co. Ltd, 1979, 46
75. Tomorrow's World, BBC 1, 12 November 1987
76. Horrobin, D F (1981) The Importance of Gamma-Linolenic Acid and Prostaglandin E1 in Human Nutrition and Medicine, J Holistic Med 3(2): 118-139
77. Graham, Judy, 'Evening Primrose Oil', Wellingborough, Thorsons 1984, 34
78. Kamen, B and S (1981) The Kamen Plan for Total Nutrition During Pregnancy

79. Colquhoun, Irene, Barnes, Belinda, 'The Hyperactive Child. What the Family Can Do', Wellingborough Thorsons, 1984

80. Hodges and Adelman (1980) Nutrition in Medical Practice, Philadelphia, W B Saunders

81. Robertson, W.F., 'Thalidomide (Distaval) and vitamin B deficiency', BMJ, 1962, 1, 792

82. Johnson, M K (1975) The Delayed Neuropathy Caused by Some Organophosphorous Esters: mechanism and challenge, Critical Reviews in Toxicology, June 289:313

83. Anon. 'Tie Deficiency in Vitamin B6 to Low Agpar', Medical Tribune, 2 April 1980, 27

84. Chaitnow, Leon, 'Candida Albicans. Could Yeast be Your Problem?', Thorsons, 198, 48

85. Stempak, J.G., 'Etiology of antenatal hydrocephalus induced by folic acid deficiency in the albino rat', Anat Rec, 1965, 151, 287

86. Arawaka, T. et al., 'Dilation of cerebral ventricles of rat offspring induced by 6 mercapto purine administration to dams', Tohoku J Exp Med, 1967, 91 143

87. Smithells, R.W. et al., 'Possible prevention of neural tube defects by preconceptual vitamin supplementation', Lancet, 1980, i, 339-340

88. Smithells, R.W. et al., 'Further experience of vitamin supplementation for the prevention of neural tube defect recurrences', Lancet, 1983, i, 1027-1031

89. MRC Vitamin Study Group. 'Prevention of neural tube defects: results of the Medical Research Council vitamin study', Lancet, 1991, 338, 131-7

90. Department of Health. 'Folic acid and the prevention of neural tube defects: report from an expert advisory group', Heywood: DoH Health Publication Unit, 1992, 21

91. Sutcliffe, Margaret, Schorah, Christopher J. et al., 'Prevention of neural tube defects', Lancet, 1993, 342, 1174

92. Fletcher, David, 'Cake recipe may prevent spina bifida', The Daily Telegraph, 13 January, 1994

CHAPTER 3

VOLUNTARY SOCIAL POISONS (OR WHAT I CALL VOSPs)

This chapter is about what I call the VOSPs, the voluntary social poisons we choose to make ourselves ill with, because we enjoy it! (At least in the early stages.)

The ones we are encouraged to use because it feels unsophisticated or excessively "do-goody" to be seen without them. Smoked and pickled old journalists rumble on about the "nanny state". The "method" schools of acting teach vomiting as an advanced level of thespianism. (We went through a period when you hardly dared to turn on the television without laying out the newspapers in front of it.)

Latterly, this seems to have died down a bit, but the theme seems to have been taken up enthusiastically by teenage revellers in town centres. Excess is "in". Sanity is "out".

SMOKING

Well, let's start with smoking.

So, how much harm does smoking really do (a) at a national level and (b) to our own tiny baby son or daughter (albeit that they may, as yet, just be a sperm with a twinkle in his tail, and an ova with a forming game plan).

There are even two ways of looking at "national". Firstly, looking at the approximately one out of three adults who smoke, and secondly at the rest of the country – the hapless taxpayers who have to shell out, year on year, to pay for the costs of their illnesses and their absenteeism from work. "*Hey*", you can hear the smokers yell, "*We pay plenty of money in taxes on our cigarettes*". Yes, but I gather there are reliable figures to show that this nothing like covers the costs that are inflicted on the NHS, and thus on the rest of us.

The truth is that the time has come when we have to learn to look at illness in a different way. Fifty years ago it was all looked upon as "*just bad luck*". You were shunted off to hospital (nice, clean, caring hospital) and visited by friends with cards and flowers, grapes and sympathy, and in due course, those who emerged fully repaired, rejoined the human race and got on with their lives.

That was then. Not too many people were ill, and by and large the NHS could cope. Not so many people were *volunteering* for illness, at younger and younger ages. Not so many people were *made* ill before they were even born. It was containable!

Now, as the rate of illness has increased, year on year, the NHS is on its knees. Bigger and bigger hospitals have been built. Many are so tall the windows have to be made so that they do not open, as we are told that changes in the air pressure could put undue strain on the structure. Far be it from me to wish to see the whole thing fall to the ground, but I feel uneasy about an entire building full of sick people hermetically sealed in with the so-called "air conditioning" blowing smells and germs from one place to another...

I am also unsure whether the modern young woman, with all the education and opportunities made available to her, wants to become a nurse or "carer", and devote her life to coping with sickness, dementia and double incontinence. Think about it.

I hear the anguish of those who have left their beloved relatives in this situation and have watched them lose their life to Clostridium Difficile (C-diff) or Methicillin-resistant Staphylococcus aureus (MRSA), in very un-ideal conditions. They may complain to their MP and we may hear a lot of rhetoric at Question Time from the green benches, or from Dimbleby's Question Time. However, have any of "those in power" ever faced *one week* of coping with these scenarios close up? I think not.

The days of the Nightingale-inspired Saints and the devout and devoted nuns are over. They are unlikely to come back. *So the point of all this is simple.* We need to learn how to keep ourselves well and, above all *sane*, if humanly possible, and we need to bring the next generation into the world *fit*. Happily, it is actually not as difficult as it may sound.

What the body needs is to have the nutrients to build and repair itself - good food, required supplements, clean water, fresh air - and to be free from the toxic factors that destroy human cells – namely, what I term *"drugs, bugs and plugs"* - voluntary Social Poisons (VOSPs), medical drugs, exogenous hormones, infections, infestations and rogue radiation. This is perfectly achievable with a bit of effort, and it is becoming even more necessary.

Now it is well known that smokers' children are much more likely to smoke than non-smokers',[1,2] so if you *are* a smoker it is probably not your fault. Your parents maybe set you up for your habit. *But,* for exactly the same reason, you can see how vital it is that *you* stop *now*, so this huge disadvantage is not passed on and on by succeeding generations until the end of time. It is in your hands.

There is a lot of scientific evidence out there that smoking causes abnormal pregnancies, illness, handicap and deformity in the babies.[3,4,5,6,7,8,9]

On average, the smokers' babies are about half a pound (226g) lighter that they would have been if their mother had not smoked.[10,11,12,13]

Both the nicotine and the lack of oxygen affect the growth of the baby, as they reduce the blood flow to the placenta and the uptake of protein.[14,15,16,17,18,19]

Researchers have also reported large areas of dead tissue in the placentas of smoking mothers. The baby is totally dependent on the placenta for his "support services", so this short changes the baby, while he is in a position where he cannot complain about it, or walk out and find a better situation elsewhere.[20,21]

Cadmium, which as we know, can damage the brain and kidneys in the newborn child, is present in large quantities in smokers' babies. The damage inflicted is not reversible.[22,23,24,25,26,27,28,29,30,31,32,33,34,35]

There is a greater risk of the baby being still-born, and of miscarriage, cleft palate and hare lip and central nervous system malformations. When you have waited as long for this precious little person as so many of you have, stillbirth or miscarriage is the very last thing you could bear. Never do anything that appreciably increases the risk. Cleft lips or palates are reversible by surgery, but it is a long and arduous process, more so for the baby, even, than for the parents. For a tiny baby, surgery is terrifying as well as painful, as you cannot explain to them what is going on. (I have been through this five times, and I cannot bear it.) Some of them with a bad cleft have lifetime problems with diction, and with a few there is some permanent disfigurement. Central nervous system aberrations can include spina bifida and mental retardation.
[36,37,38,39,40,41,42,43,44,45,46,47,48,49,50,51,52,53,54,55,56,57,58]

Many smokers' babies will be born small and early, which is agony if they have to be left behind in hospital in Special Care. This, good as many of the Special Care Baby Units (SCBUs) are, can never be as special as being with Mummy, as love is everything at this age. If you are breast-feeding, getting through the traffic to get back to him or her every three hours can become a Herculean task. (I know one mother who had to do this through the Christmas traffic for the whole of one December...) Being held up in traffic when you know your tiny person may be crying for you, and getting more and more miserable when you do not appear, is a nightmare. Prematurity is to be avoided at all costs, any mother who has been through it will tell you.

Ectopic pregnancies (where the embryo implants outside the womb, almost always in one of the fallopian tubes) are more common in smokers.[67]

This can usually lead to a tube being removed. This does not necessarily impede future fertility significantly, so long as the remaining tube is viable, but it has usually meant emergency surgery with all the panic and pain that that entails. In addition you lose the hope of *that* baby.

Last but not least, poor little smokers' children have been shown to have "poorer learning abilities" i.e. to be a bit thick![68,69,70,71,72,73,74,75,76,77,78,79,80,81,82] This is not their fault, but when they come home with a report at the end of term saying they are near the bottom of the class, and full of phrases like, "could try harder" and "does not pay attention" it is very depressing for them. Also for their parents.

The old-fashioned view was that the parents should then "give them a good talking to". Hopefully we have now moved into a more understanding era. However I would guess a lot of teenage "switching off" (girls), or bravado (boys) in class, and later sick notes and truancy, comes down to a biochemically disadvantaged brain stemming from before birth, whether through smoking, alcohol, deficiencies, food additives, pesticides – whatever. It can make for a miserable little life.

As if all these disadvantages were not hard enough for the poor little baby, if his mother continues smoking after birth, things get even more disappointing, as smoking has been shown to adversely affect milk production.[21,83] What a life! It has also been shown that physical and emotional development is slower. This can be permanent. [68,69,70,71,72,73,74,75,76,77,78,79,80,81,82]

So far we seem to have concentrated on the smoking mother. However, the adverse effects on the sperm can be just as heavy. Smoking can lower testosterone, and affect numbers of sperm, their health (normal forms) and their motility – i.e. their keenness to do their job and reach the ova. In other words, there are fewer sperm and they are not fit for purpose.[84,85,86,87,88]

Furthermore a study from Germany showed that the children of smoking *fathers* were two and a half times more likely to have a deformity.[89] Another study found facial defects to be related to paternal smoking. Yet another study has shown a smoking father to be a much increased cancer risk to their children.

On our website, the work of Tuula Tuormaa goes into all the disadvantages in detail and is backed by 155 scientific references. She leaves us in no doubt!

So what do we do?

Firstly, you need the motivation. You need to take in all of the previous pages and realise how your future child could be significantly better-looking, probably taller, certainly brighter academically, and that crucial but difficult to define area, "more together" generally. They will also be much less prone to illness. A huge amount of influence on their future lies in your hands.

Smoking

The women I talk to usually tell me that the men won't give up alcohol, and they (the women) can't give up smoking. Quite an interesting lesson in psychology really. It appears that the belief is: the men are in command –

and will make their own decisions. The women are in submission, *even to their cigarettes*. So let's disprove that last bit, and show the little brutes who is in charge!

THE BAD NEWS

- Smoking is the greatest single cause of ill health and premature death in the UK.

- Smokers have a 1 in 2 risk of getting ill and dying early from smoking.

- Smoking kills 120,000 people each year in the UK, compared to 5,000 in road accidents

- 13 people die each hour from smoking.

Over 80% of all lung cancer deaths are caused by smoking.

SOURCE: DEPARTMENT OF HEALTH, 2002

OTHER CHEMICALS FOUND IN TOBACCO SMOKE

ACETONE	WIDELY USED SOLVENT, FOR EXAMPLE IN NAIL POLISH REMOVER
AMMONIA	FOUND IN STRONG CLEANING FLUIDS
ARSENIC	A DEADLY POISON USED IN INSECTICIDES
BENZENE	USED AS A SOLVENT IN FUEL AND CHEMICAL MANUFACTURE
FORMALDEHYDE	HIGHLY POISONOUS, USED TO PRESERVE DEAD BODIES

For health practitioners who wish to give talks about smoking and fertility/pregnancy, we have a talk on PowerPoint.

So, how can we best help you to give up? There are some ideas that have been suggested, and used with success by some people, so we will pass them on.

- Firstly, giving up caffeine at the same time (coffee, tea and chocolate) is said to lessen *the cravings*. Yes, really, although I hear a few groans!

- Some people find it easiest to just throw the pack away, tell their friends what they are doing and ask for their support. If 2 or 3 of you can decide to do it together, the moral support will be helpful.

- Homoeopaths can give us what they call a remedy or nozode, comprising a minute amount of the tobacco potentised in such a way it helps to remove tobacco residues from the system. These are obtainable from Ainsworths Homoeopathic Chemists (see useful addresses list).

61

- I have been told by one successful 30-a-day quitter: You leave out one cigarette every few days, and say to yourself, "later". Starting with the first one of the day, and giving up one at a time. I think it took her 4 – 5 months, but it was a "lasting quit". She also put the money she saved in a jam jar in the kitchen and looked at it at intervals. I think in those days it was about 11p a cigarette – now, I suppose, it is much more. She found it encouraging – and useful!

- You take little protein or fruit snacks to eat throughout the day: nuts, hard-boiled eggs, fruit, mustard and cress, cheese cubes, white goat's cheese is lovely, so is organic Cheddar, celery, carrots, muesli bars. (Not as fattening as chocolate, cake, biscuits etc!)

- You have a hair analysis and get a Foresight programme. Tell us you are quitting and we will structure your programme to help as much as we can.

- See your local NHS "stop smoking nurse" and have a lung capacity test. This is very motivating I am told. It shows you how your lungs are struggling!

They also offer nicotine chewing gum, (I am told it doesn't work and its stains your teeth); nicotine inhaler (I am told this *does* help); and nicotine patches (I am told they *do* help. They gradually reduce the amount in the patch so that it tails off...)

- Helping people to stop smoking is usually a co-operative effort. Just half an hour reading through all the misfortunes that can plague smokers' children is very convincing. The most usual response is, "*I have been meaning to give up for ages, and this has really made my mind up.*"

60mg of pure nicotine placed on a person's tongue, would kill within minutes - Source: Department of Health, 2002

Quitters say it is helpful to occupy your hands and your brain cells:

So: embroidery, sewing, knitting, gross pointe, crochet – they have the advantage that you can make some money at it, once the family are "garmented up"!

There is also watercolour painting if you have a little talent, this could become another money-spinner! I guess you could write a novel, design gardens, make new curtains, and make new clothes? *Anything* to let the emerging entrepreneur take over from the addict! Think of yourself as a butterfly emerging from a chrysalis. Over to you. Good luck!

I have never smoked, so can't give you any blow-by-blow personal experience, but if you do find any extra helpful tips, do write into us, for the Newsletter and the website, and we will very much welcome your news!

I have recently read with a feeling of doom, that Indian women are enjoying the new found "freedom" of the contraceptive pill and cigarettes. I would say this is not liberation, but commercial exploitation.

Just as it needs to be explained to the Foreign Office that crashing about with tanks, bombs and guns, killing their husbands and sons, and destroying their homes is not *necessarily* increasing the happiness of the women in the Middle East, it needs to be made clear in India that causing women future infertility, cancer, and endless health problems is not doing them some huge favour.

Women do not want to be exactly like men! Only men feel this *must* be a good idea for us! We just need men to get off our backs, and let us be ourselves in our own way.

If they just stopped having (commercially lucrative) ideas about how to "transform the lives of women" that would be a liberation in itself.

We need to explain this to them.

Way back in 1980, I was rung up by a very intelligent young man from Teeside University. *"I've got some students needing to do a study"* he said. *"Is there anything we can do to help you?"*

"Can you make a rat smoke a cigarette?" I asked him. *"No problem,"* came the reply. *"You want me to get the effects of tobacco on pregnant rats then?"* *"No, on the father." "The FATHER – you think it affects the mate?" "Well, that's what I need you to find out for us." "I see...well....yes...all right."*

A year later, the following study emerged. It was with mice, not rats, and, as you see, it tells us a great deal. God bless Teeside University, and Dr Barry Hemsworth.

Teeside Study

Male mice were given daily injections of nicotine. This was calculated according to body weight and blood volume so that the amount of nicotine in their blood equated to that of a fully grown man smoking 20 cigarettes a day. Spermatogenesis in the mouse takes 11 days.

After 5 months of "moderate smoking" the first cohort of mice were mated. The female mice from these matings suffered a 16.4 in utero death rate, (equivalent to human miscarriage but with litter animals the remains are resorbed). This worked out at approximately one pup in six being lost. Of the remainder, 4.8% had suffered limb reduction deformities. (21.2% major disaster rate).

A second cohort of males were then allowed off their nicotine injections for a week and then mated. As spermatogenesis in a mouse takes only 11 days, this was roughly the equivalent of a "one third contaminated" sperm population, compared with the previous group.

63

The resultant matings from this group produced a 13.1% in utero death-rate, and a 1.6% limb reduction deformity rate (exactly one third the number of pups with malformed limbs). (A 14.7% major disaster rate.) A considerable improvement, although some nicotine was still present.

The final cohort was mated after 3 weeks entirely free from nicotine and the mother then suffered only 3.8% in utero losses, and there were no malformed limbs. (Only a 3.8% disaster rate.)

To show this more graphically:

Resorbed/Miscarried

Nicotine+	16.4%	(those given nicotine)
Nicotine ½	13.1%	(those given half the amount)
Nicotine -	3.8%	(nicotine free)

Malformed (Limb reduction deformity or missing limbs)

Nicotine +	4.8%	(those given nicotine)
Nicotine ½	1.6%	(those given half the amount)
Nicotine -	0%	(nicotine free)

[Hemsworth, BN, 'Deformation of the mouse foetus after ingestion of nicotine by the male'. IRCS Medical Science: Anatomy and Human Biology; Biochemistry: Developmental Biology and Medicine: Drug metabolism and Toxicology: Pathology: Pharmacology: Physiology: Reproduction: Obstetrics and Gynaecology. 1981. 9, 727-9]

This study is interesting for two reasons: It demonstrates that although a reduction in nicotine smoking does give some help, it is not enough. The whole process of spermatogenesis needs to take place free from this noxious element completely. It also shows us how early in spermatogenesis the sperm can be damaged. It also poses the question, *what could be achieved worldwide by healthy fatherhood?*

Currently, 1 baby in 4 (25%) of all babies in the UK are miscarried. If those born alive are 600,000 (approximate figures), then in the region of 200,000 babies perish in the womb every year. How many of these family tragedies are down to non viable sperm?

Over 5,000 babies are born every year with limb reduction deformity. (1 child in 120). How much of this could be prevented by no parent smoking?

At the very least, this should all be considered urgent for further research. However, to obtain this research, a lot of pressure will have to be brought to bear by the general public, as the wealth, and therefore the influence, of the alcohol and tobacco firms is immense. So we are unlikely to hear any more about this in the short-term. Just make up your own minds and protect your own children.

ALCOHOL

Alcohol however is a much more frequent problem. If I had one pound for every time I've heard, *"My husband definitely won't give up his beer, no way!"* I would be a very rich woman.

The most usual argument is that our mother or father drank and we are fine! Well, maybe, but probably they ate better food - less processed and less intensively farmed, so the probability is that they were much better banked up with essential vitamins and minerals. However, even so, if their offspring find they are unable to give up alcohol, this is indicative of unstable blood sugar, so it was not *really* an unqualified success! You could do even better for your lot!

Well, as with the smoking, there are a lot of good reasons for giving the baby a level playing field. Foetal alcohol syndrome, FAS, has been well documented in the last 30 years. More recently in the USA, they have studied the effects of quite small amounts of alcohol, and have identified a new category of lesser disadvantages they have called FAE (foetal alcohol effect).

More recently still, it has been queried whether a grandparent's past drinking is affecting the grandchildren. In one way this sounds like very bad news. But, on the other hand, we can stand this on its head, and say that, by abstaining <u>now</u>, you could be benefiting not only your own children, but even your future *grandchildren*!

In the Bible we are told *"the sins of the fathers will be visited upon the sons, even until the 10th generation"*. This is usually looked upon as a particularly dire, almost vindictive, threat. But I think in reality it was a *warning*. As with most biblical pointers, it was pertinent and intended to be helpful, so we may as well take it on board. Think about it. Grab a calculator. If each generation multiplies by only two, by abstaining *now* you will be helping 2,046 of your descendants to have a better life! Formidable, really!

As people so often come to Foresight when they have one very much loved, but damaged little person, I am all the time hearing, *"he is very hyperactive, he never stops all day, or all-night really, we haven't had a full night's sleep since he arrived, we take it in turns..."*

"My little girl is covered in eczema, hardly anywhere on her body is not affected..."

"One of my children is autistic. I have help with him during the day, but it is very hard..."

"My little boy has asthma. It is quite frightening sometimes. We have had to rush him to hospital for oxygen more than once...."

And so on. They all wanted to know <u>one thing</u>. Is there anything we can do to stop it happening again? They are coping manfully, but the cry is, *"we just couldn't manage with two of them like this."*

Well, yes, we do manage to produce one without problems with their cooperation, and the help of the full Foresight programme. We also help the original little one with *his or her* problems, looking for food and other allergies, for mineral deficiencies (zinc, manganese, selenium and magnesium will be low). Often copper or a toxic metal will be high – there may be a urinary tract infection, a bed in a position vulnerable to geophysical stress, and so on.

But recently, I have started to ask: *"I hope you don't mind this question, and of course you need not answer me if you do not want to, but was there, by any chance, any quite heavy consumption of alcohol in any of the grandparents?"*

I have been very interested by how many times I have heard:

"Oh my God yes, permanently awash."

"Grandfather, yes, very much so, I'm afraid."

"Yes, indeed, yes. What we went through..."

"Don't mind you asking, no, but why? Are you finding out something? Is it connected to the problems with the kids? I always thought it might be."

"Alcohol, oh my dear yes, very heavy, very heavy indeed, I think you could say."

And so on. Not too surprising really.

(a) alcohol dehydrogenase is a zinc dependent enzyme. So consumption of alcohol removes zinc from the system big-time.

(b) essential fatty acids, and most particularly omega-3, are also used up.

(c) B-complex vitamins are squandered.

If the sperm and/or the ova that creates the child are short of these elements (and a host of others also, no doubt) then the resultant babies will also be deficient. But the fascinating, but daunting, follow-through is that their minute ova and their tiny testicles may also be short, and, unless this is addressed and rectified before they start to reproduce, some of their future offspring may also suffer. (I hope some really switched-on scientists will do a study on this before too long.)

One thing we do know, is that when the mineral imbalances etc are addressed and fully corrected before conception, the children come through very well. They are intelligent and often with surprising bonuses, such as a talent for music, or chess, or drawing.... whatever.

Research has shown unequivocal answers. In one study, male mice were given alcohol for 26 days, and then sobered up for two days prior to mating. The litter size was halved, and of those who were born, 88% died within a month.[91] Another study proved that alcohol had a specific effect on the chromosomes. This would have implications for many miscarriages, as well as physical and mental handicaps.[92]

Effects on male fertility are dire; in heavy drinkers, the sperm have been noticed to have no tails. This would, of course, mean they could not reach the ova and do the deed.[93] Russian research has found abnormalities in the sperm of alcoholic men which they believe could cause abnormalities in any children they produced.[94]

Another study in 1975 found alcohol induced testicular atrophy.[95] Yet other studies have linked alcohol to problems with the production of testosterone and the function of the testicles.[96,97,98,99,100,101]

It seems to me extremely likely that this is a brilliant design mechanism of nature. If the sperm are likely to produce a physically or mentally afflicted baby, nature does her level best to ensure they cannot reach the egg and thus cannot fertilise. So many lifelong tragedies may have been averted by this excellent mechanism.

This is why, once the intake of alcohol had been temporarily interrupted, after about four months we get the ecstatic phone call we so love to hear, "*Would you believe it, I'm pregnant!*"

Sperm take approximately 116 days to "make" so this is often the timescale, between, "*he says he will give up alcohol*", and the magic moment.

The direct converse to this is the IVF scenario where the sperm are taken by force, manhandled into a saucer, made to do their duty, (against their better judgement), and then the tears because the "treatment" has failed, or later because there has been a miscarriage.

People come to us constantly having had 3, 4, 5 failed IUIs, IVFs, ICSIs and so on. The man drinking a "normal" amount, 18 to 25 units a week, say. "*Nobody ever told us it mattered. Does it really? Will it make a difference?*" Often they have spent £12,000 to £20,000 and there is still no baby (probably fortunately).

Typically, foetal alcohol syndrome (FAS) is described thus: growth retardation, meaning low birth weight, failure to thrive, and subsequent short stature, although at puberty there maybe weight gain, particularly in the girls, who tend, later in life, to be short but obese.

There are facial characteristics which included a low nasal bridge, back tilted nose, with "exaggerated epicanthic folds" (sides of nose to corner of mouth), and a flat philtrum (space between nose and mouth) and a very little vermillion for the upper lip. The openings for the eyes tend to be rather short giving a "round eyed" kittenish appearance, and there may be a squint. The ears tend to be unusual in form, sometimes simple and sometimes with the top folded down lower than normal on one or both ears.

There are often (in about 40% of cases) some muscle and skeleton defects such as bent fingers, and hip or rib cage abnormalities. Psychologically, as well as physically, the worst effects can be the genital abnormalities where it is hard to tell if a child is a boy or a girl. Some kidney abnormalities have also been detected. Nearly one in three will have a heart defect of some kind, often requiring surgery, which is sometimes fatal.

Defects of the central nervous system can range from poor hand-eye coordination resulting in excessive clumsiness, to seizures and mental retardation. As infants, they may be fretful and have difficulty suckling and feeding, making them very unsettled and difficult to rear.

The average IQ of children born with FAS is 65, well below the national average of 100. FAS is the leading known cause of mental retardation. About 70% of the children with the syndrome are hyperactive, and are prone to rocking and head banging.

When they arrive at school age there are serious problems with behaviour and quite severe learning difficulties.

The problems do not abate with age, but, it would appear that they become more severe, with difficulties with acquiring skills, keeping jobs, managing money affairs and retaining relationships.

The work of Dr Anne Steissguth of the USA, who followed the lives of her little FAS children through to adulthood makes very sad reading.

According to her, the FAS child although sometimes a bright, chirpy, giggly little thing at the outset, upon coming to the challenges of real school, will find life very stressful. He will be prone to tears and tantrums, disappointment and resentment, as his limitations become exposed, and possibly his little friends become scornful about his lack of ability.

As school continues, his inability to organise himself and fully take in everything around him, becomes more and more of a burden to him. He may clown his way through or he may become deeply depressed.

Dr Streissguth followed her little FAS patients through to maturity, and she found them more prone to alcoholism, drug-taking, living off benefits, mental illness and suicide. They found it difficult to stay in a job or a relationship. Many became destitute despite their best intentions, and the support of family and friends. These were the frank FAS children.

FAE (Foetal Alcohol Effect) is the term for the children less severely affected, but not untouched by their background. The effects can be less severe, but nonetheless, the child's life can be limited, and his ability diminished – and do we want to inflict this on Our Hero? No, we don't.

Reading the research, it is obvious that it would be a very different world we would be living in if no unborn baby were affected by alcohol. In our booklet, "The Adverse Effects of Alcohol on Reproduction", Tuula Tuormaa sums up the problems. She wrote with such dedication and such clarity that I felt I could not better it, and so I have asked her to let me use it to show you how widespread and how damaging the problems are. It is on our website, in full.

For the most part, I find that once the possible consequences of drinking prior to/during pregnancy and during breast-feeding are explained to women, they are immediately able to take in the implications.

So, what do we do?

After a lot of explanation and persuasion, almost all of the men who contact us are also convinced! Stratagems we find helpful with those who find it really hard to give up include:

• Combating Reactive Hypoglycaemia. This occurs when the pancreas is functioning at a less than optimal level. This may be because of heavy alcohol or sugar consumption in previous generations (we do not yet know this, but it would be worthy of study). This could have meant the pancreas was small or weak (poorly functioning) at birth. Or it could just be because of a childhood diet high in sugar, possibly white sugar and flour. This would have meant the pancreas was overused and undernourished.

The pancreas needs the trace minerals chromium, manganese and zinc, and plenty of the B-complex vitamins especially pantothenate and the essential fatty acids, to function properly.

If the pancreas is somewhat exhausted, the person will crave sugar, or alcohol. Indeed, they will feel unable to function adequately without a boost.

Once the alcohol (or chocolate, coffee, whatever) kick in, this causes a rise in the blood sugar, and creates a "high". If the alcohol intake is considerable there will be feelings of boundless energy, infallibility, and elation. If things have not gone "over the top", for a period the drinker will function well, physically or intellectually.

This will, however, be followed by a commensurate fall in blood sugar, and (in overt alcoholism at least) the "fall" period will be filled with fatigue, muddle, depression – sometimes by self doubt and despair – sometimes by self-pity, feelings of being exploited and righteous indignation! All not easy to live with for the long suffering relatives and colleagues! (This is a pattern that may be mirrored at a milder level in the more modest imbiber!)

A helpful measure is hair analysis, plus a tailor-made programme of supplements, which would include B-complex vitamins, chromium, zinc, manganese and omega-3 supplements to restore optimum nutrient status. Also vitamin C., garlic, milk thistle and nicotinamide to help cleanse the liver and kidneys. Drinking plenty of water, and having a good wholefood diet will help.

• Also, I would increase the intake of omega-3 oils. They are present in oily fish, also in supplements of specific fish oil, or in the flax seed oil such as High Barn Oil. Although it is said that absorption from flax seed oil can be more difficult, as it requires the body to take one more step in the conversion, I feel there are advantages in High Barn Oils as they are more reasonably priced. They are less likely to be contaminated with heavy metals than oils from deep sea fish. (The oceans are becoming depressingly polluted.)

Subjectively, I also find they do not give me a headache, and I often find the fish oils do. I am sometimes told by Foresight people that they find this too. If you get the oil capsules you can bite them, chew them for a minute to obtain all the oil, and then spit out the capsules and throw them away, which saves you having to digest the gelatine. This also tastes nice, which the fish oils do not!

•   <u>Attention to Possible Allergies</u>: Dr Theron Randolph, an American doctor with a keen interest in allergies, found that some regular drinkers had a craving for alcohol made from a substance to which they were allergic. (I think it is permissible to wonder which came first, the heavy intake of the fermented substance, or the allergy to the basic foodstuff?) Be that as it may, it is worth taking his theory on board, if there are difficulties. It has the merit of being completely harmless, easy to do, and not costing anything!

Whisky cravings: eliminate grains. (Probably wheat, oats, barley and rye). Presumably Irish whisky, eliminate potatoes. (When you eliminate potatoes it may be necessary to eliminate the whole "belladonna" family – potatoes, tomatoes, aubergines and peppers.)

Vodka cravings: eliminate potatoes etc, as above.
Wine cravings: eliminate the grape.
Cider cravings: eliminate the Apple.
I admit to feeling somewhat nonplussed regarding gin. Do we eat any relative of the juniper berry? My botany does not stretch to this, as yet, but I am very anxious to learn. Help welcomed.

•   <u>Lessening the intake of sugar.</u> It is worth noting at this point, that, when giving up alcohol, cigarettes, coffee, chocolate and sugar will make the situation *worse*. They will all tweak at the pancreas, which is already somewhat fed up.

It is possible to drink a huge range of other substances, so long as you are not allergic to them. There are alcohol-free wines and beers, so long as they do not set off any cravings again.

There are endless hot or cold milk drinks if you are not allergic to milk. If you are, you may be okay on goat's milk, rice milk or nut milks such as almond milk.

There are herbal teas, fruit juices, smoothies in huge varieties. There is Marmite (if you are not yeast allergic), and, if you are not grain allergic, beef or chicken Bovril, also Tesco's 'Beefy' which is gluten free. Soya milk has
70

become a bit suspect as they may be allowing in GM soya. However, so long as you are not a whisky craver, there is a lovely milk called Oatley.

The "Land of Milk and Honey" was, of course, the land of goat's milk and honey, and this is very possible to achieve these days, as even the most modest little corner store sells goat's milk. Maple syrup can be another idea to alternate with honey. Probably clean water is the best of the lot, and is almost certainly the most helpful to fertility!

•   Using nutrients. It is an excellent idea to take more care of the pancreas and the liver with B complex vitamins, zinc, manganese and magnesium. As the whole digestive system starts to function better, the blood sugar, and thus the brain function, becomes more stable. Caffeine and sugar need to be avoided. Protein, fruit and vegetables, with some complex carbohydrates (which means brown bread and brown rice, or stuff made with brown flour) can be taken on board. All this, plus plenty of clean water and plenty of fresh air, will go a lot of the way.

•   Combat boredom with creative ventures. *Surely we all need*: plenty of music, good books, time for planting things in the garden – perhaps painting the house or painting a picture, writing to the newspapers with your views on anything? Perhaps go to the gym or take up a sport? How about making clothes, embroidery, and tapestry, anything – just doing something creative. These things provide a "mood-lift" because they are *satisfying*. I believe these could all be more helpful than anything else.

I think we none of us spend enough time out-doors – do we? We should all be much freer to do our own creating. We were meant to be more like the birds flying about the rooftops. Wild and inventive and following our own ideas. Much less tied to routine and schedules – much more joyful about what we do – much less bored!

Isn't either loneliness or boredom somewhere at the bottom of addiction in many cases? I feel we have too little contact with animals – they were such a joy when I was part of farm life – there is more feed-back from something animate than from machinery! As we empathise with them, our basic instincts develop more, I feel. We seem to listen too much, and sing too little. Walk too much and dance too little. We do not spend enough time with little children. What do you think?

If we took into ourselves more of the stuff that makes us happy in the long term, and much less of the stuff that makes us happy for a couple of hours and then cantankerous and dreary in the long term, the whole world would have a holiday!

To get back to our subject! As with smoking, we have put an excellent summary of 124 papers on alcohol and fertility compiled by Tuula Tuormaa on our website.

We have also a PowerPoint disc to help any bold pioneers who will try to help the cause by going out there and giving talks. We need help from all of you.

If only we can rescue the next generation by seeing that they are properly nourished from the ova and sperm stage, to birth, and that the birth is accomplished with as little drug use as possible, and they are then breastfed by a drug-free mum, I think we have every hope of beating the evil of drugs.

Teenagers who have had too little energy and zest for life all through their childhood, are vulnerable to the myth of substances they are told will give them new and exciting experiences, and make them more trendy and alluring.

I recently had a Christmas card from the mother of our first ever pair of twins. One had just done his PhD, and two universities are after him for research into environmental issues. His twin sister has just been out to Africa to help build a school! The excitement and the fulfilment of hopes and dreams is on offer Out There. The young ones just need to be well enough and bright enough to take up the challenges!

Onward!

Some useful research findings:

B.M.J. Vol 286. January <u>1983</u>
Alcohol & Advice to the Pregnant Woman
<u>Californian study</u> of 32,000 pregnancies
Women taking 1-2 drinks daily the risk of miscarriage doubled when compared with non-drinkers.
<u>New York study</u> of women who drank twice weekly, only 2 drinks per occasion, had miscarriage rate of 25%
<u>Seattle study</u> on congenital abnormalities:
4 drinks per day, 19% abnormalities
2-4 drinks per day, 11% abnormalities
Fewer than 2 drinks per day, 2% abnormalities
Some criticism due to maternal age in some cases
<u>**The United States Surgeon General**</u>: "advises women who are pregnant (or considering pregnancy) not to drink alcoholic beverages and to be aware of the alcoholic content of food and drugs."

HEART DEFECTS
ACCOMPANY F.A.S.
In the history of 24 patients with FAS, 13 had a heart defect. (sic)
- ♥   7 congenital heart disease
- ♥   2 ventricular septal defect
- ♥   1 patent ductus arterioscus
- ♥   4 heart murmurs (later spontaneously corrected)

(NB there appear to be 14 from the script) (58.3%)
Accompanied by typical growth retardation, development delay and facial anomalies.

J.A.M.A. May 1976

Nutrition Reviews. February 1982
<u>Average Birth Weights:</u>
In mothers consuming alcohol throughout pregnancy:
2,786g ± 485g (6lb 2oz)

In mothers who drank previously, but abandoned alcohol upon becoming pregnant:
3,137g ± 466g (6lb 15oz)

In mothers who did not drink alcohol:
3,520g ± 419g (7lb 12oz)

CAFFEINE AND MISCARRIAGES

Drinking 3 or more cups of tea or coffee a day is associated with increased risk of miscarriage (American Journal of Epidemiology 1996)

Caffeine during pregnancy can increase the probability of chromosomal abnormality which could lead to a miscarriage. (American Journal of Obstetrics and Gynaecology 1985)

Since 1980, the US Food and Drug Administration has advised pregnant women to minimise caffeine intake, citing the dangers of possible miscarriage or having a mentally retarded baby.

Even de-caffinated coffee is linked to an increased risk of miscarriage. (American Journal of Epidemiology 1996)

References:

1. Rantakallio P (1979) Social background of mothers who smoked during pregnancy and the influence of these factors on the offspring. Soc Sci Med, 13A:423-429

2. Rantakallio P (1983) A follow-up study up to the age of 14 of children whose mothers smoked during pregnancy. Acta PediatrScand, 72:747

3. Wynn M and Wynn A (1981) The Prevention of Handicap of Early Pregnancy Origin, pp 28-33, Foundation for Education and Research in Childbearing, 27 Walpole Street, London SW3

4. Kelly J, Mathews KA, O'Conor M (1984) Smoking during pregnancy: effects on mother and the foetus. Br J Obstet Gynaecol, 91:111-117

5. US Public Health Service, 'The Health Consequences of Smoking for Women'. A Report of the US Surgeon-General, Office on Smoking and Health, US Dept of Health and Human Services, Rockville Mid, 1980

6. Abel, Ernest L., Marijuana, Tobacco, Alcohol and Reproduction, Boca Raton, F1, CRC Press, 1983, 31-33

7. Himmelberger, D.U., et al., 'Cigarette smoking during pregnancy and the occurrence of spontaneous abortion and congenital abnormality', Am J Epidemiology, 1978, 108, 470-479

8. Nieburg, P. et al., 'The Foetal Tobacco Syndrome', JAMA, 1985, 253, 2998-2999

9. Sterling, H.F. et al., 'Passive smoking in utero: its effects on neonatal appearance', British Medical Journal, 1987, 295, 627-628

10. Simpson, W.J., 'A preliminary report on cigarette smoking and the incidence of prematurity', Am J Obstet Gynacol, 1957, 73, 800-815

11. Crosby, W.M. et al., 'Foetal malnutrition: an appraisal of correlated factors', Am J Obstet Gynacol, 1977, 128, 22

12. Goujard, J., Kaminiski, C, et al., 'Maternal Smoking, Alcohol Consumption and Abruptio Placentae', Am J Obstet Gynacol, 1978, 130, 738

13. Fedrick, J., Anderson, A., 'Factors associated with spontaneous pre-term birth', Br J Obstet Gynaecol, 1976, 83, 342

14. Lehtovirta P and Forss M (1978) The acute effects of smoking on intravillous blood flow of the placenta. Br J Obstet Gynaecol, 85:729-731

15. Naeye RL (1978) Effects of maternal cigarette smoking on the foetus and placenta. Br J Obstet Gynaecol, 85:732-737

16. Longo LD (1970) Carbon monoxide in pregnant mother and foetus and its exchange across the placenta. Ann NY Acad Sci, 174:313-341

17. Longo LD (1977) The biological effects of carbon monoxide on the pregnant woman foetus and newborn infant. Am J Obstet Gynecol, 129:69-103

18. Himmelberger, D U et al (1978) Cigarette smoking during pregnancy and the occurrence of spontaneous abortion and congenital abnormality, A J Epid 108:470-479

19. Simpson, J (1957) A preliminary report on cigarette smoking and the incidence of prematurity, Am J Obstet Gynaecol, 73: 800-815

20. Stirling, H F et al (1987) Passive smoking in utero: its effects on neonatal appearance, BMJ 295:627-628

21. US Public Health Service (1980) The Health Consequences of Smoking for Women. A report of the US Surgeon General, Office on Smoking and Health, US department of Health and Human Services, Rockville

22. Ostergaard K (1977) The concentration of cadmium in renal tissue from smokers and non-smokers. Acta Med Scand, 202:193-195

23. Nandi M, Slone D, Jick H, Shapiro S, Lewis GP (1969) Cadmium content of cigarettes. The Lancet, 2:1329

24. Lewis GP, Coughlin LL, Jusko JW, Hartz S (1972) Contribution of cigarette smoking to cadmium accumulation in man. The Lancet, 1:291

25. Lewis GP, Jusko WJ, Coughlin L (1972) Cadmium accumulation in man: influence of smoking, occupation, alcohol habit and disease. J Chronic Dis, 25:717

26. Menden EE, Ella VJ, Michael LW, Petering HG (1972) Distribution of cadmium and nickel of tobacco during cigarette smoking. Environ Sci Technol, 6:830

27. Cadmium in the environment and its significance to man. U.K. Department of the Environment, Pollution Paper No:17, Her Majesty's Stationery Office, London 1980

28. Hammer DI, Calocci AV, Hasseiblad V. Williams ME, Pinkerton C (1973) Cadmium and lead in autopsy tissue. J Occup Med, 15:956

29. Schroeder HA and Winton WH (1962) Hypertension induced in rats by small doses of cadmium. Am J Physiol, 202:515

30.   Lener J and Bibr B (1971) Cadmium and hypertension. The Lancet, 1:970

31.   Kallerup HE, Kierkegord-Hansen G, Hansen JC (1976) Exposure to cadmium as a possible precipitating factor in connective tissue disease. Ugerskr Laeger, 138:1396

32.   Ward NI, Watson R, Bryce-Smith D (1987) Placental element levels in relation to foetal development for obstetrically normal births: A study of 37 elements. Evidence for effects of cadmium, lead and zinc on foetal growth, and smoking as a cause of cadmium. Int J Biosocial Res, 9(1):63-81

33.   Siegers CP, Jungblut JR, Klink F, Oberhauser F (1983) Effects of smoking on cadmium and lead concentrations in human amniotic fluid. Toxicol Letters, 19(3):327-331

34.   Ward N.I.(1994) The effect of cadmium from smoking activity (non, active and passive) on the outcome of pregnancy. Foresight Spring Newsletter, pp 0-13,

35.   Carmichael NG, Backhouse BL, Winder C, Lewis PD (1982) Teratogenicity, toxicity, and perinatal effects of cadmium. Human Toxicol, 1:159-186

36.   Meyer MB, Jonas BS, Tonascia JA (1976) Perinatal events associated with maternal smoking in pregnancy. Am J Epidemiol, 103:464-476

37.   O'Lane JM (1963) Some foetal effects of maternal cigarette smoking. Am J Obstet Gynecol, 22:181-184

38.   Zabriskie JR: Effect of cigarette smoking during pregnancy: Study of 2000 cases. Obsted Gynecol, 21:405-411, 19634039.

39.   Ravenholt RT, and Levinski MJ (1965) Smoking during pregnancy. The Lancet, 1:961

40.   Ravenholt RT, Levinski MJ, Nellist DJ et al. (1966) Effects of smoking upon reproduction. Am J Obstet Gynecol, 96:267-281

41.   Russell C, Scott TR, Maddison RN (1966) Some effects of smoking in pregnancy. J Obstet Gynaecol Br Commonw, 73:742-746

42.   Underwood PB, Kesler KF, O'Lane JM et al. (1967) Parental smoking empirically related to pregnancy outcome. Obestet Gynecol, 29:1-8

43.   Mulcahy R (1968) Effect of age, parity, and cigarette smoking on outcome of pregnancy. Am J Obstet Gynecol, 101:844-849

44.   Yerusnaimy (1964) Mothers' cigarette smoking and survival of infant. Am J Obstet Gynecol, 88:505-518

45.   Comstock GW and Lundin FE (1967) Parental smoking and perinatal mortality. Am J Obstet Gynecol, 98:708-718

46.   Perinatal Mortality Study, Ten University Teaching Hospitals, Ontario, Canada, Publ: The Ontario Department of Health, Toronto, p 173, 1967

47.   Butler NR and Alberman ED (1969) Perinatal Problems: The Second Report of the 1958 British Perinatal Mortality Survey. Edinburgh, Livingstone

48.   Kullander S and Kallen B (1971) A prospective study of smoking in pregnancy. Acta Obstet Gynecol Scand, 50:83-94

49.   The Health Consequences of Smoking: A Report of the Surgeon General: U.S. Department of Health Education and Welfare, 1039(1 0):1 23-137, 1973

50.   Meyer MB, Tonascia JA, Buck C (1974) The interrelationship of maternal smoking and increased perinatal mortality with other risk factors. Further analysis of the Ontario Perinatal Mortality Study. Am J Epidemiol, 100:443-452

51.   Himmelberger DV, Brown BW, Cohen EN (1978) Cigarette smoking during pregnancy and the occurrence of spontaneous abortion and congenital malformation. Am J Epidemiol, 108:470-479

52.   Kline JO, Stein ZA, Susser M, Warburton D (1977) Smoking: a risk factor for spontaneous abortion. N Engl J Med, 297:793-796

53.   McKean HE (1978) Smoking and abortion. N Engl J Med, 298:113-114

54.   Fergusson DM, Horwood U, Shannon FT (1979) Smoking during pregnancy. N.Z. Med J, 89:41-43

55.   Goujard S. Rumeau C, Schwartz N (1965) Smoking during pregnancy, stillbirth and abruptio placentae. Biomedicine, 23:20-22

56.   Fielding JE and Rosso PK (1978) Smoking during pregnancy. N Engi J Med, 298:337-339

57.   Kelsey JL, Theodore RH, Bracken MB (1978) Maternal smoking and congenital malformations: An epidemiological study. J Epidem Community Health, 32:103-107 .

58.   Fedrick J, Alberman E, Goldstein H (1971) Possible teratogenic effect of cigarette smoking. Nature, 231:529-530

59.   Frazier TM, Davis GH, Goldstein H et al. (1961) Cigarette smoking and prematurity: A predictive study. Am J Obstet Gynecol, 81:988-996

60.   Peterson WF, Morense KN, Kaltreider DF (1965) Smoking and prematurity: A preliminary report based on study of 7740 Caucasians. Obstet Gynecol, 26:775-779

61.   Jansson I: Aetiological factors in prematurity. Acta Obstet Gynecol Scand, 45:279-300, 1966

62.   Reinke WA and Henderson M (1966) Smoking and prematurity in the presence of other variables. Arch Environ Health (Chicago) 12:313-316

63.   Frederick J, Anderson A (1976) Factors associated with spontaneous pre-term birth. Br J Obstet Gynaecol, 83:342

64.   Simpson WJ and Linda L (1957) A preliminary report on cigarette smoking and the incidence of prematurity. Am J Obstet Gynecol, 73:808-815

65.   Lowe CR (1959) Effect of mothers' smoking habits on birth weight of their children. Br Med J, 2:673-676

66.   Herriot A, Billewics WZ, Hytten FE (1962) Cigarette smoking in pregnancy. The Lancet, *1:771-773*

67.   Chow, W (1988) Maternal cigarette smoking and tubal pregnancy. Obstet Gynecol 71: 167-174

68.   Naeye RL and Peters EC (1984) Mental development of children whose mothers smoked during pregnancy. Obstet Gynecol, 64(5):601-607

69.   Naeye RL (1981) Influence of maternal cigarette smoking during pregnancy on foetal and childhood growth. Obstet Gynecol, 57:18

70.   Rantakallio P (1978) Relationship of maternal smoking to morbidity and mortality of the child up to age of five. Acta Paediatr Scand, 67:621-631

71.   Gustavson KH, Hagberg B, Hagberg G, Sars K (1977) Severe mental retardation in a Swedish country. Neuropadiatrie, 8:293-304

72.   Butler NR and Goldstein M (1973) Smoking during pregnancy and subsequent child development. Br Med J, 4:573-575

74.   Maxwell C and Berry MD (1959) Tobacco hypoglycaemia Ann In Med, 50:1149-1157

75.   Hypoglycaemia and Personality. Br Med J, p 134, April, 20 1974

76.   Wilder J (1943) Psychological problems in hypoglycaemia. Am J Digest Dis, 10, 11:428-435

77.   Landmann HR and Sutherland RL: Incidence and significance of hypoglycaemia in unselected admissions to a psychosomatic service. Am J Digest Dis, 105-108, April, 1950

78.   Rynaerson EH and Moersch FP: Neurologic manifestations of hyperinsulinism and other hypoglycaemic states. J AM Med Assoc, 1196-1199, October 20, 1934

79.   Jones MS: Hypoglycaemia in the neuroses. Br Med J, 945-946, November 16, 1935

80.   Salzer HM: Relative hypoglycaemia as a cause of neuropsychiatric illness. J Nat Med Assoc, 12-17, January, 1966

81.   Moiers RL (1973) Relative hypoglycaemia in schizophrenia. pp 452-462, Orthomolecular Psychiatry, Eds: D Hawkins, L Pauling, W.H. Freeman & Co

82.   Virkkunen M: Reactive hypoglycemic tendency among habitually violent offenders. Nutr Rev, Suppl, 94-103, May, 1986

83.   Virkkunen M (1984) Reactive hypoglycemic tendency among arsonists. Acta Psychiatr Scand, 69:445-452

84.   Davies, Stephen, Nutritional Medicine. (1987) Pan, London

85.   Kulikauskas V. Blaustein D, Ablin RJ (1985) Cigarette smoking and its possible effect on sperm. Fertil Steril, 44:526-528

86.   Handelsman DJ, Conway AJ, Boylan LM, Turtle JR:

87.   Rantala ML and Koskimies Am (1986) Semen quality of infertile couples - comparison between smokers and non-smokers. Andrologia, 19:42-46

88. Briggs MH (1973) Cigarette smoking and infertility in men. Med J Austr, 1:616

88. Evans HJ, Fletcher J, Torrance M, Hardgreave TB (1981) Sperm abnormalities and cigarette smoking. The Lancet, 1:627-629

89. Grant, Ellen, 'The Effect of Smoking on Pregnancy and Children.', In: Guidelines for Future Parents, Witley, Surrey, 1986, 85-86

90. Carlsen, H., Guverman, A et al. 'Evidence for decreasing quality of semen during past 50 years.' BMJ 305: 609-13

91. Plant, Moira, Reported in: Gill, Kerry, 'Alcohol "safe in pregnancy"' the Times, 4 Nov 1987

92. Kaufmann, Matthew. In: Hodgkinson, Neville, 'Alcohol Threat to Babies', Sunday Times, 31 January 1988

93. Federick, J, Anderson A, 'Factors associated with spontaneous pre-term birth', Br J Obsted Gynaecol, 1976, 83, 342

94. Kauffman, Matthew, op.cit.

95. van Thiel OH, Gavaler JS, Lester R, Goodman MD (1975) Alcohol induced testicular atrophy: An experimental model for hypogonadism occurring in chronic alcoholic man. Gastroenterology, 69:326- 332

96. Ylikahri R, Huttunen M, Harkonen M, Adlercreutz H (1974) Hangover and testosterone. Br Med J, 2:445

97. Mendelson JM, Ellingboe J, Mello NK, Kuehnli J (1978) Effects of alcohol on plasma testosterone and luteinizing hormone levels. Alc Clin Exp Res, 2:255-258

98. Kucheria K, Saxena R, Mohan D (1985) Semen analysis in alcohol dependence syndrome. Andrologia, 17:558-563

99. Brzek A (1987) Alcohol and male fertility (Preliminary report) Andrologia, 19:32-36

100. Dixit VP, Agarwal M, Lohiya NK (1983) Effects of a single ethanol injection into the vas deferens on the testicular function in rats. Endokrinologie, 67:8-13

101. van Thiel DM, Lester R, Sherins RJ (1974) Hypogonadism in alcoholic liver disease: Evidence for a double defect. Gastroenterology, 67:1188-1199

Suggested reading/papers:

- Prof David W Smith, University of Washington in Seattle with references from Hanson et al, J Amer Med Assn, 1976, 235, 1458.

- Alcohol and the Safety of the Unborn Child Woollam *The Journal of the Royal Society for the Promotion of Health.*1981; 101: 241-244

- Clarren, S K and Smith, D W (1978) The Foetal Alcohol Syndrome, New England J Ned. May 1978.

- Jones, K L, Smith, D W, Ulleland, C N and Streissguth, A P (1973). Pattern of malformation in offspring of chronic alcoholic mothers, Lancet, 1, 1267.

- From Alcoholism: Clinical and Experimental Research, Vol 14, No 5, September/October 1990. Moderate Prenatal Alcohol Exposure: Effects on Child IQ and Learning Problems at Age 7½ Years. Ann P Streissguth, Helen M Barr, and Paul D Sampson.

- From The Lancet, March 14th 1981. Zinc Status of Pregnant Alcoholic Women: A Determinant of Foetal Outcome.

- From Neurotoxicology and Teratology: Vol 11 pp 493-507. Neurobehavioral Effects of Prenatal Alcohol: Part III. PLS Analyses of Neuropsychological Tests. Ann P Streissguth, Fred L Bookstein, Paul D Sampson and Helen M Barr.

- Streissguth, A P (1992) Foetal Alcohol Syndrome: Early and Long Term Consequences.

- Clarren, S K, and Smith, D W (1978) The Foetal Alcohol Syndrome. New England Journal of Medicine 298, 1063-1068

- Little, B B, Snell, L M, Rosenfield, C R, Gilstrapp, L C, and Gant, N F (1990) Failure to Recognize Foetal Alcohol Syndrome in Newborn Infants. American Journal of Diseases in Children 144, 1142-1146

- Streissguth, A P, Clarren, S K, and Jones, K L (1985) Natural History of the Foetal Alcohol Syndrome: A Ten-Year Follow Up of Eleven Patients. Lancet 2, 85-92

- Streissguth, A P, Aase, J M, Clarren, S K, Randels, S P, LaDue, R A, and Smith, D F. Foetal Alcohol Syndrome in Adolescents and Adults. The Journal of the American Medical Association 265 (15): 1961-1967, 1991.

- The Role of Zinc Deficiency in Foetal Alcohol Syndrome, From Nutrition Reviews, Vol 40, No. 2/February 1982.

- The Foetal Alcohol Syndrome and Placental Transport of Valine, From Nutrition Reviews, Vol 40, No. 2/February 1982.

- K L Jones, D W Smith, C N Ulleland and A P Streissguth (1973) Pattern of Malformation in Offspring of Alcoholic Mothers. Lancet 1: 1267-1271

- G F Chernoff (1977) The Foetal Alcohol Syndrome in Mice: An Animal Model. Teratology 15: 223-230

- W J Tze and M Lee (1975) Adverse Effects of maternal Alcohol Consumption of Pregnancy and Foetal Growth in Rats. Nature 257: 479-480

- National Institute of Alcohol Abuse and Alcoholism (1977) Critical Review of the Foetal Alcohol Syndrome. Rockville MD, Alcohol, Drug Abuse and Mental Health Administration

- The Role of Zinc Deficiency in Foetal Alcohol Syndrome. Nutrition Reviews 40: 43-45, 1981.

- Immune Deficiency and Apparently Increased Susceptibility to Infection in the Foetal Alcohol Syndrome. Nutrition Reviews 40: 45-47, 1981.

- R V Patwardhan, S Schenker, G I Henderson, N N Abou-Mourad and A M Hoyumpa Jr (1981) Short Term and Long Term Ethanol Administration Inhibits the Placental Uptake and Transport of Valine in Rats. J. Lab. Clin. Med 98: 251-262

- Alcohol and Pregnancy Outcome: D D Lewis, Director ALFAWAP Trust Fund Ltd. December 1983. Midwives Chronicle and Nursing Notes.

- Alcohol Misconceptions: Lindsay Reid. From Nursing Times, October 14, Volume 88, No. 42, 1992.

- Publ. Hlth, Lond (1984) 98, 238-241. Alcohol Related Birth Defects. Ronald Forbes, Hon. Executive Director, Alfawap Trust Fund Ltd. From The Society of Community Medicine

- Alcohol – Dr Ernest Nobel, Director of the National Institute on Alcohol Abuse and Alcoholism 1976-1978.

Regarding other drugs such as cannabis, we are so lucky to be in touch with Mrs Mary Brett, a wonderful teacher who really has her pupils' best interests at heart, and who has been spreading the word about the dangers of street drugs for many years. She is now advisor to H.M. Government on drugs.

She has been kind and generous enough to say we can use her material to give you the very best information available – and has given her article to us free of charge. A wonderful woman, we should all help her to spread the word as far as possible.

DRUGS

By Mrs Mary Brett

CANNABIS - THE FACTS

Cannabis (marijuana, pot, grass, weed, joints, spliff, hashish, blow) is a hallucinogen, a depressant and our commonest illegal drug.

How drugs work in the brain

100 billion nerve cells (neurons) may have up to 10,000 connections to other neurons in the vast brain network. Messages pass along the nerve fibres as electrical impulses, then cross the gap between the neurons (the synapse) in the form of chemicals – neurotransmitters – the brain's natural drugs. Each neurotransmitter molecule has a particular shape to fit into its receptor site on the next neuron as a key fits into a lock.

Mind-altering drugs like cannabis or more specifically THC (tetrahydrocannabinol), the ingredient that gives the "high", mimic the shape of these neurotransmitters so the brain is "fooled". Cannabis mimics

81

anandamide and also interferes with the transmission of the other neurotransmitters because THC dissolves in the fatty cell membranes and persists. Fifty per cent of the THC is still there after a week and ten per cent a month later. Traces are still detectable in hair and urine for weeks after that.

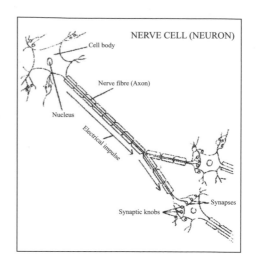

The immediate effects

Taken for euphoria, usually smoked with or without tobacco, or eaten in "hash" cakes. (But enhances the mood you're in so you may well feel worse).

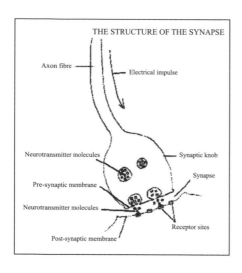

An intoxicant, like alcohol, so people should not be driving. If you have a joint today you should not be driving tomorrow. (Airline pilots on flight simulators could not 'land' their planes properly even 24 hours and more after a joint and had no idea anything was wrong.)

One 20mg joint has the same effect as being just over the legal alcohol-driving limit. The combination of cannabis and alcohol is 16 times more dangerous when driving than taking either drug alone.

Panic attacks and paranoia can occur immediately after a joint.

The long-term effects.

Just one joint per week or even once a month will ensure a permanent presence of THC. Since the other neurotransmitters are affected, new nerve connections cannot be made properly. Concentration, learning and memory are all badly affected. School grades fall, some students miss out on university places. A cannabis personality develops. Users become inflexible, can't plan their days properly, can't take criticism and struggle to express themselves. They feel lonely, miserable and misunderstood. Apathy, amotivation and dropping out are all common.

Few children, using cannabis even occasionally, will achieve their full potential.

82

Dependence.

<u>Psychological addiction</u>, the craving for cannabis is very strong.

<u>Physical addiction</u> occurs. As more and more THC is consumed, more receptor sites are made, tolerance builds as more THC is needed to get the same effect. All the receptor sites need to be satisfied, this is physical addiction. Withdrawal symptoms are not so dramatic as they are for heroin as THC persists in the body. More young people now are treated in the USA for marijuana than alcohol dependence.

There is no foolproof cure for any type of addiction.

Mental Health.

<u>Cannabis psychosis</u> has been reported in scientific papers for decades. Cannabis causes far more mental illness than drugs like heroin.

The increased risk factors for psychosis, anxiety, and depression range from 3 to 5. Schizophrenia is triggered or worsened by its use, it may even be caused. Cannabis increases the amount of the neurotransmitter dopamine in the brain. Schizophrenics have an excess of dopamine in the brain, sufferers of Parkinson's disease, too little. (One in four of us carries a faulty gene which controls the release of dopamine. If a child inherits a copy of the gene from each parent, and if they then use cannabis, the chance that she/he will develop schizophrenia rises from 1 or 2%, the norm in the population, to 15%). The presence of one gene increases the risk by 5 to 6 times.

<u>Violence and Suicide</u> A Swedish study found more suicides among pot users than those who used alcohol, amphetamines or heroin. The manner of death was more violent. A study in 2001 from Dunedin found that young male cannabis users were nearly five times more likely to be violent than non users, the risk for alcohol users was around three. Violence seems to occur with the psychosis or during withdrawal.

Other Effects on the body

Cannabis contains more cancer-causing substances than tobacco, its smoke deposits three to four times as much tar in the lungs and airways. Cases of lung cancer, bronchitis and emphysema have been reported. Rare head and neck cancers are now being found in young pot smokers. The average age for these conditions in tobacco smokers is 64.

The immune system is damaged. Fewer white blood cells are produced, many are abnormal and can't fight off infections. People are more vulnerable to disease, their illness is more severe and they stay sick longer.

Sperm production is decreased. Infertility and even impotence have been reported.

Babies born to cannabis using mothers are smaller, hyperactive, have behaviour and learning problems and are 10 times more likely to develop leukaemia.

THC interferes with the production of new cells being made in an adult body - white blood cells, sperm and foetal cells. (It causes faulty copying of DNA, and hastens cell death.)

Blood pressure and heart rates rise to the levels of real stress. Heart attacks have been reported. Two teenagers had strokes and died after bingeing on cannabis, another was left paralysed.

The Medical Argument

Medicines by law, have to be pure substances, single chemicals, so that their actions are predictable and controllable. Heroin and cocaine fall into that category. Cannabis contains around 400 chemicals.

The BMA is currently testing more of the 60 or so purified cannabinoids (substances unique to the cannabis plant) as potential medicines and that is correct procedure.

Synthetic purified THC, Nabilone, (Marinol in USA) is already available on hospital prescription but has many side-effects and is not popular among doctors.

It all started in 1979 when an American pot smoking lawyer said, "We will use the medical marijuana argument as a red herring on the road to full legalisation".

The Pro-legalisers.

Many pro-legalisers are users, or their children are. Others are libertarians who think we should be able to do what we like with our bodies. That's fine as long as it doesn't interfere with anyone else. But stoned drivers can and do kill other people. Addicts and the mentally-ill need treatment at the taxpayers expense, stoned workers are inefficient and unproductive. And passive smoking does occur.

Cannabis as a gateway drug?

Tobacco, alcohol and cannabis can all act as gateway drugs. A recent New Zealand study showed that weekly cannabis users were 60 times more likely to progress to "harder" drugs. The more they use, the greater the risk.

Almost 100% of heroin users started on pot. New research suggests that cannabis can "prime" the brain for the use of other drugs.

Relaxing the law

Holland turned a blind eye to cannabis in 1987 and is now the crime capital of Europe. The country is awash with dealers, and it is a major producer and exporter of drugs especially ecstasy.

Health and social problems have escalated and the amount allowed for personal possession has been reduced from 30g to 5g. The present Dutch government wants to close all the coffee shops. Many have gone.

Since down-classification in 2001 in the UK, regular cannabis use is still rising among 11 to 12 year old boys, older teens seem to have progressed to cocaine.

Strength

In the sixties and seventies, the average THC content of herbal cannabis was just 0.5 - 1%. Today's specially bred varieties from Holland such as skunk and nederweed, have THC contents of anything from 9-27%. These strong types are now commonly grown in the UK and are thought to account for 60% of the cannabis consumed here.

The rest of the cannabis used here is cannabis resin with a THC content of around 4 to 5%.

Drug Testing

More and more employers are testing for drugs in the workplace – cannabis will show up for weeks, and a conviction would prevent someone from getting a visa for the USA.

Quotations from the Experts:

Mental illness:

"Five years ago, 95% of psychiatrists would have said that cannabis doesn't cause psychosis. Now I would estimate that 95% say it does" (Professor Robin Murray, Director Institute of Psychiatry, London. October 2006).

"The mistake was that in its 2002 report, The Advisory Council on the Misuse of Drugs denied that cannabis was a contributory cause of schizophrenia, continued to deny this for the next two years and thus mislead ministers into repeatedly stating that there was no causal link between cannabis and psychosis". (Professor Robin Murray, letter to The Guardian, 19/01/06).

Personality:

"If the development of identity does not progress, the teenager remains at a childish level of development characterised by both a lack of independence and a deficient integration in the adult world". (Swedish researcher, Jan Ranstrom 2003)

Academic performance:

"Use more often than twice per week for even a short period of time, or use for 5 years or more at the level of even once per month, may each lead to a compromised ability to function to their full mental capacity, and could possibly result in lasting impairments" (Dr Nadia Solowij, "Cannabis and Cognitive Functioning" 1998).

Medical argument:

Dr Keith Green an American ophthalmologist, says 6 joints a day would be needed to maintain reduced eye pressure caused by glaucoma, rendering the patient incapable of any useful functioning.

The warning on Nabilone reads:

"THC encourages both physical and psychological dependence and is highly abusable. It causes mood changes, loss of memory, psychoses, impairment of coordination and perception, and complicates pregnancy".

Dr Robert Dupont, founder of NIDA (National Institute for Drug Abuse) in the USA said, "I have been apologising to the American people for the last 10 years for promoting the decriminalisation of cannabis. I made a mistake. Marijuana combines the worst effects of alcohol and tobacco and has other ill effects that neither of these two have". He added, "In all of history, no young people have ever taken marijuana regularly on a mass scale. Therefore our youngsters are in effect making themselves guinea pigs in a tragic experiment. Thus far our research clearly suggests we will see horrendous results"

Mary Brett, Former Head of Health Education, Dr Challoner's Grammar School (boys), Amersham, Bucks.

UK spokesman for EURAD (Europe against Drugs).

References can be found in "Cannabis – a general view of its harmful effects" by Mary Brett on the "Talking about Cannabis" website. June 2007.

STREET DRUGS

Marijuana – pot, cannabis
4 times more dangerous than cigarette smoking
3 times more tar in the lungs and 5 times more carbon monoxide

Psychoactive substance is tetrahydrocannabinol (THC) – steroid structure found in the sex hormones and in certain hormones of the adrenal glands. THC accumulates in the ovaries and testes.

Women – upsets menstrual cycle, tolerated and then restored.
Men – lowers blood testosterone, lowers sperm count, greater than usual impotency and diminished libido. Sperm motility affected and an increase in number of abnormal sperm.

Effects the synthesis of DNA. In animals linked with increased foetal deaths and malformations.

Cocaine & Crack
In mice – teratogenic even at non-toxic levels.
Humans – decrease in weight of foetus, higher malformation rate and increased still birth rate.

Crack is a cocaine derivative which is purer than cocaine. *Withdrawal symptoms in the new born are severe.*

Heroin
Heroin and other opiate narcotics such as opium, morphine and codeine are all extremely addictive.

Decreased fertility and atrophy of the male accessory sex organs, decreased testosterone.

3 times more stillbirths
4 times more premature births
6 times more growth problems

Babies are born addicted to the drug and have to endure withdrawal.

CHAPTER 4

CONTRACEPTION, INCLUDING THE PILL

W e will start the chapter with the work of Dr Ellen Grant. The work of Dr Grant will give you the science. What the pill does, and how it does it, and why. This is the medical viewpoint from a doctor who has been into oral contraception from the outset, and has dedicated her life to studying the effects on women's health, and on the consequences for their fertility.

HELP WITH RECOGNISING THE HAZARDS OF HORMONE MANIPULATION, AND WHY YOU NEED TO KNOW.

Dr Grant explains:

The Pill

It is probably true that no other drugs have received so much attention as the oral contraception pill (the 'Pill'). It is also probably true that the general public and much of the medical profession have never been so misled about a group of drugs. Even to the lay person, there are obvious discrepancies – for example, many gynaecologists seem unable to explain why steroids which are said to be unsafe for women over the age of 35 are safe when women reach the menopause. Logic would suggest that the risks are at least the same, if not greater with increasing age. But what are these steroids and what are their risks? Are we being deceived into believing they are safe?

What the pill is

Oral contraceptive pills generally contain two synthetic hormones (steroids), oestrogen and progestogen, in various combinations. The mini-pill contains just progestogen, and can cause irregular bleeding and has a higher chance of pregnancy with its use. But it really does not matter which type a woman is taking, because it is the ingested or injected hormones that are known to be dangerous to women's health.

How the pills work

The levels of oestrogen and progesterone in your body rise and fall during the menstrual cycle, being high towards the end of the month. Both oestrogen and progesterone remain high throughout pregnancy, thereby preventing the ovaries from preparing another egg to release. The combined pill works by confusing the body into thinking that it is pregnant, by keeping the hormone levels high. Because oestrogen alone caused irregular bleeding, a progesterone was added to the pill. The commonly prescribed mainly progestogen pills make the cervical mucus thick and sticky and the lining of the womb atrophied and thin. Both of these actions increase the contraceptive effects, making it difficult for the sperm to enter the womb or for the womb to accept a fertilised egg.

Normal menstruation is prevented – indeed, the pill is often prescribed for painful periods, on the assumption that it relieves them. It does so by stopping normal ovulatory cycles, including periods, altogether, substituting withdrawal bleeding for a normal period when the pill is stopped for a few days each month. Painful cramps due to prostaglandin release may be part of a response to inflammation and using steroid hormones to suppress this natural response does nothing to treat any inflammation of the neck of the womb.

In women of all ages, simple vitamin, mineral and essential oil supplements are a much safer way to relieve painful periods. They also carry no risk of interfering with the brain control of ovulation.

'Lies, damned lies and statistics'

The Royal College of General Practitioners' Oral Contraceptive Study was one of two large scale trials started in 1968. It is best regarded not as a clinical trial but 'as a record of the natural history of two cohorts of women, one of which has used oral contraceptives while the other has not'. Unfortunately, it has erroneously been accorded the status of a proper trial, with the interim report being quoted in the press as suggesting that the pill is a safe drug. Yet there can be no conclusion other than one which points to the pill as a dangerous drug even on the data available to date, without considering what damage could be inflicted in the long term. Unfortunately, since the 1974 Report, there has not been a comprehensive follow-up.

47,174 women were enrolled on the study during 1968 and 1969. Even from the start, the control and experimental groups were not randomised or equivalent. Obviously, the experimental (pill-taking) group did not contain women in whom illness had already rendered the pill inadvisable, so this group was likely to be healthier than the controls. The drop-out rate from the pill-users group was large, even in the first three years. By 1979, it was enormous, with only a small percentage of the original pill-users group still taking the pill. The researchers had even switched 6,000 women in the control group to the pill-users (experimental) group to boost numbers. Why had so many dropped out?

The 'big exodus' was hardly surprising, as the 1974 report showed a large number of medical conditions were increased in pill users... an increase in over sixty conditions, for example, in suicide, cancer and vascular conditions.

My detailed review to the *British Medical Journal*, complaining the 'high drop-out and side-effects rates did not justify further use of the pill', was cut to a short letter. Nor did the study measure 'total morbidity', as was claimed. It measured conditions that doctors recognised – there are a number of important conditions that many doctors do not always acknowledge, such as some allergies and widespread nutritional deficiencies.

I was not alone in my concern. As far back as 1974, a Lay Person's Guide to Better Health gave an overview of the dangers of the pill, including quotes of eminent doctors to a Congressional subcommittee. Another from R. William's book, published in 1969, said: "In fact, the pill has been shown to be capable of affecting any or all systems and organs in the body, with the greatest variety of consequences." In the same year, Barbara Seamans wrote: "Very few pill-users have the slightest notion of the potency of the drugs they are ingesting, or how the little pills may affect their own health or their still unborn children."

Dr Ellen Grant

We are also glad to be able to quote the work of Dr Paavo Airola: For further information on risks associated with the pill, Dr Paavo Airola, a world authority on nutrition and biological medicine, has listed the risks under two headings: the less serious, which are still bothersome, and those which cause serious complications. We could argue with his divisions – depression and increased susceptibility to vaginal and bladder infections are hardly 'less serious', but taking both lists together, we can gauge the detrimental effects to female health. His lists include:

'Less serious, although bothersome'
    Increased susceptibility to vaginal and bladder infections.
    Lowered resistance to all infections.
* Cramps
    Dry, blotchy skin. Mouth ulcers.
    Dry, falling hair and baldness.
    Premature wrinkling
    Acne
    Sleep disturbances
    Inability to concentrate
* Migraine headaches
* Depression, moodiness, irritability
* Darkening of the skin of upper lip and lower eyelids
* Sore breasts
* Nausea
* Weight gain and body distortion due to disproportional distribution of fat
    Chronic fatigue
    Increase in dental cavities
    Swollen and bleeding gums

Greatly increased or decreased sex drive
Visual disturbances
    Amenorrhoea (no periods)
* Blood sugar level disturbances which complicate diabetes or hypoglycaemia

'More serious complications'
    Eczema
    Gallbladder problems
    Hyperlipemia (excess fat in the blood)
* Intolerance to carbohydrates leading to 'steroid diabetes', which can lead to clinical diabetes
* Strokes
* Seven to ten times greater risk of death due to blood clots
* Jaundice
* Epilepsy
* High blood pressure
* Kidney failure
    Oedema (swelling)
    Permanent infertility
* Varicose veins
* Thrombophlebitis and pulmonary embolism
* Heart attacks
    Cancer of the breast, uterus, liver, and pituitary gland

To this list Foresight can add:
    Vitamin and mineral imbalances
    Ectopic pregnancy
    Miscarriage of later pregnancies
    Food allergies
    Genito-urinary disease, including cervicitis
    Congenital malformations in later babies
    Osteoporosis
    Ovarian and lung cancer.
    Fungal infections.

* The items that are asterisked are the ones for which there are specific warnings on the instructions which come with all packets of the pill. Obviously, for most women, this is where they will get their information. It is, therefore, very important that it is not misleading.

Yet, to return to Dr Grant as she points out, if one reads the small print (and it is SMALL PRINT) one can see that the 'facts' are presented very cleverly to minimise the adverse picture painted.

For example, in one set of instructions for use, it is claimed that 'Painful periods are in most cases abolished', implying that the user still has periods. Only further down the page is there a phrase which suggests that this is not so, when the 'period' is referred to as a 'period of bleeding resembling a menstrual "period"'. The side effects are referred to as 'occasional', which is certainly not what my colleagues and others have found. The user is advised to stop taking the pill immediately pregnancy is suspected, because of the risk of congenital abnormality. Does this advice not seem to rest uneasily with the warning earlier in the instructions and 'Not even the combined oral contraceptive can offer 100 per cent protection against pregnancy'. As malformations can arise very early in the pregnancy, stopping after pregnancy has occured will, in many cases, be too late. The text continues: 'It can be definitely concluded, however, that if a risk of abnormality (foetal malformation) exists at all, it must be very small.' In view of what is known about the effect of hormones on the foetus, this is nonsense. The teratogenic effects are underestimated because of the number of miscarriages which occur.

It is impossible, within the constraints of this book, to consider all the above in more detail, so we shall just take some of the more important aspects affecting preconception, conception and the subsequent child. However, anything which affects the health of the mother can indirectly, if not directly, affect the health of the foetus.

THE PILL AND VITAMIN AND MINERAL IMBALANCES. One of the most widespread deficiencies we have is zinc. We know it is essential for many biochemical processes in the body, and is especially important in pregnancy. Unfortunately, the pill upsets the balance between copper and zinc levels, raising copper and lowering zinc. Often, therefore, when a woman comes off the pill to become pregnant, she will arrive at conception in a zinc deficient state, which will get worse as time goes on. This can lead to problems during the gestation for mother and foetus, as well as problems for mother and infant after birth. Difficulties may include post-natal depression and lactation problems in the mother, and feeding difficulties, and later learning difficulties and developmental difficulties, especially with regard to sexual development, for the child. Excess copper has been associated with pre-eclampsia and post-partum depression, among other conditions. The pill interferes with other minerals, including especially magnesium, also iron, iodine and, probably, chromium and manganese.

Nor is vitamin metabolism left unscathed. Steroids change protein building and breakdown in the liver and change the levels of protein in the blood that carries the vitamins to the body tissues. The pill can alter the actions of the enzymes which need vitamins to function properly. The pill raises Vitamin A levels, and leads to deficiencies of B1, B2, B3, B6, folic acid and C. It may lower B12.

They married quite young as their love had been kindled when they were school children. Their life was ahead of them, a house, their careers and children. They both loved children but were careful, Margaret was on the pill. Time for children later.

When they decided to start a family, Margaret came off the pill but it didn't
continued on next page

happen. Her menstrual cycles stopped, and they were deeply distressed that there was a problem.

A previous illness had left Margaret underweight which contributed to their situation.

A family friend, a Paediatric Consultant at a local hospital suggested that they contact Foresight, as it was Foresight who had previously helped the consultant with her own fertility issues.

Both Margaret and her husband were put on the Foresight Programme. Hair was sent for analysis, the diet was tidied up, alcohol and tobacco were dropped.

The hair analysis revealed that there were high levels of mercury in both their samples, which was a result of eating much Tuna. Once this was addressed, their mercury levels dropped and previous low zinc levels began to rise. The periods returned quickly!

For 18 months they followed the programme. Their GP told them that they could try Clomid but that "*it didn't always work,*" and they would have to try IVF.

This would take longer than they wanted to wait, so, still on the Foresight Programme, six months of Clomid, and Margaret conceived and her baby daughter was born weighing 8lbs 7oz.

Margaret has continued on the programme as "it kept me healthy". Now, as they are looking to enlarge their family, both husband and wife are back on the programme.

About Foresight, Margaret said "Excellent."

Problems more likely to be encountered after pill use include:

ECTOPIC PREGNANCY.

Ectopic pregnancy, is a serious condition which is often life-threatening for the woman. This has now reached epidemic proportions in the USA and is an increasing worry in the UK. Even where the pregnancy can be successfully aborted, the woman will often have severe fallopian tube damage or even lose the tube. Some women may have low magnesium levels which may impede tubal muscular action. Some may have infections. There may also be high copper levels.

MISCARRIAGE.

Pill users have a higher risk of miscarriage, unless specific mineral and vitamin levels are restored to normal prior to conception.

FOOD ALLERGIES.

The pill is a major contributory factor to the increase in food allergy. This is not surprising as the pill compromises the immune system leaving it less able to cope with sensitivities. Its effects on liver function mean that enzymes which should help in the detoxification do not work properly, thereby exacerbating the effects of toxins from foods and chemicals to which an individual may be allergic. Nutritional imbalances, especially zinc deficiency, are major factors contributing to allergy.

GENITO-URINARY INFECTIONS.

The pill has led to an increase, not only through greater sexual freedom, but also because of its physical effects on the body. It weakens the immune system so the body is not so resistant to infection. It has led to increases in cancers, especially of the cervix, in younger women. In part, because it was given to many of them when their bodies were still growing, their cervix linings were still immature and susceptible to changes, particularly those leading to cancer.

CONGENITAL ABNORMALITIES.

Since Dr Isobel Gal first discovered that hormone pregnancy tests (which are no longer used) were associated with higher incidences of congenital malformations of the baby's central nervous system, studies have continued into the teratogenic effects of the pill and other hormones.

In the USA, researchers found limb reduction anomalies in one study, with major abnormalities, including congenital heart anomalies and neurological and neural tube disorders in another. These findings were confirmed in a major study in Europe, as well as in a number of small ones· In Australia, researchers concluded that 'the relative risk for a limb defect... was 23:9.' However, when the results of this study were subjected to more stringent statistical analysis, the risk was 30:2. Other researchers argue that "Hormonal treatment during pregnancy may be a predisposing factor in congenital heart defects". Even researchers of studies which fail to find links warn that there is a need for further studies.

FERTILITY.

The pill deliberately interferes with the hormone system to prevent pregnancy. Frequently after a woman has ceased taking it, the body's systems do not return to normal. Having had the message to switch off making certain hormones for so long, the body takes time to adjust to producing them again. Sadly for some women, the adjustment may take a very long time, or may never happen. Nutritional imbalances, especially zinc deficiency, are also often a factor.

(NB: These deficiencies are corrected on the Foresight programme, and we also suggest reflexology.)

Intra-uterine devices – the IUD, or coil

The IUD is a small device, which is inserted into the womb by a doctor. There are many shapes in use, made from toxic materials such as plastic, copper, or plastic-coated copper. Its continual presence in the womb prevents conception, though it is still not clear how. It may prevent the egg from attaching to the lining of the womb by mechanical means, or it may be by some toxic action. Its failure rate is higher than the pill. It is also quite harmful, the side effects including:

- Cramping and pain, especially during menstruation
- Ectopic pregnancy (pregnancy occurring outside the womb)
- Spontaneous abortion
- Uterine bleeding
- Blood poisoning
- Bowel obstruction
* Cervical infection (and infection of the uterus)
- Pelvic infections
- Infections in the Fallopian tubes
- Dysplasia
- Cancer of the uterus
- Anaemia
- Perforation of the uterus
- It can become imbedded in the uterus, which often means hospitalisation and even death
- Mineral imbalances, especially elevated copper and low zinc

In an attempt to overcome some of these problems, sometimes chemicals, such as progesterone or progestogen, are added. As the section on the pill has shown, though, this is not a safe practice.

Clearly, when it comes to preconception care and pregnancy, the above are undesirable. The problems associated with infections are discussed elsewhere,as are the problems of excess copper and zinc deficiency.

Conclusion

No contraceptive method which interferes with the chemistry and physiology of the body, as do the pill and the IUD, can be recommended. It is impossible to calculate how much iatrogenic illness (illness caused by medical intervention) is caused by them, especially the pill. The evidence for the harm they do is overwhelming and well documented in the medical literature. You should not be fooled by anyone who tells you otherwise! Remember that a number of countries will not permit their use.

Checklist

1. If you have never taken the pill, don't be persuaded to start.

2. If you have taken the pill in the past, it is advisable, regardless of whether or not you are pregnant, that you have a check-up with a practitioner who is trained to recognise mineral imbalances. If you are breastfeeding, it is also important.

3. Until your body is in balance, it would be preferable for you to avoid pregnancy, but by methods other than the pill.

Dr Ellen Grant.

We are grateful to Dr Grant and Dr Paavo Airola, for all of the above, which is clear and candid. Dr Grant is a very remarkable woman, a doctor with a very rare insight into the fallibility of certain aspects of the medical scenario, and a willingness to admit past mistakes. A whole generation of women (and succeeding generations) have much to thank her for.

She was one of the first people to introduce the pill to excited and grateful patients. At last, a simple solution to contraception! It seemed too good to be true - and it was.

After years of research and manipulation of the hormones, trying to find a balance that did not make women ill or threaten their sanity, she concluded that such a pill was not possible. Unable to convince her colleagues, and fearing for womankind, she left the scene.

Since then, her life has been devoted to tirelessly campaigning to warn both the general public and the medical profession of the dangers. She has faced up to hostility and rejection, but she is still there fighting. She has written two books, the Bitter Pill and Sexual Chemistry, both should be compulsory reading for young couples and for all health professionals.

Over a lifetime of closely observing the scene, she has observed the Pill to hugely increase the risk of migraine 60%, mood swings, loss of libido, allergic illnesses, weight gain, depression, inability to cope with stress, vascular disorders such as thrombosis, increased body hair and breast and cervical cancer, heart disease and disturbed protein metabolism.

Dr Grant has studied life events in Pill takers and has seen an increase in accidents and suicides, schizophrenia, violent attacks on husbands (and vice-versa), battered children, self poisoning and self injury. Some of this may relate to medicaments given to combat the depression, and the PMT, caused by the hormonal mayhem.

They had decided that they would like to get their future sorted out in terms of job security etc, before starting a family. So, for nine years, Shirlayne was on the pill. In 2002, they decided to start planning for pregnancy.

She stopped the pill and used the Persona method of Natural Family Planning so that her body could adjust itself after years on the pill. In 2003 it was time to start a family and Shirlayne conceived almost straight away. Due to constant bleeding, 4 scans were performed at the Early Pregnancy Clinic between weeks 4 and 6, by which time a miscarriage was confirmed. A second conception took place, but this was also miscarried at 10 weeks.

Flicking through a magazine, Shirlayne found Foresight, which she contacted immediately and went on the programme. Her husband, short of hair, just couldn't, on numerous occasions get enough hair for the laboratory.

Shirlayne's analysis revealed high copper levels which were addressed

continued on next page

straight away. Within 2 months she conceived and again bled. Undeterred, Shirlayne continued with the Foresight Programme and a Foresight Baby girl was born at 43 weeks weighing 7lbs 13oz, Apgar 10.

Not wanting a large gap between babies, once back on the programme, Shirlayne fell pregnant again and this time bled for only 1 week. Her pregnancy was very easy with no nausea at all. Foresight Baby girl 2 was born weighing 8lb 11 oz, Apgar 10. Whilst the recent baby was on both mixed breast feeding and solids, Foresight Baby 3 was conceived. The first two babies had been born by caesarean section but the scar had began to rupture so Foresight Baby girl 3 was also born by caesarean section at 36 weeks. 6lbs 1 oz.

Shirlayne asked us why Foresight is not known about more. It's a shame people only contact Foresight when they find it difficult to get pregnant. Such good and sensible advice.

There was a brief trial of men being put on a male version of the Pill. However, this was very soon abandoned as the men complained of headaches and shrunken testicles. The experiment was instantly halted and has not been repeated!

Children born after pill use are more prone to birthmarks, skeletal abnormalities, (deformities of the skeleton such as cleft palate and spina bifida), reduced IQ, and learning difficulties such as dyslexia and ADHD.

These problems will be mainly due to the fact that the pill raises the level of copper in the body and lowers the level of zinc, manganese and B6.

(As is discussed elsewhere in this book, these deficiencies can be righted in time by the full Foresight programme.)

However, every problem we examine does make us realise how very much at risk the general population is, and how it is no wonder that we have a generation of children, riddled with deficiency, allergic illness, behavioural problems and inability to learn.

A further article by Dr Ellen Grant on The Pill is given in Appendix 1.

Not long after trying for a baby, Jane conceived, but the joy was short lived when at around 12 weeks bleeding began. A fault in chromosome 22 was detected and a termination at 25 weeks was organised. Determined, they approached a fertility specialist who organised an IUI. When that failed, both Jane and her husband were told not to worry, to forget about it. "It will work out all right".

Three years later they went for IVF, this too failed. At 37 years of age they travelled abroad for another IVF, sadly nothing happened.

On their return to the UK, Jane, as determined as ever, began to search for information on pregnancy and came across Foresight listed in the back of one of the books that she had read. Foresight was contacted, and both of them began the programme.

continued on next page

Painful periods led her to get information on herbs and to try acupuncture. She got involved in natural products, changed her diet and bought organic food where possible. Both followed the programme for the next 3 years taking their supplements including lots of zinc. They didn't worry any more, exercised regularly and generally went on with their lives.

Being aware of her cycle, Jane found that she was late. She had gone on to day 44. She took two tries at a pregnancy test, because she couldn't believe what she saw! When she spoke to her husband, he already knew. "I told you so!" was what he said!

A baby boy 9 lb 3oz and 57cm long was safely delivered. "He's into everything, very determined, growing fast, and loves his food. We prayed, people in church prayed. I am nearly 40 years old. He is our miracle baby". It had taken ten years!

So what are my own feelings about the development of life for women since the advent of the pill? I was part of the pre-Pill generation, and I have watched life unfold over nearly 80 years.

The line we were all sold over the pill was that it "heralded a new deal for women". A brighter era had dawned.

Family size could be limited to manageable; as there would be choice about how many children you had in your family. You would decide, in view of the mother's health and the financial viability exactly when you had your babies. "Every child a wanted child" was the battle cry. (Every pill a profit to the industry concerned, of course!)

The public believed this was the end of poverty, as everything would be under control. The household budgets would be manageable. Women would no longer be exhausted, harassed, and strapped for cash. It would be a land of happiness and plenty.

So far, so good. (It could have been, if they had gone for *natural family planning* of course! More anon on this.)

Fast forward to what has *actually* happened. Let's face it, the "libertarians" rushed forward with what they called "free love". This meant, in reality, sex free *from* love. Men then felt free to seduce their secretaries or other friend's wives, or anyone else in the frame. Let's face it, in very short order, there were many, many more deserted wives, loveless unions and single mothers left to fend for themselves, and do most of the upbringing of one or more children on their own.

So much for less hardship and less exhaustion! On the heels of this sad little revolution comes the era of teenagers and older sleeping around, living alone or cohabiting without bothering with marriage. Lots of sexually transmitted disease, and lots of girls and women ill with the side effects listed by Ellen Grant, and without *even* having the information about where the PMT and the explosive mood changes were coming from!

Lots of babies born out of wedlock, and, if no babies at an early stage, later a Holocaust of broken dreams, with the infertility and/or miscarriage, the premature births and little fellows who aren't quite right. Again, the lost hopes of the women who tried to wait to have their little children, until the marriage that never came, or came too late, the panic and the tears and sometimes the bitter disappointment.

"You can have it all", the girls are told. "You have your career, and when you are well established, you will have a double income household and will be able to afford childcare".

Spinster school-mistresses have, I suspect, their own agenda in promoting admiration of the woman who has a "fulfilling career" and lives alone in a small flat with a couple of cats. Their school rises in the "tables" if more of their pupils make it to university. Not that there is anything against universities as such. It is just the using of the girls to further their own cause, and the artificial damming-up of the natural flow of love and maternal feelings, that everyone appears to accept as "part and parcel" of the deal.

Their blandishments, the manipulation of the hormones that control emotional development, and the whole feminist movement seems to have confused an entire generation of young women. They are encouraged to suppress their natural instincts – then the chemicals take over and more brutally do this for them.

Not that I am against University for those of academic inclination who *really want* to go there. I am just wary of whose agenda it is? Young women are so pressurised. Is it better to spend four years pursuing a career where most of the posts may be taken, where you are competing with bright and ambitious young men, and end up with a mountainous debt that may well take another several years to pay off?

Or, might it be happier to have a less pressurised job for 4 years, saving up for your home and working towards making your *own* dreams come true?

To fall in love, to marry, to have your children – along with, if you wished, puppies, kittens, to love your house and garden and love looking after your family – that is doing what comes naturally. The joy grows inside you as your body matures, and natural hopes and desires play like music in every cell of your body.

Babies are wonderful. The happiest –and the most joyfully chaotic days of your entire life will be spent bringing up a young family! It is a huge, growing, developing, loving experience for everyone. It is what a young woman's body wants to do. To make love, get pregnant, have babies and breast-feed and nurture them until they grow up. Every little animal in the wild is doing the same!

So what have the problems been? Why has loving and laughing gone out of fashion with so many people? Because, given the chance, hormones develop naturally in growing women, and are the secret orchestra that plays their body music for them, and all their thoughts and dreams and future plans dance to their body music.

So what happens when you switch the music off?

Initially, the hormones given in the first pill were very strong. Women I knew told me they felt sick all the time like pregnancy sickness. Another side-effect was that it reduced the libido. Not a happy effect at the beginning of married life.

Those who realised the connection complained...

Then a small amount of testosterone was added to the Pill. Just to *"switch the libido on again."*

The effects were gradual and subtle. But the change was tangible after a time. Women journalists "dared" to say that they were not enjoying motherhood. That it was getting in the way of their careers. It became fashionable to abandon the idea of having babies, and whinge about the "glass ceiling".

The DINKYS started to appear. "Double income, no kids yet." The estate agents chorused with joy. It has been their all-year Mardi Gras. They have not passed up this opportunity.

In 1961, my husband and I bought a holiday home on the south coast for £5,400. About 10 years later, we sold it for £15,000. In 2005, when I was going to return to the area, I mentioned the house to an estate agent, and he told me it had just been sold for £330,000. What a ridiculous state of affairs, really! What a fleecing of us all!

The truth is that instead of women marrying, and happily starting their families when they wished to, (as envisaged at the outset of the Pill era), they are harassed, exploited, overworked and cash-strapped as seldom before!

They are forced to become wage earners for the best fertile years of their young lives. They have to chemically crush their natural fertility, and all the precious dreams and the thrust and excitement that goes with it. Many of them have to sit tapping away at a computer all day long, to get enough money to pay for a much smaller house or flat than a previous generation had for far less money.

Many of them who have given birth are having to put their children, and even very young babies into childcare, whether they want to or not. Even if a husband is doing his bit manfully, the mortgages or rents are so astronomical. It takes their combined efforts to pay this and all the other bills - which have risen too, as all the country's other employees also have to keep a roof over their heads!

Some women are deeply unhappy about having to hand over their beloved babies into the care of strangers, and most of them find it stressful. A few years ago, the National Council of Women did a survey, and found that 94% of women who had small children and were doing a job, were finding it stressful, and almost all of them would have preferred to be at home with their children. 94% of women, not as happy as they could be, and dare I say 100% of children, not very happy either.

When apart all day, the maternal/baby bond does not develop as love should develop. Many of the children are disoriented and unhappy, and gradually they become unmanageable. It is not normal or natural for a tiny child to be parted from its own mother. Anyone who has been with animals will tell you how a lamb will bleat for its mother; how a foal will whinney to be returned to the mare; how piglets will squeal for the sow. This is normal and natural.

When I was a child in Wales, the way you took a cow and a calf to market was to put the calf in the pony trap, and get in and trot off. The cow would trot behind as she would never let the calf be taken out of her sight.

<u>We do not want to lose this instinct</u>. Love is what life is all about. It is indefinably precious and far reaching. It fuels family love, it fuels understanding for others, it fuels all positive emotions. It is the basis of how a parent can influence a child. This is called "up-bringing".

I fear that the pill cocktail with its testosterone fillip just puts this age-old instinct right off.

Women are finding fertility hard. Far too many cannot have the baby of their dreams. Many have found previous pregnancies hard, and have had many health complications, followed by a long and difficult labour. Sometimes they have the baby successfully, but the milk does not come in. I am told about their struggles with previous pregnancies, every day. In many cases, a baby has been born prematurely, some tragically, do not survive, and some have lifelong disabilities.

Many of these sad happenings are directly due to the fact that the contraceptive pill induces copper to rise in the body, and due to the imbalance, the elements zinc and manganese, fall. Copper and zinc/manganese, are biochemical antagonists, and as one rises, the others will fall. (Pfeiffer, Bryce-Smith, Grant).

Lack of both zinc and manganese has been found to eliminate the maternal instinct in laboratory animals. (Carl Pfeiffer and Oberleas and Caldwell). Rats deprived of zinc have a long and difficult labour, which is otherwise unusual in rodents. They have litters of young, and so in the normal way the young are commensurately smaller and easier to produce. After the birth, if she is deficient, the rat mother will go down to the far corner of the cage, and curl up in a ball, pull her tail over her nose, and switch off. She will not go near the litter to feed them or clean them up, or pull them back into the nest if they fall out. All the usual loving attention a mother rat instinctively gives to her babies is entirely absent.[1]

The same thing happens exactly, if she is kept short of manganese.[2] The rat pups are left to die – unless the laboratory assistant finds them a foster mother. It is interesting that, even when given a replete foster mother, this exercise is not very successful. Zinc/manganese deficient youngsters are poor suckers, and their general development is much slower than rats who received sufficient zinc/manganese in the womb.

Their coats are sparse, they are slow to gain weight, late to cut their teeth, and slow to leave the nest. I think we can conclude, life is a struggle for them.

The work of Professor Bert Vallee of Harvard University Medical School,[3] again researching with rats and rabbits etc, showed that zinc deficiency/copper excess could lead to premature birth. He demonstrated that in the third trimester of pregnancy, the copper rose in the body and the zinc was all gathered in from the bloodstream and given to the placenta.

As the copper (which is a brain stimulant) rose, and the zinc fell to a certain ratio, the phenomenon of birth was started, and the labour went ahead. With the small rodents, they ate their placentas immediately after the birth. As the placentas were so rich in zinc, within 96 hours, the copper/zinc balance was restored in the blood. As the zinc level rose, the rat pups became calmer and were more easily satisfied and settled to sleep better.

Professor Derek Bryce Smith when he was at Reading University, tested a large number of human placentas and found the zinc content was between 350-600mg. At Foresight, we are usually giving about 60mg a day at the time of birth, and we find this prevents any depression, and means the milk comes in very well. The milk is satisfying and this means a happy baby as well!

We find non-Foresight mothers with postpartum depression recover in three to four days, when adequate zinc – 100mgs a day - is given. This will filter through to the milk also, in the quantities required, and then the baby will settle to sleep.

The combination of zinc/copper imbalances, resulting from copper in the drinking water (coming from copper water pipes), and the contraceptive pill, causing the woman's body to retain it, is all a major modern woman's health hazard, and it can affect all areas of her life.

These problems, and the fact that the zinc lost in the placenta is not replaced, (unless supplemented at the time), leads to a whole range of mental illnesses in women. This may lead, in some cases, to her being put on benzodiazepine, valium, Prozac etc. Much long-term mental illness, abandonment of children, breaking up of marriages etc, stems from this.

A lot of conditions in children born after pill use, such as eczema and asthma, are partly due to lack of zinc. (In asthma, lack of selenium and essential oils, is also involved) and epilepsy can often be lack of zinc, magnesium and manganese. (Underwood,[5] Pfeiffer,[1] Brostoff,[6] Passswater & Cranton,[7] Saner,[8] Ward,[9] Williams[10])

We constantly do hair analysis in the previous children of couples who come to us, where there are problems. The imbalances in the children reflect those in their parents, but they are usually more severe in the children, and are often producing chronic illnesses and/or aberrant behaviour.

Conditions such as dyslexia, ADHD, and hyperactivity always show up with a low hair zinc. It is since the pill and copper water pipes, (also mass vaccination), that these problems have suddenly appeared, having virtually not been there in previous generations. They will continue to escalate, unless we take steps to reverse them. Each generation will suffer more severely than the previous one. (Grant,[11] Ward[9]).

It is almost certainly due to this huge prevalence of zinc deficient children that the vaccinations are causing such appalling problems. Zinc is needed to fire up the immune system. Therefore introducing foreign substances into the bloodstream will call for more and more zinc every time it happens.

These events can result in the immune system making huge and sudden demands for zinc leading to flare ups of eczema, so it has now been suggested that overtly eczematose children are excused vaccination. However some whose poor zinc levels are manifesting in other ways, or whose levels are borderline, will still be vaccinated, and will still suffer.

The small intestine is normally covered with a lining that is a rich in an enzyme called alkaline phosphotase. This is a zinc dependent enzyme, i.e. it needs a zinc co-factor. (Enzymes all have a cofactor, which is usually, although not always, a mineral. The cofactor, I have been told, is like the outboard motor on a dinghy. Without it, the enzyme *"does not work."*)

With zinc deficiency, therefore, the working of the small intestine is deprived of alkaline phosphotase and is usually therefore severely compromised in function.

Hence, if the vaccines do not cause the body to call in the zinc from the skin, (giving the poor little child the nightmare of itching eczema), it will call for zinc from the alkaline phosphotase in the gut, (and the poor little mite will have diarrhoea.)

The diarrhoea will give the body a shortage of *every* essential nutrient before too long. So about a couple of weeks after vaccination, the child's development will start to regress. The child will also feel desperately ill, exhausted and distraught, and will have what are described as "tantrums", "night terrors", etc.

The parents will find the child "difficult", the child may just continue to regress into autism, or sometimes, in the most tragic of cases, about 16 days after the event, into "cot death".

Dr Viera Scheibner, Ph.D., Principal Research Scientist Brataslava University[12] (Rtd) has noticed that the adverse reaction to vaccination has a measurable rhythm to it. The children were worse on the 3rd, 6th, 11th, and 16th day after the jab. It seems each time the body called for the zinc (and possibly other nutrients we know less about, very possibly vitamin A or C) the response took a little longer.

The skin, the intestine, and probably the brain itself, would need to relinquish zinc it could ill afford. The immune system acts on the rest of the body rather like a poor but much loved relation who keeps on suffering terrible "bad luck events". (Certainly through no fault of its own!) Unfortunately, it keeps having to be "propped up and sustained" until the long-suffering family are driven slowly bankrupt! Hence the huge increases in many diverse childhood conditions in the last couple of generations. Too much is demanded from a tiny body for the amount of nutrients there are to go round. (Part of the story is the Pill having created the paucity in the first place.)

There is another aspect of this much trumpeted "freedom" for women that is not all unadulterated benefit. Abortion. "The woman's right to choose" – to destroy her baby. It seems to be less well recognised that the motivation behind this is usually the *man's* wish to choose – to whistle off into the middle distance and not to feel any responsibility, love or protective feelings towards either the woman or their baby.

We need to think about this more than we do. Most women love their baby from the moment they know it is there. To a lot of women, having to kill their baby, and have it removed from their body by force, is a cruel and devastating experience. This may not be a very modern way to look at it, but women are not modern inventions. They go back a long way. They have very deep feelings that are not entirely obliterated either by present day "culture" or by the hormonal manipulation provided by the Pill. (Rather like dying the hair – the surface changes in appearance, but the real stuff still grows out.)

Write and tell me if I am wrong, but most of the women who talk to me when they have been through this experience are still sad that it happened, even many years on.

Some fear that the womb was damaged and this is why they are having problems conceiving now. Many are still lonely for the baby they lost. If they are aware that he/she is alive in the life to come, they miss them, and are deeply frustrated not to have been able to know and love them. They are often aware of how old the child would be now, and know the "birthdays" and so on.

My own belief is that most abortion is the product of love-free sex, which is usually deeply disappointing for a woman. All of this lifestyle really stems from the emotional immaturity in the male partner which, in many cases, is largely due to lack of zinc, manganese, B-vitamins and omega-3s!

It has become part of the "macho" age we live in for politicians to boast of 30 conquests, and flourish before the cameras. However, I would like to ask if at least 29 of these women were not rather disappointed? We don't see much below the surface, do we? But we are entitled to wonder! And you are all entitled to rethink many aspects of life on behalf of your own generation, and those to come.

Yet another aspect of the pill promoted "culture" is the influence the little dollops of testosterone have had on the maternal instinct, and the way this has been perceived by the male psychiatrist.

Overlying the normal hormonal ebb and flow around the cycle with a daily clobbering of hormones from outside the body (be they from another animal, or manufactured in a laboratory) is *bound* to change the mood. You cannot "turn off" the role of the ovaries and the uterus, and not "turn off", or drastically alter, a large portion of the woman's emotions.

"Mood swings" is even acknowledged on the list of side effects put on the Pill box! What exactly is a "mood"? It is the amount you love, the way you handle relationships, the way you care, the way you react? The feelings behind everything you do?

If you are in minute-by-minute contact with someone who is so dependent, and so needs your love, as a baby or small child does, how does this affect his/your emotional development together? Have the "scientists" ever thought of this one?

Then we have the psychiatrists telling us that all mass-murderers had terrible mothers who gave them no affection and ruined their emotional lives, causing them to erupt into violence they were unable to contain.

Yes, well. I would go back a lot further than that. What affected the *mothers* so badly – the Pill, lack of zinc, (remember how the zinc deficient rats treated their litters)? Maybe the mothers too had smoking, alcohol drinking, and pesticide contaminated parents? Maybe during their infancy, their brains were bashed by a thimerosol cocktail every few months? Copper water-pipes (in certain areas) have a lot to answer for. So do food additives, medications, fluoride, vaccinations, etc, etc, with all of us.

Let's *understand* where it all comes from. Let's stop the blame game. Let's just put it all right for the next generation. Let's try and tidy everything up for them, so they start with a clean slate.

It is a lot of effort, but it's not too expensive or impossible. Onward!

So what do we do?

Well, Foresight has worked out a programme that we are offering to you, that can reverse the damage. Information on the diet - to make it replete in all the vitamins and trace minerals.

106

> *All bliss*
> *Consists in this,*
> *To do as Adam did*
> From The Apostasy by Thomas Traherne (1637 – 1674)

How to avoid the plague of the contraceptive pill and the copper coil! Learn Natural Family Planning (NFP) from Colleen Norman so you need never risk using them again.

Colleen will tell you how to reliably control your fertility without the need for the pill. She has an excellent website where you will find everything you want, including, hopefully, the name of your nearest natural family planning teacher.

This, in Colleen's own words is how she describes the approach for us:

Natural family planning
Fertility control by education not intervention.

There are basically two approaches to fertility control. The standard clinical approach has been to encourage couples to believe they are permanently fertile and insist that a method of contraception is in use every time they make love. This "continuous contraceptive approach" is certainly effective but there is a price to be paid, in health risks with some methods, and reduction of satisfaction levels with others. Since in fact there are only a few days in each monthly cycle when a woman is fertile, many couples regret this "blunderbuss" approach of continuous contraception, where each day is treated as highly fertile, and are seeking alternatives.

The alternative approach which is therefore enjoying increasing publicity and demand is to offer couples a programme of education in fertility awareness, teaching them to identify accurately those few fertile days in each cycle. The couple can then build a natural loving sexual relationship around the fertility cycle, including at the fertile days if they wish to plan a pregnancy, and avoiding them if pregnancy is not desired at that moment. It provides an efficient means of fertility control which is non-invasive and therefore free of side-effects and health hazards. This can be termed the "ecological approach", otherwise known as the fertility awareness method, or natural family planning.

Past myths. The main objection to this second approach has been its reputed unreliability. The reasons for the high failure rates associated with the old "Calendar Rhythm Method" needs to be understood, but must not be confused with modern techniques of natural family planning, which on WHO statistics has a biological failure rate of virtually Zero. Back in the 1940s when the rhythm method was developed, the accepted fertility facts were that a woman always ovulated 14 days before the onset of her next period, that her egg lived for three days, and that sperm also lived for up to three days. (None of these facts is actually correct!) A woman was required to calculate the date of her next period, then count back 14 days to her estimated day of ovulation. To avoid pregnancy, couples were told to avoid intercourse for four days before and after that date.

The reasons for the high failure rate (declared in all studies to be 33%) are obvious – irregular cycles, and misinformation.

The egg, in fact, is fertilisable for only 8-24 hours, but sperm can live up to 6 days given certain circumstances. The luteal phase (the time between ovulation and menstruation) is not a fixed gap of 14 days, but can be as short as 10 days for some women, and as long as 16 days for others. How does a woman know which one, she has? No calculation method could embrace so many variables.

Yet despite all that, it is amazing how many couples have used this method with success. I am meeting them all the time in NFP clinics! The old fashioned calendar calculation method, with all its inaccuracies, is of course still used in most sub fertility clinics, where couples are told to have intercourse 14 days before the period is due, which is too late for some, and too early for others.

New Knowledge. A step forward in the identification of ovulation came in the 1950's with the introduction of the Temperature Method, perfected by Prof. John Marshall, a consultant neurologist in London. If a woman was prepared to take her temperature for a few mornings each month, before getting up, and at approximately the same time, with a special fertility thermometer, she would find that her body temperature was at a lower level *until she ovulated.*

After ovulation her temperature would rise and stay at a higher level for the next 2 weeks. If she had conceived, her temperature would continue to stay up, providing her with a free proof of pregnancy. If she had not conceived, her temperature would fall with the onset of her period and a new fertility cycle would start, repeating each time this biphasic temperature pattern. Prof. Marshall's studies showed that if a couple waited till 3 high temperatures had been recorded after ovulation, the failure rate for the rest of the luteal phase was very low. In the 1970's Prof. Tietze in his international review of all methods of contraception ranked the Temperature Method (Post Ovulation only) as a "highly efficient" method of contraception, *comparable to sterilisation or a high dose pill.*

The limitations of the method were that, though it accurately confirmed the event of ovulation, and released nearly half the average cycle for infertile intercourse, it gave no warning of an approaching ovulation. When couples had intercourse based on Calendar Rhythm calculations before ovulation, the failure rate jumped from virtually zero to 19%! The Temperature Method is also used in sub fertility clinics, but its benefits are often lost when couples are told to have intercourse when the temperature dips and again when it rises. The temperature could "dip" on any day if she took it earlier than usual. If she waits till the rise, hormone assays have shown that the rise can be delayed up to 48 hours after ovulation. Since the egg is fertilisable for as little as 8-24 hours, it could well be a case of closing the door after the horse has bolted!

What was needed, both to plan and avoid pregnancy successfully, was a sign obvious to a woman that her egg was ripening in her ovary. Here we are indebted to a team of doctors and researchers in Western Australia, headed by Drs. John and Evelyn Billings, who began to study the pattern of vaginal discharge in women. After years of double-checking their work with hormone assays, this is what they learnt:

As the egg-sac (follicle) starts ripening in the ovary, a hormone called estrogen is produced, which stimulates glands in the neck of the womb (cervix) to produce a wet, slippery, relatively clear mucus discharge. This mucus is alkaline and neutralises the acidity in the vagina, enabling sperms to survive in it. It is also rich in nutrients which attract and feed the sperm prolonging their life for several days. Its thin watery nature has a molecular structure that produces a swimming lane structure through which sperm can migrate out of the vagina and into the cervix at incredible speed, and thereafter upwards towards the ripening egg. The mucus increases in flow for approximately the 6 days that the follicle takes to fully ripen. It produces a sensation of wetness and lubrication at the external opening of the vagina which most women cannot fail to notice. When ovulation is imminent, the wet slippery mucus can become so clear that it looks like raw egg-white. This mucus is vital for sperm, which can live minutes or hours at most without it. But once in this mucus, the sperm can live for 3-6 days inside the neck of the womb.

As the egg is released, the mucus, having done its work, dries up and forms a plug in the neck of the womb to prevent the passage of any more sperm upwards. In that way the womb cavity is kept clear ready to receive the baby down the fallopian tube should it be conceived. The womb lining becomes very thick and spongy, ready for the baby to implant into it. However, some 10 to 16 days after ovulation, if there is no baby implanted in that lining, then the, lining is washed away in menstruation, and a new fertility cycle starts. For this reason many older midwives used to speak of the menstruation as "the weeping of the disappointed womb".

The accuracy of the mucus symptom as an indicator of ovulation is beyond doubt. The hormone assays of James Brown in Melbourne, now supported by ultrasound studies in many centres, my own included, have all shown that the subjective observations of simple women, (even those with minimal education levels in developing countries,) are as accurate in identifying ovulation as tests for L.H. peak. When these observations of mucus patterns are combined with minimal use of the Temperature Method, the biological failure rate of Natural Family Planning is virtually zero. The user failure rate as with all methods can be higher. So whenever I am asked the question *"How successful is NFP in preventing pregnancy?"* my answer is always the same: *"It is as successful as you make it. If you stick with the rules, it works. If you take risks, the failure rate is high because you are using the potentially fertile days".*

It goes without saying that mucus observation is vital to couples experiencing sub fertility. It frees them from inaccurate calculations and temperature charts that are only useful in retrospect. Instead it allows them to identify their potentially fertile phase, no matter how short or inadequate it may be, and enables them to maximise their chances of conception.

Couples who in all other aspects of their lives are usually trying to live in harmony with nature rather that in destructive conflict. Yet they often come up against a brick wall when seeking a natural solution to the most intimate area of their lives, their sexual relationship and the control of their fertility. There are at last several good books on the subject and simplified charting systems to help couples use the method successfully. Having used natural methods over 25 years of marriage, I am convinced of the benefits of NFP for modern society. I hope I have given you food for thought and dispelled some of the prejudice against natural methods·

If you would like further information about charting the fertility cycle, please contact me enclosing cheque or P.O for £4 and I will send you literature and the address of your nearest NFP teacher.

Mrs Colleen Norman. 218 Heathwood Road, Heath, Cardiff. CF4 4BS. Tel: 02920 754628. www.fertilityet.org.uk

We all owe a huge debt of gratitude to Colleen as well. She is totally dedicated and has worked for most of her life to bring NFP to those who need and wish to use it.

One more thing - Colleen is constantly in need of new people to train as Natural Family Planning teachers. If the thought of becoming a teacher appeals to you, you will need a course of 4 weekends, usually working all day on the Saturday and for the morning on the Sunday. On her website Colleen advertises where and when these courses will be taking place. She will be absolutely delighted to hear from you, if you would like to attend one. More anon.

Colleen's way of doing things is the right one. The likelihood of unintentional pregnancy using the method as she describes, is down to about one baby per hundred – which means only about one family in four will be blessed with one little "afterthought"! (And my daughter and I are both so pleased that ours happened!)

However, I do know that some of you will find the five days of abstinence very hard. So, as a Black Protestant (as we were called in Tudor times), I am happy to suggest the cap or the diaphragm, used with a little Manuka honey, at these times.

Honey has a natural anti-candida agent, (as mould would not be welcome in a beehive!) A very enlightened doctor, Dr Pam Tatham of Durham, always says "Do not put anything into the vagina that you would not be prepared to eat!" It also seems a little more sperm-friendly. I always hope they are so happy eating honey, they just forget their original goal!

It has to be understood, this adapted approach is probably a little less sure of success than Colleen's stricter regime, but then again I always think another baby is the happiest thing that can happen in any family!

Another huge advantage of taking on board Colleen's knowledge is, of course, that when you intend to conceive you can use your expertise to make sure you do so as soon as possible!

110

Yet another huge advantage is that your life is entirely under your own control. Your moods, your dreams, your hopes, your loves are your own. You are not being altered and manipulated by some little white pill – made somewhere miles away by somebody who does not even know you!

Yet another advantage, the hormones from your urine entering the water table are not polluting the planet, and perhaps inadvertently causing infertility to wildlife – or PMT or cancer, migraine, premature birth or other agonies to foxes, rabbits, sparrows, bees – who knows? We do not know what we are doing, do we?

We all need to wonder what this huge uncontrolled dose of extra hormones is doing to our own species. There is the Pill, then fertility drugs, then HRT, and since all of this has been pouring into the biosphere there has been such a huge increase in paedophilia and we gather much exchange of pornography on the internet. Children are being abducted, school girls and prostitutes get murdered, all sorts of chillingly aberrant sexuality seems to be on the increase. *Why*?

Do we know how much in the way of aberrant hormones accidentally found their way into these strange, troubled minds? Was their mother on the Pill for many years before they were conceived? Were they fed on breast-milk laced with pill-hormones? Were they fed on beef-burgers from American steers fed "growth hormones". Was their drinking water awash with female hormones? Was it in the fish which were fished out of similarly suspect river water with very damaged genitalia? Are we eating fish who have had similar problems?

Let's all of us try to struggle back onto the road to "Natural". We have no idea what we are doing otherwise.

Remember, there is a Supreme Love that can make a butterfly sperm that can effortlessly reproduce the resplendent wing colours every time.... Let's put more faith in Him and our own natural instincts than in blessed little scientists in their white coats. We are more complex than they realise.

Let's help Colleen to get the word around how we can control our fertility ourselves, and help the Planet to remain a normal, cheerfully fertile spinning miracle as we do so.

How about a Campaign for Real Women? The men are very busy with their Campaign for Real Ale. How about we up the game a bit?

PS: Do you ever feel that people who are "trained" are exactly like a *train*? Going along a railroad that can only go in one direction, not left, right, up, down, like a bird among the trees.

Life should be lived much more by instinct – the eternal wisdom we carry inside us like the birds, and the foxes and rabbits, like the mice in the fields....

Do you ever feel we can be over-educated, and under-loved? Too much sitting at a school desk, then an office computer. Too little interaction with other people – particularly with small children, dogs, cats, horses? Is life too sterile and too boring? Too much paperwork? Too little humour?

At the end of the day are we all being "trained" to chuff along the rails, and make a contribution to some great amorphous commercial giant organisation – to help the Alan Sugars of this world get to "the top of their game" – rather than enjoying our own family?

Are we all being "trained" to live a life we do not really enjoy living? What is going on here? Do we need to step back and have a think about it?

Onward!

References:

1. Pfeiffer "Zinc and Other Micronutrients" 1978. New Conran, Keats Publishing Co. LCCC No. 77-91327

2. Oberlas D, Calswell DF, Prasad AS, 1972 International Journal of Neurobiology, Academic Press

3. Vallee B, 1965, Chapter Zinc, Mineral Metabolism, Vol II B., London Academic Press

4. Bryce-Smith D, 1981, Environmental Influences on Parental Development, Thessaloniks Conference

5. Underwood EJ, 1977, Trace Elements in Human and Animal Nutrition, New York Academic Press. ISBN 0-12-709065-7

6. Bostoff J, Gamlin L, 1989, The Complete Guide to Food Allergy and Intolerance, New York Crown Publishers

7. Passwater R and Cranton E, 1983, Trace Elements, Hair Analysis and Nutrition, New Conran Keats Publishing. ISBN 0-87983-265-7

8. Saner G et al, 1985, Hair manganese concentrations in newborns and their mothers. American Journal of Clinical Nutrition 41

9. Ward NI, 1995, Preconceptual Care and Pregnancy Outcome, Journal of Nutritional and Environmental Medicine 5

10. Williams RJ, 1973, Nutrition Against Disease, London, Bantam LCCCN 70-166201

11. Grant ECG, 1994, Sexual Chemistry, Understanding Our Hormones, the Pill and HRT, London, Cedar. ISBN 0-7493-1363-3

12. Scheibner V, 2000, Behavioral Problems in Childhood, the Link to Vaccination, Griffin Press, Netley, South Australia. ISBN 0-9578007-0-3

CHAPTER 5

GENITO-URINARY INFECTIONS

A fter the Voluntary Social Poisons, and the Hairy Hormones, which all come loosely under the term of Drugs, we come to the Bugs.

This chapter is about the health disruptors that can undermine, in some cases, your general feeling of "wellness", and, as we know, anything that does this can also be undermining your fertility.

Any type of illness causes you to activate the immune system. This calls for vitamins A, B2, folic acid, zinc, manganese, etc etc. All the good guys who work for us tirelessly around the clock are squandered as they chase armies of unnecessary bugs.

The genitourinary infections are known as GUI. Things like Chlamydia, which everybody has now heard of, are alarmingly prevalent, and the damage they do to couples and their babies' health seems to be catastrophically under-estimated.[1,2,3,4]

During World War Two, we were left in no doubt about the danger of venereal disease (VD), as it was then called. Every post office, train station, public convenience or bus stop had posters in A3 size, listing the symptoms and advising on the whereabouts of the nearest VD clinic. The government recognized that they could not afford to be coy about it, as many of the service men would be bringing home "a packet" and the women needed help on what to do.

Well, I would think today that the prevalence is much greater than in yester year, but this much needed information is not so "in your face" as it used to be![4]

What is out there, and what it does, remains, in essence, exactly the same, however and my proviso on how to tackle it would be:

  a. Ring your local large hospital and ask if they have a Genitourinary Medicine (GUM) Clinic. They probably do, but if they do not, they will be able to tell you where the nearest one is. A second string to your bow is to check Yellow Pages, where you may find Family Planning and Sexual Health Clinics, (out of seven so listed in our

Yellow Pages, only one appears to be directly relevant, but your area may be luckier.) There is also a Helpline on 0845 3101334. Make an appointment and if possible both of you should go. If one partner is reluctant, then at least one of you should go. If the partner who attends is clear, then it is more likely that the other one will be, but this is not infallible. Do your best. If the partner who attends has an infection, then it is extremely likely that you both have. At least get the second partner to take the treatment.

b.   Once you have the diagnosis, you can take the antibiotic given by the Clinic or you can consult a homoeopath for a homoeopathic remedy. Ainsworths Homoeopathic Chemist, in London, (see useful addresses) has remedies for many of them, ready and waiting. Whatever, <u>both</u> take the remedy.

c.   Once you have taken the solution of your choice, leave it for 3 weeks, then return to the Clinic to check that this has solved it. If not, repeat the remedy and recheck again.

d.   At the same time, (or directly afterwards if your homoeopath thinks this is preferable) take 3 gms of Vitamin C and 100mg of zinc for a couple of weeks, (plus Vitamin A of 5,000iu for three days while you have your period.)

If you have had the infection for a while, it may later be advisable to have the patency of your fallopian tubes checked, as if the bugs have travelled up the tubes this can cause blockages.[5,6,7,8,9] Sometimes an experienced reflexologist can tell if the tubes are not in a good state. Sometimes they can increase the peristaltic action, a little bit, to get them to evacuate mucus and pus, and this way it may be possible to clear them. For this reason I would make reflexology your second port of call, after a diagnosis, and obtaining the remedy.

Now for all the detailed scientific information.

For the scientific nitty-gritty, I think I can do no better than to reproduce Gail's excellent chapter of 1994 which also includes other infections that could affect the course of the pregnancy and the outcome.

We have long recognised that certain diseases can adversely affect the foetus (e.g. German measles), or cause sterility (e.g. mumps). But we often overlook the importance of genito-urinary infections, which include sexually transmitted diseases.   Clearly, any infection in the baby at the start of its life is serious.[10,11,12,13,14,15,16,17,18,19,20,21] We have seen that stress increases the need for nutrients – nutrients which are needed for the development of the sperm, egg or foetus.[22,23,24,25,26,27,28,29,30,31,32,33,34,35] Thus, infection can indirectly affect the development. It may, of course, have direct effects, causing sight problems (eye infections) or brain damage (as in some meningitis cases).

In this chapter we review some of the literature on the genito-urinary and other infections.

Toxoplasmosis (not a GUI but important none-the-less)

This is an infection which may result from eating raw or insufficiently cooked meat and raw fish, or from contact with cat faeces or cat litter or by eating foods soiled by animal carriers of the toxoplasma gondii, the organism which causes toxoplasmosis.[36,37] (Ideally you should be screened before becoming pregnant.) If it is contracted in the first half of pregnancy, it may cause the baby to suffer from hydrocephalus, eye problems, psychomotor retardation, convulsions, microphthalmia, and intercerebral calcifications (calcium deposits in the brain). In the second half of pregnancy, the damage it may cause to the foetus is likely to be less severe. If diagnosed early, toxoplasmosis can be treated with antibiotics which do not harm the baby. If you think you may be carrying the organism or if you have flu-like symptoms then you should see your doctor immediately. You may have to convince your doctor of the necessity of a test since not all GPs think the test is reliable and not all know that the infection can be treated.

Cytomegalovirus (CMV)

Caused by one of the herpes viruses, this can have serious problems for men, women and infants. It is linked with low sperm count and inflammation of the testicle.[38] Prenatally, it can cause miscarriage. Some 3,000 babies are estimated to be infected each year, 300 of them being left with a subsequent handicap.[39,40] It is the most commonly known viral cause of mental retardation, though it may also be responsible for other conditions. These include microcephaly, psychomotor retardation, developmental abnormalities and progressive hearing impairment,[41] respiratory illness, jaundice, small size for gestational age, failure to thrive and eye infections.[42]

Mumps

For the fertile male, mumps can cause inflammation of the various parts of the sex organs, leading to eventual sterility in some cases. But it can also affect the foetus. An excess of diabetes was found among people exposed to the infection in the mother's womb in the first three months of pregnancy. By the age of 30 years, researchers had found a 15-fold increased risk of developing diabetes.[43] (NB: This will almost certainly have been due to the loss of vitamins and minerals caused. Any infection causes significant over-use of nutrients. Foresight would compensate and problems would be much less likely.)

Listeriosis

Listeriosis infection is caused by Listeria monocytogenes, an organism widely distributed in the environment. The most likely source of the infection for humans is food. Pregnant women are advised to avoid eating soft, ripened cheeses (Brie, Camembert and blue-veined types). All cook-chill meals and ready-to-eat poultry should be heated until very hot. They should never be eaten cold. In 1988, out of 291 reported cases, 115 were associated with pregnancy. Among these were 11 miscarriages, 9 stillbirths and 6 neonatal deaths.[44] Abortion, stillbirth or premature labour may occur soon after signs of maternal infection. Congenital Listeriosis and acquired neonatal infection may be present as pneumonia, septicaemia or meningitis. Studies suggest *'up to a third of neonates may die and a third suffer long-term neurological damage.'*[45] Another paper has reported about a 50% mortality rate if Listeriosis infection occurs in the new-born period.[46] (So we avoid insufficiently heated "ready meals" by avoiding "ready meals" *anyway*, and we give a wide berth to blue cheeses, which can cause candida anyway!)

Influenza

There is some debate about whether prenatal exposure to influenza is associated with an increased risk of later schizophrenia. Some studies show no risk, while others show an association. In one study on 3,827 schizophrenic patients born in England and Wales between 1938-1965, the researchers found that females, but not males, exposed to influenza five months before birth can have a significantly greater rate of adult schizophrenia. They cannot explain the gender difference.[47]

Well, we think can: Mothers would have used up zinc, fighting off the flu. The males, who need much more zinc, would have died or been miscarried. If the females survived, they would have been zinc deficient. Carl Pfeiffer's work shows zinc deficiency to be a major factor in schizophrenia.

Genito-urinary infections

Sadly, the number of people suffering from genito-urinary problems continues to rise. There are many reasons – increased use of the pill and IUD, poor nutritional status, leading to a weak immune system, and earlier sexual activity, to mention but a few. Greater sexual freedom, leading to more partners, has certainly increased the risk of infections,[48] though some genito-urinary conditions occur even among couples who are completely faithful to each other (e.g. candidiasis and e-coli). Most of the infections can have dire consequences for fertility, sterility, and the foetus, not to mention the general health of the sufferer. We have not explained the symptoms of the various conditions, because they are not always apparent. If, however, you think there is any chance, whatsoever, that you may have an infection, especially if you have an unpleasant or coloured discharge, you should visit your local Genito-urinary medicine clinc. (NB: Why wonder? It is worth just checking out anyway.)

Urinary tract infections

Bacteriuria infections include cystitis, pyelonephritis and asymptomatic bacteriuria. Bacteriuria are detected in 2-10% of pregnant women, a similar number as in non-pregnant women. In non-pregnant women these infections frequently clear up spontaneously, but this is not so in pregnant women, where the clear-up rate is lower. If not cleared with medical help, such infections can lead to spontaneous miscarriage.[49] (NB: They will steal zinc, once again, so check out <u>before</u> the conception.)

Common sexually transmitted diseases:

VIRUSES	Wart (HPV)
	Herpes
	Cytomegalovirus*
	Hepatitis B*
	AIDS
MYCOPLASMA	Mycoplasma hominis*
	Ureaplasma urealyticum*
BACTERIA	Chalmydia trachomatis
	Gonorrhoea
	E. coli*
	Entercocci
	B. streptococci
	Gardnerella
	Bacteroides
	Mixed anaerobes } Anaerobes
	Syphilis
	Haem influenza
	Haem Strep
	Staph Aureus
	Strep Millerii
FLAGELLATES	Trichomonas
FUNGI	Candida – thrush*

*Indicates the condition is not exclusively sexually transmitted in adults.
The only normal vaginal bacterial known is Lactobacillus

Adapted from Grant, Ellen, Unpublished, 1988

Candidiasis (thrush)

The yeast, candida albicans, occurs naturally in the body, and in healthy people it causes no problems. It is well known as the cause of thrush, both oral, which is common in babies, and vaginal. But it is now recognised that an overgrowth of the yeast can be a contributory factor in many other conditions.[50,51] In some cases this may arise as a condition secondary to viral or bacterial infections which thrive because of a weakened immune system. The use of antibiotics kills off both good and bad organisms in the gut and other mucous membranes, allowing the yeasts, which are not killed off, to proliferate. Symptoms of chronic candidiasis are many. Those such as allergies and sensitivity to food and/or chemicals, cravings for refined carbohydrates and/or alcohol, and alcohol intolerance, irritable bowel syndrome, iron or zinc deficiency can affect nutritional status and may therefore compromise reproductive outcomes[52] (though, as we have said before, any symptom which shows an adverse state of health could do this). One authority has said that there was a doubling of new cases of genital candidiasis reported between 1971 and 1975.[53] Such candidiasis may also cause painful intercourse and possibly provide a hostile environment for the sperm. With treatment for both partners, which includes anti-fungal agents and nutritional therapy, most of the symptoms can be relieved. Short courses of Vitamin A, which protects the mucous membranes, have been found to be helpful, as has the local application of yoghurt. (You should take a maximum of up to 20,000 iu for three days; This should be reduced to 2,000iu before conception. The larger dose should be taken during menstruation to be certain pregnancy has not occurred. Then, postpone conception for a couple of months, to be sure it is out of your system.)

Chlamydia

Chlamydia trachomatis is a nasty pathogen (disease-carrying organism) which is thought to be the most common sexually transmitted pathogen in the Western industrialised world. It is responsible for a great deal of sexually transmitted infection, as well as infertility, and ill health in infants.[54] *Since the symptoms are not always obvious, the woman may not even realise she has it, until her health is very much undermined.*

In men, chlamydia, as it is usually called, causes between one-third and half of non-gonococcal urethritis, although it often occurs together with gonorrhoea.[54] It can also cause inflammation of the prostate tubes, a painful and potentially sterilising infection, or even of the rectum, testes and *vas deferens*.[55,56,57,58,59,60,61,62,63,64,65,66,67,68] In women, it is a major cause of pelvic inflammatory disease (see below), cervicitis, cervical cell dysplasia and urethral syndrome.[69] When it spreads from the cervix to the womb lining,[70] it may induce endometriosis. If it goes on to the Fallopian tubes, it can cause salpingitis, which can result in blocked tubes and infertility.[71,72,73,74,75,76,77,78,79,80,81,82] If the tubes are partially blocked there is a risk of an ectopic pregnancy, which can be very serious. More antibodies are found in infertile couples than in fertile ones.[83]

One study has shown an incidence of 1.9% among 7,305 pregnant women. However, when the sample was restricted to women under 25 years of age who had at least one risk factor as identified in the study (young age or nulliparity or a new sexual partner in the last year) 81.7% were positive.[84] The authors recommend pre-screening criteria could optimise the use of specific diagnostic tests. (NB: No, just screen *everybody*!)

For women coming for abortions, the researchers concluded that 'Estimated costs of hospital admissions for complications of chlamydial infection were more than double the cost of providing a routine Chlamydia screening programme and prophylactic treatment.'[85,86,87,88,89,90,91]

In children, at least 50 per cent of infants born to chlamydia positive women are likely to develop infections. One study quoted a 61 per cent rate of infection, with a 44 per cent rate of clinical disease in infants born to infected mothers. Prematurity may result, and other main problems are conjunctivitis, found in 25-50 per cent of exposed infants, and pneumonia in 10-20 per cent. Rhinitis, otitis media, proctitis and vulvitis have also been reported. For example, in one study, exposed infants had twice the rate of pneumonitis and *recurrent otitis media* (which can lead to hearing defects) in their first six months of life. Those who had pneumonitis had higher subsequent rates of gastroenteritis. The researchers concluded: *'These results suggest that appreciable outpatient infant mortality may be associated with maternal infection with chlamydia trachomatis and that it may either cause or promote the occurrence of early recurrent otitis media and gastroenteritis.'* Another study found chlamydia trachomatis in the infant's pharynx and conjunctiva, the mother's cervix and the father's urethra. The researchers recommended searching for chlamydial infections in preterm infants with atypical respiratory disease even if delivered by caesarean section. (NB: Yes, but this is too late, isn't it? Search for it in prospective parents and *stop this happening* in the future.)[92,93]

Gonorrhoea

Caused by the bacteria, *Neisseria gonorrhoea-gonococcus*, this is one of the most contagious diseases there is. Often symptoms pass unnoticed, but if it is not treated, it can have very serious consequences for men, women and infants.

In men it can lead to sterility and low sperm counts. In the female, it is a major cause of pelvic inflammatory disease, which may lead to sterility. It also seems to leave her more vulnerable to chlamydial infections.[94]

If a woman has suffered from gonorrhoea, she is likely to be tested during pregnancy (N.B: though with good preconception care, she should be free from infection before conceiving). At least one researcher has found that prolonged rupture of the membranes and later chorioamniocentesis in infected women predisposes the baby to acquire the infection. There are also risks of prematurity with infected women.[96]

Infections in the newborn are common if the mother is infected, as the bacteria are passed to the baby during its passage through the birth canal. Conjunctivitis is the most common problem, as the conjunctiva comes into contact with the infected cervix during birth – this can lead to a serious discharge with risks to sight, including blindness.[97] Other parts of the body may also suffer, with infections of the umbilicus, the anogenital area, or nose and throat. There may be arthritis or meningitis.[98]

Herpes

There are various types of herpes virus, causing a number of conditions, some of which we have already mentioned. However, it is the herpes simplex virus which causes the condition known commonly as 'herpes'. There are two similar types – Type 1 causes sores around the mouth and nose, often referred to as 'cold sores', and, more rarely, in the eyes or genital or anal area. Type 2 causes sores in the genital and anal area and, more rarely, on the mouth. Genital infections caused by Type 2 are more severe.

Small sores appear which can be quite painful. There may be itching or pain on urinating. The symptoms clear but further attacks usually occur.[99]

It is very important for a woman to tell her doctor if she has or has had genital herpes as it could affect the birth procedure. A caesarean section may be advised where there is an active sore in the vagina or on the cervix.[99] If the waters break, a path is created for the virus to reach the baby, so a caesarean section should be done quickly.[100] The virus may also be passed to the baby after birth by kissing if one has a cold sore or if there are sores on the breasts during breastfeeding. It is rare for the foetus to be infected in the womb and this would generally result in a miscarriage.[100]

Researchers have concluded that herpes 'can result in spontaneous abortion, congenital and perinatal infections in the infant, or disseminated infection and death in the mother'. The frequency of risk factors is unknown. In their study there was a 40 per cent incidence of serious perinatal disease or illness. Some of the infants whose mothers became infected in the last three months of pregnancy had perinatal morbidity such as prematurity, intrauterine growth retardation, and neonatal infections with herpes Type 2.[101]

The main problem is the baby's immature immune system may not be able to cope with the virus and this can lead to an overwhelming infection, resulting in encephalitis with consequent brain damage, or eye infections, with eye damage. There may be jaundice, pneumonia with breathing difficulties, or even spells with no breathing at all. Microcephaly, microphthalmia and intracranial calcification have also been reported.[102] There have been reports of physical impotence in men who suffered from herpes and proctitis, which then resulted in nerve inflammation. [102]

Syphilis

This is a very dangerous infection although now, thankfully, comparatively rare. Fortunately it responds to *early* treatment. In both sexes it can lead to sterility and damage to many vital organs, including the heart and brain. The brain damage leads to psychiatric problems.

Syphilis is transmitted from the mother to the foetus via the placenta, thus making it prenatal rather than congenital, though in the child it is usually referred to as 'congenital syphilis'. It only occurs when the mother's syphilis is not diagnosed and treated, making it now comparatively rare as most women's blood is screened at the antenatal stage.[103] (Of course, if you have followed the Foresight programme you will have been screened before conception.)

Without treatment one third of the babies will be born healthy, one third will be aborted or stillborn, and one third will have congenital syphilis. Stillbirths will occur if the maternal infection is present very early in pregnancy and if there is so great a dose of the organism responsible that the foetus succumbs to infection.

120

The baby suffering from congenital syphilis may appear healthy at birth, though occasionally there may be a rash. However, failure to thrive and gain weight, often the first clinical signs of early congenital syphilis, becomes apparent two to eight weeks after birth. There may be weight loss and often the baby has a wizened appearance, like an old man. Other symptoms include skin lesions, mucous membrane lesions, visceral lesions, enlarged liver and/or spleen, abdominal swelling, meningitis, and bone lesions.

Mycoplasmas, including ureaplasma urealyticum

These organisms are the smallest free-living pathogens, capable of causing a wide range of problems in humans.[104,105,106,107,108,109,110] In the reproductive system, mycoplasma hominis and ureaplasma urealyticum are the most commonly cultured. A direct relation between the frequency of venereal infection and serum antibody levels has been found.[111] One authority writes: Mycoplasmas, which commonly reproduce when the subject's health is impaired, can cause attacks of vulvovaginitis, genital irritation and urinary frequency. Symptoms may persist for twenty years or even longer.'[112]

In men, ureaplasma urealyticum is a major cause of non-gonococcal urethritis, which can lead to infertility,[113] non-specific urethritis (NSU), prostate and kidney disease. Higher concentrations have been found in the genital tracts of sterile couples than in fertile couples.[114] In women, pelvic inflammatory disease can result if the mycoplasmas, including ureaplasma urealyticum, are allowed to proliferate. Scarring may lead to infertility. Miscarriage and premature birth are also associated with them.[115,116,117] Of the common organisms ureaplasma urealyticum is the most frequently implicated in repetitive abortions.[118]

Genital mycoplasma infection is difficult to eradicate and prospective parents who have such a condition may have to be patient.[119] Women need local treatment of the cervix.

Pelvic inflammatory disease

This can be gonococcal, chlamydial, or non-gonococcal, non-chlamydial in type. It is sometimes misdiagnosed so that tests for all types should always be conducted. Treatment for one type may be ineffective against another. For example, antibiotics for gonorrhoea do not cure chlamydia. One study found a high incidence of non-gonococcal infection among the male partners of women with PID. Over three-quarters of the males were showing no symptoms.[120] The men never admit to symptoms in any case. It does not mean they do not need to attend a clinic.

The consequence of untreated PID include sub-fertility, sterility, menstrual difficulties, chronic abdominal pain and ectopic pregnancy.[121] The risks of tubal infection leading to infertility seem to be related to the number of types and infection. In one study, even after treatment with antibiotics, a single tubal infection, including chlamydia, produced a 12.8 per cent infertility rate, two infections produce a 35.5 per cent infertility rate, while for three it is a 75 per cent rate.[122] Catterall reports that: 'If the statistics are correct there is a 50 per cent chance of relapse..., a one in three chance of being sterile, a 25 per cent chance of dyspareunia (painful intercourse) and a 10 per cent chance of ectopic pregnancy'.[71,72,73,74,75,76,77,78,79,80,81,82]

Genital warts – condyloma accuminata

These are caused by a virus called 'papilloma virus'. The symptoms may only be warty nodules which may not be readily apparent. Some types of the virus have been linked with cervical cancer and may therefore affect reproduction.[123] By 1987, one in six women attending Islington family planning clinics had a positive smear. One in three had either cell abnormalities and/or the cancer wart-virus.[124] (It is not clear, though how representative a group this is, compared with the general population.)

Trichomoniasis

This condition is caused by the organism trichomonies vaginatis. Women may suffer from excessive (itchy) vaginal discharge, while the newborn may have fever, irritability and fail to thrive.[125]

Hepatits B

Hepatitis means 'inflammation of the liver'. Type B, one of three types, can be spread through sexual contacts or contact with body fluids, such as blood, urine and saliva, so it is not just sexually transmitted. Like chlamydia and gonorrhoea, it is possible to have it without any symptoms. Treatment may be slow, being bed rest and nutritional therapy. Vaccination is available to some people, although at least one authority has advocated screening for everyone, with vaccination as appropriate, because it is a serious condition leading to neonatal deaths.[126] It can also lead to an increase in food and chemical sensitivities in the mother, which may affect a baby who is being breastfed. At least one authority has argued that 'the cost-benefit of screening is difficult to assess, but it is likely to be substantial'[127]. (NB: Need we always be so *obsessed with cost*? How about mother-benefit and baby-benefit from preconceptual screening of parents? The health benefit would pay off handsomely surely?)

AIDS – Acquired Immune Deficiency Syndrome

First recognised as a distinct syndrome in 1981 the human immunodeficiency virus (HIV) which is generally thought to cause it was identified in 1983. By September 1993, 20,590 people in the UK had tested HIV positive. Since 1982, 8,115 people have been diagnosed as having AIDS, of whom 5,553 have died. These figures are acknowledged to be under-estimates. Treatments have now improved so that HIV positive people, if treated early, may find there is a delay in the onset of symptoms. Even 8-10 years of health is possible in the West.

There is some debate as to whether or not pregnancy will increase the risk of developing AIDS-related complex or the risk of the baby being infected in the womb in asymptomatic women. Early studies suggested a risk.[128] Other studies suggested no discernible effect.[129] NB: This was written in 1994. This is not an area that we have a great deal of knowledge about, so it may not be as accurate now as it was then, ie the figures relate to them. But it reflects the trend.

Gardnerella

There has been some debate about whether or not the presence of anaerobic bacteria, including Gardnerella, in such abnormal amounts as to cause the condition bacteria vaginosis, can have an adverse outcome in pregnancy. Researchers at Northwick Park Hospital found that 'late miscarriage and preterm delivery are associated with the presence of bacteria vaginosis in early pregnancy. This is independent of recognised risk factors such as previous preterm delivery.'[130]

Gail Bradley's Conclusions

Many infections can be damaging, either to the reproductive tract, the sperm, ova, or foetus. We have written about the most common infections individually, but unfortunately they often occur in combination, and this multiplies the risks of damage. In one study, mycoplasma hominis was found in 30-50 per cent of vaginal cultures of sexually active women, with ureaplasma urealyticum in 60-80 per cent of cultures. Another study looked at the incidence of six infections in pregnant adolescents. They were aged 13-17 years, all from very poor socio-economic backgrounds and in their third trimester. The results showed that only five appeared to be free from all the infections being considered, while 34 per cent had trichimonas, 38 per cent candidiasis, 70 per cent mycoplasma homini and 90 per cent ureaplasma urealyticum. Chlamydia trachomatis was found in 37 percent of 115 specimens. Gonorrhoea was originally present in 12 subjects early in pregnancy, but only in one in the third trimester. Three had evidence of genital herpes infection and three others evidence of papillomavirus infection.[131]

A survey of 109 patients attending a Hertfordshire Foresight doctor for preconception care confirmed the importance of screening. Of 32 men tested between 1989 and 1991, 15 had one or more infections. These included B Streptococci, Chlamydia, ureaplasma, enteroccus, Staph Aurius, candida, E coli, Klebsella, anaerobic bacteria, Haem influenza and Strep milleri. 77 women were tested, showing a total of 39 positive cervical swabs and 22 positive chlamydia antibodies. Infections identified included B Streptococci, ureaplasma, mycoplasma, anaerobic bacteria, candida, Gardnerella, E coli, Strep millerii, Strep aureus, 80.

A study of 400 women attending another clinic for abortion revealed 28% had anaerobic bacteria, 24% candida, 32% chlamydia, 0.75% trichmonas and 0.25% gonorrhoea.[132]

While the immune system may cope with one mild infection, if there are multiple infections, it is likely to be unable to withstand such an onslaught. There is also the risk that not all infections will be treated, even if symptoms persist. Comprehensive screening is vital and it is sensible that, where possible, a colposcope should be used as it is a superior technique for at least one condition[133] and thought to be a better technique for others.[134] If you suspect that you may have an infection, attend a Genito-Urinary Medicine Clinic for a full examination with the appropriate swabs taken and the use of a colposcope. This may mean travelling a bit.

However, in view of the many adverse effects of genito-urinary infections, it is worth making an effort to get the best treatment available. Any infections or cell abnormalities on the cervix should be diagnosed and treated *before pregnancy* as the rise in hormones during pregnancy increases these problems. The extra artificial hormone stimulation given to infertile women is especially likely to cause a flare-up of cervical or pelvic infection.[135]

Checklist

1. Have you had your rubella status checked?

2. Avoid eating raw meat and fish. Wash cats' dishes separately. Do not allow cats on cooking surfaces. If you are pregnant, do not handle soiled cat litter.

Regarding GUIs:

3. Always ask for a genito-urinary examination if you suspect any infection of if you are having difficulty conceiving. For women this should involve the use of a colposcope.

4. If a genito-urinary infection is diagnosed it is vital that both partners receive treatment and follow-up checks.

5. The male partner should have the semen and/or prostatic fluid checked for infection. Urine screening alone is inadequate.

So What Do We Do?

As many infections are symptomless they therefore may be unsuspected. However, we now know what devastation and long term damage they can cause to the baby. Just get checked out, <u>whatever</u>. Our Hero is worth it! There is a way through the minefield! Check with your local Genito-urinary Medicine Clinic. Track them down through the local hospital, yellow pages (sexual health), or on the web. You may not have anything, but better safe than sorry.

Onward!

References:

1. Dunlop EMC (1980) Chlamydial infection; terminology, disease and treatment. Recent advances in sexually transmitted diseases, Churchill Livingstone, Edinburgh, London, New York, 101-119

2. Department of Health and Social Security: Sexually transmitted diseases. In: On the state of public health: The annual report of the Chief Medical Officer of the DHSS for the year 1978, London HMSO, 6, 1980

3. Royal College of Physicians Committee on Genitourinary Medicine (1987) Chlamydial diagnostic services in the United Kingdom and Eire: current facilities and perceived needs. Genitourin Med 63: 371-374

4. Catterall RD (1981) Biological effects of sexual freedom. The Lancet, 315-319, February 7

5. Eliard T, Brorsson JE, Hamark B et al (1976) Isolation of chlamydia trachomatis infection in patients with acute salpingitis. Scand J Infect Dis., 9: 82-85

6. Kane JL, Woodland RM, Forsey T et al (1984) Evidence of chiamydial infection in infertile Women with and without fallopian tube obstruction. Fertil Steril, 42:832-838

7. Padjen A, Nash LD, Fiscelli T (1984) The relationship between chlamydial antibodies and involuntary infertility. Fertil Steril, 41: 975-985

8. Brunham RC, MacLean IW, Binns B et al (1985) Chlamydia trachomatis: its role in tubal infertility. J Infect Dis, 152: 1275-1282

9. Miller PR. Taylor-Robinson D, Furr PM, Toft B, Allen J (1985) Serological evidence that chlamydia and mycoplasmas are involved in infertility of women. J Reprod Fertil, 73:237-240

10. Cates W., Wasserheit JN (1991) Genital chlamydial infections: Epidemiology and Reproductive sequelae. Am J Obstet Gynecol. 164:1771-1781

11. Martin DH, Koutsky L, Eschenbach DA et al (1982) Prematurity and perinatal mortality in pregnancies complicated by maternal Chlamydia trachomatis infections. JAMA, 247: 1585-1588

12. Heggie AD, Lumicao GG, Stuart LA et al (1981) Chlamydia trachomatis infection in mothers and infants. AJDC, 135: 507-511

13. Frommell GT, Rothenberg R, Wang SP et al (1979) Chlamydial infection of mothers and their infants. J Pediatrics, 95: 28-32

14. Hammerschlag MR. Anderka M, Semine DZ et al (1979) Prospective study of maternal and infantile infection with Chlamydia trachomatis. Pediatrics, 64:142-148

15. SchachterJ, Grossman M, Holt J et al: Prospective study of chlamydial infections in neonates. The Lancet, 377-380, August 25, 1979

16. Schachter J, Grossman M, Holt J et al (1979) Infection with Chlamydia trachomatis: Involvement of multiple anatomic sites in neonates.J Infect Dis, 139: 232-234

17. Schaefer C, Harrison R, Boyce T, Lewis M: Illnesses in infants born to women with Chlamydia trachomatis infection. AJDC, 139: 127-133, February, 1985

18. Zuher M, Naib MD (1970) Cytology of TRIC agent infection of the eye of newborn infants and their mothers' genital tracts. Acta Gytologica, Vol:14, No:7, 390-395

19. Rees E, Tait IA, Hobson D, Byng RE, Johnson FWA (1977) Neonatal conjunctivitis caused by Neisseria gonorrhea and Chlamydia trachomatis. Br J Vener Dis, 53: 173-179

20. Rees E, Tait IA, Hobson D, Karayiarinis P, Lee N (1981) Persistence of chlamydial infection after treatment for neonatal conjunctivitis. Arch Dis in Childhood, 56: 193-198

21. Watson PC, Gaidner D: TRIC agent as a cause of neonatal eye sepsis. Br Med J, 3: 527 1968

22. Foster RK, Dawson CR, Schachter J (1970) Late follow-up of patients with neonatal inclusion conjunctivitis. Am J Opthalmol, 69: 467

23. Beem MO, Saxon EM (1977) Respiratory tract colonization and a distinctive pneumonia syndrome in infants infected with Chlamydia trachomatis. N Engl J Mod, 296: 306-310

24. Frommell CT, Bruhn FW, Schwatzman DJ (1977) Isolation of Chlamydia trachomatis in infant lung tissues. N Engl J Mod, 296: 1150-1152

25. Tipple MA, Saxon EM, Radkowski MA, Beem MO (1977) Clinical characteristics of Chlamydia trachomatis pneumonia. Podiatric Res, 11:508

26. Arth C, Von Schmidt B, Grossman M, Schachter J (1978) Chlamydial pneumonitis. J Pediatrics, 93: 447-449

27. Embil JA, Ozere RU, MacDonald SW (1978) Chlamydia trachomatis and pneumonia in infants: report of two cases. Canad Med Assoc J, 119: 1199

28. Hammerschlag MR: Chlamydial pneumonia in infants.

29. N Engl J Med, 298: 1083 1978

30. Hallberg A, MUrdh P-A, Persson K, Ripa T (1979) Pneumonia associated with Chlamydia trachomatis infection in an infant. Acta Paediatr Scand, 68: 765-767

31. Harrison HR, English MG, Lee CK, Alexander ER (1978) Chlamydia trachomatis infant pneumonitis: comparison with matched controls and other infant pneumonitis. N Engl J Med, 298: 702-708

32. Harrison HR, Taussing LM, Fulginitis V (1982) Chlamydia trachomatis and chronic respiratory disease in children. Pediatr Infect Dis, 1: 29-33

33. Tipple MA, Beem MO, Saxon EM (1979) Clinical characteristics of the afebrile pneumonia associated with Chlamydia trachomatis infection in infants of less than six months of age. Pediatrics, 63: 192-197

34. Hammerschlag MR. Hammerschlag PE, Alexander ER (1980) The role of Chlamydia trachomatis in middle ear effusion in children. Pediatrics, 66: 615-617

35. Chang MJ, Rodriquez WD, Mohla C (1982) Chlamydia trachomatis in otitis media. Pediatr Infect Dis, 1: 95-97

36. Aspock, H., 'Toxoplasmosis'. In: Prenatal and perinatal infections. EURO reports and Studies, 93, 43-51

37. Cengiz, Dincer, Rotc, Firat, Soylemez, Firide, 'Tackling the threat of toxoplasmosis', Midwife Health Visitor and Community Nurse, 1991, 27(7): 199-220

38. Alder, M.W., ABC of Sexually Transmitted Diseases, London, BMA, 1984, 48

39. Hanshaw, J.B., 'Developmental abnormalities associated with congenital cytomegalovirus infection', Adv Teratology, 1970, 4, 62

40. Elek, S.D., Stern, H., 'Development of a vaccine against mental retardation caused by cytomegalovirus infection in utero', Lancet 1974, 1, 1-5

41. Dahle, A.J., et al., 'Progressive hearing impairment in children with congenital cytomegalovirus, infection', J Speech Hear Dis, 1970, 44, 220

42. Blattner, Russel J. 'The role of viruses in congenital defects', Am J Dis Child, 1974, 128, 781-786

43. Fine, P.E.M., et al. (1985) 'Infectious diseases during pregnancy: a follow-up study of the long-term effects of exposure to viral infection in utero. Studies on medical and population subjects'. HMSO

44. Acheson, D (1989) Letter from the Chief Medical Officer on listeria and food. Department of Health and Social Security. Letter ref PL/CMo (89) 3, 16 February

45. Hay, M., 'Neonatal listeriosis and ventriculomegaly: two case reports', Maternal and Child Health, 1989, 14(1): 14-15

46. Gellin, B.G.B., Broome, C.V., 'Listeriosis' JAMA, 1989, 261: 1313-1319

47. Noritoshi, Takei, Sham, Pak, et al., 'Prenatal exposure to influenza and the development

48 Catterall, R.D., 'Biological effects of sexual freedom', Lancet, 1981, 315-319

49. Nicholas, N.S., Urinary tract infections in pregnancy, Maternal and Child Health, October, 294-297

50. Truss, C., Orion, Missing Diagnosis, MD Inc., 1983

51. Crook, William G. (1983) The Yeast Connection, Professional Books

52. Davies, Stephen and Stewart, Alan, Nutritional Medicine, London, Pan, 1987, 360

53. Hurley, Rosalind. Reported in Davies, S., op. cit., 364

54. Schacter, Julius and Grossman, Moses, 'Chlamydia', in: Infectious Diseases of the Foetus and Newborn Infant, Jack Remington and Jerome O., Klein, eds. W.B. Saunders Co., 1983

55. Dunlop EMC, Waughan-Jackson JD, Darougar S, Jones Chlamydial infection: incidence in "non-specific" urethritis. Br J Vener Dis, 48: 425-428, 1972

56. Holmes KK, Hansfield HH, Wang SF, Wentworth BB et al (1975) Etiology of non-gonococcal urethritis. N Engl J Med, 292: 1199-2005

57. Oriel JD, Reeve P, Wright JT, Owen J (1976) Chlamydial infection in male urethra. Br J Vener Dis, 52: 46-51

58. Alani MD, Darougar S, Mac D, Burns DC.et al (1977) Isolation of Chlamydia trachomatis from the male urethra. Br J Vener Dis, 53:88-92

59. Bowie WR, Wang SP, Alexander ER, Floyd J et al (1977) Etiology of nongonococcal urethritis: Evidence of Chlamydia trachomatis and Ureaplasma urealyticum. J Clin Invest, 59: 735-742

60. Jacobs NF, Arum ES, Krauss SJ (1977) Nongonococcal urethritis: the role of Chlamydia trachomatis. Ann of Int Med, 86: 313-314

61. Waughan-Jackson JD, Dunlop EMC, Darougar S et al (1977) Urethritis due to Chlamydia trachomatis. Br J Vener Dis, 53: 180-183

62. Wong JL, Hines PA, Brasher MD, Rogers GT et al (1977) The etiology of nongonococcal urethritis in men attending a venereal disease clinic.J Am Vener Dis Assoc, 4:4-8

63. Berger RE, Alexander ER, Monda GD, Ansell J et al (1978) Chlamydia trachomatis as a cause of acute "idiopathic" epididymitis. N Engl J Med, 298: 301-304

64. Pierroud HM, Miedzbrodzka K (1978) Chlamydial infection of the urethra in men. Br J Vener Dis, 54: 45-49

65. Stamm WE, Koutsky LA, Benedetti JK, Jourden JL et al (1984) Chlamydia trachomatis urethral infections in men: Prevalence, risk factors and clinical manifestations. Ann Intern Med, 100:47-51

66. Terho F (1978) Chlamydia trachomatis in nonspecific urethritis. Br J Vener Dis, 54: 251-256

67. Stamm WE, Cole B (1986) Asymptomatic Chlamydia trachomatis urethritis in men. Sex Transm Dis, 13: 163-165

68. Suominen J., Gronroos M., Terho P., Wichmann L. (1983) Chronic prostatitis, Chlamydia trachomatis and infertility. Int J Andrology, 6:405-413.

69. Mardh, P.H., 'Medical chlamydiology: a position paper'. Scandinavian Journal of Infectious Diseases (supp 32), 1981, 3-8

70. Mardh, P.H., et al., 'Endometriosis caused by chlamydia trachomatis'. Br J Vener Dis, 1981, 57-191

71. Sellors JW, Mahony JB, Chrnesky MA et al (1988) Tubal factor infertility: an association with prior chlamydial infection and asymptomatic salpingitis. Fertil Steril, 49: 451-457

72. Kelver ME, Ngamani M (1989) Chlamydial serology in women with tubal infertility. Int J Fertil, 43: 42-45

73. Reniers J, Collet M, Frost E et al (1989) Chlamydial antibodies and tubal infertility. Int j Epidemiol, 18: 261-263

74. Cates W, Rolfs RT, Aral SO (1990) Sexually transmitted diseases, pelvic inflammatory disease and infertility: an epidemiologic update. Epidemiol Rev, 12: 199-220

75. Minassian SS, Wu CH, Jungkind D, Gorcial B et al (1990) Chlamydial antibody as determined with an enzyme-linked immunosorbent assay, in tubal factor infertility. J Reprod Med, 35: 141-145

76. Svensson L, MUrdh P-A, Ahlgren M, Nordenskjold F (1985) Ectopic pregnancy and antibodies to Chlamydia trachomatis. Fertil Steril, 44: 313-317

77. Brunham RC, Binns B, McDowell J, Paraskevas M (1986) Chlamydia trachomatis infection in women with ectopic pregnancy. Obstet Gynecol, 67: 722-726

78. Hartford SL, Silva PD, DiZehera GS et al (1987) Serologic evidence of prior chlamydial infection in patients with tubal ectopic pregnancy and contralateral tubal disease. Fertil Steril, 47: 118-121

79. Walters MD, Eddy CA, Gibbs RS, Schachter J et al (1988) Antibodies to Chlamydia trachomatis and the risk of tubal pregnancy. Am J Obstet Gynecol, 159: 942-946

80. Chaim W, Sarov B, Sarov I, Piura B et al (1989) Serum IgH and IgA antibodies to chlamydia in ectopic pregnancies. Contraception, 40: 59-71

81. Chow JM, Yonekura MU, Richwald GA et al (1990) The association between Chlamydia trachomatis and ectopic pregnancy: A matched-pair, case-control study. JAMA, 263: 3164-3167

82. Shermark I, Daling J, Stergachis A et al (1990) Sexually transmitted disease and tubal pregnancy. Sex Trans Dis, 17: 115-121

83. Moore, D.E., et al., 'Association of Chlamydia trachomatis with tubal infertility', Fert Ster, 1980, 32, 303-304

84. Alary, Michael, Roly, Jean R., et al., 'Strategy for screening pregnant women for chlamydial infection in a low prevalence area'. Obstet Gynecol 1993, 82: 399-404

85. Blackwell, Anona L., Thomas, Philip D., et al., 'Health gains from screening for infection of the lower genital tract in women attending for termination of pregnancy', Lancet, 1993, 342: 206-210

86. Miller Br, Ahrons S, Laurin J, MUrdh P-a (1982) Pelvic infection after elective abortion associated with Chlamydia trachomatis. Obstet Gynecol., 59:210-213

87. Westergaard L, Philipson T, Scheibel J (1982) Significance of cervical Chlamydia trachomatis infection in postabortal pelvic inflammatory disease. Obstet Gynecol, 60;322-325

88. Ovigstad E, Skang K, Jerve F et al (1983) Pelvic inflammatory disease associated with Chlamydia trachomatis infection after therapeutic abortion. Br J Vener Dis, 59:189-192

89. Osser J, Persson K (1984) Post-abortal pelvic infection associated with

Chlamydia trachomatis and the influence of humoral immunity. Am J Obstet Gynecol: 150;699-703

90. Barbacci MB, Spence MR, Kappus EW et al (1986) Post-abortal endometritis and isolation of Chlamydia trachomatis. Obstet Gynecol, 68:686-690

91. Southgate LJ, Treharne JD, Williams R (1989) Detection and treatment and follow-up of women with Chlamydia trachomatis infection seeking abortion in inner city general practices. Br Med J, 299: 1136-1137

92. Alexander ER, Chandler JW, Pheiffer TA et al (1977) Prospective study of perinatal Chlamydia trachomatis infection. In: Hobson DC, Holmes KK, Eds. Nongonococcal urethritis and related infections. Am Soc Microbiology Washington D.C. 148

93. Chandler JW, Alexander ER, Pheiffer TA et al (1977) Opthalmia neonatorum associated with maternal chlamydial infection. Trans Am Acad Opthalmol Otolaryngol, 83: 302-308

94. Cherry, Sheldon H., Planning Ahead for Pregnancy, London, Viking, 1987, 75

95. Brooks, Geoffrey F., 'Neisseria gonorrhea infections in children'. In: Gonaccal Infections, Geoffrey F, Brooks and Elizabeth A. Donegan, eds. E. Arnold, 1985, 132

96. Israel, K.S., et al., 'Neonatal and childhood gonoccal infections', Clin Obs Gyn, 1975, 18, 143-151

97. Brooks, op. cit., 133-134

98. Scarrel, P.M., Pratt, K.A. 'Symptomatic gonorrhea during pregnancy', Obstet Gynaecol, 1968, 32, 670-673

99. Health Education Council, 'Herpes. What it is and how to Cope', Health Education Council 1985

100. Sack, Stephen L., The Truth About Herpes, Vancouver, Verdant Press, 1986, 87

101. Brown, Zane A., et al., 'Effects on infants of a first episode of genital herpes during pregnancy', New Eng J Med 1987, 317, 1246-1251

102. Sacks, op. cit., 78-80

103. Schofield, C.B.S, Sexually Transmitted Diseases, London, Churchill Livingstone, 1972

104. Braun P, Lee YH, Kiem JO et al (1971) Birth weight and genital mycoplasmas in pregnancy. N Engl J Med, 284: 167-171

105. McCormick WM, Rosner B, Lee YH (1973) Colonization with genital mycoplasmas in women. Am J Epidemiol 97: 240-245

106. Shurin PA, Albert S, Rosner B et al (1975) Chorioamnionitis and colonization of the newborn infant with genital mycoplasmas. N Engl J Med, 293: 5-8

107. Harrison RF, Hurley R, deLouvois J (1979) Genital mycoplasmas and birth weight in offspring of primigravid women. Am J Obstet Gynecol, 133: 201-203

108. Ross JM, Furr PM, Taylor-Robinson D et al (1981) The effect of genital mycoplasmas on human growth. Br J Obstet Gynaecol, 88: 749-755

109. Embree JE, Krause VW, Embil JA, MacDonald S (1980) Placental infection with Mycoplasma hominis and Ureaplasma urealyticum: Clinical correlation. Obstet Gynecol, 56: 475

110. Friberg J, Gnarpe I: Mycoplasma in human reproductive failure. Am J Obstet Gynecol, 23-26 May, 1973

111. Cassell, Gail, ed. 'Ureaplasmas of humans: with emphasis on maternal and neonatal infections'. Pediatric Infectious Disease, 1986, 5, 6, Suppl

112. Sutton, Grahame, 'Genital Infections', Midwife, Health Visitor and Community Nurse, 1982, 18(2), 42-45

113. Walton, Pauline, 'New antibiotics in fight against genital disease', Doctor, 11 September 1980.

114. Friberg, J., Gnarpe, H., 'Mycoplasma and human reproductive failure', Am J Obstet Gynaecol, 1973, 116, 23-26

115. Gibbs, Ronald S., 'Microbiology of the female genital tract', Am J Obstet and Gynecol, 1987, 156, 491-495

116. Kudsin, RB, Driscoll SC, Pelletier PA (1981) Ureaplasma urealyticum incriminated perinatal morbidity and mortality. Science, 213:474

117. Quinn PA, Shewchuck MD, Shuber J et al (1983) Serologic evidence of urealyticum infection in women with spontaneous pregnancy loss. Am J Obstet Gynecol, 145:245-249

118. Simpson, Joe Leigh, 'Foetal Wastage'. In: Obstetrics, Normal and Problem Pregnancies, Gabbe, Steven, et al., eds., New York, Churchill Livingstone, 1986, 665

119. Sutton, Grahame, op. cit.

120. Jacob, Martha, et al., 'A forgotten factor in pelvic inflammatory disease: infection in the male partner', British Medical Journal, 1987, 294, 869

121. Grant, Ellen, The Bitter Pill, London, Corgi, 1975, 174

122. Westrom, L., 'Effect of acute pelvic infectious disease on fertility', Am J Obstet Gynaecol, 1975, 121, 707-713

123. Health Education Council, Guide to a Healthy Sex Life, 1985, 22

124. Hollingworth, Barton, et al., 'Colposcopy of women with cervical HPV type 16 infection but normal cytology', Lancet, 1987, 2, 1148

125. Corbett, Margaret-Ann and Jerrilyn, H. Meyer, The Adolescent and Pregnancy, 1987, Boston, Oxford, Blackwell Scientific Publications, 1987

126. Dulfer, Susan, 'Hepatitis B and the newborn: a case for vaccination', Maternal and Child Health, 1987, 12, 206-212

127. Chrystie, Ian, Summer, Debsorah, et al., 'Screening of pregnant women for evidence of current hepatitis B infection: selective or universal?', Health Trends 1992, 24(1): 13-15

128. Minkoff, H., Nanda, D., et al., 'AIDS-related complex: follow-up of mothers, children and subsequently born siblings', Obstet Gynaecol, 1987, 69: 288-91

129. Lindsay, S., Alger, Farley, John J., et al., 'Interactions of human immunodeficiency virus infection and pregnancy', Obstet Gynaecol 1993, 82: 787-96

130. Hay, Pillip E., Lamont, Ronald F., et al., 'Abnormal bacterial colonisation of the genital tract and subsequent preterm delivery and late miscarriage', BMJ 1994, 308: 295-8

131. Hardy, P.H., et al., 'Prevalence of six sexually transmitted disease agents among pregnant inner-city adolescents and pregnancy outome', Lancet. 1984, 2, 333-337

132. Nevison, Jenny. Unpublished paper. Details available through Foresight.

133. Schneider, A., et al., 'Colposcopy is superior to cytology for the detection of early genital human papillomavirus infection', Obstet Gynaecol, 1988, 71, 236-241

134. Sutton, Graham E., Personal Communication

135. Grant, Ellen, Personal Communication, April 1988

CHAPTER 6

ALLERGIES AND INTESTINAL PARASITES

Food Allergy is any adverse reaction to food in which the immune system is demonstrably involved.

False Food Allergy denotes a special kind of non-immunological reaction, seen with particular foods in which the food triggers the mast cells directly. The immune system is not at fault and the body does not overproduce IgE but the end result is with symptoms the same as allergy.

Food Intolerance means any adverse reaction to food, other than false food allergy, in which the involvement of the immune system is unproven because skin-prick tests and other allergy tests are negative. This does not exclude the possibility of immune reactions being involved in some way, but they are unlikely to be the major factor producing the symptoms.

Food Sensitivity is employed as the umbrella term for all non-psychological adverse reactions to food.

Food Aversion means the dislike and avoidance of a particular food for purely psychological reasons.

(Jonathon Brostoff 1989)

The incidence of allergic illness in children has risen enormously in the last 50 years. We all need to examine the many possible contributing reasons for this, if we are going to be effective in reversing this trend. Do not believe officialdom's suave explanations, "We are now better at diagnosis". Rubbish. The problems were not there to *be* diagnosed until the environment became so problematic that a lot of illness was created.

In my school of over 200 girls in wartime Britain (1940s), I remember only one person who had any form of allergy; she reacted to strawberries by coming out in a rash. In my Nursery Nursing days, I knew well over 100 children in the Nursery, many from very less-than-ideal backgrounds, but the allergic illness etc was not around. In the 1950s I worked in a prep school, and over the years knew about 180 boys. Only one, who had been born very prematurely, had a very occasional attack of asthma. All the boys ate well, but there was no obesity, nor hyperactivity, dyslexia, eczema, epilepsy, asthma, and so on.

So what has changed *so much* that we now *accept* that one in 4 children has learning difficulties, one in 7 carries an inhaler in case of an asthma attack, and many carry a syringe in case of threatened anaphylaxis? We know that 2,000 die each year as the result of asthma. We are also told one in 5 has eczema.

Way back in the 1990s, when Gail and I first wrote the book, we said: "We are now seeing an escalation of diet related diseases. There have, for example, been increases in the incidence of allergic illness, anorexia/bulimia and mental disorders." Now the problem has escalated even more, rather than receded. WHY?

As we have mentioned earlier, maintaining optimum health in the modern environment is putting together the pieces of an enormous jigsaw, but a large area we need to study particularly is how to produce an allergy-free generation! So what are the possible causes of this huge influx of illness which has only arrived in the last 40-50 years? *There has to be an answer.*

The 21st Century environment is high in toxins. These are: (a) inhaled, such as traffic effluent, cigarette smoke, organophosphate pesticides (both from agriculture, and from indoor uses such as moth-proofing and fire-retardants, and flea drops for pets, house dust mites' faeces, pets' dandruff, good old pollen etc;) (b) ingested such as hazardous food additives, pesticides on food, fluoride from water, alcohol/caffeine, aluminium, artificial hormones, growth promoters, the Pill, fertility drugs and medicines, and; (c) worst of all inflicted, such as vaccines and immunisations, bacteria and viruses (albeit supposedly more or less dead) with the carriers such as the lymph from calves, chicks or aborted foetuses they are aluminium or peanut oil they are floated in or thimerosal they are preserved with. Also there are injections of antibiotics, and mercury amalgam fillings in our teeth.

All, or any, of these may result in an over-responsive immune system.

At the time we wrote our last book, it has to be admitted that we did not link allergic illness/behavioural problems very closely with vaccination. The hazards of the bug/animal lymph/mercury cocktail had not become so apparent. It should have been obvious that its effect on zinc levels in the children would be catastrophic. But the impact had not really been felt as it has today. However, after Neil Ward's work, in particular, the link was clearer – when zinc goes down, for whatever reason, behavioural problems arise.

Children's brains and central nervous systems cannot cope without zinc. In the mid 1950s the country started to recognise dyslexia, hyperactivity and cot death. This has lead on to lethal allergic reactions, such as death due to asthma or anaphylaxis, to fits and ADHD and into full blown autism.

Do we now have "subclinical autism"? Children so out of control that they are knifing each other, alcoholic in their teens, and so many on drugs, even from so called "middle-class" families? (MPs are "down grading" drugs they know their own children are dabbling with, to keep them out of prison?) Is the present deterioration of behaviour down to what is loosely termed "allergic reaction"?

It has been recently discovered that a group of Makaque monkeys were given the whole programme of immunisations/vaccinations normally given to American children, and they became hyperactive and violently aggressive. Not typical monkey-moods at all.

The MMR was started in this country in 1988. People aged one at that time, are now 21 years old. Is this the age group where the knife-carrying, binge drinking into oblivion, the drugging, the gangs – the children described by the press as "feral" – all started? I think so.

The Government should not be considering fining the parents – *it should be compensating the entire family.* Blaming "absent fathers" is invalid and a red-herring. During the Second World War, almost all fathers were "absent" but no children behaved in this way. I know. I was there.

The unborn child is deficient, allergic and full of toxic substances as never before. Remember the 287 toxic substances reported in the press as found in amniotic fluid a short while ago? However, we can work away to keep our Hero safe from all of the possible hazards and also warn our friends!

There are also the problems of nutrient deficiencies, and the hazards of early weaning.

Many problems can be due to deficiencies of needed nutrients, such as Vitamin A, B vitamins, zinc, chromium, manganese, selenium and others. These are required as co-factors for enzymes. As I have said before, the co-factor is rather like an outboard motor on a dinghy. It makes it "go"! Without it the enzyme, (which is needed to protect the skin, linings of the lungs, the brain etc, and / or to digest and process the food) can't function properly.

Why should babies and small children be short of these essential nutrients? Partly because, as explained earlier, so much modern food is lacking in nutrients and partly because of a lack of information at crucial times. This meant the parents were short of these nutrients. *Firstly*, during the pre-conception period when the egg was "ripening" or getting ready to be shed, and the sperm were being formed and matured ready to get down to business. *Secondly*, during the pregnancy, when mistakenly mothers can be persuaded to totally forgo Vitamin A, and when pregnancy sickness can be an additional problem. *Thirdly*, while breast-feeding, when possibly the mother is very busy and may be too tired to cook, especially if she is short of nutrients in the first place, which exacerbates the fatigue. This is a very usual scenario with the modern baby, where there has been no Foresight work-up.

Sometimes a hair analysis and a comprehensive nutrient programme –

vitamins given with Zinc, Manganese and Selenium, and with Omega-3 oils – can be all that's needed to improve the health of both mother and baby and nip things in the bud.

Our mothers' hard work on the Foresight programme can usually pre-empt these and a whole host of problems. (Especially exhaustion in the mother, and allergies leading to much vocal complaining by the baby!) This means breast-feeding will go ahead happily, and much cow's milk allergy can be avoided.

Because, if early weaning has been necessary, this again can be a factor that starts allergy off. If a baby is weaned on to cow's milk formula this will often be the start of eczema, wheezing, colic, vomiting and/or diarrhoea. I have known of cases where this has all continued throughout childhood, with no end of medical drugs being taken to try to prevent the allergic symptoms and the vomiting. Not until the child was 16 years old, in one case, and 23 years in another, was the cow's milk stopped and the vomiting brought to an end. (NB: Some children diagnosed as "anorexic" may simply be allergic.)

Breast-milk is the natural food for a human baby. Cow's milk, the food that is perfectly constituted for the calf, (although now available modified and adapted to some degree) is still less than perfect for the human baby. This could mean that each successive generation finds it less easy to handle. "Bottle feeding" has by now been around for about 100 years, so we need to give this some thought.

Then again, with cow's milk itself, there have been some very dramatic alterations in its production since the World War II days, when we used to milk by hand into a galvanised bucket, and pour it into the individual enamel Billy-cans at the farm gate. We never heard of "milk allergy" in the village in those days. (We would have known, as we heard of *everything* at the farm gate! What a different world!)

Now, cows are machine milked. There are long lengths of rubber tubing (does this give off PCBs?). This is cleaned with Milton, which is a bug-destroyer. The milk then goes into tankers, which are cleaned with another germicide. Do these bug-bugging chemicals end up in the milk? In what quantity? If so, what effect do they have on human intestinal flora? Are enzymes or vitamins destroyed in the milk? (We **do** know that when milk is pasteurised, this destroys lysine, which is an 'essential' amino acid and cannot be made in the human body).

We **do** know that these days cows are not fed exclusively on grass, hay and mangle-worzle tops, as was the case sixty years ago, but are fed on cow-cake which contains grains. Some seem to thrive on this, but some have projectile diarrhoea, (and you don't want to be standing behind them when this occurs). Is this a sort of bovine coeliac condition? Has this any link to the fact that some coeliacs cannot take cow's milk?

We also know that cows are now milked when they are pregnant. This means there are different hormones released into the cow's blood and hence into the milk. During the War in Wales, this never happened. The cow was "dried off" and rested for 8 weeks before being taken to the bull again. It was believed that the milk was "unwholesome" if the cow was pregnant. The cows lived long and productive lives.

I remember one cow who was still being milked aged 22 years. We held them all in great affection. Now they are slaughtered at 5 years. They are just regarded as milk machines.

In the War, all the young men had gone away "to fight" – it was just the old men and the children and the women. The old men I knew could not read or write, they used to bring things into the house for my mother to read to them. But they were so wise, so compassionate, so strong, so gentle, so humorous, so kind to everybody. So good to the animals. And nobody was allergic to our milk.

In addition to what may be in the milk, we have recently been told that babies' plastic feeding bottles give off bisphenal A, a by-product of the plastic, and furthermore some babies are allergic to latex, (the teats are made of latex). So one way and another, it is hard to win through with bottle-feeding. Especially if you are the baby.

For optimum breastfeeding, I would stick to the full Foresight programme, and the breastmilk is likely to be more plentiful, and breast-feeding will be less tiring. Breastfeeding mums put a lot of their precious nutrients into the milk. The 2am feed usually goes on for about 6 to 8 weeks, before their little tummies are big enough for them to tank up and sleep a bit longer. This is quite tiring enough, without running short of nutrients.

Lactation failure, as the medics call it, is just the whole scenario running mothers ragged because they have too little B complex vitamins, zinc etc to keep them on top of things. Remember, the rats on the "Rat Purina Chow" were fine. They had litters of 12-14 babies, and they all thrived. The poor deprived rat mothers with low zinc etc, were the ones that opted out of motherhood and made a run for it. They retreated into the far corner of the cage and curled up with their tail over their nose. Presumably this was post-partum depression, plus "lactation failure" or they would have gone back to the nest. Nutrients to keep things going do not get the positive press they deserve, but they can be the golden solution for avoiding much maternal misery, and allergy in the children.

To return to the matter in hand, other major allergens are the gluten grains, (wheat, oats, barley and rye). Many more people are being diagnosed with either wheat intolerance or coeliac condition. This, in one way, is rather good news for those of us, like myself, who are coeliac! Providing gluten-free food is now a growing industry, and all the supermarkets have a thriving gluten-free section and the products are delicious! Waiters are sympathetic when you dine out, and even some fish and chip shops provide gluten-free batter! Progress! (However, for all that, it would certainly be a benefit to most people *not* to have this particular bug-bear). Nevertheless, if you suffer "irritable bowel syndrome" and are constantly told it is "stress" or "nerves" (the fashionable non-diagnosis) I would try going onto a gluten and/or milk-free diet for a few months so see if things clear up. There is nothing to lose, the alternative food is good, and you will come to no harm. If this does not answer, then it could be candida or intestinal parasites, keep on searching until you have the answer!

On the whole, milk allergics are tired, heavy, lethargic, have black rings under their eyes, and are prone to fatigue, bloating and diarrhoea, also to catarrh and snoring. Gluten allergics also suffer diarrhoea, and tend to be a bit hyperactive, argumentative, (do you find other people very irritating?) thin, (sometimes to the point of anorexia) with itchy eyes, irritable skin, poor sleeping patterns, possibly up and down all night to urinate, sometimes "workaholics".

There is some evidence recently that there may be alcoholic parents or grandparents behind coeliac disease. I have known at least five or six families where this applies. However, whether the alcoholism caused such zinc-deficiency in the dependants that this precipitated the allergic condition; or whether the person with the alcoholism was an undiagnosed coeliac, it is hard to say. I would be very interested to have any feed-back on this one.

Be that as it may, if allergy seems likely to be in your family for whatever reason, I would avoid eating much gluten or dairy in the preconception period, and during pregnancy and breast feeding. I would also leave it until at least 9-10 months before introducing it, very cautiously, to the baby. "Rice Dream with Calcium" is a good milk substitute for the pregnant or breast feeding mother. Or goat's or sheep's milk, both of which appear to be less allergenic to most people.

Other very common intolerances are caffeine (in coffee, tea, chocolate and cola) and sugar. The unborn babies are better if these are kept right to a minimum. Caffeine has been closely linked to increased risk of miscarriage, and sugar could be the trigger to gestational diabetes.

One cheerful hot drink is Marmite, (but not too strong, so as not to give too much salt), also, if you are not gluten intolerant, Bovril, both beef and chicken flavoured. Or Tesco's "Beefy" which is gluten-free. The green/herb tea unit in the supermarket seems to grow every week, and it is possible to grow mint, sage, basil, dill, fennel etc in pots, and make your own herb teas. For cold drinks, juice, smoothies, goat's milk, Rice Dream, Provomil, Oatly, almond milk and others are out there if you are milk allergic. Horlicks, Ovaltine, etc are a bonus for those who are neither gluten nor milk allergic – lucky them!

We should note here that some herbs are contraindicated during pregnancy, for example:

138

- Saw Palmetto - when used orally, has hormonal activity
- Goldenseal - when used orally may cross the placenta
- Dong Quai - when used orally, due to uterine stimulant and relaxant effects
- Ephedra - when used orally
- Yohimbe - when used orally
- Pay D' Arco - when used orally in large doses; contraindicated
- Passion Flower - when used orally
- Black Cohosh - when used orally in pregnant women who are not at term
- Blue Cohosh - when used orally; uterine stimulant and can induce labor
- Roman Chamomile - when used orally in medicinal amounts
- Pennyroyal - when used orally or topically
- Red Raspberry Leaf - There is some controversy about whether this should be used throughout pregnancy or just in the second and third trimester, so many health care providers will remain cautious and only recommend using it after the first trimester. I think maybe just at the very end, as it contains copper, and this can bring on early contractions, which could mean premature birth.

It would be wise to check the internet yourself for current thinking on all herbal teas.

Some people are allergic to citrus fruits and this can give diarrhoea, sneezing, skin problems – from a vague "little itch" which seems to have no visible origin, to full-blown eczema, and even arthritis. Some people react to just orange, or just lemon, etc. Some are allergic to *any* citrus fruit.

Some react to the "belladonna" family which consists of tomatoes, potatoes, peppers and aubergines. Tomato ketchup may start a reaction, or baked beans in tomato sauce. Again, some people may just react to one of them, some to the whole family.

Another huge source of "allergies" using the word in its broadest sense, is the ubiquitous "food additives" which seem to lurk in everything you pick up unless it is straight raw food. To cut a long story short, the Hyperactive Children's Support Group (run by Sally Bunday, and until her death, her wonderful old mother, Vicky Colqhoun) and Foresight have been campaigning about the E numbers for over 30 years. At v-e-r-y long last, there seem to be faint stirrings at Government level (Spring 2008: six have just been banned!). In 1984 we brought out "FIND OUT", our little booklet pointing out the numbers and names and the reactions the additives produced.... asthma, eczema, diarrhoea, epilepsy, migraine, cancer.... and so on. In 2003 FIND OUT was updated. Alas, none of the dangerous ones had been banned. However more dubious ones had been introduced, and a few of the ones about which there had been "conflicting reports" had now been confirmed as health hazards. In 2004, FIND OUT was translated into French and Spanish by a very enterprising multilingual Frenchwoman, and 70,000 copies have been sold on the Continent, to date!

Many of these additives produce hyperactivity which can ruin the life of the child, and cause much disappointment and anxiety to the whole family.

Since the banning of the six "worst offenders", (Tartrazine, Sunset Yellow etc) in the recent Government initiative, those allowed in the UK include:

- 48 which cause hyperactivity

- 82 which cause digestive disorders

- 54 which cause asthma

- 53 which cause skin rashes, urticaria, eczema

- 36 which cause insomnia

- 52 known as suspect for cancer

- 30 known as suspect for liver and/or kidney disorders

The list does not end there, but if these noxious substances were removed from the tax-payers' food supply, might we all be having to pay a great deal less tax?! Should we not have some say in the matter? The current NHS drugs' bill is said to be £8billion (National Audit Office, 2006). Not to mention the bills regarding the remedial teaching, the detention centres and the prisons. Paid for by *us*, remember. Why should we be ignored for 30 years? Well, at the very least get a copy of FIND OUT and use it ostentatiously!

Some of these additives are made by the same companies who make a fortune out of Ritalin and many similar medications. It must be a very lucrative exercise. This can be confirmed by nosing about on the Web, by spiders with enough curiosity!

People on Government committees are usually asked to declare their interests in businesses whose interests might conflict with the matters under discussion, for example, the Pharmaceutical Industry. Most will declare a number of investments, but will continue to be allowed to take part in the proceedings that make the decisions on what is permitted.

In 1987, Dr Neil Ward, of the University of Surrey, linked hyperactivity both to nutritional deficiencies and food intolerances. Ward surveyed the parents of 486 hyperactive children and 172 non-hyperactive controls. The parents of the hyperactive children reported that more than 60% exhibited increased behaviour problems when exposed to synthetic colourings and flavourings, preservatives, cow's milk, and certain chemicals. In contrast only 12% of parents of the controls reported a connection between food additives or colourings and worsened behaviour.

Ward identified a subgroup of hyperactive children with known sensitivities to synthetic food colours, and exposed the children to these chemicals. Of 23 exposed to the food colouring tartrazine, 18 responded by becoming overactive, 16 became aggressive, 4 became violent, and several developed eczema, asthma, poor speech, or poor coordination. In contrast, only one control subject showed minor behavioural changes after drinking tartrazine. Two other colourings, "sunset yellow" and amaranth, also caused significant behavioural effects in hyperactive subjects.

For years, Vanessa had many health problems attributed to both Candida and Endometriosis. The Endometriosis needed laser treatment followed by medication. Systemic Candidiasis was diagnosed, which also included the ovaries and this was proving to be obstinate to modern medicine. No medical solutions helped. Lots of antifungal medicines were prescribed but to no effect. For 5 years Vanessa turned to all sorts of complementary remedies including exclusion diets. With this history, Vanessa and her husband believed that they would need extraordinary preconceptual help if they were to have a baby. They did not want to go down the usual route of IVF, IUI, and ICSI. They wanted a natural conception and birth.

Searching for preconceptual care on the internet, they found Foresight, and started on the programme. Vanessa's first hair analysis showed she had high copper levels but all other minerals were next to normal. Her husband's on the other hand, reflected much lower mineral levels especially that of zinc. Unfortunately their mineral levels improved sufficiently to allow an unplanned conception to take place, but not enough to carry the pregnancy to full term and a miscarriage occurred a few weeks later.

Taking care, and after two more cycles of hair analysis and supplements, Vanessa conceived naturally which lead to a healthy baby boy. "Smiley Miles is in very rude health, chatty, active, very charming, like Daddy." says Mummy.

Ward uncovered one possible explanation for the food colouring's effects. The hyperactive children in the study had statistically lower zinc and iron levels than controls. Therefore, when hyperactive children known to be sensitive to the colourings tartrazine and "sunset yellow" were exposed to these chemicals, their blood serum zinc levels dropped markedly. "Several studies," Ward notes, "have shown that zinc-deficient animals are more prone to stress and are aggressive when compared with normal cases." Previous research also has strongly linked tartrazine to hyperactivity. I am sure that if the additives can do this to a five year old child, it makes us all shudder to think what they may be doing to the unborn.

I would get "FIND OUT" from us, and take it shopping with you. I would flourish it in front of the supermarket staff, and suggest that they introduce it to their managers. The more interest we can get at commercial level, the more likely we are to get the additives controlled. A great many of those allowed in the UK are forbidden in other EU countries. Why can the British Government never take on board the *useful* things the EU does, and only concur when they make really silly regulations? It is a mystery – except that the establishment is doubtless more sympathetic to big business moguls, with whom they can identify and socialize, than they are with the little children suffering from unnecessary illnesses.

I am sure you have gathered by now, there are many modern causes of ill-health which are interacting. Two steps may need to be taken.

Firstly, deficiencies can make you more prone to developing allergies. Defences can be weakened if the immune system is undermined by zinc and other deficiencies. Enzyme systems may be compromised.

Secondly, and directly conversely, the allergies may lead to the deficiencies. Irritation from detergents can make the skin sore, and this will call for zinc, oils and vitamins A, E, and B. Inhaled pesticide, smoke and/or flame retardant can irritate the lungs and create a demand for selenium, and vitamins A and E to soothe them. Organophosphate pesticides will also create a shortage of manganese, as they inhibit the uptake from the gut. Calcium and zinc are used up in driving lead out of the body and so on. These minerals are needed to make enzymes work, but being so overworked, they are then not there to "do their stuff".

Do you or anyone in your family have asthma, eczema, migraine, epilepsy, insomnia, depression, ME, or irritable bowel syndrome? Try in the first instance using FIND OUT and WATCH IT as you shop. It could be as simple as a noxious additive! Be sure also to "eat organic" and you will shortly get rid of a lot of pesticides!

If, after a few weeks, you are not clear of the symptoms, try eliminating the food groups we have talked about. Milk, gluten-grains, belladonna family, caffeine, citrus. About two out of three times it is *that simple*. (Then if in doubt, check with a Nutritional Therapist that your replacement diet is adequate.)

Often people know their allergens, but have not really bothered to acknowledge them! I often hear: *"Really? Yes I'd always thought oranges gave me a headache, but I thought, no they can't because they are meant to be good for you, aren't they?"*

I think cheese makes my eczema worse, definitely. Would this mean that milk affects me, too?"

"I always feel a lot better when I'm slimming and I don't eat bread."

They just need a bit of encouragement to take it the rest of the way! This way, it doesn't cost anything to get it right! If this does not answer, get back to us for the address of a doctor who understands testing for allergies. For further information on detecting allergies, see the appendix.

To summarise:

Ever increasing pollution of the biosphere has brought with it an ever increasing cascade of adverse reactions (allergies, intolerances) especially in the very young and/or the zinc deficient and the undernourished, whose enzyme systems and immune systems lack the needed support. Babies and small children who fall into both categories are particularly unlucky. Breast feeding offers the best protection for babies. Making breast milk is much easier if you have everything you need in the way of vitamins and minerals, to do so and keep yourself going. This avoids post-partum depression (exhaustion and feelings of inadequacy) which appear if you have not enough nutrients for energy, plus enough to supply "happy-making" milk! When milk is satisfying and abundant, then weaning onto "solid" foods can be done very gradually at the baby's own pace, and this will help to avoid making a whole load of allergies in the next generation!

On the following few pages there is more help from Gail Bradley:

Allergy

In 1906 Clement von Pirquet, a pioneer in the study of immunisation, defined allergy as 'observable altered reactions to environmental substances'.[1] Unfortunately, as more research was done on allergy, allergists split into two camps: those who believed the answers lay in closely studying the immune system and those who were more concerned with considering a wider perspective.

Immunologists had discovered that when a foreign body enters the blood, the host body produces special protein substances called antibodies, which circulate in the blood and bind with the foreign body to neutralise it. An allergic person produces more antibodies than is necessary, and these irritate various tissues, causing a range of conditions, including asthma, eczema and hay fever. Immunologists can check for four types of reaction, using blood tests. If one or more is not positive, then allergy is said not to be present. Knowing this, it is surprising that the medics are so willing to inject tiny babies with half-dead bugs, aluminium animal serum, mercury and so on. This adds credence to Dr Viera Scheibner's idea that allergy follows on the backs of the vaccination programmes.

However, only some of the people have been found to have symptoms which fit this diagnosis. What about the many others who experience 'observable altered reactions'? Even now, some doctors will use the following logic: since it is not allergy and other tests reveal nothing, the symptoms must clearly not exist. They must therefore, be imaginary. The patient is neurotic, a hypochondriac, a nuisance!

Not all doctors trod the immunologists' path. There were still some who continued to follow through the ideas of Francis Hare, a British psychiatrist who wrote a book in 1905 call *The Food Factor in Disease*.[2] But they were few, and they failed to convince the medical establishment of their ideas, so that today most of them are found in private practice.

Some doctors decided on new approaches and theories on the basis of studies they read in medical journals. Yet we saw in Chapter 4 that even reputable journals sometimes publish very bad research. This has also happened in the field of allergy. Many research projects assume that if there is no quick reaction to a test, allergy is not present. In food allergy this may be quite erroneous. Sometimes a person may not react to a food for many hours, even days. In critical analysis of a study reported in the *Lancet*,[3] Jennifer Masefield has highlighted some of the study's weaknesses:[4]

Dried encapsulated foods used for double-blind provocation tests may not give accurate results, because the actual state of the food may be the important factor. Some people can tolerate cooked cabbage but react to raw cabbage. The preparation of food can alter the allergen.

Often certain food reactions are only caused by food combinations, so testing of foods in isolation will not produce a reaction.

If an allergic person has not been exposed to an allergen for a long period he/she may have lost sensitivity to it. However, reactions may return after repeated exposures. In a multiple allergic patient who is repeatedly changing his/her diet to maintain better health, the sensitivity swing will make food allergy tests give difference responses at different phases of the sensitivity level, for each excluded allergen or ingested allergen. This can give very confusing results, leading to an assumption of psychosomatic illness. If an allergen is excluded for only a few days, sensitivity is initially heightened and will show on testing.

At least two states in the USA have passed laws requiring examination for undiagnosed organic conditions either causing or exacerbating psychiatric symptoms.[5] Many studies are now linking allergy with conditions such as migraine, epilepsy and hyperactivity.[6,7] Self-help groups are increasing in number, and more doctors are becoming interested.

Relevance in preconception care

As Gail Bradley wrote for us many years ago -

Foresight clinicians pay special attention to allergy for a number of reasons:

If a prospective parent is suffering from a food allergy, health is impaired, and there may be malabsorption which will generally lead to nutritional deficiencies.

Allergies in either prospective parent seem to lead to allergies in their offspring, which can seriously impair development.

Clearing up allergies may mean that drugs do not need to be taken to alleviate the symptoms caused by the allergens.

Allergies may cause excessive mucus which can lead to blocked Fallopian tubes, which cause infertility.

If the mother's allergies are not resolved and she is breastfeeding, she may find her baby suffering, e.g. from colic, because of a masked cow's milk allergy in the mother.

144

So what do we do?

Investigating allergy

There are a number of ways of investigating allergy, with varying degrees of effectiveness. We list below some of the main ones.

1.   The clinical history is most important and, ideally, should include reference to the wider family, especially parents. Allergic symptoms may have been present early in life, may alter and not be diagnosed as the cause of later problems found in, for example, the hyperactive, learning disabled child, the delinquent teenager, and/or the aggressive husband who abuses his wife and children.

2.   Questionnaires can be useful in identifying symptoms. The list of symptoms is extensive. Indeed, it is this very wide range which makes some doctors so sceptical, and the investigation so difficult.

3.   Cytotoxic blood tests, performed by skilled technicians, are approximately 75 per cent reliable for food allergy only, so can give useful guidance.

4.   Skin prick tests and sublingual testing, which are sometimes used, are unreliable for food allergy.

5.   Miller Provocation testing, a form of skin test, is more reliable and can be used to establish dosage for treatment.

6.   Elimination and rotation diets are the most reliable methods. Many doctors specialising in ecological medicine (sometimes called clinical ecology or environmental medicine) put patients on a special diet to check for allergies. Depending on what the clinical history and questionnaires have revealed, it may mean cutting out all dairy produce and cereals, including refined carbohydrates. Basically this means eating meat and vegetables and the more unusual fruits such as pears. But not all meat and vegetables may be allowed. Often a patient will be asked to eat just lamb and game to start with if it is suspected that beef, pork and/or poultry may be allergens.

Easier than this is just eliminating one food group and noting the effects. This is often tried with the major allergens, which tend to be the foods/drinks most commonly ingested in a country, such as wheat, yeast, chocolate, tea, coffee, citrus fruit, eggs and milk in the UK.

If this does not improve the situation you may wish to try a rotation diet, designed to give each specific food only one day in, say, five or seven days. The following rotation diet has worked well with many Foresight patients. It should be used in conjunction with a food diary, in which every food and drink taken is noted, with the time. There should be a separate column for comments, which will include any effects felt, either physical or emotional, and the time they were experienced. This is very important, since we have said that the reaction may not be immediate. Remember, you are going to have to play detective, so you want all the evidence you can collect. (You may first wish to try the diary without the rotation diet.)

A word of warning: whatever type of diet you try, be it elimination or rotation, when you come off an allergen you are usually going to suffer some sort of withdrawal symptoms that will make you feel worse. It may be similar to having a hangover, as you are often addicted to the foods to which you are allergic. Persevere, because you are going to feel better than ever once you are over the effects! It is probably wise to start your new diet when the next few days are free of pressure.

If you do find allergies, seek advice from one of the self-help organisations, a nutritionist who understands allergy, or a doctor who is experienced in nutritional medicine, to ensure that your diet and nutritional supplements provide all the nutrients you require. This is especially important if you are planning a pregnancy or are pregnant.

Do not despair! You will find there are many alternatives to our usual foods, which will add interest and variety to your diet. If you look in your local healthfood or wholefood store you will see many different types of flour, grains and milks. You may also find that your allergies change over time, and if you sort out your nutritional imbalances, allergies sometimes become a thing of the past.

Always try to choose an organically grown food, free of additives.

The rotation diet is designed to give each specific food only one day in seven. The diet eliminates the most common allergens, cow's milk, grains and eggs. Also, all stimulants such as coffee, tea, chocolate and the sugars. No drink should be taken except the juice of the day and water. All foods must be boiled in plain water, steamed, plain grilled or cooked in the oven in a covered dish. No fats, oils, gravies are to be used. During the trial period NO FOOD OTHER THAN THOSE LISTED MAY BE TAKEN AT ALL.

A rotation diet for the detection of allergy

Monday	Tuesday	Wednesday	Thursday
Chicken	Pork	Lamb	Turkey
Banana	Sago	Brown rice	Maize
Pineapple	Dates	Rice flour	Cornflour
Beetroot	Apple	Orange	Leeks
Spinach	Pear	Grapefruit	Onions
Swiss chard	Lettuce	Satsuma	Asparagus
Pineapple juice	Endive	Mandarin	Chives
	Chicory	Lime	Grapes
	Artichoke	Carrot	Sultanas
	Sunflower seeds	Celery	Grapejuice
	Apple juice	Parsnip	
		Parsley	
		Orange or grapefruit juice	

Friday	Saturday	Sunday
Fish	Rabbit	Beef
Millet	Lentils	Potato
Millet flakes	Green beans	Potato flour
Cabbage	Peas	Tomato
Savoy cabbage	Blackeyed peas	Aubergine
Brussel sprouts	Broad beans	Cucumber
Brocoli	Mung bean shoots	Marrow
Cauliflour	Plums	Melon
Kohl rabi	Peaches	Tomato juice
Swedes	Apricot	
Avacado	Cheery	
Figs	Prines	
Water	Prune juice	

During the first week of the diet adverse reactions may take place due to the withdrawal of cow's milk, etc, if these are allergic substances. For a few days the reactions may be quite strong, akin to alcohol withdrawal in the first few days of abstinence.

The participant may be more hungry than usual, however, and it is important to have enough food available.

The diet will have ensured a fast of six days from any offending food so the reaction to the allergen will probably be fairly immediate and may take the form of a running or stuffed-up nose, headache, stomach pain, feeling of bloatedness, extreme lethargy, irritability, etc. The day this occurs can be marked on the diet sheet. It is then possible to test the foods eaten on this day one at a time.

Having thus worked out a basic diet of 'safe' foods, it will then be possible to test common allergens, such as cow's milk, eggs, the gluten grains – wheat, oats, barley, rye – and other fruits etc. After three weeks' abstinence the reaction may be strong, and at first only a small quantity of the substance should be given. If the reaction is very severe, a teaspoonful of bicarbonate of soda in water will help alleviate the symptoms. After an adverse reaction a return to known safe foods for a few days will be necessary before testing for another possible allergen. After a few weeks it should be possible to identify all food allergies in this way.

The treatment of food allergies will depend on a number of factors, including how extensive the allergies are. You may be able to get by with simple elimination, though this is no cure. There are various desensitising methods, ranging from drops to injections. The most practical and successful is probably enzyme potentiated desensitisation, though, as with all methods it does not work for everyone.[8] Any doctor who is practising as a clinical ecologist, or using a nutritional approach in his work, will be able to diagnose and treat you. You will not be able to get desensitisation done except by a doctor. (If you ring Foresight HQ, we may be able to advise on someone not too far from you.)

Allergies to chemicals, such as food additives, pesticides and chemicals used in the workplace and home, may also be present. These are often difficult to diagnose and eliminate.[9] (See Chapter 10.)

Coeliac condition

There is a condition in which the sufferer cannot metabolise gluten, a protein found in wheat, barley, oats and rye. It can cause severe physical and mental symptoms if it is not diagnosed, mainly because of the severe deficiencies arising from the malabsorption. condition has been found to exacerbate infertility problems, especially in zinc deficient women. Treatment is by avoidance of gluten-containing grains.

Malabsorption

Malabsorption is not a disease or illness in itself, but the result of other conditions such as allergies, infections, disease, candidiasis, nutritional deficiencies and toxic metal excesses, irritable bowel syndrome, Crohn's disease and colitis. Clearly, if you are not absorbing nutrients properly, you are likely to have nutritional deficiencies which can affect pregnancy outcome. Your hair analysis and other tests may reveal a malabsorption pattern. It is important that you seek medical help, or go to a qualified nutritional therapist.

References:

1.   Von Pirquet, Clement, 1906
2.   Hare, Francis, *The Food Factor in Disease*, 1905
3.   'Food Allergy: How Much in the Mind', *Lancet*, 1983, 1, 1259-1261
4.   Masefield, Jennifer, 'Psychiatric Illness caused or exacerbated by Food Allergies', 1988 (unpublished paper)
5.   Anon., Oregon Enacts America's First Law to Diagnose Underlying Organic Causes of Mental Illness, *Int J Biosocial Res*, 1984, 6(1), 13
6.   Grant, E.C.G., 'Food Allergies and Migraine', *Lancet,* 1979, 1, 966-968
7.   Egger, J., et al., 'Controlled Trial of Oliantigenic Treatment in the Hyperkinetic Syndrome', *Lancet*, 1985, 1, 540-545
8.   Eagle, Robert, *Eating and Allergy,* Wellingborough, Thorsons, 1986. This book gives an excellent survey of food allergy, including useful sections on diagnosis and desensitisation.
9.   Mansfield, Peter, Munro, Jean, *Chemical Children*, London, Century, 1987. This book gives an overview of how harmful pollutants, including chemicals, can affect children

PARASITES

Irritable bowel syndrome is present in about 20% of people (both male and female) who come to Foresight. The term encompasses abdominal pain, inflammation of the gut-wall, bloating, flatulence, diarrhoea and malabsorption of nutrients.

In many cases, if allergies or coeliac condition have been eliminated as possible causes, there can be candida or intestinal and other parasites. Stomach parasites include helicobacter, often responsible for stomach ulcers. Parasites from the drinking water include cryptosporidium, about which we are usually warned when there is an outbreak. Intestinal ones we have had detected in Foresight people are blastocystic hominis, giardia lamblia, the homely threadworms and some amoebic-type buglets.

All or any of these need to be coped with ahead of the pregnancy, as the diarrhoea and inflammation can cause gross discomfort, and will result in malabsorption of essential nutrients. This could, at best, severely compromise the health of the future baby, and at worst it could precipitate a miscarriage

Your Foresight Practitioner can arrange for a stool test. This will give you the diagnosis. You can then obtain help from a trained herbalist, a homeopath (we can suggest one if you ring us), or from Ainsworths Homeopathic Chemists.

DIY preparations that have been found to be helpful are Paraclear, a herbal preparation, and Citricidal, a preparation made from grapefruit seeds. One of our most experienced doctors suggests 600mg of garlic every day for three months. After any treatment, or self treatment, test again to make sure it has been successful.

Be careful to avoid starting a pregnancy until you are certain it has completely cleared up. It can take three to six weeks, as the parasites lay eggs which later hatch out and restart the colony! The treatment is therefore a series of carefully timed doses, and needs to be done accurately.

To Summarise

If allergy doesn't turn out to be the whole answer, seek out a nutritional therapist, get her to arrange a stool test and this will tell you if you have candida albicans (a mouldy infestation of the gut) or some other type of parasite. She, or others, can then advise you further on combating these with diet and herbal remedies.

Within a few months there should be a Brand New You, feeling much brighter and stronger – and able to stay that way for the rest of your life. Commensurately, your ova, or sperm, as the case may be, will also be brighter, stronger, better nourished, and more purposeful!

News on a recent experimental approach:

Read on for a very new approach to parasites from our colleague, Lynn Alford-Burow. This has not yet been tried and tested, as have other Foresight approaches. However, we have decided to include it in the book as it is a painless procedure and can do no harm. We will be interested, as always, to

receive feedback, good or bad, by those who decide to take the plunge and put this to the test.

Parasites and infertility – Hair follicle DNA testing and treatments with consideration to health during pregnancy. by Lynn Alford-Burow Dip ION, MBANT

Foresight hair mineral tests often show very low levels of nutrient minerals despite a 'reasonable' diet. They may have many symptoms such as headaches, bloating, low energy, mood changes, depression, irritability, coughs, food allergies, anaemia, leaky gut, diarrhoea, constipation, itchy bottom, dark circles around the eyes, skin rashes, aches and pains, exhaustion, disturbed sleep and insomnia. Many are frequent travellers or have made a major trip abroad during a gap year. All of these factors have an association with parasitic infections, there could of course be other causes needing investigation.

Why are parasites so common?

Approximately 1 in 6 people in the UK, if tested, are shown to have one or more parasites. It is not necessary to travel to far-flung countries to pick up parasites or even to have a stressed lifestyle. Parasites aren't always the big visible tropical types, many common varieties are microscopic single cells.

Contaminated drinking water even in the UK, is a common source, with Cryptosporidium parvum and hominis constantly monitored but outbreaks frequently found[1]. Both plant and animal foods carry parasites, and cleaning and cooking methods together with a trend for pre-packaged salads and ready meals, often do not destroy them before ingestion. Other culprits can be overcrowding in cities, pets, farms, poor food handling, restaurant meals, exotic foods, poor hygiene, antibiotics, sexual practices, rodents and houseflies.

Contaminated water and food can spread the problem to our pets and livestock. Animals become infected by parasites on their fur, by exposure to infected animal wastes. Forgetting to wash your hands after handling or cleaning up after your animal could transmit a parasite to you. Pets are a wonderful part of our lives, yet pets, like humans, are often victims of serious infections that can unintentionally be passed on to their owners. Animals are major carriers of parasites, and some physicians, let alone the general public, are unaware of this fact. Experts have projected that of the 110 million pet dogs and cats in this country, over half may be infected with at least one or more different kinds of parasites so the potential for transmission of parasitic infection from animals to humans is extremely high. We regularly worm our pets but never think to treat ourselves, although for thousands of years, indigenous peoples have understood the anti-parasitic properties of locally available plants and use them regularly.

Bear in mind that man has lived in close proximity with domestic and farmed animals for thousands of years and probably been a host to many organisms without compromising his health and fertility. Modern lifestyle has changed all that. High sugar consumption and processed diets, additives, drugs - street and prescription-chemicals, radiation and heavy metal toxins, candida and stress make an environment that encourage parasites to take hold and thrive. Mercury slowly leaking from dental amalgam (silver-coloured) fillings can be a cause of low stomach acid, poorly digested food and a toxic home in the gut for parasites to settle.

If a couple are infertile, there is a good chance that one and probably both of them are infected with some sort of pathogen. In my experience more than half of subfertile women are testing positive for a pathogen robbing them of nutrients.

What do parasites do to us?

When given an environment they can thrive in, parasites rob the host of essential nutrients lowering resistance to disease and obstructing fertility. Sometimes more than one variety of pathogen is present adding to the burden on the host.

Most parasites exist in three stages – eggs, hatchlings and adults. Adults in the gut lay eggs from which hatchlings emerge as small as white blood cells and travel through the gut wall lodging anywhere in the body including the brain, liver, kidney, muscles, organs, not only the digestive tract. Parasites do not have a digestive system of their own and rely on our digested food to thrive. Adult parasites produce waste in the gut including a toxic chemical called phenol. Phenol breaks down the gut lining creating gaps in the mucous membrane allowing rubbish to enter the bloodstream creating inflammatory conditions both within the gut – Dysbiosis, colitis and so on – and in distant regions of the body – arthritis and so on. Hatchlings produce ammonia, a brain irritant responsible for mood changes, irritability, disturbed sleep and brain fog.

Parasites live a parallel life inside our bodies, feeding off either our own energy, our own cells or the food we eat depleting our immunity and leaving us open to other viral, bacterial or chemical assault, and even feeding off the health supplements we use.

Types of parasite

From single cell microscopic organisms (protozoa) such as trichomonas vaginalis; roundworms, pinworms, and hookworms (nematoda) to multi-cellular 6 metre tapeworms (cestoda); and flukes (trematoda), the number of varieties are in the hundreds. Experts claim that 'some type of worm is already in the intestines of over 75 percent of the world's population', but most unwanted infestations go unnoticed by the host and may even stay for decades.

The **protozoa** are single cells with two or three phases - cysts, trophozoites, flagellates. They inhabit fresh water, soil, power plant discharges, heated swimming pools, contaminated food, sewerage and can be found in the brain, intestines, skin, eye, lung, vagina, prostate or systemically. Entry is by the skin, mouth, genitalia, nose and lungs. Examples – dientamoeba fragilis, giardia lamblia, trichomonas vaginalis, toxoplasma gondii, pneumosystis carinii, entamoeba histolytica, leishmania, plasmodium malariae.

Toxoplasmosis is of particular note as if infected during a pregnancy, possibly from faeces in cat litter, contaminated soil or water, eating undercooked meat or eating unwashed produce from infected soil, the mother can pass the infection to her child in the womb. The risks to the child can be hydrocephalus, eye problems or brain damage. Protozoa can be a cause of pneumonia which can induce premature births.

Nematodes are multicellular parasites in worm and egg form using an intermediate host such as arthropods, mosquitos, fish, beetles, flies and rodents before gaining entry by skin or mouth into the definitive host – humans, pigs, rodents, cats and dogs. They can be found in intestines, liver, lung, brain, eye, lymph system, body cavities or under the skin. Examples – roundworm, pinworm, hookworm, threadworm, trichinella spiralis and filiaris.

Hookworms have been the cause of some stillbirths. Threadworms are very common in young children with 40% becoming infected, teachers are susceptible to catching them. Fortunately they aren't transferred from cats and dogs but any human can pick them up even through dusty air. Typical symptoms are itchy bottom and disturbed sleep, it may be possible to see them by sticking sellotape to the child's bottom before he gets out of bed.

Cestoda are the tapeworms from cysts or eggs found in beef, pork, fish and also dog and cat fleas. Proglottids, one segment of tapeworm, contain both male and female reproductive organs. Entry is by mouth and they are found in the small intestine.

The **trematodes** such as liver fluke, intestinal fluke, lung fluke and bilharzia are leaf-shaped flatworms requiring two intermediate hosts through fish, molluscs, larvae, vegetation, crab, crayfish. Flukes start as larvae from infected snails which can penetrate human skin or are ingested by mouth from cysts. In man they can be found in intestines, bladder, bile ducts and lungs.

Diagnostic methods

Two symptoms in particular are a red flag to consider testing for parasites – itchy bottom and teeth grinding at night. There are many good laboratories offering stool tests but these can be expensive and can give false negatives because they only examine the stool. Since pathogens can exist anywhere in the body and even when in the gut remain buried in the gut lining, many would never be found by stool testing. Purged stool tests can be more successful but would be dangerous in pregnancy. Blood antibody tests look for specific types such as toxoplasma gondii, entamoeba histolytica and flukes but may miss giardia or amoeba for example. Misdiagnosis of symptoms can create chronic ill-health and lead to infertility or other disease states.

The hair DNA test performed by Dr Sam Shohet of Harley Street London (around £75 from Integral Health www.integralhealth.org 020 7467 8322) using a Cellular Frequency Scanner can find parasitic infection when it is of primary concern, from just a few hairs. The test is quick, convenient and has proved to be very accurate. As long as one hair has a good root ball on the end, the damage to DNA can be identified. The test shows parasites if present but only if they are the priority to treat first. The problem may not be parasites however as candida has similar symptoms and the convenience of the test is that it will always show what is causing the most damage so there is no need to do a separate test to look for candida or something else. It is possible to have candida and parasites at the same time, but the major of these would be the first priority.

How the hair follicle DNA test is said to work

An accurate energy assessment is made from the cells contained within the root of your hair. Sometimes viral, bacterial, chemical, radiation or heavy metal toxicity will show instead of parasites, if these are the priority for treatment, saving the need for other tests. Results will also show which foods are causing intolerances and which foods are safe to eat. Remember this test should be done in addition to the Foresight hair mineral test, and is not intended to replace that information.

The protocol for treating parasites is accurately calculated in the results of the hair DNA test, generally over a timespan of six weeks but all results are individual. It is clear to the patient what they have to do, however the treatment may not be practical for all patients as dietary advice must be very strictly followed. Supplements can be expensive at around £200 for a six week treatment. The products specified from the test results are made up for the person, so for example, person A with a diagnosis of parasites will get a completely different food list of what to eat and not to eat and a different supplements list from person B with a diagnosis of parasites. The hair DNA test prescription can avoid mistakes in dosages and timing as the quantities are worked out specifically for you.

The herbal treatment prescribed must not be used alongside any other supplement, even the Foresight ones, during eradication of parasites. Anyone using medication will need advice from the laboratory and their doctor. If instructions are followed accurately, I find excellent results with chronic symptoms vanishing.

Afterwards a hair DNA retest is advised to check for underlying problems, just in case. Then continue with Foresight method and supplements to prepare your body for excellent reproductive health.

When to treat

A severe infestation of parasites is likely to cause complications during pregnancy, childbirth and/or breastfeeding to both mother and child. Pre-conception is the ideal time to test, treat and eradicate parasites and regain health and immunity. It has always been common practice to give anti-parasitics to livestock, pregnant bitches and subsequent pups, but any herb or commercial product could not be tested or guaranteed safe during a human pregnancy and should not be used. Prescription anti-parasitic drugs are used with caution because of the risk of side effects. This window of time before trying for pregnancy is perfect to deal safely with these invaders. The would-be mother must understand that it is imperative not to accidentally become pregnant.

Other ways to treat parasites

Traditional methods include colonic cleanses and enemas to old-fashioned purging and sitting in a bowl of warm milk. Parasites thrive on all milk products so they must be removed from the diet during any treatment. Sugars, starchy foods, refined foods, grains, and high glycemic load foods all create a parasite canteen. Where parasites are seen, the mainstream treatment of the highly toxic metronidazole[2] antibiotic can lead to reinfestation through dormant eggs hatching out later. Metronidazole has been found to double chances of premature birth[3]. There are other side effects so it is always worth considering alternative safe options.

Parasites need to be starved and killed off, ideally supervised by a herbalist or nutritional therapist using natural safe methods. Powerful **anti-parasitic herbs** such as wormwood, dogwood, black walnut, horsetail, goldenseal, sage, cloves, thyme, tansy, barberry, olive leaf, castor oil and grapefruit seed extract require careful calculation for the individual as there can be side effects. You can purchase off-the-shelf internal cleansing kits readily from the internet or health stores.

Very high doses of **sodium ascorbate**, a type of vitamin C, are used to purge parasites before amalgam removal by some dental experts. Dr. Hulda Clark, PhD, ND, invented a battery operated **electronic zapper** apparently capable of killing parasites in five minutes.

Bentonite clay, montmorillonite from volcanic ash, is a traditional treatment for drawing toxins out, parasites can't reproduce in the presence of clay. There are many claims for its use from eliminating allergies, adsorbing microwave radiation, curing poisonous bites to repairing cataract damage, but large quantities need to be swallowed in water or juice and it can't be taken alongside medication. It works best with psyllium husk powder for additional fibre.

Because parasites, along with other pathogens are anaerobic – unable to live in an oxygen environment, **oxygen therapy** supplements such as magnesium peroxide that introduce oxygen into cells throughout the body are able to gradually clean up the bowel. Follow up with friendly bacteria like bio-acidophilus.

Around the world many **foods** are used as anti-parasitics and to prevent reinfestation – garlic, coconut, pumpkin seeds, watermelon seeds, papaya seeds, pomegranate seeds, linseeds, beetroot, raw carrots, even raw brown rice is chewed.

Since parasites are highly contagious, other members of the family will need testing with treatment and lifestyle changes to prevent reinfestation.

So what do we do?

Outcomes

The good news is that parasites should not affect a healthy body. Good health includes strong protective gateways to the body – saliva, stomach acid, digestive enzymes, gut sIGA, skin, lungs and blood. Diagnose parasitic presence if need be, improve the diet by removing the foods parasites love. Eat healthy organic foods, wash vegetables in vinegar, cook meats and fish thoroughly, be scrupulous with washing hands and use lemon juice and vinegar on kitchen and bathroom surfaces. Remove chemicals in the home and garden, avoid chemicals in cosmetics and personal products, avoid all possible radiation, check dentistry amalgams are not leaking with a holistic mercury-free dentist.

Do use herbal remedies regularly, get plenty of exercise, remove any environmental toxins to starve them out and kill them off and improve your overall health to boost fertility.

©Lynn Alford-Burow Dip ION, MBANT 2008. Cinnamon Health, Cinnamon House, 49 Worton Gardens, Isleworth TW7 4BD. 020 8568 4797 Mob: 07949 085688 lynn@cinnamonhealth.co.uk

NB: It is important not to confuse hair follicle DNA testing with the hair mineral analysis, which is a completely different analysis.

Most of the Foresight practitioners can also offer help in the old fashioned way of obtaining a stool test and approaching the cure with the usual preparations of herbs, garlic, and substances such as Citricidal. For the address of Foresight nutrition therapists, apply to Foresight HQ.

References:

1. "Guidance on Assessing Risk from Cryptosporidium Oocysts in Treated Water Supplies" – Drinking Water Inspectorate www.dwi.gov.uk

2. www.physchem.ox.ac.uk Safety data - Metronidazole - Harmful if swallowed(!), may act as a carcinogen.

3.   A Shennan et al, A randomised controlled trial of metronidazole for the prevention of preterm birth in women positive for cervicovaginal foetal fibronectin: the PREMET Study: British Journal of Obstetrics and Gynaecology January 2006 113 (1), 65–74

CHAPTER 7

HAIR MINERAL ANALYSIS

"Hair analysis provides an accurate assessment of the concentration of minerals in the body — those that are toxic in any amount, those that are essential, and those that are necessary in small amounts, or toxic in larger amounts. This non-invasive technique readily determines exposure to toxic substances such as mercury, lead and cadmium. The correlation between mineral concentrations in the internal organs of the body and levels in the hair is much more reliable than the correlation between intracellular mineral concentration and the levels found in serum and urine specimens. Normal trace element concentrations, as detected in the serum or the urine, may be quite variable; however, hair analysis gives accurate readings of the intracellular concentrations of these substances."

From the book "Prescription for Nutritional Healing", by James Balch, MD (Member of the American Medical Association and Fellow of the American College of Surgeons)

Hair mineral analysis is arguably the most important part of the Foresight programme. It is one of the main reasons why I founded Foresight.

In the 1970s, the outstanding paediatrician Dr Beth Lodge-Rees was on one of her memorable visits. My friend Gilly Gibbons and I had taken her to see Winchester Cathedral. On our way home we were discussing the formidable strength and determination of the men who carried and placed all the enormous stones that made it. All done with sheer beef and willpower as there was not the machinery to help them, other than ropes and pulleys,...well, we need Rupert Hart-Davies to show us, but we reckoned the strength they needed was phenomenal..... We were surmising about their diet...

"We are linking the quality of muscle meat now to the trace mineral content of the diet" said Beth, "They are taking samples of hair from the animals in the slaughterhouses. They are finding the levels of the essential elements in the hair relate to the quality of the meat. It seems to me that this could be a good way of looking inside people without the complication of cutting them open. I am thinking about this. I am wondering if there is some way I could do this for my kids".

"YES!" we all said together. "There will be!" We were so excited we nearly drove off the road!

Beth went back to the States, and within the year she and Dr Gary Gordon had started "Mineralab", the first of the hair analysis laboratories. They were both in agreement that hair was the ideal sample material. Hair takes in the nutrients that are present in the blood at a steady pace. Those that enter the hair follicle grow out in the hair, where they are bound into the structure. Thus a one-inch sample of hair will give a good rough history of what has been going on in the body for approximately the previous 7-8 weeks. In most cases this is the most useful record to be able to examine. With the body fluids such as blood, saliva and urine, they are all in a constant state of flux. The blood is transporting minerals to an organ, or to storage in fat or bone. Thus a sample will show what was in the last meal. Urine will show what is being thrown out of the body. Saliva is somewhat akin to blood. About a quarter of all American doctors, I have been told, now use hair analysis routinely.

Once we heard that the American lab had opened, we sent hair from hyperactive and allergic children and found, when we gave them the minerals they needed, we could help them a great deal.

A number of pioneering doctors, who were into diet, allergies and natural therapies generally, became interested, and a few years later two of them, Dr Stephen Davies and Dr Alan Stewart, set up "Biolab" with Dr John McLaren Howard in London. Some years after this, Foresight contributed to obtaining an analytical instrument and started working with it at the University of Surrey with Dr (now Professor) Neil Ward. We then did the Study, which is published on our website and also found at Appendix 6. (Also see Appendix 4)

As you will see, in this particular Study we had 367 couples who participated, and we achieved 327 babies, (89% success rate), all in good health, with no miscarriages or other mishaps along the way. As you will also see, the data gave us a whole lot of other information regarding the parents' mineral status when they came to us, and how this related to in their previous medical and reproductive history.

We have used this information ever since, and built upon it. It was a great shame it could not be published in the Medical Journals, but they rejected it on the grounds that there was no control population.

A "control population" would have had to be duped with fake pills called "placebos", and this would have meant they would have been denied the supplements they needed. This would have put their babies at risk. The researchers would then have counted the index population's babies, and the placebo babies (or lack of babies, or miscarriages or whatever disaster occurred). This would have given them a "scientific study", and a lot of very sad parents and possibly dead or damaged babies. This is something Foresight will never do.

Unfortunately, current medical training imposes these Draconian strictures, and a world of useful knowledge and healing gets blocked from the medics, which would otherwise be very helpful to them, - and to us all. This serves the interests of the pharmaceutical industry, who fund the medical schools, as the more people are "below par", who have deficiencies, toxic metals or undiagnosed allergic illnesses, etc, the more drugs get taken and the more money they make.

Back to the Matter in Hand:

Background information

These are the things it is useful to know if you are doing analysis. Some minerals will "over-ride" or drive down others in the body if they become too dominant. Others act synergistically and help the absorption/use of another.

Some of them use the same "binding sites" in the intestines. I feel this may act as a type of rough homeostatic mechanism for keeping them in balance? i.e. if too much of something has been taken in, maybe they shut down for that mineral and open up for another? (Empirical observation seems to point to this.)

However, if, due to environmental factors, the body gets swamped with a rogue element (such as lead, mercury or cadmium), then much needed elements can be denied absorption and then the body is in trouble. Needless to say, most of the sources of unfortunate environmental factors are man-made, albeit often inadvertently, but fortunately almost all of the excess levels are reversible, although it takes a little time.

For example, the most obvious of these is lead. When we were first doing hair analysis (in the late 1970s) it was quite usual to see 5-7ppm in the hair, even of children. Due to the tireless campaigning of Professor Derek Bryce-Smith for lead-free petrol, (which was successful after 29 years!) the average lead level in hair has fallen to approximately 2-3 ppm, and now only approximately 17% of people who come to us have a level that is of concern, even for reproduction.

Lead damage to the foetus can include malformations such as spina bifida and mental retardation, hyperactivity, ADHD and autism.[1,2,3,4,5,6,7,8,9,10,11,12,13,14]

So now I think we should look at some charts. In an ideal situation the needed trace minerals should be at or above the recommended values, and the toxic ones below the threshold values, as shown on the chart. We get people's levels as near to this ideal as we can.

Selenium protects the lungs, so smoking always reduces levels of selenium.[15,16] Selenium is also necessary for sperm production, and is a mineral that guards against cancer and chromosome damage.[17,18,19,20] This could be one of the reasons – perhaps the main reason – why children of fathers who smoke are more prone to cancer.[21] Also why parents who smoke are more likely to have Down's syndrome children.[22,7,8]

These were just the few of the hair analyses that demonstrate the problems confronting the modern sperm and ova! They may be short of the minerals that they require to form themselves properly, and they may be clobbered by toxic metals that damage or totally destroy them.[23,24,25]

The human body is quite volatile, and the levels of trace minerals are in a constant state of flux. Each meal, and with some minerals each breath, brings a fresh influx, and minerals are lost in outward breath, perspiration, urination and bowel movements.

Minerals are carried round the body by the blood and lymph, and all the body fluids vary round the day, which is why hair is the most stable sample for information on mineral status.[26,27,28]

The hair gathers available minerals from the blood, which is transporting minerals around the body; excesses and paucities are therefore quite well reflected in the hair. A sample about an inch long reflects the mineral history of the previous 6-8 weeks, which makes it quite a stable reading, as it is not fluctuating and altering every few hours, as with blood, sweat, urine, saliva etc.[9,29,30,31,32,33,34,35,36,37]

However, we all need to be aware of some aspects of hair analysis:

If the supplements significantly enhance the health of the person taking them, this may increase the rate of growth of the hair.[8] Faster growing hair may contain somewhat lower levels of some of the minerals we are looking at. This is, in fact, likely to be a more valid reading of the body status, than the more optimistic levels shown in the reduced growth of the first sample! Further supplementation can achieve good levels even in the normally growing hair. These are then the optimum levels for healthy pregnancy.

If there has been a high level of a toxic metal – lead, cadmium, mercury or aluminium – or an over-high level of the essential mineral copper – you will be given 2-6 "Vitamin C with Garlic" to take it down. This can tend to take other minerals down also. This will be partly due to enhanced bowel actions, which may hasten the transit time of the food. It will also owe something to the ability of the body to coat (chelate) the toxic substances with a non-toxic substance such as zinc or selenium to carry them safely through the liver and kidneys and out of the body. This will mean that, even though we have given some zinc and selenium, these may also have gone down along with the toxins. As the programme continues, they will return to normal.

It is the policy of the body to store any toxic metal to which it is exposed in large quantities, until such time as circumstances are more favourable to cope with the overload. When B complex vitamins and minerals such as zinc, selenium, manganese, calcium etc, enter the body, sometimes these tissues start to evacuate large stores of lead, cadmium, mercury etc into the blood. This will take some months, rather than weeks, to clear, so the second hair chart may show some dumping of toxins. The more that is released, the better, as the quicker we can get it to leave the body, the better.

However, be very careful not to become pregnant until this has been fully achieved. All of the toxic metals, if present in large amounts, can cause health problems with the baby. Do not be tempted to try to leave the metals "in storage" however, as in response to pregnancy hormones they would be released into the body, and could not be kept away from the developing embryo.

Sadly, we often see high levels of toxic metal in people who have come to us after the birth of a malformed baby. If only this work was done with one and all routinely, prior to every pregnancy, so much suffering could be avoided.

The body has ways of balancing the levels of the minerals so that no single one will predominate in the body. Zinc, selenium and manganese all share binding sites in the intestine. You therefore need to take a little of one when you take any other of these, (ie. if you are taking zinc, you need to balance it with a little selenium, even if it does not show a low level in this reading, or the selenium will go down). Magnesium will enhance the utilisation of calcium, so giving either, without enough of the other, can result in the levels of the neglected element going down. It is not an easy matter to get the balance exactly right, and, with zinc in particular, one can sometimes struggle for several programmes. A lot may depend on the levels of lead, copper etc in the drinking water and even the house dust, and nutrients in the diet. *Levels are often slow to rise in people who do not give up alcohol.* If we suggest that water and/or dust are tested it is worth doing this at an early stage.

As you may have gathered, it is not always easy to achieve perfection in a short space of time. This is why it is unwise to take a hair analysis to an inexperienced person for interpretation. One can understand why they may be non-plused or dismissive!

Nevertheless, the babies who are ultimately born free from a toxic load of dangerous substances, and able to use any vitamin or mineral they require for their mental and physical integrity, are, unsurprisingly, perfectly formed and mentally and emotionally exceedingly bright.

I have devoted my life to making it possible for you to achieve this, because I know it is worth it. Be patient. We will get there.

People have to use up their precious stores of essential minerals to chelate the toxins. As a toxin is released from storage, it will be wrapped around with zinc or similar to go safely through the liver or kidney. This stops the toxic metal from causing damage as it makes its way out of the body. However, it may also deplete an already parlous zinc level! So as you detoxify, you also have to back up with the essential minerals to hang on to them, as best you can!

Yet another problem is that organophosphate pesticides inhibit the uptake of manganese. Therefore low manganese can indicate there is some organophosphate contamination. Organophosphates are a nerve poison, so it is as well to clear them from the body before pregnancy. (Or at any time, as they can cause epilepsy and have been linked to illnesses such as MS, ME, Parkinson's and Alzheimer's disease.) We give nicotinamide as it is the only substance known to take organophosphates out through the liver, according to M K Johnson of the Medical Research Council, who has made a study of this.

It is best to be doing all the other components of the full Foresight programme as you are taking the supplements. If you improve the diet this backs up the supplements and makes success likely to happen more quickly. This helps us all, as you are all understandably impatient for Our Hero to make his appearance! (If things do not move at speed, I can take a lot of hassle!)

Tobacco and alcohol both increase the load of toxic metals, and cannabis is the worst of the lot! Smoking produces a lot of lead and cadmium, and lowers selenium. Alcohol removes zinc, and considerably slows down liver and kidney function, making it more difficult to get rid of toxic metals. Cannabis can deposit aluminium, and high levels of manganese and nickel on some occasions. The weed also appears to be full of both lead and cadmium, among other toxins.

The pill causes women to retain copper and lose zinc, and sometimes also magnesium and manganese. (Pfeiffer and Grant).

Mercury from dental amalgams or from eating tuna etc, can lower positive minerals, especially selenium. The genitourinary infections, allergies and candida (which overuse zinc and cause malabsorption,) and, of course, intestinal parasites, all lower the essential minerals.

Electromagnetic pollution (increasing all the time) is now believed to lower levels of zinc.

Many environmental chemical nasties do the same – including aluminium from deodorants and fluoride from toothpastes, food additives, pesticides, toxins from cosmetics etc, and medical drugs.

So there is every good reason for taking all the information on board, and doing everything you can. If we pull together we can get there sooner! When you see your programme of vitamins and minerals you may find it a bit daunting. If so, just start with one or two every day, and work up gradually. You will find you soon get used to it, and as you get into the full lifestyle, you will feel so much more energetic and on top of things, and it will all swing into place.

Food supplements need not be confused with medical drugs, although they may be much the same shape, and come in the same type of container! If you find it hard to swallow those capsules, they can be opened and their contents mixed with food. Most people seem to find the capsules easier to swallow than the old fashioned tablets, but this is a very subjective judgement!

Apart from the Vitamin C and Garlic, which contains two herbs, the ingredients in the Foresight range are just simple nutrients, given in quantities well below "mega" doses and packed with organic vegetable powder. There are no artificial colourings, flavourings, preservatives, fillers, etc.

The only large doses sometimes given are 2-6 of the Vitamin C and Garlic, as a cleanser of toxic metals and/or excess copper. This capsule contains garlic and milk thistle, which are excellent liver-supporting herbs. The level of Vitamin C is well within the range advised by Linus Pauling, and also by Carl Pfeiffer, both of whom were world renowned for their work with nutrient therapies.

Some people find that large doses of Vitmain C can cause loose stools, especially if it is given to clean out lead, cadmium and/or copper. This is partly due to the metal that it coming out in the stool. If this becomes tiresome, drop the Vitamin C for 3 days, and then start again, using one tablet for the first few days, and then working up gradually to using just as much as you can tolerate comfortably. This may make the process a little slower, so allow a few more weeks before retesting.

Some people find the zinc can be a little nauseating. If this is a problem, I would drop it for 3 days and then take one with meals, and work up over a few days, to find how many you can tolerate. Most people find they can get used to them. We have added ginger to the zinc to help to counteract any nausea with the bigger doses, and given a mixture of zinc citrate (absorbed in the stomach), zinc amino acid chelate and zinc picolinate. We believe that this has made it easier to handle, but again reactions are very individual.

It is extremely important that zinc levels in the hair are up to at least 175ppm – preferably 185ppm, to ensure both a healthy conception and a smooth pregnancy. Copper excess, coupled to zinc deficiency, can cause miscarriage or premature birth. However, if you feel you need to spread the programme out over a longer time-span, by all means do, but this may mean it is a longer time before conception would be advisable.

Whatever you do, let us know when you retest exactly what you have taken and for how long. Then we can look at the retest results in the light of this information. This makes it so much easier for us to help you.

Energy levels soar on the programme, I am often told. Quite a lot of people said they got promotion at work while on the Foresight programme! Others have told me: *"the house and garden are tidier than ever before, they don't know what's hit them."*

Interesting to think the little birds in the trees are also making their nests when they get to this bit! (Little male birds bring their partners lots of titbits as part of the courting ritual. Instinct is a wonderful thing. Presumably this tenderness gives her tiny ovaries the boost they need to spring into action!)

As the season arrives when they are foraging around gathering up little bits of moss and feathers to line their nests, people often tell me they are making a quilt, or re covering a lampshade, or washing the curtains, and I feel we are all part of one enormous explosion of love and life, and it is all enormously hopeful and jolly!

As the work gathers momentum, I hope you will all join us in trying to take this work forward, as, just as the fertility can be repaired, so can many general health problems.

I know that we can turn the general health around in so many families where the children are hyperactive or "awkward" most of the time, due to the lack of Preconceptual care.

In the same way, unwillingness to work, the "sick-note culture" would respond to deficiencies, allergies, addictions and so on being addressed with hair testing and nutrients. Much chronic illness is likely to be due to lack of nutrients coupled to an overload of toxins, compounded by a significant intake of Voluntary Social Poisons to try to combat the general malaise and gloom!

Thirty years of reading hair analyses and hearing about the outcomes of our programme at first hand has convinced me that balancing the minerals is the key to excellent reproductive health. As with all animals, fertility flows from abundance and well-being.

Getting rid of the toxic metals prior to pregnancy means the babies are guarded against deformity and brain damage. Getting the necessary minerals up to speed means they develop optimum physical and mental abilities.

As you become more familiar with the charts, the patterns will become more obvious. Low levels right across the board can show an inadequate diet – whether because of poor food choices: *"I have to admit that I love Mars Bars – yes, I eat one for my lunch every day. No, I don't eat breakfast, I don't have the time...."*; or because of anorexia: *"I don't want to look fat like my sister....."*; or because of undiagnosed gluten or milk allergy: *"I have an upset tummy two or three times a week – some days I have diarrhoea up to six times, my doctor says it is nerves, he's given me some tranquillisers and told me not to think about my bowels but I can't really stop it, - it just seems to happen anyway......"*

These people will have all their minerals very low – particularly zinc.

Other charts will show up with high copper and lead, and we will need to test the tap water.

Sometimes there is a high aluminium – their deodorant may need to be changed. The very high mercury levels are usually seen in the dentists and dental nurses. High lead and cadmium are in the smokers – low zinc, again, will be linked to alcohol consumption or chronic illness. Low manganese

164

indicates organophosphate pesticide contamination. Low chromium relates to high sugar concentration. And so on!

The high toxic metals send all the needed nutrients down. At first, as you supplement things, they will all move around a bit – introducing helpful vitamins will make the body perk up and use things to repair itself – or just to give more energy!

"I've been getting a lot of praise at work – goodness, my supervisor said, I was really getting down to it!"; "My husband has just been promoted – he was quite surprised really, but he's done so well lately. I said to him that it was the vitamins, but he's not going to admit it, because he was so against taking them...!"

"We've started running together in the evenings, and our little dog is so pleased. He thinks he persuaded us...."; and as for the stories about the babies.....- don't start me! But isn't this how it was all meant to be?

A lot of you say to me, *"When the kids grow up, I'm going to start doing natural health work. How do we learn about it?"* Well, I think we're going to have to organise this because I think there could be a whole army or you out there, and you could be quite unstoppable! Join us and get the Newsletters, and we can take it from there. Nutritionists, Homeopaths, Naturopaths, Reflexologists, Acupuncturists, Herbalists – anyone can expand their area of expertise, and, as it were, "learn all the other bits", or find out who you can cooperate with to round off your programme. To all of you who are practitioners, (or would like to be), I would suggest you meet Colleen Norman, if you possibly can, and I would also look at Alf Riggs' video, come to one of our Information Days and meet Roy Riggs.

If you are a nutritionist or a naturopath, you could team up with a homeopath and a reflexologist, and all areas of the work can be covered.

There are satellite courses for hard-pressed mums who want to start from scratch, and there are courses on organic gardening and cooking – and if there is not the time, there are some wonderful books available.

What we have all got to do is find ways of helping people remove the road-blocks between where they are now, and their perfect fertility and perfect health. We need to spread the word!

You remove one road-block when you get the tap water right. You remove another when you stop smoking. You remove another when you change your deodorant. You remove another when you get them not to use copper algaecide at the swimming pool. You remove another when you bath the dog and get rid of at least some of the anti-flea drops, and so on.

Then you build up the bridges you need to cross with nutrients and organic food, and clean water, and the genuine goodwill that goes with it all!

On another tack, but still relevant, we are told that thousands of people are "malingering" and living off benefits because they pretend to be ill, so as not to have to work. *I don't believe it*.

They would probably all get better in a few months if (a) we cleared their toxic metals, and (b) we supplemented the minerals they needed, and (c) we did the rest of the Foresight programme with them!

They start off feeling below par, and because of poor brain development leading to lack of success at school, they see themselves as rather thick. They are depressed and embarrassed about this, and either take to alcohol and street drugs, or "go to the doctor" and get put on tranquilisers. Either way, their lives and their brains are bombarded with toxins, which makes them feel worse, and perform worse. With women, this may be all further compounded by the contraceptive pill.

As the cycle continues, they feel worse and worse. Some may have allergies due to early weaning. Some may have parasites. Some may have "foetal tobacco syndrome" or "foetal alcohol syndrome". Others may be bombarded by electrosmog from nearby pylons, mobile phone masts, tetra masts. This may keep them awake at night, and then they may be given sleeping pills which then join the other medicaments in plaguing their already harassed liver.

We need an army of New Health Pioneers to get them back on their feet, and having the courage and the energy to live real lives.

Exhortation won't do it. Nutrients would. Can we get the Powers-That-Be to see this? Can we get our country back to sanity? The challenge is to get the next generation born road-worthy!

Those of you who are young, energetic and intelligent – help them! Just telling people about the Foresight Programme is a step forward. Do *what* you can, *however* you can!

TOXIC METALS

Also known as heavy metals.
What they do, and how we stop them doing it.

Gail Bradley and I collected together all this research and wrote almost all of this in the 1980s. It is as significant today as it was then. The modern environment is like a minefield for the poor little foetus, but, with care, we can clear a path for him, and he can flourish! By testing the hair, seeing what toxic substances, if any, are present in the prospective parent's samples, we can see what needs to be done.

All trace elements can be toxic if consumed in sufficient quantities. However, the term "toxic metal" generally denotes "those elements not recognised as having an essential function and known to have well documented deleterious effects." (Lodge Rees, 1983)

Man has been utilising these metals for building and industrial purposes for hundreds of years, but in this century new processes and products have meant a huge escalation in use. The result is widespread pollution with sometimes serious effects on health. The injurious effects of lead were recognised by the Victorians and lead was widely taken to procure abortion. In the 1980s, largely due to the unremitting effort of Professor Derek Bryce-Smith, the environmental effect was acknowledged with the introduction of lead-free petrol.

Although the dangers of cadmium are highlighted in discussions on soil levels, there was little apparent concern until very recently over its major source, cigarette smoking.

Dentists have been aware of the risks of mercury for decades now,[64,65] yet some still continue to use amalgam fillings. Those at greatest risk are dentists and their assistants, and dentist's spouses. Recently an association has been formed to campaign for compensation for dental nurses affected by mercury (www.mercurymadness.org).

The possible toxicity of aluminium has been highlighted in respect of Alzheimer's disease,[88] but UK hospitals, especially those dealing with the mentally ill and geriatrics, serve large amounts of tea, a high source of aluminium. Aluminium serving pans are also still used in some institutions. The use of deodorants and antiperspirants grows, and these are sometimes high in aluminium salts, although it is possible to find them without. Once again, we need to read the labels and also tell the shop managers about it, if you are the pioneering type!

There is the continual interaction between the elements in the body — and it is the beneficial relationship between the individual elements that is important in health. There are only a small number of studies which review these interactional effects as the work is difficult and expensive; but Bryce-Smith and his colleagues pursued it.[2,12,37,90] There is also the problem common to government health departments and the medical industry; the assumption that something is safe until it is proved otherwise. What is needed is a major shift to assume the opposite, namely that something with toxic potential is dangerous until proved safe! *NB: Seventeen years on from when this was originally written, we are still waiting for this shift!*

The major toxic metals which are known to adversely influence pregnancy outcome include lead, cadmium, aluminium and mercury. Also over-high levels of copper can be problematic.

Aluminium

Sources: The major sources of aluminium include antacids (they are a stomach irritant – these are some of the many self perpetuating medicaments - antiperspirants, food additives, and anti-caking agents found in milk substitutes and baking powder. Pearly, glittery cosmetics, especially eye cosmetics. Some toothpastes use it as an abrasive. In some places aluminium flocculants are added to the water to collect up the peaty particles, sometimes the "comb" that is meant to catch it all as it leaves the reservoirs is damaged, and becomes ineffective, and there is some leakage of the gel into the mains water. If a patient's hair level is high, the water from their taps should be tested. Aluminium saucepans and other cooking utensils impart some metal if they are in contact with food, especially leaf vegetables, rhubarb, apple and other acid fruits. The pans seem polished when you have cooked them! Aluminium pressure cookers, although now relatively rare, are worse than ordinary pans. Kettles and aluminium teapots were potent sources, but happily in the last 17 years, there has been a shift away from aluminium kitchenware, though some people may still have old family possessions! Work at the University of Wales at Cardiff suggests that the major UK food source of aluminium is tea, since the tea plant thrives on alum soils, so the soil is fed with alum. Foil-wrapped foods, can be sources. Foil-wrapped fats and acid foods are the worst.[7,8,31,32,106] Food microwaved in aluminium foil containers is very bad news. Modern anti-perspirants contain aluminium. Check this out.

Effects on health: Aluminium is easily absorbed, accumulating in the arteries. A study has shown that people living in areas with a high level of aluminium in the drinking water face a 50 per cent greater risk of developing Alzheimer's disease.[105] (Many who develop Alzheimer's in other areas may be suffering from pollution from any of the above sources.) How many people with chronic indigestion, likely to be due to an undiagnosed milk or gluten intolerance, habitually take ant-acids for example? The aluminium they contain is a stomach irritant, leading to them needing another tablet a short time later. (The only one that does not, "Nulacin", contains gluten!). Also check vaccines.

The following food additives are allowed in this country: E173 Aluminium (c.1 77000) known to cause kidney stress and said to be "not safe" for the brain. It is forbidden in Australia. E554 Aluminium Sodium Silicate is implicated with Alzheimer's disease, as is E556 Aluminium Calcium Silicate, E541 Sodium Aluminium Phosphate; Acidic Aluminium Phosphate Basic is unsafe for babies or people suffering from kidney or heart problems. There can also be skin reactions. It is also known to be a neurotoxin. As this is not suitable for babies under 6 months, it is advisable for pregnant and lactating mothers to avoid it also. E559 Aluminium Silicate – has been implicated in Alzheimer's disease, which is hugely on the increase. *We should all be reading labels while we can!* Take FIND OUT and WATCH IT with you when you go shopping.

It is known that aluminium can destroy vitamins as it readily combines with other substances. It irritates and weakens the lining of the gut. Excessive amounts can lead to constipation, colic, excessive perspiration, loss of appetite, nausea, skin problems and fatigue. Adverse effects associated with the body's attempts to clear itself, in which aluminium salts are found in small quantities in the blood, include paralysis and areas of numbness, with fatty degeneration of the liver and kidney, as well as symptoms of gastrointestinal inflammation. Thus it seriously compromises nutritional status. It has been linked with kidney problems in babies, with researchers concluding that formula feeds should be aluminium-free for neonates and infants with reduced kidney function, in fact for *any* infants! Soya milk has been withdrawn for infants due to high aluminium levels. It has been associated with behavioural problems and autism. For the same reason it **is vital that pregnant/breastfeeding mothers do not use anti-perspirants.** Mice fed large doses had no symptoms, *but* the next three generations of offspring had growth defects. (Cowdry 1989, Nutrition Search Inc 1975, Freundlich 1985, Lodge Recs 1979, Ward 1992)

We recommend that the Hair Mineral analysis level should not exceed 2 parts per million.

Cadmium

Sources: The main sources of cadmium are cigarette smoking – your own or even passive smoking. (NB: The new law regarding no smoking in the pubs is Very Good News!)

Cadmium is in processed foods, since in the refining of flour the zinc in the germ and bran layers is mainly removed, leaving a higher cadmium to zinc ratio.

It is widely used in manufacturing industries, including particularly those concerned with paints, dyes, batteries, television sets and fertilisers. Artists or housepainters should be aware that it is in yellow and red paints. Artists should not lick their brushes, as this can lead to tongue and throat cancer, also depression. Housepainters or those scraping down old paint need to wear protective gear, including masks and rubber gloves. It is found in shellfish from polluted waters and galvanised containers and can be released by coal-burning. It can come from burning rubber. This can occur where old rubber tyres are burnt to dispose of them, and on race-tracks, as the rubber can burn off the tyres as the pressure is on!

Effects on health: It is highly dangerous as it accumulates in the kidneys and liver slowly, unless nutritional measures are taken to remove it or reduce absorption. It particularly builds up in people who are deficient of Vitamins C, D, B6, zinc, manganese, copper, selenium and/or calcium.[7,8,106,108]

Cadmium is known to damage the unborn in animal studies.[7,8] Elizabeth Lodge Rees[32] reported cleft palate and/or lip, other facial malformations and limb defects in a number of species, testicular and ovarian necrosis,[110] and renal disorders.[109] This will explain why cleft lip and palate is more common in the children of smokers. In research studies, she noted pregnant animals developed toxemia, an observation which lead her to wonder if "one might suspect that toxemia in humans may be due to excess cadmium and/or a lack of nutrients that counteract the effect of cadmium". She also mentioned that in humans it was associated with proteinuria, as well as low birth weight and small head circumference in the baby. Cadmium accumulates in the placenta, causing placental necrosis if large amounts are absorbed.[31] It also crosses the placenta. It has been found to impair reproduction in mice.[109,110]

The importance of zinc in counteracting the effects of cadmium has been demonstrated in animal research on the effects of cadmium on the testes. Pre-treatment with zinc can abolish some of the adverse effects, though it does not reverse others. When cadmium is injected subcutaneously into female rats it produces marked changes in the ovaries, the adverse effects initially increasing over time, though the ovaries do return to normal eventually, when the cadmium leaves the body.

It seems likely from these observations that smokers' semen will contain excess cadmium, and that this could adversely affect their partners' ovaries. One more good reason for *everyone* to stop smoking!

Foresight recommends that the hair mineral analysis level should not exceed 0.14 parts per million. (And when it does, we take steps to do something about it!) NB: Cadmium is known to accumulate in the kidneys, and we frequently see high levels in people suffering from high blood pressure. If people were always given a hair analysis before being given medical drugs, so often the solution would be obvious. Cadmium can be removed from the body with Vitamin C, garlic, milk thistle and B-complex vitamins, especially nicotinamide.

Mercury

Sources: The main sources of mercury are dental fillings, pesticide and fungicides, fish and industrial processes. The larger the fish, the greater the concentration, with tuna and swordfish being the most common sources in the UK. Some large marine mammals ingest high levels of mercury. I have found that people who consume tuna fish on a regular basis tend to have quite high levels of mercury in their hair. 'Freshwater' fish can also be contaminated if the river has been polluted by factory effluent, or water run-off from fields which have been treated with mercury-containing agrochemicals.

It is found in slimicides used in paper manufacturing to stop the growth of slime moulds.

It is in some cosmetics and other toiletries, antiseptic sprays, make up removers, eye moisturiser and mascara. The worst dangers of all have come from the vaccines where mercury was used as a preservative. The recent work of Dr Viera Scheibner of Australia, in her book 'Behavioural Problems in Childhood – The Link to Vaccination', who has followed research all over the world, makes clear that the damage done to the human brain, and therefore the human mind, by vaccines has been incalculable. Some of this was due to the mercury preservative Thymiseroal, although in part there may also have been problems with the viruses themselves, and with the animal lymph in which they were "floated". (More anon on this.)

A well known London dentist, Dr Victoria Lee, has long been concerned about the mercury saga, and has made a huge study of the whole subject. She said to me: "The phials which contain the vaccine have enough for 5 shots. Mercury is a heavy substance. It will fall to the bottom of the phial. The fifth baby is likely to be the unlucky one. He will get a big wallop of mercury. Is this why one child in 5 now has learning difficulties? I think so."

Although it may not be the full answer, it may be a big piece in some children's biochemical jigsaw.[64,65]

Dr Viera Scheibner also has evidence of how the most severe reactions occur approximately 16 days after the vaccination/immunisation. She has investigated thousands of cot deaths, and believes that apnoea attacks and cot deaths cluster around this inauspicious date. This needs much further – urgent – research.

The major controversy around the dangers of mercury concerns mercury-containing amalgams used in dentistry.[64,65] Dentists have been aware of mercury poisoning for many years. We have found that the people with the highest mercury in their hair are dentists, dental nurses, and dentist's spouses or partners. Unfortunately, the seminal fluid is an excretory route for toxic metals. This means that a wife often suffers from toxic effluent coming from her husband's occupation. The American Society of Dental Surgeons was opposed to mercury amalgams 150 years ago! Norway, Sweden and Denmark now ban mercury in dental work. It is time Britain followed suit.

<u>Effects on health</u>: There are three basic forms of mercury, elemental, non-

organic and organic. The elemental and non-organic forms tend to be slowly absorbed and readily excreted, unlike the organic form which is easily absorbed and slow to be eliminated. Thus the main dangers lie in the organic, especially methyl mercury, although there are some conditions linked to elemental mercury. These include psychological disturbances, oral cavity disorders, gastro-intestinal, cardiovascular, neurologic, respiratory, immunological and endocrine effects. In severe cases there are hallucinations and manic-depression. Organic mercury exposure is linked with psychological symptoms which can develop into paralysis, vision, speech and hearing problems, loss of memory, lack of coordination, renal damage and general central nervous system dysfunctions. Eventually death can occur. Not exactly what you need put into your mouth on a permanent basis. Nevertheless, the British Dental Association refuses to admit it is harmful. However, there is an Association for Mercury Free Dentists who have a website: www.mercuryfreedentistry.org.uk (The British Society for Mercury Free Dentistry, The Weathervane, 22a Moorend Park Road, Cheltenham, GL53 0JY, Telephone: 01242 226918.)

I would contact them for help with finding a dentist who does not use mercury.

Metallic mercury vapour has been reported to affect men exposed to it in a serious way. In one study of nine men, exposed after an accident, all complained of loss of libido, lasting in some cases up to eight years. One reported temporary impotence for eighteen months.[65] (NB: Should we regard this as a failsafe mechanism of nature as toxic sperm can produce damaged children? Nature can be far more aware than we are.)

The damage mercury can cause to the foetus was highlighted in the Japanese tragedy of Minamata, in which 23 children were born with cerebral palsy-like symptoms, varying from mild spasticity to severe mental retardation, blindness, chronic seizures, and death. Their mothers, free from symptoms themselves, had been exposed to mercury while pregnant. Mercury is readily passed through the placenta and foetal blood often contains concentrations 20 per cent greater than the maternal blood. Foetal brain tissue concentrations may be four times higher than the mother's brain tissues. In the Minimata incident, adults and older children were also affected with a total of 46 dying.[24,64]

Animal work by Dr Joan Spyker[111] suggests that the adverse effects may be long-term. Mice exposed in utero did not appear outwardly different from controls until they were about 18 months old (middle-aged). The experimental mice then contracted severe infections, implying an immune system impaired prenatally. They lost all semblance of normality, ageing quickly and prematurely.

Only extensive investigation, magnifying the brain tissues 48,000 times, showed slight damage to the individual cells — yet this slight damage was responsible for their problems. Dr Spyker has pointed out that the Minamata victims are deteriorating just as the animal model predicted.[24,64,112]

Lead

Lead has been known to be toxic to animals and humans for centuries and its use has been so great, it has been impossible to escape ingesting or inhaling it.

Sources: It is found in foods and in water which has coursed though old lead piping, or through lead-glazed earthenware mains. Sometimes it is found in copper piping where the joins of the pipes have been formed with lead-containing alloys.

Where high lead does arise now, it is often in conjunction with high copper, and is coming from the tap water. Joining copper piping to a lead connecting pipe from the mains, and/or joining copper pipes with a lead containing solder, are now both illegal. However, this simply means that builders/plumbers cannot do this anymore. *It does not mean* that these problems have been rectified in the properties already built. I think from what we see on a daily basis, that in the region of 10-20% of homes still have these problems. It should be part of the remit of the surveyors to look for this when the properties change hands. Better still, all houses should have a water survey as a starting point for the government's new drive forward on health! Expensive, maybe, but *what* it could save the NHS! One of those things I feel that the army could do, very efficiently. (Rather than being deployed to bomb and shoot people and to drive tanks into their houses, in the name of preventing terror!)

Cigarette smoking can increase lead uptake significantly, from the lead arsenate used as an insecticide in the production of tobacco. Occupational exposure can be a hazard, as lead is used in a number of industries.[7,8,113,114,115] Builders can be high in lead from scraping down old paint, from roofing felt and from cement.[113] Artists can get it from certain paints. Particular occupations such as making windows with "leaded lights", stained glass windows, glazing pottery or making cathode ray tubes for TV sets can put workers at risk.

Some black hair dyes, such as "Grecian 2000" and black hair extensions, used when making hair into little plaits all over the head, can contain lead and/or cadmium. Always check, and reject those that do. There is also a substance called "Morgan's Pomade" that contains a lot of lead. On no account use it. Lead may also be in some powdered inks.

It is illegal to put lead into cosmetics in this country, but some people import a type of mascara made in India or Pakistan that contains it. Although it is illegal over here, people have too little understanding of *why* this is so. The danger to the babies needs to be fully explained, preferably on television.

Animal research suggests that nutritional status may be a factor in lead absorption. Diets low in calcium, iron, zinc, selenium and manganese may actually enhance lead uptake. However, one study also suggests that cow's milk may increase absorption, since, although it is high in calcium; it is low in other trace minerals such as iron.[116] The fact that lead can be removed from the body by nutrients further supports the idea that nutritional status is important.

Safety levels: There is no agreement on safety levels of lead in the body. Some researchers (who I find easy to believe) say that no level can be assumed to be safe. The Government sets limits for industry and the environment which are lowered from time to time as more is revealed about its toxicity.[1] One problem in deciding toxicity levels is that for a long time there were no officially agreed ways to measure levels. Blood levels are not reliable as the lead is passed quickly into other tissues. Hair analysis is now accepted as a reliable guide, and is available through Foresight. Foresight recommends that the hair reading should be no more than 1.4ppm, (part per million). None at all would obviously be the ultimate goal, but this is unlikely to be achievable in the present environment.

Further information on the effects of lead toxicity on health: It is now accepted that levels of lead in the body which do not manifest symptoms of "classical lead poisoning" may still have significant effects on the body.[7,8,117,90] Chronic "low" lead exposure is implicated as a significant causative or contributory factor in a wide range of conditions, including cardiovascular disease, renal and metabolic disease, immune dysfunction, and a multiplicity of vague symptoms, such as lethargy, depression, muscle aches and pains, and frequent infections. Cancer can occur in the babies born to mothers with significant amounts of lead in their systems. Developmental abnormalities and learning, behavioural and central nervous system dysfunction in schoolchildren later in life are also linked to raised lead levels during the pregnancy.[1,3,5,113,117,118,119,120] Lead interferes with the normal functioning of many trace elements, especially by inhibiting zinc-dependent enzymes, making its effects widespread. Other enzyme systems are also vulnerable. High childhood blood lead levels and smaller stature have been shown to be highly correlated.

Lead can affect both male and female reproductive abilities. Men exposed to high levels in their work have been found to be at risk of low sperm count, with more sperm likely to be misshapen and less mobile.[7,8,45,90,113,114,121,122] High rates of infertility, miscarriage, and stillbirth, congenital abnormalities including microcephaly, convulsions, early deaths and chromosomal abterations have been reported in their children.[2,7,8,12,90110,117,118,119]

In women, lead's capacity for inducing abortions has long been known — *it was used for this purpose* about the turn of the century with, sometimes, blindness and brain damage in surviving babies as unwanted results. It was also this danger that eventually ensured women were not employed to work with lead.

In 1977, a study by Wibberley[13] at the University of Aston in Birmingham, of placental lead levels showed that there were greater amounts in the placentas of malformed stillbirths and neonatal deaths compared with normal babies surviving longer than a week. In the same year, two other researchers reported higher levels of lead (and cadmium) in stillbirths, using rib and pre-ossified cartilage for the analyses.[2]

Needleman and his colleagues found that the relationship between lead exposure in utero and congenital abnormalities to be associated "in a dose-related fashion with an increased risk for minor abnormalities."[125]

Prenatal exposure can result in lead intoxication in the new-born. In a study which measured the level of lead in umbilical cord blood at birth, subsequent mental developmental testing at the ages of 6 months and 12 months showed that the higher the level of lead the lower the test scores. At neither age were scores related to *current* blood levels. The researchers concluded:

"Prenatal exposure to lead levels *relatively common among urban populations* appear to be associated with less favourable development through the first year of life."[117]

Another longitudinal study by the same researcher, which concerned lead exposure and early cognitive development, concluded, "It appears that the foetus may be adversely affected at blood lead concentrations *well below* 25 ug/dl, the level currently defined by the Centre for Disease Control as the highest acceptable level for young children."[117]

Research by Doctors McConnell and Berry suggest why this should happen. They found that in rats lead tends to derange the development of the brain in a unique way, interrupting the process of forming neural connections. Other studies have shown that other parts of the brain closely involved with learning processes are also susceptible to damage by lead. Animal research with monkeys has confirmed that learning abilities are affected. In one study, monkeys in their first year of life showed no physical signs of toxicity, but all the lead-exposed ones showed performance deficits on reversal learning tasks. The researchers report that the effects are not the result of delayed maturation:

"...Data currently being collected in this laboratory indicate that the deficit can be observed at least three years beyond the final dosing. It therefore appears likely that this deficit represents a relatively permanent characteristic of the chronically lead poisoned monkey."[3]

The most widely quoted study on the effects of lead on children is that done by Needleman[125] and his colleagues. They showed that at levels below those which were considered to produce symptoms of toxicity, the performance of children in the classroom was adversely affected. A wide range of behaviours was examined, including distractibility, persistence, dependence, organisational ability, hyperactivity, impulsiveness, frustration, day dreaming, ability to follow, and overall functioning, and it was found that the higher the lead level, the poorer the performance in every measure. Other studies have also indicated the negative effects of lead on learning abilities and classroom behaviour. In a follow-up study, Needleman and his colleagues checked 132 students over an

11 year period, (ending in 1989) concluding that the harmful effects of lead persist beyond childhood and the mental impairment from lead poisoning may be permanent. Decreased hand-eye co-ordination and shortened reaction times, as well as physical effects were seen in 45 adolescents and young adults with hair levels considered to be normal, with problems starting at levels as low as 10 ppm. Most laboratories class up to 15 ppm as "normal". His work was published in the New England Journal of Medicine.[126]

A number of other studies have also suggested a link between hyperactivity and raised lead levels. In one, 13 children with no apparent cause for their hyperactivity were examined. Their behaviour improved when their lead levels were reduced using lead-chelating medication. A Danish study linked high levels with minimal cerebral dysfunction (MCD) — learning disabilities are often linked with hyperactivity or MCD.
1,2,4,5,6,9,10,11,13,14,24,37,90,107,110,113,117,119,121,123,124,125,126,127,128,130

They always enjoyed the weekend papers. On such an occasion, an article relating to age spots, mineral deficiency analysis and Foresight registered with Alison. Thinking no more about the article, life went on as usual. After trying for six months for a baby, conception occurred. Unfortunately at 6 weeks the baby miscarried. Although they were trying, no further conception took place, so several months later, tests revealed that all was normal. With these findings, they were referred to a hospital for further investigation. They were informed that there would be blood tests as well as other investigations of the fallopian tubes; antibiotics, pain killers, x rays and dyes injected into the body. All in the name of searching for reasons for infertility.

Both Alison and her husband had a science back ground, yet this did not feel right, too uncomfortable, and too invasive. Both knew that there must be an alternative. Remembering the particular article they had read a while back, Alison searched for the article, and luckily she found it.

Foresight was contacted. After speaking to Nim, who was so calm and supportive, they both started on the Foresight Programme. "After all, we had nothing to lose".

Their first Hair Mineral Analysis revealed that both had high Lead levels and low Zinc levels. The analysis was scientific and they became "very dedicated" to the programme. The second analysis revealed that mineral levels had improved sufficiently for conception in about 3 months. Three months later, prompted by "a feeling" out came the pregnancy test. All Alison could hear from upstairs was "oh!" shortly followed by "OH! Yes you are pregnant. It works!" At the appointed time, a 6lb 14oz baby boy was born to them.

Multi Element Studies

As far back as 1969 it was reported that "Cadmium teratogenicity is dramatically augmented by lead when they are administered concurrently."[11] Lead and cadmium often occur together. Their concentrations in hair and blood show strong positive correlations and their overt symptoms of toxicity are not unalike. These similarities have led some researchers to the view that "it is possible that some of the deleterious effects attributed to lead in correlation studies may instead be due to cadmium." They conducted a study on hair cadmium and lead levels in relation to cognitive functioning in children, in which the results showed that hair cadmium and lead levels were significantly correlated with intelligence tests and school achievement, but not with motor impairment scores. Statistical analysis suggested that "cadmium has a stronger effect on verbal IQ than does lead and that lead has a stronger effect on performance IQ than does cadmium."[11]

Professor Bryce-Smith and his colleagues, aware of the inadequacies of single element studies, reviewed the levels of four elements, lead, cadmium, zinc and calcium, in stillbirths' bones and cartilage. They found that cadmium concentrates in the stillbirths were ten times greater than the levels normally found in human bones. Lead levels were also raised. Low calcium and zinc were sometimes associated with these marked elevations.[2]

Research has shown that lead and cadmium can also cause problems for the neonate. A much larger study by Bryce-Smith and his colleagues studied 36 elements. In 1981, Professor Bryce-Smith reported that for all the elements being studied, the levels of foetal and maternal blood were about the same for most elements. Only in lead levels was there a difference, with the foetal level about 95% of the maternal. He explained this thus:

"This means that the placenta passes all elements, both nutrients and toxins, to the foetus from the maternal circulation with little or no selectivity or filtering effect. We can see no evidence for a significant barrier to protect the foetus from inorganic toxins such as mercury, arsenic, and antimony; and there is only a slight, but significant ($p=0.01$) barrier in the case of lead for normal births only."[1]

Having begun by analysing nine tissues, including maternal and foetal (umbilical) cord whole blood and serum, amniotic fluid, placenta, and scalp hair from the mother and neonate, later on they decided that the *placental* element levels showed the clearest correlations with indices of foetal development for supposedly "normal" births. Thus it was with this tissue that they continued the investigation.

In the first written report on the final 37 elements studied, the researchers observed highly significant negative relationships between placental cadmium and lead levels, and birth weight, head circumference and placental weight. The smaller the birth weight, head circumference and placental weight was, the higher the level of cadmium and lead. There was a statistically significant positive correlation between lower placental cadmium and lead levels where birth weights were less than 3,000g. For higher birth weights, the correlation, though still positive, was not significant. Placental zinc showed significant relationships with birth weights up to 3,000 g and head circumference of less than 34 cm, i.e. the lower the level of zinc, the lower the birth weight and the smaller the head circumference. With respect to other elements, there was "a weak positive correlation between placental iron and head circumference, and stronger but negative correlations for chlorine, vanadium, and lanthanum." However, placental levels of iron did not correlate with birth weight, nor were the iron levels or birth weights significantly raised in those mothers receiving iron supplements. Indeed, the results in iron and zinc lead the researchers to suggest that more emphasis should be paid to zinc supplementation than to iron. The final point made in the paper states that, "In cases of cadmium, lead, and zinc, biological, neurobehavioral, and biosocial studies in which the levels of all three elements are measured may prove more informative than those involving single elements."[12,37,90]

Much the same conclusion was reached by the researchers who conducted further investigation into lead, cadmium, and cognitive functioning. Looking at the protective effects of zinc and calcium against toxic metals, they found that higher zinc levels seemed to protect against the effects of cadmium, while calcium did the same against lead. They concluded: "The results suggest that the effects of heavy metal pollutants on cognitive function cannot be adequately assessed without concurrently evaluating the status of essential nutrients with which these toxins are known to interact metabolically."[129]

(The Foresight research, from the 1980s conducted by the University of Surrey, is reproduced in full on our website, in Appendix 6 and summarised in Appendix 4.)

Detoxifying the Body

The preferred method of detoxification must be nutritional since it does not have the same potential for harmful side effects as drugs. EDTA (ethylenediaminetetraacetic acid) is sometimes used by doctors in acute poisoning but it has disadvantages as it also removes many essential minerals at the same time.

Vitamin C and zinc supplements were used successfully in reducing blood lead levels of psychiatric outpatients in one study.[118] The treatment was also found to reduce blood copper levels. Subjects included some hyperactive children.[129] Vitamin C has also been shown to lower cadmium levels in birds.[118]

Calcium helps prevent absorption, as well as removing lead from the tissues. Vitamin D is necessary for calcium metabolism and to help displace lead from the bones. Vitamin B1, taken with a B-complex, provides protection against lead damage. Lecithin can also help in protection, while Vitamin A helps to activate the enzymes needed for detoxification. Trace elements, in addition to zinc, which are protective, include chromium, selenium and manganese. In the diet, peas, lentils and beans act as detoxifiers. Algin, found in seaweeds, attracts lead in the gut and carries it out of the body. Yoghurt, garlic, onions, bananas and fruits such as apples and pears which contain pectin (especially the pips) help to reduce absorption, as well as detoxifying.[131] Vitamin E may also reduce lead poisoning. (Nutrition Search Inc 1979) In animal studies exposure to sunlight has been found to help remove toxic metals.[132]

At Foresight, once we have found levels that need detoxifying, we give our cleansing capsule "Vitamin C and garlic" (see below for the formula), with Nicotinamide. We also give the dietary advice as above, and after four months we retest to see if the levels of toxins have fallen to acceptable levels. If not, we continue a little longer, until they have. This way, the sperm and ova that make the future baby are ready to do so.

Vitamin C, garlic, milk thistle, Vitamins BI and B12 have been formulated as a cleansing tablet "Vitamin C with Garlic". This is usually used in conjunction with Nicotinamide, to enhance liver function, and Magnesium, Zinc and other cleansing minerals.

The Foresight vitamins and minerals have been specially formulated by the FORESIGHT nutritional advisers for preconception, pregnancy and lactation to provide a balance of essential nutrients. These may be used in conjunction with other supplements, where need is indicated by the test results. The organisation has had thirty years of experience in trace mineral supplementation to restore optimum levels and cleanse the toxic metals. We are here to help!

The longer I live, the more I hate the cruelty of animal testing, but at the same time, the more I realise the benefits that we could gain, as a species, if we just took on board what all these researchers and all these poor little rodents have uncovered for us.

Don't let all this work and all this suffering have been in vain. We are able to test for lead and all the other toxic metals. We are able to eliminate them. Even those 'in high places' are prepared to cede that hair analysis is a useful guide to toxic metals. When we get the toxic metal levels to an acceptable level before the conception takes place, I believe we see the human child as he/she was meant to be. Look at our "case histories" – chess players, musicians with exceptional ability, scholarship winners. Little people with sunny natures, robust health and a zest for life. As a species, we human adults make the environment so problematic in the first place! *They* have the right to expect we study the research and sort this out for them.

All I wonder is, why have we all had to wait for so long? The research Gail wrote out for us so eruditely in the last few chapters was all done in the 1970-80s. Why is everybody not tested as a matter of course before every pregnancy? How long is it going to take us to get it right?

Read on, so you become really informed about what each and every mineral does to both you and your future baby, and then you can pass this crucial information on to your GP, midwife, health visitor, and to your family and friends.

So *then* what do we do? Be sure to have hair analysis and get it all sorted!

Ruth had a fantastic job as a picture restorer at the Fitzwilliam Museum in Cambridge. She was leaving her home in North London each morning at 5.30am to drop Tom, her husband, at his job in the City, and then she would drive to Cambridge.

They had been trying for a baby for two years, but she was exhausted. Her husband worked very long hours so Ruth was left doing everything in the house as well as having a full time job. She realised that she was going to have to change her lifestyle and give up her job in Cambridge if she was to get pregnant.

For the next year Ruth rested during the day, did a few chores, cooked dinner and went to bed at 9.00pm. After a year passed she concluded that she was not going to get pregnant naturally. She had a session of IUI and her FSH levels were so high that it was decided that she was going to have to have IVF.

Two embryos were implanted and Beatrice was born.

Two years passed with no further conception. It was then that Ruth contacted the La Leche League, who suggested Foresight.

Ruth's hair mineral analysis revealed that both she and Tom were extremely low in essential minerals, especially zinc, cobalt and iron. Both Ruth and Tom were PhD chemists from Oxford who thought they were pretty healthy. They did not smoke, drink or go out for late nights, yet it "never occurred" to them to check their nutrition levels.

Ruth's diet was very good as she was still breast-feeding Beatrice. It was a huge relief to both of them to know that they were taking the right supplements. These were checked every three months and adjusted as changes in their nutritional status were revealed. Although Tom struggled, Ruth was very strict in taking her supplements. Knowing that she was on the Foresight programme, and having some acupuncture meant that she could relax a bit.

Three months later Ruth conceived again, and gave birth to her first Foresight baby, a little boy.

Although they have two healthy children, they plan to have a large family while they are still young enough, and will be "using the Foresight programme again very soon".

ESSENTIAL MINERALS

This chapter includes a lot of the work from our previous book, as it comprises some of the excellent research that was done in the 1970s and early 1980s into the role of specific nutrients in reproduction. Here and there it has been updated, or commented upon by myself in 2008!

So many of you say to me in our telephone calls, *"But is it all _really_ important? How do you know?" "_Why_ does zinc deficiency matter?" "What does selenium actually _do_?" "Will it _really_ help my husband's sperm count?" "My mother thinks you are just making money out of us." "My husband is very sceptical, I'm afraid. He isn't going to do it."* And so on.

So please read on. We are not making money out of you. I have worked *voluntarily* for 30 years. My motivation is that I want you all to have healthy babies. _I love babies_. That is the momentum behind Foresight. Read on!

CALCIUM is needed for the formation of strong bones and teeth, and for controlling blood clotting mechanisms and proper nerve and muscle function. Other functions include assisting in muscle growth and strength, maintaining blood balance and acting as a catalyst in enzyme reactions. It is said it may help to protect against allergies, viruses and tooth decay.[34,105,132]

Calcium can sometimes run up very high. I find this usually relates directly to the level of calcium in the water or dust, so it is a natural happening rather than a metabolic fault. In the hair, the ratio of magnesium to calcium should be 1:10, so if the ratio of magnesium is lower than 1:10, we give some extra magnesium. This helps the body use the calcium as it should. High calcium without the balancing magnesium can be at a bit of a loose end in the body, and can form into kidney stones, gallstones, etc. Magnesium will help to pack it into the bones, joints etc where it is meant to be. This also helps to guard against arthritis, osteoporosis, etc.[23,34,132]

For pregnancy, we need plenty of calcium as we women are expected to build a little skeleton approximately 21 – 22 inches long, ("unfolded", a newborn baby is approximately one third as tall as his mummy); and a skull, (containing a good little working brain) of about 13 – 14 inches round, (nearly two thirds the size of his mummy's).

All to be done in *nine months*! No yelling down the phone that we can't *possibly* finish it for another three months, as with the books! The deadline is absolute. It is not under our control.

So, calcium is vital for the growing of the foetus and the well-being of the mother. Davis recommends giving it, in conjunction with Vitamin D, during labour to ease pain.[137] It can ease leg cramps, and help sleeping. Calcium is lost from the bones during bed rest and also while on high protein diets. People affected will need to supplement the diet and to choose foods with high levels.

Lack of calcium can cause rickets, allergy, tooth decay, insomnia, back pain, osteoporosis, osteomalacia, irritability, nervousness, tension, uneven heartbeat, indigestion, stomach cramps and spasms, constipation, premenstrual tension, and cramping of the uterus (ie very painful periods).[34,105,134,135,137]

Unfortunately, due to modern farming practices and what is called "increased efficiency in dairying", cows are now milked while they are pregnant. At this time, the milk contains the hormone that releases calcium from the bones, in order to give it to the growing calf they are gestating. This may make the milk less helpful as a source of calcium as once released, it can be excreted! We find that often people who consume a lot of dairy products are very *low* in calcium (and very surprised by this). Unfortunately, even people producing organic milk now abuse the cows in this way.

FOETAL DEFICIENCY

Government documents state: "signs of calcium deficiency are manifest in the bones and teeth of all young animal species, including humans. Effects include stunted growth, poor quality bones and teeth, and bone malformation."[34,105,135]

Low levels in the baby are associated with low birth weight and low scores on developmental tests. Premature babies tend to have low levels.

Rickets, tooth decay and a high raised palate. The high raised palate leads to cramping of the middle brain, possibly lessening the blood supply and subsequently to learning difficulties like dyslexia. See Dr June Sharpe's study.

A Small Study of Palate Height
conducted for Foresight by Dr June Sharpe of Godalming, Surrey, UK, in the 1970s.

Palate Height - Normal Primary School - 95 Children Seen

Palate Height	Percentage
Normal	73%
Marginal	9%
High	18%

Palate Height - School for Children with Learning Difficulties - 95 Children Seen

Palate Height	Percentage
Normal	31%
Marginal	5%
High	64%

Palate Height - Home for Mentally Subnormal Children - 13 Children Seen

Palate Height	Percentage
Normal	15%
Marginal	15%
High	70%

N.B. I think this breaks down to only 2 mentally subnormal children seen had a normally developed palate.

Good sources: kelp, carob, bone broth, green vegetables, Brazil nuts, hazelnuts, almonds, dolomite, brewer's yeast, yoghurt.

Inhibitors: Foods containing oxalic acid (sesame seed hulls, rhubarb, spinach) and phytic acid (soda, unsoaked muesli and unleavened bread) can reduce availability.

Calcium is best taken with Vitamins A, C, D, essential fatty acids, iron, magnesium and phosphorous. (Nutrition Search Inc 1979)

The month of June was just two months after the wedding, and when they decided to start a family. By September, Catherine had lost her baby due to a "blighted ovum". Six months later, another miscarriage came at about 7 weeks. Devastation, loss of confidence and a reluctance to get pregnant again gripped Catherine.

As the months rolled on, Catherine read about Foresight, sent off for the Foresight Information Pack, and with her husband, went straight on to the programme.

The first Hair Mineral Analysis revealed that her husband had raised levels of heavy metals Aluminium, Lead and Mercury. His levels of Zinc, Calcium, Magnesium and Selenium were very low. Catherine's analysis revealed that she, too, had raised levels of Lead and Mercury, and her Magnesium levels were very low. A supplement programme was devised to rectify heavy metal toxicity and to increase the levels of important vitamins and minerals for each of them.

Six months later, after missing a period, a pregnancy test proved positive. Now she was scared. Scared of miscarrying again, and worried that the stress from being scared was affecting her pregnancy. Too scared to be excited, and too scared to feel pregnant until she got over the three month barrier. Following the Foresight programme throughout the pregnancy and having reflexology, the pregnancy held, and a son was born weighing 6lbs 13oz. He was followed in quick succession by a baby girl at 8lbs 7oz.

Catherine says: It made such sense. There was a reason for the miscarriages. I definitely felt healthy and I was actually doing something positive to ensure a safe pregnancy. If we were to have a third baby, I would definitely use Foresight again".

MAGNESIUM is needed for the production and transfer of energy, muscle contraction, proper nerve function, protein synthesis, the functioning of many enzymes and the absorption and use of calcium.[8,136]

Deficiencies cause involuntary muscle movements, such as spasms and twitching, convulsions, insomnia, panic attack, allergy, impaired protein synthesis, premenstrual tension, painful periods, poor memory, confusion, disorientation, hyperactivity, irritability, anxiety, nightmares, increased sensitivity to noise, irregular heartbeat, leg and foot cramps, bedwetting and depression. Pregnancy aggravates any deficiency.[7,8,23,133]

A deficiency is said to contribute to painful uterine contractions at the end of pregnancy. It may also be associated with miscarriage or premature birth. Rats fed low magnesium diets give birth to smaller pups with a higher rate of congenital deformities.[138] They also develop calcium deposits and other abnormalities in the heart cells. Stones may form in the kidneys. Women with low levels tend to abort more or have low birth weight babies.[7,8,137,138,139] Magnesium deficiency is very common.[105]

FOETAL DEFICIENCIES: Congenital abnormalities, calcium deposits, anorexia (failure to suck), convulsions and perinatal death. There is a condition "Williams' Syndrome", where calcium is found to be deposited in the brain causing mental retardation. It would be interesting to know if this has been linked to lack of Magnesium.

Good sources: Nuts, kelp, green vegetables, seafoods, eggs, milk, whole grains, dolomite. Epsom salts can be added to the bath water to get absorption through the skin.

Magnesium is best taken with Vitamins B6, C, D, calcium, phosphorous, protein. [105. Also: 29,34,112,137,140,141,142,143,144,145,146,147]

POTASSIUM is needed to regulate blood pH, to acidify urine, and for proper nerve and muscle functioning. It is involved in the utilization of enzymes. It may be involved in bone calcification. Together with sodium, it maintains the fluid balance in the body and may help the transportation of nutrients into the cells. It is necessary for growth.

A deficiency causes disorientation, listlessness, low blood sugar, nervous irritability, insomnia, oedema, headaches, irregular heartbeat, bone and joint pain, constipation, cramping of muscles, weakness and fatigue. *It is linked to poor sperm motility.* In the embryo, it may cause abnormalities in the kidneys. Deficiency may result from too much sodium chloride (salt), too little fruit and vegetables, some diseases and some medical treatments. Potassium chloride has been used successfully in the treatment of colic and diarrhoea in adults as well as children.[7,8,31,136,34,105,138]

FOETAL DEFICIENCY: Possibly low blood sugar, which will lead to a disinclination to suck, and/or constipation in the newborn.

According to the EVM (Government) Report 2008, Potassium exerts a beneficial effect on hypertension by lowering blood pressure. Potassium is a co-factor of many enzymes and is required for secretion of insulin by the pancreas. (Most) potassium is found in muscle and the skeleton. Also, there are high concentrations in the blood, central nervous system, intestine, liver, lungs and skin. Keeping levels steady may help to prevent diabetes.

Over-high levels of potassium and sodium together in the hair can indicate some interruption of liver and kidney function. We suggest checking for a urine infection when we see this. However, it will also be present if the liver and kidneys are stressed by clearing toxic metals, such as lead. If this is the cause, when the toxic metal has gone from the system, the potassium and sodium levels will settle back to normal. (E.Lodge-Rees 1984)

Good sources: Brewer's yeast, wheat germ, whole grains, vegetables, fruit, nuts., milk, fish, shellfish, beef, chicken, turkey, liver. Potassium is best taken with Vitamin B6, sodium.[105]

CHROMIUM is needed for the regulation of the glucose tolerance factor, in combination with nicotinic acid and some proteins. Glucose is required for every bodily function – it is the body's fuel. Chromium is also necessary for the synthesis of fatty acids and cholesterol.

A deficiency may be linked with heart disease.[22] It can lead to poor sugar handling, which can contribute to reactive hypoglycaemia, causing sugar cravings, which can lead to diabetes and/or obesity and/or alcoholism. Sugar and alcohol consumption will reduce chromium. Deficiency has also been linked to arteriosclerosis and hypertension.[7,8,12,29,34,35132,142,147,148]

Chromium is not easily absorbed, though it is readily removed from the body. Even a small deficiency will be serious.

FOETAL DEFICIENCY: It has been linked to eye abnormalities, and possible later development of diabetes.[149]

Good sources: Brewer's yeast, black pepper, liver, whole grains, wheat germ, vegetables, butter, beer, molasses.[150,151,152,153,154,155,156,157,158,159,160,161,162,163]

COBALT is an essential part of Vitamin B12. There is a possible relationship between cobalt and iodine. It is necessary in B12 for the normal function of all cells, but especially red blood cells, and has been used in the treatment of pernicious anaemia. It activates some enzymes. Deficiency is associated with pernicious anaemia and maybe with slow growth and goitre.[149,105] It can be present where there is a Vitamin B12 deficiency in vegans and vegetarians, or in people eating a diet high in refined carbohydrates, or consuming much alcohol.[7,8,34,23,133]

Cobalt is present in blue paints/colourings and high levels are sometimes seen in people using blue glasses and/or blue patterned plates. We are not sure how much this matters, but usually advise them to change to another type of crockery or glassware in case it is harmful.

Good sources: Although it is said that cobalt can only be taken by humans in the form of Vitamin B12, Underwood points out that organ meats and muscle meats each contain more than can be accounted for as a part of Vitamin B12. Green leafy vegetables are a rich source if the soil they were grown in was rich, but others include meats, brewer's yeast, seafood, nut, fruit and whole grains.

At Foresight we supplement with B12 to enhance levels of cobalt. Cobalt is more effective when taken with copper, iron and zinc.[105]

COPPER aids the development of brain, bones, nerves and connective tissue. It is involved in many enzyme systems, and is essential in the production of RNA. In practice it is the only necessary mineral that goes much above the normal value and has sometimes to be brought down.[105,142,149] This is directly due to copper water pipes, or occasionally to the use of copper-containing algicides in swimming pools. Use of the contraceptive pill (and other hormonal drugs) causes women to retain copper, so this compounds the hazards. Any of these factors may just overwhelm the normal homeostatic mechanisms and give the body more copper than it can cope with. It has to be brought back to normal before the start of the pregnancy or it can prevent conception, or cause miscarriage or premature birth. More anon.

It is however, an essential mineral. Deficiency can cause porous bones, loss of hair, de-myelination, heart damage and anaemia.[7,8,34,62,63]

In the foetus of a number of animals, copper deficiency can result in depressed growth rate, de-pigmentation, anaemia, fine, fragile bones, ataxia, small brain and perinatal mortality. In rats, infertility has been noted. Skeletal and cardiovascular defects, central nervous system disorders, and steely wool hair (failure of melanin formation) have also been reported.[34,105,149]

At this moment in time, 2008, however, copper deficiency is extremely rare, and copper in excess is common and can be toxic.

While copper water pipes are the norm, it is unlikely that copper deficiency will be seen. Copper excess is present in about 1 couple in 10 who come to Foresight. Almost always this can be corrected within four months to a year, although there have been two exceptions in couples where the drinking water was exceptionally high. This can be due to the soil being very acid, or due to corroding pipes that have been soldered together with a lead-containing solder. Heating water in an Ascot (or similar) water heater can add to the copper. If you have been using a water filter for several weeks and see the white contents of the cartridge change to bluish green, there is likely to be a significantly high level of copper and the water should be checked. Many people have excess copper in their bodies due to drinking or bathing in water with a very high level. Where there is a blue-green stain on the surface where a tap has been dripping, this is verdigris and will indicate the water is quite high in copper. We normally suggest that tap water from all sources used, is tested at our laboratory if either partner has a hair level of over 30ppm. Then we can tell if any/which taps are the source. There are now so many different types of filter on the market, the best plan is to go on the internet and look for one that suits the problem. Ie, in some cases a "whole house" filter is needed, in other houses it may just be the shower or a single tap. If there are high levels of lead and copper together, then there may be a corroding pipe. This is usually due to a position where two pieces of copper piping are joined with a lead-containing solder, or the old lead connecting pipe running from the mains to new copper piping at the boundary stop-cock has been left in place. (This is illegal but quite often you find one still there!) You need a plumber to advise you.

However, as people become more aware of this, ABS plastic, and even (very new!) glass pipes are being used. So we may need to be more aware of the symptoms of copper deficiency in the future, as the environment changes for certain people. Meanwhile we have to soldier on. There are stainless steel and fibre-glass tanks available, also ABS plastic pipes, which are hard plastic and are said not to leak dioxins into the water.

I am told (2008) that manufacturers are now making glass water pipes, but as yet I do not know where to obtain them. In due course "further news will follow" on our web site, I hope!

Copper kettles, pans and jewellery are occasionally other sources. There may be external contamination of hair samples by some Henna dyes and rinses, and from swimming-pool water where the pool has been treated with a copper-containing algaecide. For an accurate hair reading the patient should cease the contamination for six weeks before having a hair mineral analysis.

Good sources: Shellfish, Brazil nuts, organ meats, dried legumes, dried stone fruits and green vegetables. It is best taken with cobalt, iron and zinc.[105]

Important things to know:

The top level of copper you need in your drinking water – or bathing water – if you are a woman, is 0.2 ppm. You absorb copper as you drink, and also when you bath. In women, copper can accumulate in the ovaries, where it is a stimulant. You do not need to be short of copper, as the ovary needs it to ovulate, but you do not want to *overload* it, as this can be a cause of cancer, particularly breast or ovarian cancer, or of failure to ovulate. I often see high copper in women struggling with obesity. As it could stimulate the ovaries to produce extra oestrogens it could lie behind some cases of obesity. This needs further study. Many women find their weight rises, without changes in diet or exercise patterns, when they go on the Pill, and after childbirth. This is all linked to the hormones being jiggled around, and high levels of copper may be relevant.[7,8,62,63]

The legal limit for copper in the water was set at 3 ppm. This, I suspect, was to avoid any trouble for the water authorities! It is about 15 times what women really need. This all needs urgently to be studied and the limit to be revised. We suggest changes if the level is over 0.2ppm.

As we said earlier, excessive levels of copper may be embryo-toxic or teratogenic (they can make the baby ill, cause a malformation or damage the brain). They are known to produce behavioural symptoms, such as uncontrollable rages and are linked with pre-eclampic toxaemia in the mother. Copper levels rise naturally during pregnancy, so if a woman conceives with a raised level she is at risk of overloading her body. This can lead to a premature birth. The ratio of copper to zinc in the blood is normally 1:14-17.[7,8,164] Professor Bert Vallee, working with small rodents, found that in the third trimester of pregnancy the zinc was transferred into the placenta at an increasing rate, and therefore the ratio of copper to zinc increased in the circulating blood. Once the copper had risen to a certain level in relation to the zinc, then this stimulated the brain, and the phenomenon of birth started to take place.[161,162,163,164,165,166,167,168]

Over the last 30 years we have confirmed that the level of copper rises in the hair as the pregnancy progresses. An "old wives tale" is that raspberry leaf tea will bring on labour if the baby is overdue. Raspberry leaf tea contains a lot of copper. (Old wives often knew a thing or two!) Another theory is to scrub and then suck a copper coin. Either/both are certainly worth a try before resorting to injections of hormones, pessaries, or having "the waters" artificially broken.

Many girls with a high copper level and a history of infertility come to us. As we increase the levels of zinc, manganese and selenium, the copper level tends to normalise. However, we do advise testing the tap water. Changing the pipes does sound a bit drastic, but believe me; anything is better than risking a very premature birth.

High copper levels in the woman can lead to postpartum depression, and have been linked to premature birth in a number of animal studies. Raised levels are associated with low levels of manganese and zinc, deficiencies of which are known to cause birth defects.[7,8,24,112] Foresight recommends a hair reading of no more than 18—24 ppm to start a pregnancy.[12,29,34,35,36,37,129149164,169,170,171,172,173,174,175,176]

Copper is a brain stimulant (Pfeiffer, Pfeiffer and la Mola, Pfeiffer and Hoffer). It can lead to feelings of euphoria, and heightened emotions of all descriptions. Anybody reading this who has ever given birth will know we are all flying high for the first few hours after birth – this must be one of the reasons why a home birth must be such a blissful experience – for the baby as well, I would guess. Also, this was why the baby being taken to cry its little heart out at the far end of a long hospital corridor, (as was the case 50 years ago), was such agony.

However, in the laboratories, what happens with the little rodents, (who are so much more in touch with their deepest wisdom than we are,) is they eat the placentas where all the zinc has been stored, and within 96 hours of birth, their copper/zinc levels are all back to normal balance. Evidently, nature reckons about 4 days of being high as a kite is enough to make sure of the mother-baby bonding, and that the long-term relationship is ensured.

It is interesting that the Red Indian culture allows the mother to spend 19 days in her own tepe, being waited on by female relatives, as a recovery/milk stabilising/baby bonding period.

188

I feel we could learn a lot from all of this. I think all new mothers would benefit enormously from rebalancing of the zinc levels. While we have copper water pipes I do not think this will happen automatically. So I would suggest, unless people are already on a comprehensive Foresight programme, they take at least 60mg zinc a day for 10 days following birth. This also helps to ensure good, satisfying breast-milk, and then the baby sleeps well, which is always a major mercy!

Post-partum depression is total exhaustion plus excess copper chasing much needed zinc/manganese out of the system. Rat mothers who are short of zinc or manganese, desert the scene, and go down to the far corner of the cage and roll up in a ball. They do not want to feed their pups, clean them up, or retrieve them if they fall out of the nest. If nobody intervenes, the pups are left to die. Presumably no lactation occurs.

Changes in "fashion" and "culture" are much more lead by environmental factors impinging on brain biochemistry, than by philosophers, politicians, writers or whoever. If the zinc galvanised plumbing on which we won the war had been left in place – what a different world we would be living in! *Think on*, all you young ones!

IODINE is necessary for the formation of thyroxin and triodothyronine, hormones produced by the thyroid. Thyroxin is necessary for growth, mental and physical development and the maintenance of health. Most people are aware that too little iodine can cause goitres, but a deficiency is also associated with fatigue, lethargy, susceptibility to cold, loss of interest in sex, slow development of the sex organs, anorexia, slow pulse, low blood pressure, rapid weight gain, high blood cholesterol, death from heart disease and cancer of the thyroid.

Deficiency in the pregnancy can result in cretinism in children, a congenital disease with mental and physical retardation. However, if iodine is given soon after birth, many of the symptoms are reversible.[34,105,137,177]

Good sources include water, iodised salt, watercress, onions, kelp, shellfish, and mushrooms and dark leafy vegetables if they are grown on soil rich in iodine.

Too much iodine can also have serious consequences for health.[105,149]

IRON is needed to make haemoglobin, the substance in the red blood cells, which carries oxygen in the blood. It also aids resistance to infection. It helps supply oxygen to the muscles. It helps in protein digestion and also in respiratory function.

Need in pregnancy increases because the number of red blood cells increases by 30 per cent. Since it is thought that most women do not have a large enough store before pregnancy, many women are given supplements. This can be quite unsatisfactory if other nutrients are not given as well, since iron is not absorbed well without Vitamin C and needs to work with other vitamins and minerals. Also, iron given alone can cause loss of other essential minerals, such as zinc, manganese, chromium, selenium and cobalt.

It is quite common for pregnant women to be "diagnosed" as short of iron on the strength of a blood test, when this may not be the case. In early pregnancy, women are often very thirsty, and drink a lot of water. The blood is then quite diluted for a short while. Then the water is taken into the placenta and used to make "the waters" (amniotic fluid). Then the blood will return to normal.

The huge doses of NHS iron (200mg or 150mg of ferrous sulphate) usually make women feel sick and make them horrendously constipated (which is hugely uncomfortable and difficult to manage in pregnancy). Ferrous sulphate is the least absorbable form of iron in any case. However, in 2008 NHS practices are being reviewed by the EVM and smaller doses of iron are being suggested. Possibly in the region of 60mg. This is better, but still too high.

We find about half the people who come to us prior to pregnancy have some shortage of iron. We use our own tablets giving 7mg or 9mg iron amino acid chelate. Thus we can give 7mg, 9mg, 14mg, 16mg or 18mg, according to what they need, and one of these doses will achieve adequate iron levels, without the side effects.

Shortage of iron can lead to weakness, excessive fatigue, depression, headache, pallor, lack of appetite, mental confusion and poor memory. Iron-deficient people will absorb two to three times more lead than non-deficient people. Deficiency can occur in women due to losses during menstruation. Deficiency is not quite so common in men, but it does occur. Also it is often present in children, particularly if they are eating a diet which includes white flour and white sugar.

In the foetus, severe iron deficiency can cause eye defects, slow growth, bone defects, brain defects and neonatal mortality.[105,135,136,178,34,137,180,7,8]

Blood donors of both sexes are at risk of iron deficiency, so giving blood when you are planning a pregnancy should be avoided.

The usual test for iron is using blood. However, since the body will draw on its stores from the tissues and bone to maintain the amount circulating in the body, blood is not the best way of checking levels, so we prefer to use hair samples.

Good sources: Organ meats, kelp, brewer's yeast, molasses, wheat germ, beans, nuts, dried fruit, poultry, fish, almonds, parsley, egg yolk, lean meats, whole grains, vegetables. The iron of egg yolk is poorly absorbed unless taken with a food containing Vitamin C. Thus, a glass of fresh orange juice with an egg is a good source of iron.[105]

MANGANESE is needed for numerous enzyme reactions, bone growth and development, lipid metabolism, and nerve function. It is necessary in the formation of thyroxin (see iodine) and in blood clotting. It has been found to contribute to a mother's maternal instincts and love, through its role in certain enzymes. A deficiency has been found to cause epilepsy, depression and schizophrenia.[179]

Manganese is sometimes very high, often in combination with a highish lead. Usually this will be from scraping down paint..... the powers-that-be made lead in paint illegal in the 1960s, and replaced it with manganese. This was a Good Thing, as they say in "1066 and All That". BUT older houses stayed full of lead paint, of course, and evidently it is still not yet all scraped off nationwide! Therefore, we quite often see high levels of lead and manganese together in the hair of DIY enthusiasts! Manganese is not a toxic metal, but I am never too happy about something being wildly out of the average range, so I would always wear a mask and rubber gloves when you scrape off, whatever you are uncovering!

Nonetheless, deficiency is the more serious hazard, and more usual.

Although its function in reproduction is not understood, there is no doubt that a deficiency can affect foetal development. In a study of hair levels of manganese, babies with congenital malformations had significantly lower levels of manganese than babies without malformation. (Saner 1985) There were also similarly significant differences in the mineral levels of the mother's hair.[36,149,180]

In rats it has been shown that in the least severe stage of deficiency, there is an increase in the number of offspring born with ataxia. In the second, more serious stage, the young are born dead or die shortly after birth, while in the third, most serious stage, the animal will not mate, and sterility results. This is also seen in hens. In the male rat and rabbit with severe deficiency there is sterility, and also absence of sex drive, in association with degeneration of the seminal tubes and lack of spermatozoa. In the young there may be faulty cartilage and bone matrix formation and heart and neural function problems. Animals from mothers who are deficient show difficulty with behavioural tasks.
8,149,34, 36,180, 181,182,183, 184,185,186, 187,188,189, 190,191,192, 193,194,195, 196,197

FOETAL DEFICIENCY: Malformation of the inner ear (impaired hearing), impaired balance, ataxia, bone malformation, lack of co-ordination, head retraction, and, tremor, lack of righting reflex, epilepsy.

It was also noted by Pfeiffer[7,8], and by Oberleas and Caldwell[180], that lack of manganese could lead to rejection of the baby by the mother. This is too often overlooked. It has major bearing on post partum depression. It needs to be remembered that *organophosphate pesticides* can inhibit the uptake of manganese by the blood, due to their inhibition of function of the choline-containing enzymes which are necessary for the transfer of manganese from the gut to the blood. It is therefore *particularly important* to avoid these noxious chemicals during pregnancy and at around the time of birth.

Unfortunately a lot of shop–bought cut flowers are rather heavily treated with bug-killers. We are trying to encourage people to grow their own, also florists to stock those that are organically grown. Beware of you and the baby being surrounded by commercially grown floral tributes, however lovingly presented!

Try and raise awareness of the dangers of pesticides. As new parents, you are particularly likely to be getting together a new home with new carpets, furnishings and perhaps even bedding (see chapter on pesticides). It is possible to get these chemical-free from places such as Healthy House, Green Fibres and others. People need to know this. Other manufacturers need to be informed so that organic becomes the norm.

Manganese is the only trace element that carries oxygen to the mitochondria of the brain cell. The mitochondria is the small inner part of the cell that organises how it works. Without oxygen this does not function properly. It seems likely that the widespread use of OPs on our food (as well as aluminium contamination) is at least partially responsible for the huge rise in cases of Alzheimer's disease. This does need further research urgently. Meanwhile, those of us who *think* buy organic food!

Good sources: Nuts, whole grains, seeds, leafy green vegetables, brewer's yeast, egg, liver, parsley, thyme, cloves, ginger, tea.

It is best taken with Vitamins B1, E, calcium, phosphorus and choline.[105]

NICKEL is found in high concentrations in DNA and RNA and in all the body's tissues and fluids. Most of the work on it has been focused on animals. It is needed for the action in the enzyme urease. In studies, deficiencies have been linked with reproductive failures, early infant deaths, and growth problems. In the rat, it is associated with the metabolism of copper and manganese. It may have a role in hormonal control and as an enzyme co-factor. High levels are found in the blood of patients who have suffered heart attacks. It is thought that the damaged heart muscles release the nickel. Low levels are decreased in those with cirrhosis of the liver or chronic uremia. Deficiency is found to have a negative influence on growth and life expectancy and to impair iron metabolism.[7,8,149198,199,200,202]

FOETAL DEFICIENCY: (animal studies) Heart defects, kidney defects, liver defects, neonatal death. (Nielson, Anke) EVM (Government) papers say deficiency is associated with reduced growth, impaired reproductive function and reduced haematopoiesis. As lambs and piglets with nickel deficiency were seen to die early, it may be associated with cot death.

Good sources include organ meats, dry beans, lentils, nuts, buckwheat, grains and vegetables and kelp supplements.

Nickel jewellery is occasionally found to cause dermatitis.

PHOSPHORUS is the second most abundant mineral in the body, being found in every cell. As it functions with calcium, both being the main constituents of bone, it is important that its balance with calcium is maintained. It plays a part in almost every chemical reaction in the body, in the utilisation of carbohydrates, proteins and fats, in muscle and nerve function, digestion, kidney function, and proper skeletal growth. It is found in important substances called phospholipids, which break up and transport fats and fatty acids. Among their many functions is to regulate the promotion of the secretion of glandular hormones.

Deficiency is rare, since it is found in artificial fertilisers. It is also a common ingredient in many food additives and soft drinks. The right way to ensure balancing it with calcium and other minerals is to obtain it from the whole foods.[7,8,105,137]

Good sources: Brewer's yeast, whole grains, bread, cereals, meat, fish, poultry, eggs, seeds, nuts.

Phosphorus is best absorbed when it is eaten as part of food containing Vitamins A, D, essential fatty acids, calcium, iron, manganese and protein.[105]

SELENIUM, like Vitamin E, with which it is associated in some functions, is a powerful anti-oxidant which helps to prevent chromosomal damage in tissue culture. Such damage is associated with birth defects and cancers. It is a vital part of an important enzyme which helps the body to fight infections. In animals and chickens, deficiencies are associated with slow growth, cataracts, infertility, loss of hair and feathers, degeneration, nutritional muscular dystrophy, swelling and haemorrhages, pancreatic atrophy, and liver necrosis.

Also seen are increased sensitivity to inhaled allergens, linked to asthma and rhinitis. It is also linked with muscle weakness. In human cell culture it is required for growth, so it will be necessary for normal growth. Selenium will combine with toxic metals such as cadmium to remove them from the body, so it is useful for detoxifying. It may be important in preventing cot deaths. In the USA in the 1970s about a quarter of the babies who died each year were found to be deficient in selenium and/or Vitamin E. Most of them were bottle-fed.[7,8,149] Fluoride is known to be antagonistic to Selenium. The EVM Report states that there are beneficial effects of selenium intake on AIDS symptoms, male fertility, skin disorders, anxiety and asthma.[201,203,204]

DOWN'S SYNDROME.

In very recent experiments in USA cells were grown in vitro (in a test -tube). When the medium they were grown in was kept short of selenium, they were affected in a characteristic way. The relevant chromosome split, making the Trisomy 21 phenomena that is found in the cells of those suffering from Down's Syndrome.

When I heard of this experiment I took from my files the hair analyses of the youngest three Down's syndrome children I had tested, (Ages 11 months to 2½ years). All three had no measurable selenium in the hair. I then looked at the hair analyses of three mothers who had previously given birth to Down's Syndrome babies. Two had almost no measurable selenium; the third had a low level of selenium, but her child was by then 7 years old, so she had possibly had time to make up some of the deficiency.

Another finding we seem to make quite consistently with the Down's Syndrome children when tiny is that they have a high level of toxic metals. This is usually lead, cadmium or aluminium, but I have seen one over-high copper. Any of these metals, if way out of line, could use up the selenium, as the body uses selenium to clear the toxic metals.

I have heard of three half-Chinese Merseyside children with Down's Syndrome whose Chinese fathers all came from a part of China where the soil is lacking in selenium. The mothers in each case were English.

This evidence is anecdotal, but all points to the involvement of selenium deficiency compounded/caused by a high level of toxic metal in the body.

American research has linked low selenium in the mother with increased risk of chromosomal damage, which can lead to not only Down's syndrome, but also Patou's syndrome or Edward's syndrome in the baby. For this reason we are meticulous in obtaining an optimum level of selenium prior to conception, especially in our older mothers. As fluoride is antagonistic to selenium, we also suggest using fluoride-free toothpaste, and not drinking the tap water if it has been fluoridated. Adequate selenium levels have been found to be essential to sperm development.[201,203,204]

Anti-dandruff selenium-containing shampoos however, if used in the bath, or more often than the makers recommend, can produce an excess of selenium in the body which can drive down other needed minerals. For this reason they should be used with caution. They are also liable to confuse the hair analysis, so we often have to reject the findings and ask for another sample in eight weeks time, when the hair has grown sufficiently to give us an uncontaminated sample. This can be very frustrating to keen prospective parents!

The upside of this is that a footbath with a selenium shampoo in it can help to raise the levels if they are low in the hair. (But do not use on the hair as this will confuse the analysis!) It is possible that some Xerox copying machines can also produce selenium in the atmosphere.

Good sources: Butter, smoked herring, wheat germ, brazil nuts, brewer's yeast, whole grains, garlic, fish offal, eggs, cereals and liver. For the baby, human milk is an excellent source.

Selenium is most effective when taken with Vitamin E.[105]

SILICON is critical in the formation of connective tissues, bones, the placenta, arteries and skin, keeping it impermeable. It has been found to be essential for growth and skeletal development in rats and chickens.[34,149]

Good sources: whole grains, wholemeal bread, alfalfa, vegetables (especially the skins), pectin and hard water.

VANADIUM is present in most tissues in the body and is rapidly excreted into urine. It is thought to exert some influence on lipid metabolism by inhibiting cholesterol formation. It is part of the natural circulatory regulation system. Deficiency in animals results in impaired bone development, reduced growth, and disturbance of blood metabolism, decreased reproduction and increased perinatal mortality, and reduced fertility in subsequent generations.[149,199]

Good sources: Buckwheat, parsley, eggs, sunflower seed oil, olive oil, olives, rice, green beans, vegetables.

ZINC is needed for the health and maintenance of hormone levels, bones, muscles, sperm and ova, also eyes, organs, and teeth.[7,8,37,112, 133,136,134, 149,164,173, 175] It is important in healing. It is needed for the functioning of at least 200 enzymes. It is an important component of semen.[7,8] It is necessary to stabilise RNA. It is needed in Vitamin A metabolism.[174,175] It is essential for brain development and function.[149,142,173, 35,7,8, 34,180, 129,172] Caldwell and Oberleas have shown in rats that 'even a mild zinc deficiency has a potential influence on behaviour, despite an apparently adequate protein level in the diet.'[170]

In the male, zinc can increase the size of the penis and testes in growing boys. It also increases sperm motility and helps to prevent impotence.[7,8] Zinc deficient sperm are unable to penetrate the ova.

Lack of zinc is associated with loss of the senses of taste and smell, both of which affect appetite. This can be a major contributing cause of anorexia, also "food fighting" in toddlers. Probably a wise strategy of nature's to prevent the child eating food for which the digestive tract did not have the required enzymes. Each enzyme needs a co-factor to "make it work", and many different enzymes need zinc (I believe it is over 200). The intestine is lined with alkaline phosphatase which is a zinc dependant enzyme. It is not a good idea to try and force children to eat – it is upsetting for both parties and causes tension at mealtimes, which prolongs the problem. It is better to give them zinc and B-complex vitamins, and let the natural appetite return. Ziman drops, (zinc, manganese and B6) selenium and multivitamin drops can help here! (Available from the Foresight Resource Centre).

In animals who have lacked zinc in the womb, high rates of miscarriage (resorption), and, in the surviving babies, eye problems, brain malformation, cleft palate, cleft lip, club feet, stillbirth and urinary-genital abnormalities have been found. Low levels in maternal rats have been associated with learning problems and behavioural problems in their offspring (ie they cannot find their way out of mazes, and become aggressive and panicky). With all the concern about a general weakening of the immune system, it is worrying to note that in an experiment with mice, damage occurred to the immune system of offspring whose mothers were zinc deficient. The damage persisted even when supplements of zinc were given.[34,37,149, 164, 170,171, 172,173, 175,180]

Low zinc status in the female rat can result in lack of ovulation and menstruation. In humans it is a factor in infertility, and low birth weight.[7,8,176] Low plasma levels of zinc in mid-pregnancy have been associated with more complications at delivery and a high incidence of malformations.[120,205,206]

Deficiency also inhibits Vitamin A metabolism.[174,175] Due to this there is inhibition of the immune system, and children will suffer more allergies and more infections, and infections will be more serious. Deficiencies have been found in children with learning disabilities, especially dyslexia and hyperactivity.[62,63,169] Low levels were found in the hair of children suffering from anorexia, poor growth and hypogeusia (loss of taste).[1,2,7,8, 12,37, 62,63,105, 110,146,170, 171,172,173, 205,207] We always see low levels of zinc and manganese in children suffering from autism. The condition improves as these are corrected. The response varies, but in most cases, it is well worth the effort involved.

The EVM Report stated: Zinc is an essential constituent of more than 200 metalo-enzymes. Zinc deficiency results in poor prenatal development, growth retardation, impaired nerve conduction, and nerve damage, reproductive failure, dermatitis, hair loss, diarrhoea, loss of appetite, loss of taste and smell, anaemia, susceptibility to infections, delayed wound healing and macular degeneration (which will lead to impaired sight.) *NB: Despite the above, no recommendations were given for national testing or supplementation!*

Zinc supplementation will help with lowering excess levels of copper and lead. As mentioned before, these are very commonly seen due to copper plumbing soldered together with a solder containing lead. Although this is now illegal, the joins were never removed from houses where this had been done. So, by now, the pipes have corroded and are releasing both lead and copper into the water.

When these minerals appear together in the hair, (which we see several times a week, or sometimes it is just high copper) we test the water from all over the house. Sometimes it is just the shower - it is useful to know *what* is coming from *where*. We found one high copper was due to a kettle with a copper element. (If it is copper alone it is sometimes from a swimming-pool, due to the copper containing algaecide.) Wherever it is coming from, this needs to be detected and corrected, or it will not be possible to get the zinc level to rise sufficiently. Copper and lead contamination will continually lower it again.

Filters can be obtained and fitted − see useful addresses and also the internet. Pipes can be changed to ABS plastics. Recently I heard that glass pipes are now being produced. The zinc/copper balance is the most important factor in restoring menstruation/ovulation, and also in raising the sperm count to a viable level. I often say to couples *"You don't need a doctor, you need a plumber!"*

If the ovaries have been idle for a long time, however, in order to remind them what they are there for, it is often a good idea to have some reflexology. The combination of nourishment, freedom from toxins, and stimulation is often successful. I have heard that acupuncture can also be helpful. We find most people prefer reflexology, however.

Good sources: Oysters, whole grains, meat, brewer's yeast, wheat germ, fruit, vegetables, nuts, fish, poultry, shellfish. It is best taken with Vitamin A, calcium, copper and phosphorus.[105] Also, manganese and Vitamin B6 (Pfeiffer).

Multi-element studies

Multi-element studies are few. One such study was the the Foresight research conducted at the University of Surrey (1993). This confirmed that the mineral status in the female and male is closely linked to their reproductive ability. Of special importance in relation to problems in conception were calcium, magnesium, potassium, iron, zinc, chromium, manganese and selenium. Raised levels of lead, cadmium, aluminium and possibly mercury inhibited reproductive success. Sperm problems were most notably associated with lower levels of zinc and possibly selenium, and with high levels of lead and cadmium, especially for malformed sperm. Poor motility was linked with low levels of calcium, magnesium and potassium. (Also mobile phone use – more anon.)

In females there were significant differences between those who had had normal births and those showing previous problems related to pregnancy, including infertility, miscarriage, therapeutic terminations, stillbirths, small-for-date or low birth weight and malformations. The data demonstrated that, in general, those having malformed babies or stillbirths showed high levels of toxic metals and low levels of essential elements. Dr Neil Ward found that those women with no previous problems had higher zinc levels than those who had previous problems. (Ward 1993).

In another study, zinc levels were tested in women suffering from post-partum depression, and from a control population. The zinc levels of all those with depression were very significantly less than for the ones who did not suffer depression. This study was conducted by Dr John Nichols, MD, of Guildford, Surrey, but I do not have the reference.

Good zinc levels contribute very significantly to quick and clean healing of birth abrasions of the vagina. They lessen the chances of painful engorgement, and encourage abundant lactation. They also significantly lessen the fatigue due to broken nights, as the baby sleeps better, and they also lessen the chances of cracked nipples and picking up an infection.

Any long term debilitating illness is distressing, especially so when you are contemplating starting a family. Alison's injury had left her with damaged nerves in both arms and neck. How could she cope with a baby? Babies are so demanding and she was very ill.

A Naturopath was consulted who suggested that her mercury fillings were removed, and that she saw a Nutritional Therapist. Although the mercury fillings removal had not made her feel much stronger, she and her husband decided to get on with starting a family.

The Nutritional Therapist who happened to be a Foresight Practitioner, put Alison on to the Foresight Programme, which included a diet which eliminated foods identified through a food intolerance test.

Hair mineral analysis revealed neither of them had any heavy metal toxicity but both husband and wife were generally low in most minerals. It took four hair tests before their mineral levels were good enough for Nim to advise them to go ahead. Alison conceived within a month and was safely delivered of a beautiful baby girl weighing 7lbs 9.5 oz with an Apgar of 9.

"The birth was the most amazing thing. Everything and more than you could expect."

"Advice given by Foresight was extremely professional and very friendly."

Zinc is the king of all the nutrients, in my estimation, but it is not the only one. As you have seen from the above, which is all from bona-fide, scientific research from all over the world, keeping up the levels of nutrients can make the whole difference between a joyful birth, babyhood and childhood, and an anxious, miserable one beset with a whole host of physical and mental problems.

We now have the knowledge, so we can now make the choice.

Onward!

Here are some of our interesting charts/histories and outcomes. Most couples have several charts, but it would take up too much room to put whole histories in this book. So mainly I am showing the initial charts and telling you the eventual outcome.

I have chosen those with particular problems and environmental difficulties.

As you will see, in many cases there would have been a series of tragic outcomes unless we had been able to look at hair analysis – high copper and leads, low zincs, seleniums and manganeses are rife. They would be impossible to detect – and then trace back to their source - any other way.

If this method were used world-wide, what a very different world we could soon be living in.

Herewith some typical – and some less typical – hair charts and some brief histories that go with them:

Record 1

Brief outline: Couple who came to us after 5 years of infertility. They had a high copper and slightly raised lead which is typical of a household where there is a corroding pipe. Zinc was not too bad, so she conceived shortly after starting the programme, as the copper was not quite down as far as we like it, we compensated with a good zinc supplementation programme all through the pregnancy. She had a little boy weighing 8lb, followed 18 months later by his little sister at 8lb 2oz.

Female aged 38, first test.

	Your results	Recommended values	
Calcium:	975.00	400.00	mg/kg
Magnesium:	38.14	40.00	mg/kg
Potassium:	73.80	75.00	mg/kg
Iron:	33.15	38.00	mg/kg
Chromium:	1.64	1.20	mg/kg
Cobalt:	0.32	0.23	mg/kg
Copper:	40.72	22.00	mg/kg
Manganese:	2.62	1.70	mg/kg
Nickel:	1.44	1.10	mg/kg
Selenium:	2.32	2.25	mg/kg
Zinc:	169.40	185.00	mg/kg
		Threshold values	
Aluminium:	1.51	2.00	mg/kg
Cadmium:	0.10	0.12	mg/kg
Mercury:	0.17	0.14	mg/kg
Lead:	2.79	1.40	mg/kg
Molybdenum:	0.22	0.18	mg/kg
Vanadium:	0.14	0.18	mg/kg
Arsenic:	0.15	-	mg/kg
Sodium:	110.77	94.00	mg/kg

Record 2

The next charts are those of a lovely Irishwoman who came to us with a very high copper and low selenium.

Luckily this had made her infertile, as the low selenium would have posed a very real chance of any baby having Down's Syndrome. When she retested, 9 months later, she told us that she was already pregnant but we breathed a sigh of relief as, as you see, the selenium had got back to normal – and the copper had fallen quite a bit. Catholics don't wait, but she had been very lucky!

Copper goes up during a pregnancy, so this was quite a normal level for the circumstances. A few months later a beautiful daughter was born weighing 9lb 9oz.

Female aged 42, first test.

	Your results	Recommended values	
Calcium:	799.00	400.00	mg/kg
Iron:	33.66	38.00	mg/kg
Magnesium:	66.00	40.00	mg/kg
Potassium:	72.11	75.00	mg/kg
Sodium:	80.86	94.00	mg/kg
Chromium:	1.02	1.20	mg/kg
Cobalt:	0.33	0.23	mg/kg
Copper:	47.70	22.00	mg/kg
Manganese:	3.59	1.70	mg/kg
Molybdenum:	0.12	0.18	mg/kg
Nikel:	0.72	1.10	mg/kg
Selenium:	1.49	2.25	mg/kg
Vanadium:	0.15	0.18	mg/kg
Zinc:	165.52	185.00	mg/kg
		Threshold values	
Aluminium:	1.62	2.00	mg/kg
Cadmium:	0.57	0.12	mg/kg
Lead:	1.56	1.40	mg/kg
Mercury:	0.11	0.14	mg/kg

Third test.

	Your results	Recommended values	
Calcium:	647.00	400.00	mg/kg
Iron:	34.49	38.00	mg/kg
Magnesium:	60.07	40.00	mg/kg
Potassium:	69.89	75.00	mg/kg
Sodium:	68.16	94.00	mg/kg
Chromium:	0.91	1.20	mg/kg
Cobalt:	0.26	0.23	mg/kg
Copper:	34.18	22.00	mg/kg

Record 2 *continued*

	Your results	Recommended values	
Manganese:	1.78	1.70	mg/kg
Molybdenum:	0.10	0.18	mg/kg
Nikel:	0.75	1.10	mg/kg
Selenium:	2.27	2.25	mg/kg
Vanadium:	0.14	0.18	mg/kg
Zinc:	165.36	185.00	mg/kg
		Threshold values	
Aluminium:	1.32	2.00	mg/kg
Cadmium:	0.12	0.12	mg/kg
Lead:	1.62	1.40	mg/kg
Mercury:	0.11	0.14	mg/kg

Record 3

This lady had been suffering infertility for 4½ years. She had been through 3 IUIs, and 2 IVFs. During the second IVF an artery was cut during egg retrieval. To aid her recovery she was put on a lot of medical drugs. Her husband smoked 70 cigarettes a week.

As you see, her copper was too high, and her selenium and zinc were frighteningly low. She would never have carried a normal baby with these levels.

Her husband gave up smoking, and she took her Foresight programme, and in due course, along came their little girl, 7lb 10oz and beautiful!

Female aged 42, first test.

	Your results	Recommended values	
Calcium:	1383.00	400.00	mg/kg
Iron:	39.71	38.00	mg/kg
Magnesium:	130.90	40.00	mg/kg
Potassium:	149.70	75.00	mg/kg
Sodium:	1910.80	94.00	mg/kg
Chromium:	0.94	1.20	mg/kg
Cobalt:	0.25	0.23	mg/kg
Copper:	40.03	22.00	mg/kg
Manganese:	1.60	1.70	mg/kg
Molybdenum:	0.07	0.18	mg/kg
Nikel:	1.18	1.10	mg/kg
Selenium:	0.61	2.25	mg/kg
Vanadium:	0.12	0.18	mg/kg
Zinc:	135.00	185.00	mg/kg
		Threshold values	
Aluminium:	1.62	2.00	mg/kg
Cadmium:	0.57	0.12	mg/kg
Lead:	1.56	1.40	mg/kg
Mercury:	0.11	0.14	mg/kg

Second test.

	Your results	Recommended values	
Calcium:	425.00	400.00	mg/kg
Iron:	42.96	38.00	mg/kg
Magnesium:	49.27	40.00	mg/kg
Potassium:	66.75	75.00	mg/kg
Sodium:	74.04	94.00	mg/kg
Chromium:	0.90	1.20	mg/kg
Cobalt:	0.21	0.23	mg/kg
Copper:	28.36	22.00	mg/kg
Manganese:	1.16	1.70	mg/kg
Molybdenum:	0.10	0.18	mg/kg
Nikel:	0.71	1.10	mg/kg
Selenium:	1.82	2.25	mg/kg
Vanadium:	0.12	0.18	mg/kg
Zinc:	162.02	185.00	mg/kg
		Threshold values	
Aluminium:	1.50	2.00	mg/kg
Cadmium:	0.13	0.12	mg/kg
Lead:	1.30	1.40	mg/kg
Mercury:	0.09	0.14	mg/kg

Record 4

One month after this one they conceived.

Couple with plenty of problems! Very low zinc and selenium. They had 2 failed IVFs, 3 failed ICSIs. The husband had only 3% of normal sperm. They followed through with 3 charts. One month after the third chart they conceived and had a little boy, 6lb 11oz.

Female aged 39, first test.

	Your results	Recommended values	
Calcium:	1096.00	400.00	mg/kg
Iron:	37.25	38.00	mg/kg
Magnesium:	79.63	40.00	mg/kg
Potassium:	69.20	75.00	mg/kg
Sodium:	72.75	94.00	mg/kg
Chromium:	1.31	1.20	mg/kg
Cobalt:	0.22	0.23	mg/kg
Copper:	21.45	22.00	mg/kg
Manganese:	1.56	1.70	mg/kg
Molybdenum:	0.13	0.18	mg/kg
Nikel:	2.13	1.10	mg/kg
Selenium:	1.96	2.25	mg/kg
Vanadium:	0.12	0.18	mg/kg
Zinc:	152.93	185.00	mg/kg

Record 4 *continued*

	Your results	Recommended values	
		Threshold values	
Aluminium:	1.26	2.00	mg/kg
Cadmium:	0.16	0.12	mg/kg
Lead:	1.84	1.40	mg/kg
Mercury:	0.21	0.14	mg/kg

Third test (female)

	Your results	Recommended values	
Calcium:	400.00	400.00	mg/kg
Iron:	38.91	38.00	mg/kg
Magnesium:	45.83	40.00	mg/kg
Potassium:	69.01	75.00	mg/kg
Sodium:	71.84	94.00	mg/kg
Chromium:	1.69	1.20	mg/kg
Cobalt:	0.22	0.23	mg/kg
Copper:	22.32	22.00	mg/kg
Manganese:	1.42	1.70	mg/kg
Molybdenum:	0.15	0.18	mg/kg
Nikel:	1.48	1.10	mg/kg
Selenium:	1.67	2.25	mg/kg
Vanadium:	0.15	0.18	mg/kg
Zinc:	169.28	185.00	mg/kg
		Threshold values	
Aluminium:	1.43	2.00	mg/kg
Cadmium:	0.12	0.12	mg/kg
Lead:	2.39	1.40	mg/kg
Mercury:	0.15	0.14	mg/kg

Male aged 41, first test.

	Your results	Recommended values	
Calcium:	400.00	400.00	mg/kg
Iron:	38.91	38.00	mg/kg
Magnesium:	45.83	40.00	mg/kg
Potassium:	69.01	75.00	mg/kg
Sodium:	71.84	94.00	mg/kg
Chromium:	1.69	1.20	mg/kg
Cobalt:	0.22	0.23	mg/kg
Copper:	22.32	22.00	mg/kg
Manganese:	1.42	1.70	mg/kg
Molybdenum:	0.15	0.18	mg/kg
Nikel:	1.48	1.10	mg/kg
Selenium:	1.67	2.25	mg/kg

Record 4 *continued*

	Your results	Recommended values	
Vanadium:	0.15	0.18	mg/kg
Zinc:	169.28	185.00	mg/kg
		Threshold values	
Aluminium:	1.43	2.00	mg/kg
Cadmium:	0.12	0.12	mg/kg
Lead:	2.39	1.40	mg/kg
Mercury:	0.15	0.14	mg/kg

Third test (male)

	Your results	Recommended values	
Calcium:	494.00	400.00	mg/kg
Iron:	40.39	38.00	mg/kg
Magnesium:	57.80	40.00	mg/kg
Potassium:	72.69	75.00	mg/kg
Sodium:	87.36	94.00	mg/kg
Chromium:	1.09	1.20	mg/kg
Cobalt:	0.20	0.23	mg/kg
Copper:	23.06	22.00	mg/kg
Manganese:	1.41	1.70	mg/kg
Molybdenum:	0.17	0.18	mg/kg
Nikel:	1.21	1.10	mg/kg
Selenium:	4.37	2.25	mg/kg
Vanadium:	0.14	0.18	mg/kg
Zinc:	185.00	185.00	mg/kg
		Threshold values	
Aluminium:	1.26	2.00	mg/kg
Cadmium:	0.09	0.12	mg/kg
Lead:	1.39	1.40	mg/kg
Mercury:	0.11	0.14	mg/kg

Record 5

This couple came to us after a failed IVF. The infertility may well have been due to a raised copper level in the first place. These could have come from former use of the contraceptive pill, used where the tap water was high in copper from the piping. The pill causes women to retain copper. It is unfortunate that this danger is not more widely acknowledged. The legal limit for copper in the water is 3ppm. In fact, women will start to accumulate it at higher than 0.2ppm, sometimes even when not on the pill.

With this in mind, it is really important that hair analyses are done before they are put on to the drugs used for IVF. Hormonal drugs are liable to send it even higher. This will make failure to implant or a very early miscarriage inevitable.

However, in this case, we worked away to bring the copper down, and in 2003 a further IVF resulted in twin boys!

Record 4 *continued*

Female aged 40, first test.

	Your results	Recommended values	
Calcium:	588.00	400.00	mg/kg
Iron:	50.34	38.00	mg/kg
Magnesium:	71.37	40.00	mg/kg
Potassium:	76.19	75.00	mg/kg
Sodium:	78.54	94.00	mg/kg
Chromium:	1.46	1.20	mg/kg
Cobalt:	0.35	0.23	mg/kg
Copper:	122.20	22.00	mg/kg
Manganese:	1.87	1.70	mg/kg
Molybdenum:	0.24	0.18	mg/kg
Nikel:	0.93	1.10	mg/kg
Selenium:	2.03	2.25	mg/kg
Vanadium:	0.21	0.18	mg/kg
Zinc:	196.71	185.00	mg/kg
		Threshold values	
Aluminium:	2.06	2.00	mg/kg
Cadmium:	0.11	0.12	mg/kg
Lead:	2.83	1.40	mg/kg
Mercury:	0.17	0.14	mg/kg

Record 6

Mrs MC came to us having one little son aged 3 years, but having the agonising history of 3 lost babies prior to his birth, and one miscarriage and a stillbirth since he was born. They were a couple with great courage, and they did not want him to be an only child.

They both had very low zinc, which would have explained the tragic outcomes – but then the stress and demands on her body of six pregnancies and five bereavements could also have explained the low zinc.

We also called in Roy Riggs to check out the house and re-arrange the furniture as necessary. 17 months after they first contacted us, her second little boy was born – 8lb 1oz and extremely photogenic! His brother was delighted he had a little brother to play with!

Female aged 31, first test.

	Your results	Recommended values	
Calcium:	410.00	400.00	mg/kg
Magnesium:	39.10	40.00	mg/kg
Potassium:	70.87	75.00	mg/kg
Iron:	71.00	38.00	mg/kg
Chromium:	1.14	1.20	mg/kg
Cobalt:	0.19	0.23	mg/kg

Record 6 *continued*

	Your results	Recommended values	
Copper:	22.37	22.00	mg/kg
Manganese:	1.68	1.70	mg/kg
Nikel:	0.70	1.10	mg/kg
Selenium:	2.12	2.25	mg/kg
Zinc:	154.88	185.00	mg/kg
		Threshold values	
Aluminium:	1.78	2.00	mg/kg
Cadmium:	0.08	0.12	mg/kg
Mercury:	0.16	0.14	mg/kg
Lead:	1.91	1.40	mg/kg
Molybdenum:	0.18	0.18	mg/kg
Vanadium:	0.15	0.18	mg/kg
Arsenic:	0.02	-	mg/kg
Sodium:	80.80	94.00	mg/kg

Male aged 36, first test.

	Your results	Recommended values	
Calcium:	323.00	400.00	mg/kg
Magnesium:	35.05	40.00	mg/kg
Potassium:	91.34	75.00	mg/kg
Iron:	68.60	38.00	mg/kg
Chromium:	1.38	1.20	mg/kg
Cobalt:	0.22	0.23	mg/kg
Copper:	21.27	22.00	mg/kg
Manganese:	1.62	1.70	mg/kg
Nikel:	0.69	1.10	mg/kg
Selenium:	1.90	2.25	mg/kg
Zinc:	145.67	185.00	mg/kg
		Threshold values	
Aluminium:	1.54	2.00	mg/kg
Cadmium:	0.07	0.12	mg/kg
Mercury:	0.14	0.14	mg/kg
Lead:	1.52	1.40	mg/kg
Molybdenum:	0.17	0.18	mg/kg
Vanadium:	0.15	0.18	mg/kg
Arsenic:	0.03	-	mg/kg
Sodium:	135.65	94.00	mg/kg

Record 7

Mrs RA came to us in 2006 having been trying for a baby for just over a year. Her chart was excellent, but her husband's chart was very low in zinc, and slightly low in a few other things, despite his having been assured his sperm count was normal and his motility was good. (Do male doctors not like to be the bearer of bad news, I often wonder?)

So many women seem to have had all sorts of intervention, sometimes including surgery and even more traumatic psychological probing, before we pick up the low zinc, alcohol or the mobile phone use by the husband.

Luckily, it was only a low zinc level, and a urinary infection (as indicated by the high sodium/potassium), both quite easily detected and dealt with, and 15 months later their little girl was born, 7lb 13oz!

Female aged 30, first test.

	Your results	Recommended values	
Calcium:	896.00	400.00	mg/kg
Magnesium:	48.32	40.00	mg/kg
Potassium:	82.29	75.00	mg/kg
Iron:	51.74	38.00	mg/kg
Chromium:	1.15	1.20	mg/kg
Cobalt:	0.26	0.23	mg/kg
Copper:	22.31	22.00	mg/kg
Manganese:	1.53	1.70	mg/kg
Nikel:	1.26	1.10	mg/kg
Selenium:	2.21	2.25	mg/kg
Zinc:	183.38	185.00	mg/kg
		Threshold values	
Aluminium:	2.53	2.00	mg/kg
Cadmium:	0.13	0.12	mg/kg
Mercury:	0.06	0.14	mg/kg
Lead:	1.38	1.40	mg/kg
Molybdenum:	0.17	0.18	mg/kg
Vanadium:	0.22	0.18	mg/kg
Arsenic:	0.03	-	mg/kg
Sodium:	102.34	94.00	mg/kg

An excellent chart at the outset.

Male aged 35, first test.

	Your results	Recommended values	
Calcium:	381.00	400.00	mg/kg
Magnesium:	39.50	40.00	mg/kg
Potassium:	179.20	75.00	mg/kg
Iron:	36.63	38.00	mg/kg
Chromium:	2.15	1.20	mg/kg
Cobalt:	0.22	0.23	mg/kg
Copper:	20.08	22.00	mg/kg
Manganese:	1.65	1.70	mg/kg
Nikel:	0.08	1.10	mg/kg
Selenium:	2.45	2.25	mg/kg
Zinc:	147.31	185.00	mg/kg
		Threshold values	
Aluminium:	2.28	2.00	mg/kg
Cadmium:	0.12	0.12	mg/kg
Mercury:	0.08	0.14	mg/kg
Lead:	2.27	1.40	mg/kg
Molybdenum:	0.30	0.18	mg/kg
Vanadium:	0.16	0.18	mg/kg
Arsenic:	0.06	-	mg/kg
Sodium:	301.10	94.00	mg/kg

Record 8

Mrs PT came to us after tragically losing her previous baby at 23 weeks of pregnancy due to fibroids and a spontaneous rupture of the membranes. This was deeply upsetting, especially as she and her husband were both approaching 40 years and had been trying for a family for 6 years.

We tested hair and found her copper and mercury were a little bit raised, but his were much more significantly so. He stopped eating tuna, stopped alcohol, and they both went on the programme. They tested the tap water and found the overnight standing water was 1.800ppm and the en-suite shower water was 1.467ppm. Although the legal limit is 3ppm, we find that people (women in particular) usually start to accumulate it if the level is over 0.2ppm. By which token, probably about 10% of houses in this country have levels of copper that are too high for women's health and fertility.

However, they did everything we suggested and, after 6 months, Mrs PT found she was pregnant and in due course along came a big, bonny, bouncing boy, 8lb 12oz!

Record 8 *continued*

Female aged 39, first test.

	Your results	Recommended values	
Calcium:	381.00	400.00	mg/kg
Magnesium:	39.50	40.00	mg/kg
Potassium:	179.20	75.00	mg/kg
Iron:	36.63	38.00	mg/kg
Chromium:	2.15	1.20	mg/kg
Cobalt:	0.22	0.23	mg/kg
Copper:	20.08	22.00	mg/kg
Manganese:	1.65	1.70	mg/kg
Nikel:	0.08	1.10	mg/kg
Selenium:	2.45	2.25	mg/kg
Zinc:	147.31	185.00	mg/kg
		Threshold values	
Aluminium:	2.28	2.00	mg/kg
Cadmium:	0.12	0.12	mg/kg
Mercury:	0.08	0.14	mg/kg
Lead:	2.27	1.40	mg/kg
Molybdenum:	0.30	0.18	mg/kg
Vanadium:	0.16	0.18	mg/kg
Sodium:	301.10	94.00	mg/kg

Male aged 39, first test.

	Your results	Recommended values	
Calcium:	327.00	400.00	mg/kg
Magnesium:	32.70	40.00	mg/kg
Potassium:	76.67	75.00	mg/kg
Iron:	39.10	38.00	mg/kg
Chromium:	1.59	1.20	mg/kg
Cobalt:	0.16	0.23	mg/kg
Copper:	68.78	22.00	mg/kg
Manganese:	1.20	1.70	mg/kg
Nikel:	0.37	1.10	mg/kg
Selenium:	1.89	2.25	mg/kg
Zinc:	176.00	185.00	mg/kg
		Threshold values	
Aluminium:	1.71	2.00	mg/kg
Cadmium:	0.07	0.12	mg/kg
Mercury:	0.59	0.14	mg/kg
Lead:	1.30	1.40	mg/kg
Molybdenum:	0.00	0.18	mg/kg
Vanadium:	0.00	0.18	mg/kg
Sodium:	90.71	94.00	mg/kg

Record 9

Mrs PK came to us in 2006. She already had 2 children, but after that sadly had suffered 2 miscarriages and a termination for a malformation that was not compatible with life. Her two little daughters were looking forward to a baby and she did not want to disappoint them.

We did hair analysis and there were the usually deficiencies and high copper. Although she has not used the Pill for over 7 years, in the days of copper water pipes a high copper is all too common, and is a contributory cause of so many miscarriages and premature births. Whole lakes of tears must have been shed and so many families denied their happiness, by copper from the water pipes.

As well, as there had been this horrendous malformation, we advised giving up mobile phones and calling in Roy Riggs to check out the house. With everybody's combined efforts, their little son arrived, to everybody's delight, weighing 8lb 9oz!

Female aged 44, first test.

	Your results	Recommended values	
Calcium:	972.00	400.00	mg/kg
Magnesium:	60.18	40.00	mg/kg
Potassium:	68.82	75.00	mg/kg
Iron:	48.78	38.00	mg/kg
Chromium:	1.15	1.20	mg/kg
Cobalt:	0.56	0.23	mg/kg
Copper:	41.60	22.00	mg/kg
Manganese:	2.00	1.70	mg/kg
Nikel:	1.89	1.10	mg/kg
Selenium:	1.69	2.25	mg/kg
Zinc:	162.88	185.00	mg/kg
		Threshold values	
Aluminium:	1.73	2.00	mg/kg
Cadmium:	0.32	0.12	mg/kg
Mercury:	0.12	0.14	mg/kg
Lead:	1.85	1.40	mg/kg
Molybdenum:	0.15	0.18	mg/kg
Vanadium:	0.24	0.18	mg/kg
Arsenic:	0.01	-	mg/kg
Sodium:	75.23	94.00	mg/kg

Record 10

Mrs LD came to us in January 2006. She had no difficulty in conceiving, but unbearably, she had suffered 4 miscarriages.

The first charts showed both partners had very low zinc – also rather low selenium, magnesium and manganese and in Mrs LD's case, low calcium and iron. All bad news.

They supplemented with a will, and things began to improve quite rapidly. Sadly, when they next conceived, they suffered a fifth miscarriage. We called in Roy Riggs to look at the house for electromagnetic pollution – which, with hindsight, we feel we should have suggested earlier. Roy advised them to sleep in a different bedroom, as he found there to be underground streams running under the place where their bed was standing. These can send up electromagnetic currents that can disturb hormone levels, among other things. They also use a "barefoot bedmat" which can go across the end of the bed, and "earth" their bodies as they sleep. They continued with their programme.

14 months later their glorious (very good looking!) little boy was born, 8lb 8oz!

Female aged 28, first test.

	Your results	Recommended values	
Calcium:	406.00	400.00	mg/kg
Magnesium:	33.13	40.00	mg/kg
Potassium:	70.60	75.00	mg/kg
Iron:	43.70	38.00	mg/kg
Chromium:	0.90	1.20	mg/kg
Cobalt:	1.18	0.23	mg/kg
Copper:	20.51	22.00	mg/kg
Manganese:	1.21	1.70	mg/kg
Nikel:	0.58	1.10	mg/kg
Selenium:	1.76	2.25	mg/kg
Zinc:	149.43	185.00	mg/kg
		Threshold values	
Aluminium:	1.20	2.00	mg/kg
Cadmium:	0.12	0.12	mg/kg
Mercury:	0.06	0.14	mg/kg
Lead:	1.25	1.40	mg/kg
Molybdenum:	0.10	0.18	mg/kg
Vanadium:	0.13	0.18	mg/kg
Arsenic:	0.01	-	mg/kg
Sodium:	83.76	94.00	mg/kg

Record 10 *continued*

Male aged 28, first test.

	Your results	Recommended values	
Calcium:	336.00	400.00	mg/kg
Magnesium:	31.60	40.00	mg/kg
Potassium:	95.87	75.00	mg/kg
Iron:	31.67	38.00	mg/kg
Chromium:	0.86	1.20	mg/kg
Cobalt:	0.25	0.23	mg/kg
Copper:	18.18	22.00	mg/kg
Manganese:	1.06	1.70	mg/kg
Nikel:	0.76	1.10	mg/kg
Selenium:	1.66	2.25	mg/kg
Zinc:	146.02	185.00	mg/kg
		Threshold values	
Aluminium:	2.93	2.00	mg/kg
Cadmium:	0.08	0.12	mg/kg
Mercury:	0.06	0.14	mg/kg
Lead:	1.58	1.40	mg/kg
Molybdenum:	0.17	0.18	mg/kg
Vanadium:	0.12	0.18	mg/kg
Arsenic:	0.04	-	mg/kg
Sodium:	114.32	94.00	mg/kg

Female aged 28, second test.

	Your results	Recommended values	
Calcium:	431.00	400.00	mg/kg
Magnesium:	38.37	40.00	mg/kg
Potassium:	73.62	75.00	mg/kg
Iron:	38.90	38.00	mg/kg
Chromium:	1.00	1.20	mg/kg
Cobalt:	0.21	0.23	mg/kg
Copper:	20.55	22.00	mg/kg
Manganese:	1.34	1.70	mg/kg
Nikel:	0.59	1.10	mg/kg
Selenium:	2.42	2.25	mg/kg
Zinc:	172.57	185.00	mg/kg
		Threshold values	
Aluminium:	1.40	2.00	mg/kg
Cadmium:	0.13	0.12	mg/kg
Mercury:	0.08	0.14	mg/kg
Lead:	1.57	1.40	mg/kg
Molybdenum:	0.16	0.18	mg/kg
Vanadium:	0.14	0.18	mg/kg
Arsenic:	0.01	-	mg/kg
Sodium:	89.96	94.00	mg/kg

Record 10 *continued*

Male aged 28, second test.

	Your results	Recommended values	
Calcium:	311.00	400.00	mg/kg
Magnesium:	30.16	40.00	mg/kg
Potassium:	80.67	75.00	mg/kg
Iron:	35.91	38.00	mg/kg
Chromium:	1.14	1.20	mg/kg
Cobalt:	0.23	0.23	mg/kg
Copper:	18.97	22.00	mg/kg
Manganese:	1.26	1.70	mg/kg
Nikel:	0.78	1.10	mg/kg
Selenium:	2.36	2.25	mg/kg
Zinc:	207.96	185.00	mg/kg
		Threshold values	
Aluminium:	3.15	2.00	mg/kg
Cadmium:	0.10	0.12	mg/kg
Mercury:	0.09	0.14	mg/kg
Lead:	2.45	1.40	mg/kg
Molybdenum:	0.28	0.18	mg/kg
Vanadium:	0.16	0.18	mg/kg
Arsenic:	0.03	-	mg/kg
Sodium:	81.13	94.00	mg/kg

Record 11

Mrs GA rang us after getting her first programme and told us that she had no intention of taking all those pills, and was it safe to take the 2 Multivitamin and Mineral tablets?

We explained that as she had been on the Pill for a number of years her copper was very high, and consequently her manganese, selenium and zinc were very low. An over high copper will often cause this. If the minerals had stayed this way, conception would have been very unlikely, and had it occurred, miscarriage would have been very likely. Lack of manganese can cause central nervous system difficulties, deafness and epilepsy in a baby. Lack of selenium carries a Down's Syndrome risk, and lack of zinc can mean a whole list of possible deformities and behavioural problems.

She decided to take the supplements and in 10 months she conceived and by the end of the year had her son, 8lb 6oz, as a very welcome Christmas present. She stayed on the full programme, once convinced, but declined to have any further hair tests! However, within two years a baby sister arrived, weighing 8lb 4oz.

Record 11 *continued*

Female aged 29, first test.

	Your results	Recommended values	
Calcium:	688.00	400.00	mg/kg
Magnesium:	42.96	40.00	mg/kg
Potassium:	70.62	75.00	mg/kg
Iron:	41.37	38.00	mg/kg
Chromium:	1.76	1.20	mg/kg
Cobalt:	0.21	0.23	mg/kg
Copper:	73.90	22.00	mg/kg
Manganese:	1.22	1.70	mg/kg
Nikel:	1.47	1.10	mg/kg
Selenium:	1.50	2.25	mg/kg
Zinc:	169.47	185.00	mg/kg
		Threshold values	
Aluminium:	1.50	2.00	mg/kg
Cadmium:	0.08	0.12	mg/kg
Mercury:	0.10	0.14	mg/kg
Lead:	1.83	1.40	mg/kg
Molybdenum:	0.13	0.18	mg/kg
Vanadium:	0.11	0.18	mg/kg
Sodium:	71.58	94.00	mg/kg

Female, second test.

	Your results	Recommended values	
Calcium:	507.00	400.00	mg/kg
Magnesium:	34.99	40.00	mg/kg
Potassium:	67.80	75.00	mg/kg
Iron:	32.96	38.00	mg/kg
Chromium:	1.10	1.20	mg/kg
Cobalt:	0.17	0.23	mg/kg
Copper:	56.36	22.00	mg/kg
Manganese:	1.08	1.70	mg/kg
Nikel:	1.01	1.10	mg/kg
Selenium:	2.10	2.25	mg/kg
Zinc:	163.59	185.00	mg/kg
		Threshold values	
Aluminium:	1.89	2.00	mg/kg
Cadmium:	0.09	0.12	mg/kg
Mercury:	0.07	0.14	mg/kg
Lead:	1.42	1.40	mg/kg
Molybdenum:	0.11	0.18	mg/kg
Vanadium:	0.13	0.18	mg/kg
Sodium:	106.42	94.00	mg/kg

Record 11 *continued*

Female, third test.

	Your results	Recommended values	
Calcium:	626.00	400.00	mg/kg
Magnesium:	44.83	40.00	mg/kg
Potassium:	72.80	75.00	mg/kg
Iron:	51.06	38.00	mg/kg
Chromium:	1.13	1.20	mg/kg
Cobalt:	0.21	0.23	mg/kg
Copper:	27.69	22.00	mg/kg
Manganese:	1.24	1.70	mg/kg
Nikel:	1.47	1.10	mg/kg
Selenium:	2.34	2.25	mg/kg
Zinc:	180.81	185.00	mg/kg
		Threshold values	
Aluminium:	1.67	2.00	mg/kg
Cadmium:	0.09	0.12	mg/kg
Mercury:	0.09	0.14	mg/kg
Lead:	2.88	1.40	mg/kg
Molybdenum:	0.15	0.18	mg/kg
Vanadium:	0.14	0.18	mg/kg
Sodium:	111.20	94.00	mg/kg

Record 12

A couple in an old house with lead water pipes and paint. She had fibroids, cystitis, asthma and eczema. They had been trying for a baby for six years. Her husband who had migraine and low sperm count (luckily). Once again nature had stepped in to prevent the conception of a lead damaged child. It took over a year to get the lead down, then they conceived and had a little boy.

Female aged 42, first test.

	Your results	Recommended values	
Calcium:	562.00	400.00	mg/kg
Iron:	41.93	38.00	mg/kg
Magnesium:	55.61	40.00	mg/kg
Potassium:	67.90	75.00	mg/kg
Sodium:	67.29	94.00	mg/kg
Chromium:	6.67	1.20	mg/kg
Cobalt:	0.44	0.23	mg/kg
Copper:	36.00	22.00	mg/kg
Manganese:	3.02	1.70	mg/kg
Molybdenum:	0.25	0.18	mg/kg
Nikel:	3.21	1.10	mg/kg
Selenium:	1.73	2.25	mg/kg
Vanadium:	1.02	0.18	mg/kg
Zinc:	161.00	185.00	mg/kg

Record 12 *continued*

	Your results	Recommended values	
		Threshold values	
Aluminium:	3.43	2.00	mg/kg
Cadmium:	0.078	0.12	mg/kg
Lead:	35.64	1.40	mg/kg
Mercury:	0.15	0.14	mg/kg

Male aged 43, first test.

	Your results	Recommended values	
Calcium:	292.00	400.00	mg/kg
Iron:	54.15	38.00	mg/kg
Magnesium:	31.82	40.00	mg/kg
Potassium:	94.55	75.00	mg/kg
Sodium:	117.92	94.00	mg/kg
Chromium:	2.18	1.20	mg/kg
Cobalt:	0.25	0.23	mg/kg
Copper:	20.69	22.00	mg/kg
Manganese:	3.13	1.70	mg/kg
Molybdenum:	0.18	0.18	mg/kg
Nikel:	8.35	1.10	mg/kg
Selenium:	1.84	2.25	mg/kg
Vanadium:	0.21	0.18	mg/kg
Zinc:	165.00	185.00	mg/kg
		Threshold values	
Aluminium:	3.24	2.00	mg/kg
Cadmium:	0.23	0.12	mg/kg
Lead:	33.56	1.40	mg/kg
Mercury:	0.18	0.14	mg/kg

Record 13

Extreme low levels in husband. Note the extremely low zinc, selenium and calcium.

Seven years infertility. Sperm count 30 - 100, abnormal forms 87%. Three failed IUI. One failed IVF. He smoked 20 cigarettes a week and drank 30 units per week. (She drank 15 units per week). She had been on four different fertility drugs. They did not retest and I have not heard that there was ever a baby.

Male aged 39 years, first test.

	Your results	Recommended values	
Calcium:	303.00	400.00	mg/kg
Magnesium:	47.54	40.00	mg/kg
Potassium:	65.81	75.00	mg/kg
Iron:	42.35	38.00	mg/kg
Chromium:	1.61	1.20	mg/kg

Record 13 *continued*

	Your results	Recommended values	
Cobalt:	0.19	0.23	mg/kg
Copper:	18.46	22.00	mg/kg
Manganese:	1.55	1.70	mg/kg
Nikel:	0.60	1.10	mg/kg
Selenium:	1.70	2.25	mg/kg
Zinc:	95.54	185.00	mg/kg
		Threshold values	
Aluminium:	1.40	2.00	mg/kg
Cadmium:	0.07	0.12	mg/kg
Mercury:	0.41	0.14	mg/kg
Lead:	2.46	1.40	mg/kg
Molybdenum:	0.23	0.18	mg/kg
Vanadium:	0.31	0.18	mg/kg
Arsenic:	0.30	-	mg/kg
Sodium:	81.99	94.00	mg/kg

Record 14

Mrs TS came to us after quite a rough ride with 10 years of infertility which has included 5 failed IUIs and 1 failed ICSI. She has been through a lot of being told to "relax" and "not to think too much about it" – what could be more stressful?

We did the two hair analyses. Hers was not too bad, but her husband's showed a very low zinc level, and also low magnesium. The copper, lead, mercury and aluminium were up a little, which could account for that.

A look at the tap water – buying a Boots filter jug – no more tuna fish, no more aluminium deodorant, a hefty programme of supplements, and no alcohol!

Fifteen months later they contacted us again. They had eliminated the toxins from their environment, "cut down" on alcohol (?), but had not taken the supplement programme, although they had been "concentrating on eating a good diet".

This was a bit frustrating for us, but as Mrs TS was now rising 40 years, we were able to persuade them to actually *take* the full programme and eliminate alcohol.

13 months later, along came a beautiful baby girl, weighing 8lb 7oz!

Male aged 39 years, first test.

	Your results	Recommended values	
Calcium:	428.00	400.00	mg/kg
Magnesium:	34.51	40.00	mg/kg
Potassium:	84.44	75.00	mg/kg
Iron:	48.13	38.00	mg/kg
Chromium:	1.17	1.20	mg/kg
Cobalt:	0.33	0.23	mg/kg

Record 14 *continued*

	Your results	Recommended values	
Copper:	28.21	22.00	mg/kg
Manganese:	1.68	1.70	mg/kg
Nikel:	1.19	1.10	mg/kg
Selenium:	2.72	2.25	mg/kg
Zinc:	154.15	185.00	mg/kg
		Threshold values	
Aluminium:	3.72	2.00	mg/kg
Cadmium:	0.13	0.12	mg/kg
Mercury:	0.38	0.14	mg/kg
Lead:	3.22	1.40	mg/kg
Molybdenum:	0.28	0.18	mg/kg
Vanadium:	0.18	0.18	mg/kg
Arsenic:	0.03	-	mg/kg
Sodium:	104.59	94.00	mg/kg

Male aged 43, first test.

	Your results	Recommended values	
Calcium:	380.00	400.00	mg/kg
Magnesium:	40.48	40.00	mg/kg
Potassium:	73.70	75.00	mg/kg
Iron:	34.71	38.00	mg/kg
Chromium:	1.71	1.20	mg/kg
Cobalt:	0.19	0.23	mg/kg
Copper:	25.39	22.00	mg/kg
Manganese:	1.87	1.70	mg/kg
Nikel:	0.61	1.10	mg/kg
Selenium:	2.16	2.25	mg/kg
Zinc:	160.84	185.00	mg/kg
		Threshold values	
Aluminium:	2.16	2.00	mg/kg
Cadmium:	0.09	0.12	mg/kg
Mercury:	0.25	0.14	mg/kg
Lead:	2.44	1.40	mg/kg
Molybdenum:	0.14	0.18	mg/kg
Vanadium:	0.14	0.18	mg/kg
Arsenic:	0.04	-	mg/kg
Sodium:	72.27	94.00	mg/kg

Record 15

Mrs JR came to us in January 2007 having tragically suffered first a miscarriage and then a stillbirth at 7½ months.

We did a hair analysis and found a lead level that was not compatible with a healthy pregnancy, and rather too much cadmium and mercury

Sometimes when one heavy metal such as lead is holding up liver and kidney function, we find some of the others tend to accumulate too. The zinc and selenium are always brought down, as they get used up in clearing out the toxins. Her husband needed to stop smoking to clear the air in the house too.

Four months later, things were all much better, but there was still an obstinate little bit of lead and mercury to part with. We pressed on!

A couple of months later she rang to say she was pregnant and terrified! Partly because of the previous stillbirth, partly because she was 43 years old.

I told her lots of Foresight mums are older than that! We did another hair test, and gave the zinc, manganese and iron that she needed.

Her little boy was born 12 days early, but weighing in at 7lb 1oz, and in very good health. He was breast fed for 8 months. Everybody did well!

Female aged 42, first test.

	Your results	Recommended values	
Calcium:	834.00	400.00	mg/kg
Magnesium:	88.74	40.00	mg/kg
Potassium:	59.52	75.00	mg/kg
Iron:	37.14	38.00	mg/kg
Chromium:	1.10	1.20	mg/kg
Cobalt:	0.22	0.23	mg/kg
Copper:	26.73	22.00	mg/kg
Manganese:	4.01	1.70	mg/kg
Nikel:	0.97	1.10	mg/kg
Selenium:	1.82	2.25	mg/kg
Zinc:	167.11	185.00	mg/kg
		Threshold values	
Aluminium:	1.74	2.00	mg/kg
Cadmium:	0.23	0.12	mg/kg
Mercury:	0.22	0.14	mg/kg
Lead:	8.86	1.40	mg/kg
Molybdenum:	0.00	0.18	mg/kg
Vanadium:	0.00	0.18	mg/kg
Sodium:	94.20	94.00	mg/kg

Beautiful Babies

Female aged 43, second test.

	Your results	Recommended values	
Calcium:	474.00	400.00	mg/kg
Magnesium:	61.09	40.00	mg/kg
Potassium:	89.23	75.00	mg/kg
Iron:	33.61	38.00	mg/kg
Chromium:	0.93	1.20	mg/kg
Cobalt:	0.18	0.23	mg/kg
Copper:	21.39	22.00	mg/kg
Manganese:	1.42	1.70	mg/kg
Nikel:	0.76	1.10	mg/kg
Selenium:	2.62	2.25	mg/kg
Zinc:	178.89	185.00	mg/kg
		Threshold values	
Aluminium:	1.52	2.00	mg/kg
Cadmium:	0.08	0.12	mg/kg
Mercury:	0.23	0.14	mg/kg
Lead:	2.58	1.40	mg/kg
Molybdenum:	0.00	0.18	mg/kg
Vanadium:	0.00	0.18	mg/kg
Sodium:	139.16	94.00	mg/kg

Female aged 43, third test.

	Your results	Recommended values	
Calcium:	875.00	400.00	mg/kg
Magnesium:	71.28	40.00	mg/kg
Potassium:	65.54	75.00	mg/kg
Iron:	33.34	38.00	mg/kg
Chromium:	0.08	1.20	mg/kg
Cobalt:	0.09	0.23	mg/kg
Copper:	21.86	22.00	mg/kg
Manganese:	1.57	1.70	mg/kg
Nikel:	0.70	1.10	mg/kg
Selenium:	2.55	2.25	mg/kg
Zinc:	169.86	185.00	mg/kg
		Threshold values	
Aluminium:	1.46	2.00	mg/kg
Cadmium:	0.08	0.12	mg/kg
Mercury:	0.11	0.14	mg/kg
Lead:	2.24	1.40	mg/kg

Record 16

Some people are adamant that they will only take a limited number of supplements. "I'm not taking all of these, which are the most important?" they ask me.

As you see, this doesn't work very well! Over 13 months of just taking 6 pills, and making very small adjustments to his alcohol intake, the situation has changed very little!

We can't work miracles. All we can do is tell you what you need, based on 30 years of experience. The rest is up to you. In this instance, the husband went on drinking "a reasonable amount", and there was no baby.

Male aged 42 years, first test.

	Your results	Recommended values	
Calcium:	263.00	400.00	mg/kg
Magnesium:	26.14	40.00	mg/kg
Potassium:	77.47	75.00	mg/kg
Iron:	48.96	38.00	mg/kg
Chromium:	1.71	1.20	mg/kg
Cobalt:	0.21	0.23	mg/kg
Copper:	20.60	22.00	mg/kg
Manganese:	2.40	1.70	mg/kg
Nikel:	1.08	1.10	mg/kg
Selenium:	2.22	2.25	mg/kg
Zinc:	89.06	185.00	mg/kg
		Threshold values	
Aluminium:	8.88	2.00	mg/kg
Cadmium:	0.13	0.12	mg/kg
Mercury:	0.17	0.14	mg/kg
Lead:	5.28	1.40	mg/kg
Molybdenum:	0.22	0.18	mg/kg
Vanadium:	0.26	0.18	mg/kg
Sodium:	71.92	94.00	mg/kg

Male aged 43, fourth test, (13 months later)

	Your results	Recommended values	
Calcium:	311.00	400.00	mg/kg
Magnesium:	32.33	40.00	mg/kg
Potassium:	81.82	75.00	mg/kg
Iron:	38.85	38.00	mg/kg
Chromium:	1.87	1.20	mg/kg
Cobalt:	0.16	0.23	mg/kg
Copper:	19.95	22.00	mg/kg
Manganese:	3.44	1.70	mg/kg
Nikel:	1.02	1.10	mg/kg
Selenium:	2.01	2.25	mg/kg

Record 16 *continued*

	Your results	Recommended values	
Zinc:	117.00	185.00	mg/kg
		Threshold values	
Aluminium:	5.56	2.00	mg/kg
Cadmium:	0.17	0.12	mg/kg
Mercury:	0.10	0.14	mg/kg
Lead:	3.46	1.40	mg/kg
Molybdenum:	0.19	0.18	mg/kg
Vanadium:	0.29	0.18	mg/kg
Sodium:	89.67	94.00	mg/kg

Record 17

These are the charts of a couple who had two miscarriages before coming to Foresight. Being 39 years old, she was in an agony of impatience as people so often seem to think that the Sword of Damocles descends on their 40th birthday! (Incidentally this is not true; we have had beautiful babies with ladies who were 45 – 46 years old.)

Nonetheless, this person was in a great hurry, and by the time we got this chart back from the laboratory she had conceived again. As you will see, her selenium was very low. As we feared, the baby was Down's Syndrome, but the pregnancy ended quickly in miscarriage, which saved the trauma of making the decision to terminate.

She continued with the Foresight programme, but before she got around to retesting, another surprise conception too place. Happily, levels were better by then, although not quite optimum, so her little girl arrived perfect, just a little small at 6lb 14oz.

Female aged 37, first test.

	Your results	Recommended values	
Calcium:	463.00	400.00	mg/kg
Iron:	33.41	38.00	mg/kg
Magnesium:	60.85	40.00	mg/kg
Potassium:	69.37	75.00	mg/kg
Sodium:	68.40	94.00	mg/kg
Chromium:	1.21	1.20	mg/kg
Cobalt:	0.17	0.23	mg/kg
Copper:	20.53	22.00	mg/kg
Manganese:	1.18	1.70	mg/kg
Molybdenum:	0.13	0.18	mg/kg
Nikel:	1.36	1.10	mg/kg
Selenium:	1.61	2.25	mg/kg
Vanadium:	0.13	0.18	mg/kg
Zinc:	175.34	185.00	mg/kg

Record 17 *continued*

	Your results	Recommended values	
		Threshold values	
Aluminium:	1.36	2.00	mg/kg
Cadmium:	0.17	0.12	mg/kg
Lead:	1.26	1.40	mg/kg
Mercury:	0.05	0.14	mg/kg

Female aged 38, second test.

	Your results	Recommended values	
Calcium:	374.00	400.00	mg/kg
Iron:	41.06	38.00	mg/kg
Magnesium:	45.79	40.00	mg/kg
Potassium:	68.60	75.00	mg/kg
Sodium:	69.29	94.00	mg/kg
Chromium:	0.79	1.20	mg/kg
Cobalt:	0.17	0.23	mg/kg
Copper:	19.63	22.00	mg/kg
Manganese:	1.23	1.70	mg/kg
Molybdenum:	0.18	0.18	mg/kg
Nikel:	0.60	1.10	mg/kg
Selenium:	3.42	2.25	mg/kg
Vanadium:	0.14	0.18	mg/kg
Zinc:	173.00	185.00	mg/kg
		Threshold values	
Aluminium:	1.34	2.00	mg/kg
Cadmium:	0.10	0.12	mg/kg
Lead:	1.24	1.40	mg/kg
Mercury:	0.06	0.14	mg/kg

Male aged 37, first test.

	Your results	Recommended values	
Calcium:	330.00	400.00	mg/kg
Iron:	40.92	38.00	mg/kg
Magnesium:	39.99	40.00	mg/kg
Potassium:	73.54	75.00	mg/kg
Sodium:	91.89	94.00	mg/kg
Chromium:	1.38	1.20	mg/kg
Cobalt:	0.21	0.23	mg/kg
Copper:	30.22	22.00	mg/kg
Manganese:	2.96	1.70	mg/kg
Molybdenum:	0.15	0.18	mg/kg
Nikel:	2.03	1.10	mg/kg
Selenium:	1.91	2.25	mg/kg

Record 17 *continued*

	Your results	Recommended values	
Vanadium:	0.20	0.18	mg/kg
Zinc:	158.62	185.00	mg/kg
		Threshold values	
Aluminium:	3.37	2.00	mg/kg
Cadmium:	0.10	0.12	mg/kg
Lead:	1.24	1.40	mg/kg
Mercury:	0.06	0.14	mg/kg

Male aged 37, first test.

	Your results	Recommended values	
Calcium:	330.00	400.00	mg/kg
Iron:	40.92	38.00	mg/kg
Magnesium:	39.99	40.00	mg/kg
Potassium:	73.54	75.00	mg/kg
Sodium:	91.89	94.00	mg/kg
Chromium:	1.38	1.20	mg/kg
Cobalt:	0.21	0.23	mg/kg
Copper:	30.22	22.00	mg/kg
Manganese:	2.96	1.70	mg/kg
Molybdenum:	0.15	0.18	mg/kg
Nikel:	2.03	1.10	mg/kg
Selenium:	1.91	2.25	mg/kg
Vanadium:	0.20	0.18	mg/kg
Zinc:	158.62	185.00	mg/kg
		Threshold values	
Aluminium:	3.37	2.00	mg/kg
Cadmium:	0.08	0.12	mg/kg
Lead:	1.42	1.40	mg/kg
Mercury:	0.12	0.14	mg/kg

Record 18

This lady lived over a carpet shop. Carpets are usually full of organophosphate pesticides, used as mothproofing, fire-retardants etc. Her low manganese made it look likely that there was some degree of contamination going on. These chemicals can out-gas significantly. Under these conditions, as you see, it is very difficult to get manganese levels to improve.

We advised manganese and lecithin granules to improve absorption. She became pregnant rather sooner than expected, but we compensated with a very comprehensive programme throughout the pregnancy and her baby was born perfect, although small, due to the lack of zinc and manganese, at 5lb 12 oz.

Record 18 *continued*

Female aged 37, first test.

	Your results	Recommended values	
Calcium:	612.00	400.00	mg/kg
Iron:	43.30	38.00	mg/kg
Magnesium:	43.27	40.00	mg/kg
Potassium:	74.00	75.00	mg/kg
Sodium:	74.29	94.00	mg/kg
Chromium:	1.54	1.20	mg/kg
Cobalt:	0.22	0.23	mg/kg
Copper:	19.84	22.00	mg/kg
Manganese:	1.18	1.70	mg/kg
Molybdenum:	0.18	0.18	mg/kg
Nikel:	1.57	1.10	mg/kg
Selenium:	1.74	2.25	mg/kg
Vanadium:	0.14	0.18	mg/kg
Zinc:	155.11	185.00	mg/kg
		Threshold values	
Aluminium:	1.29	2.00	mg/kg
Cadmium:	0.08	0.12	mg/kg
Lead:	1.15	1.40	mg/kg
Mercury:	0.11	0.14	mg/kg

Female aged 37, second test.

	Your results	Recommended values	
Calcium:	645.00	400.00	mg/kg
Iron:	34.57	38.00	mg/kg
Magnesium:	63.46	40.00	mg/kg
Potassium:	71.75	75.00	mg/kg
Sodium:	69.80	94.00	mg/kg
Chromium:	1.40	1.20	mg/kg
Cobalt:	0.18	0.23	mg/kg
Copper:	21.78	22.00	mg/kg
Manganese:	1.03	1.70	mg/kg
Molybdenum:	0.11	0.18	mg/kg
Nikel:	1.17	1.10	mg/kg
Selenium:	2.26	2.25	mg/kg
Vanadium:	0.26	0.18	mg/kg
Zinc:	165.05	185.00	mg/kg
		Threshold values	
Aluminium:	1.18	2.00	mg/kg
Cadmium:	0.11	0.12	mg/kg
Lead:	1.75	1.40	mg/kg
Mercury:	0.09	0.14	mg/kg

Record 19

The chart of a prospective father who lives on a farm in the West Country where there is a landfill site just across the road from his house. There is a fume pipe emerging from this noxious dump that "issues" smoke (blowing out lead, cadmium and manganese) day and night. His wife and tiny daughter are similarly contaminated. We battled for some time with this, and he is heavily engaged with the local authorities regarding it, but has so far not had a sympathetic hearing.

I think his plight demonstrates how necessary it is for hair analysis to become a part of mainstream medicine and environmental monitoring. Nobody should be left in this position, entirely blameless, but polluted round the clock.

As you can see, there was heavy manganese and lead. We have not been able to get rid of it.

Were they living in a flat, we would advise them to move. With a large farm with livestock etc, it is really not so easy.

The child is aged 2½ years, and was also badly polluted and reacting to it.

Male aged 53, first test.

	Your results	Recommended values	
Calcium:	376.00	400.00	mg/kg
Magnesium:	58.90	40.00	mg/kg
Potassium:	125.60	75.00	mg/kg
Iron:	40.73	38.00	mg/kg
Chromium:	1.72	1.20	mg/kg
Cobalt:	0.44	0.23	mg/kg
Copper:	19.96	22.00	mg/kg
Manganese:	37.66	1.70	mg/kg
Nikel:	1.86	1.10	mg/kg
Selenium:	2.19	2.25	mg/kg
Zinc:	124.00	185.00	mg/kg
		Threshold values	
Aluminium:	4.56	2.00	mg/kg
Cadmium:	0.76	0.12	mg/kg
Mercury:	0.06	0.14	mg/kg
Lead:	12.33	1.40	mg/kg
Molybdenum:	0.33	0.18	mg/kg
Vanadium:	0.63	0.18	mg/kg
Sodium:	196.10	94.00	mg/kg

Record 19 *continued*

Male aged 53, second test.

	Your results	Recommended values	
Calcium:	356.00	400.00	mg/kg
Magnesium:	58.93	40.00	mg/kg
Potassium:	158.90	75.00	mg/kg
Iron:	34.08	38.00	mg/kg
Chromium:	1.35	1.20	mg/kg
Cobalt:	0.39	0.23	mg/kg
Copper:	20.44	22.00	mg/kg
Manganese:	42.36	1.70	mg/kg
Nikel:	0.57	1.10	mg/kg
Selenium:	1.70	2.25	mg/kg
Zinc:	140.00	185.00	mg/kg
		Threshold values	
Aluminium:	2.09	2.00	mg/kg
Cadmium:	0.27	0.12	mg/kg
Mercury:	0.06	0.14	mg/kg
Lead:	6.60	1.40	mg/kg
Molybdenum:	0.36	0.18	mg/kg
Vanadium:	0.47	0.18	mg/kg
Sodium:	189.90	94.00	mg/kg

Male aged 54, third test.

	Your results	Recommended values	
Calcium:	599.00	400.00	mg/kg
Magnesium:	140.50	40.00	mg/kg
Potassium:	231.17	75.00	mg/kg
Iron:	52.21	38.00	mg/kg
Chromium:	1.51	1.20	mg/kg
Cobalt:	0.51	0.23	mg/kg
Copper:	21.11	22.00	mg/kg
Manganese:	37.10	1.70	mg/kg
Nikel:	1.04	1.10	mg/kg
Selenium:	2.80	2.25	mg/kg
Zinc:	169.74	185.00	mg/kg
		Threshold values	
Aluminium:	3.28	2.00	mg/kg
Cadmium:	0.16	0.12	mg/kg
Mercury:	0.09	0.14	mg/kg
Lead:	7.46	1.40	mg/kg
Molybdenum:	0.41	0.18	mg/kg
Vanadium:	0.30	0.18	mg/kg
Sodium:	390.60	94.00	mg/kg

Record 19 *continued*

Girl aged 2½, first test.

	Your results	Recommended values	
Calcium:	290.00	400.00	mg/kg
Magnesium:	31.50	40.00	mg/kg
Potassium:	81.20	75.00	mg/kg
Iron:	47.40	38.00	mg/kg
Chromium:	2.12	1.20	mg/kg
Cobalt:	0.31	0.23	mg/kg
Copper:	20.90	22.00	mg/kg
Manganese:	3.28	1.70	mg/kg
Nikel:	1.38	1.10	mg/kg
Selenium:	2.69	2.25	mg/kg
Zinc:	131.00	185.00	mg/kg
		Threshold values	
Aluminium:	3.35	2.00	mg/kg
Cadmium:	0.20	0.12	mg/kg
Mercury:	0.12	0.14	mg/kg
Lead:	9.16	1.40	mg/kg
Molybdenum:	0.36	0.18	mg/kg
Vanadium:	0.36	0.18	mg/kg
Sodium:	77.70	94.00	mg/kg

Record 20

This lady came to us in 2002. She was coming because she had various nervous system conditions. She had previously had a baby born with brain damage who did not survive.

It transpired that both she and her husband's manganese levels were exceptionally low and upon enquiry, we found that she had 2 cats that were treated with organophosphate drops on the back of their necks, as a protection against fleas. This is a horrible practise, and I have heard of dogs and cats having epilepsy and even of two kittens that have been born spastic as a result of this. These cats were often on her lap and she stroked and cuddled them frequently.

The best we could suggest was to bathe the cats, wash their bedding and so on. This helped. As you see, when she retested six months later, after a supplement programme, things were getting better. The work of Saner et al, has demonstrated CNS damage in children who are short of manganese, including such deformities as spina bifida occulta.

The organophosphates have been shown to prevent the uptake of manganese, so should not be used in a domestic situation, or in food production, or in practices such as sheep dipping. This can contaminate wool and mutton, and, if the dip is disposed of by being put into the rivers, they can later contaminate the ground water and hence our tap water. The potential for tragedy is unlimited, although unlikely to be traced back to the source.

See also the chart of the husband who was the "second lap" in the evenings.

After quite a long time on the programme, things were improving very slowly. They decided to go for IVF with manganese still rather low. Luckily they had a little boy, 5lb 13oz and no damage. We compensated with zinc and manganese throughout the pregnancy, but he was still very small.

Female aged 50, first test.

	Your results	Recommended values	
Calcium:	338.00	400.00	mg/kg
Iron:	36.92	38.00	mg/kg
Magnesium:	38.56	40.00	mg/kg
Potassium:	78.95	75.00	mg/kg
Sodium:	126.70	94.00	mg/kg
Chromium:	1.06	1.20	mg/kg
Cobalt:	0.19	0.23	mg/kg
Copper:	23.05	22.00	mg/kg
Manganese:	0.89	1.70	mg/kg
Molybdenum:	0.15	0.18	mg/kg
Nikel:	1.44	1.10	mg/kg
Selenium:	3.47	2.25	mg/kg
Vanadium:	0.14	0.18	mg/kg
Zinc:	154.78	185.00	mg/kg
		Threshold values	
Aluminium:	1.03	2.00	mg/kg
Cadmium:	0.13	0.12	mg/kg
Lead:	2.11	1.40	mg/kg
Mercury:	0.20	0.14	mg/kg

Male aged 49, third test.

	Your results	Recommended values	
Calcium:	335.00	400.00	mg/kg
Iron:	32.11	38.00	mg/kg
Magnesium:	32.10	40.00	mg/kg
Potassium:	71.02	75.00	mg/kg
Sodium:	80.73	94.00	mg/kg
Chromium:	1.10	1.20	mg/kg
Cobalt:	0.18	0.23	mg/kg
Copper:	29.40	22.00	mg/kg
Manganese:	0.74	1.70	mg/kg
Molybdenum:	0.13	0.18	mg/kg
Nikel:	0.73	1.10	mg/kg
Selenium:	2.51	2.25	mg/kg
Vanadium:	0.10	0.18	mg/kg
Zinc:	158.99	185.00	mg/kg

Record 20 *continued*

	Your results	Recommended values	
		Threshold values	
Aluminium:	1.19	2.00	mg/kg
Cadmium:	0.07	0.12	mg/kg
Lead:	2.83	1.40	mg/kg
Mercury:	0.16	0.14	mg/kg

Record 21

This child is autistic. The mother is a printer. The child is full of lead, therefore calcium, selenium and zinc are very low. This is typical of autism.

Boy aged 5 years, 2 months, first test.

	Your results	Recommended values	
Calcium:	292.00	400.00	mg/kg
Magnesium:	33.70	40.00	mg/kg
Potassium:	72.30	75.00	mg/kg
Iron:	42.00	38.00	mg/kg
Chromium:	1.96	1.20	mg/kg
Cobalt:	0.39	0.23	mg/kg
Copper:	19.60	22.00	mg/kg
Manganese:	2.71	1.70	mg/kg
Nikel:	1.24	1.10	mg/kg
Selenium:	1.60	2.25	mg/kg
Zinc:	110.00	185.00	mg/kg
		Threshold values	
Aluminium:	4.24	2.00	mg/kg
Cadmium:	0.36	0.12	mg/kg
Mercury:	0.06	0.14	mg/kg
Lead:	6.68	1.40	mg/kg

Record 22

This boy suffers from dyslexia and hyperactivity. Note the very low zinc and selenium.

Boy aged 16 years, 9 months, sixth test.

	Your results	Recommended values	
Calcium:	292.00	400.00	mg/kg
Magnesium:	33.70	40.00	mg/kg
Potassium:	72.30	75.00	mg/kg
Iron:	42.00	38.00	mg/kg
Chromium:	1.96	1.20	mg/kg
Cobalt:	0.39	0.23	mg/kg
Copper:	19.60	22.00	mg/kg
Manganese:	2.71	1.70	mg/kg
Nikel:	1.24	1.10	mg/kg
Selenium:	1.60	2.25	mg/kg
Zinc:	110.00	185.00	mg/kg
		Threshold values	
Aluminium:	4.24	2.00	mg/kg
Cadmium:	0.36	0.12	mg/kg
Mercury:	0.06	0.14	mg/kg
Lead:	6.68	1.40	mg/kg

References

1. Bryce-Smith, D (1979) Environmental trace elements and their role in disorders of personality, intellect, behaviour and learning in children. Proceedings of the second New Zealand Seminar on Trace Elements and Health, University of Auckland, 22-26 January

2. Bryce-Smith, D (1977) lead and cadmium levels in stillbirths, Lancet i:1159

3. Bushnell, P J and Bowman, R E (1977) Reversal deficits in young monkeys exposed to lead, Pharm Biochem and behaviour 10: 733-747

4. Garnys, V et al (1979) Lead Burden of Sydney Schoolchildren, University of New South Wales

5. Gittelman, R and Eskenazi, B (1983) Lead and hyperactivity revisited, Arch Gen Psychiat 40: 827-833

6. Lin-Fu, J S (1973) Vulnerability of children to lead exposure and toxicity Eng J Med 289: 129-1233

7. Pfeiffer, C (1975) Mental and Elemental Nutrients New Canaan, Keats Publishing Co

8. Pfeiffer, C C (1978) Zinc and Other Micronutrients New Canaan, Keats Publishing Co

9. Phil, R O and Parkes, M (1977) Hair element content in learning disabled children Science 198: 4214

10. Singh, N et al (1978) Neonatal lead intoxification in a prenatally exposed infant, J Paediat 93(6): 1019-1021

11. Thatcher, R et al (1982) Effects of low levels of cadmium and lead on cognitive functioning in children Arch Envir Health 37(3): 159-166

12. Ward, N I et al (1987) Placental element levels in relation to foetal development for obstetrically "normal" births: A study of 37 elements, evidence for effects of cadmium, lead and zinc on foetal growth and smoking as a source of cadmium, Biosocial Res 9(1): 63

13. Wibblerley, D G et al (1977) Lead levels in human placentas from normal and malformed births, I Med Gen 14(5): 339-345

14. Yale, W et al (1985) Teachers' ratings of children's behaviour in relation to blood lead levels, Br J Dev Psych 2: 285-306

15. Robinson, M F (1982) Clinical effects of selenium deficiency and excess. In: Clinical, Biochemical, and Nutritional Aspects of Trace Elements (Ed: AS Prasad) pp 325-343, Alan Liss Inc, New York, New York, US

16. Levander, O A (1982) Selenium: Biochemical Actions, Interactions, and some human health implications. In: Clinical, Biochemical, and Nutritional Aspects of Trace Elements (Ed: AS Prasad) pp 345-368, Alan Liss Inc. New York, US

17. Shamberger and Frost, D V (1969) Possible protective effect of selenium against human cancer. Can Med Assoc J, 100:682

18. Schrauzer G N (1977) White DA, Schneider CJ: Cancer mortality correlation studies, III, Statistical associations with dietary selenium intakes. Bioinorg Chem, 7:23

19. Ip C and Ganther HE (1993) Novel strategies in selenium chemoprevention research. In: Selenium in Biology and Human Health. (Ed RF Burk), pp 169 Springer Verlag, NY, US

20. Clark L C (1996) et al: Effects of selenium supplementation for cancer prevention in patients with carcinoma of the skin. JAMA, 276:1957-1963

21. Clark L C (1997) Recent developments in the prevention of human cancer with selenium. Selenium-Tellurium Development Assoc Bulletin, November

22. Passwater, R (1980) Selenium as a Food Medicine, New Canaan, Keats Publishing Co

23. Davies, S and Stewart, A (1987) Nutritional Medicine, London, Pan

24. Elkington, J (1985) The Poisoned Womb, Harmondsworth, Viking

25. Gordon, G F (1980) Hair Analysis: Its Current Use and Limitations Part II, Let's Live, October: 89-94

26. Klevay, L M (1978) Hair as a Biopsy Material Progress and Prospects, A Intern Med 138: 1127-1128

27. Laker, M (1982) On determining trace element levels in man: the uses of blood and hair Lancet ii: 260-262

28. Balch & Balch

29. Lodge Rees, E (1983) Trace elements in pregnancy In: J Rose (Ed) Trace Elements in Health, London, Butterworths

30. Lodge Rees, E (1981) The concept of preconceptual care, Intern J Envir Studies 17: 37-42

31. Lodge Rees, E (1983) Prevention versus problems in pediatric science In: The Next Generation, Foresight

32. Lodge Rees, E (1979) Aluminium Toxicity as Indicated by Hair Analysis, I Orthomol Psychiat 8(1): 137-143

33. Maugh, T H (1978) Hair: A Diagnostic Tool to Complement Blood Serum and Urine, Science 202: 1271-1273

34. Passwater, R and Cranton, E (1983) Trace Elements, Hair Analysis and Nutrition New Canaan, Keats Publishing Co

35. Rose, J Ed: (1983) Trace Elements in Health London, Butterworths (and Samarawickrama, G)

36. Saner, G et al (1985) Hair manganese concentrations in newborns and their mothers, Am J Clin Nut 41: 1042-1044

37.   Ward, N I (1993) Preconceptual care questionnaire research project, In press Details from Foresight

38.   Hornsby, M (1993) Insecticide might be "mad cow" link, The Times, 21st August

39.   Roberts, D (Undated) Pharmacology and toxicology of organophosphorus pesticides, Offprint available from Foresight

40.   Johnson, M K (1975) The Delayed Neuropathy Caused by Some Organophosphorus Esters: Mechanism and Challenge, Critical Reviews in Toxicology, June 289: 313

41.   Andrews, S H (1981) Abnormal reactions and their frequency in cattle following the use of organophosphorous warble fly dressing, The Veterinary Record 109: 171-175

42.   Duffy, F H et al (1979) Long-Term Effects of an Organophosphate upon the Human Electroencephalogram, Toxicology and Applied Pharmacology 47; 161-176

43.   Duffy, F H and Burchfield, J L (1980) Long Term Effects of the Organophosphate Sarin in EEGs in Monkeys and Humans, Neurotoxicology 1: 667-689

44.   Erlichman, J (1993) Sheep dip alarm likely to force ban, The Guardian 26 October

45.   Whorton, M D et al(1977) Infertility in male pesticide workers, Lancett:1259-61

46.   Woffinden, B (1994) Cows: mad or poisoned? Living Earth and The Food Magazine, 184:10

47.   Campbell, J M and Harrison, K L (1979) Smoking and Infertility, Med J Aust 1; 342-343

48.   Briggs, M H (1973) Cigarette Smoking and infertility in men, Med J Aust 1:616

49.   Himmelberger, DU et al (1978) Cigarette smoking during pregnancy and occurrence of spontaneous abortion and congenital abnormality, A. Epid 108: 470-479

50.   Evans, H J et al, (1981) Sperm abnormalities and cigarette smoking, Lancet, i: 627-629

51.   Tuormaa, T (1994a) The Adverse Effects of Tobacco Smoking on Reproduction, A Review from the Literature, Foresight (Also reprinted in Int J Biosocial Med Res, 14:2)

52.   Simpson, J (1957) A preliminary report on cigarette smoking and the incidence of prematurity, Am J Obstet Gynaecol, 73: 800-815

53. Abel, Ernest L (1982) Marihuana, Tobacco, Alcohol and Reproduction, Boca Raton, CRC Press

54. Brzek, A (1987) Alcohol and male fertility (preliminary report), Andrologia 19: 32-36

55. Kaufman, M In: Neville Hodgkinson, Alcohol Threat to Babies, The Sunday Times 31 January

56. Kucheria, K et al (1985) Semen analysis in alcohol dependence syndrome Andrologia 17: 558-563

57. Rosett H,et al (1983) Patterns of Alcohol Consumption and Foetal Development, Obstet Gynecol, 61: 539-546

58. Streissguth, A P (1991) What every community should know about drinking during pregnancy and the lifelong consequences for society, Substance Abuse, 12(3): 114-127

59. Tuormaa, T (1994) The Adverse Effects of Alcohol on Reproduction, A Review from the Literature, Foresight

60. US Surgeon General's Advisory on Alcohol and Pregnancy (1981) FDA-Drug Bulletin 11(12) July

61. Wynn A and M (Undated) Should Men and Women Limit Alcohol Consumption when Hoping to have a Baby? London, The Maternity Alliance

62. Grant, E (1985) The Bitter Pill, London, Corgi

63. Grant, E (1994) Sexual Chemistry: Understanding our Hormones, the Pill and HRT, London, Cedar

64. Kupsinel, R Mercury Amalgam Toxicity A Major Common Denominato Degenerative Disease, J Orthomolecular Psychiat 13(4): 240-257

65. Ziff, S (1985) The Toxic Time- Bomb, Wellingborough, Thorsons

66. Alary, Michael et al (1993) Strategy for screening pregnant women for chlamydial infection in a low prevalence area, Obst Gynecol 82: 399-404

67. Catterall, R D (1981) Biological effects of sexual freedom Lancet i: 315-319

68. Eilard, T et al (1976) Isolation of chlamydia in acute salpingitis, Scand J Infectious Dis (Suppl 9), 82-84

69. Friberg, J and Gnarpe, H (1973) Mycoplasma and human reproductive failure, Am I Obstet Gynecol, 116: 23-26

70. Mardh, P H (1981a) Medical chlamydiology: A position paper, Scan J Infect Dis (Supp 32):3-8

71.   Fromell, G T et al (1979) Chlamydial infections of mothers and their infants, J Pod 95(1):28-32

72.   Mardh, P H et al (1981b) Endometriosis caused by chlamydia trachomatis, Br J Vene Dis, 57-91

73.   Schofield, C B S (1972) Sexually transmitted diseases, London, Churchill-Livingstone

74.   Rhodes, A J (1961) Virus and Congenital Malformations: Papers and Discussions presented at the First International Conference on Congenital Malformations, Philadelphia-Lippincott

75.   Westrom L (1975) Affect of acute pelvic infectious disease on fertility, Am J Obstet Gynecol, 121: 707-7 13

76.   Wolff, H et al (1991) Chlamydia trachomatis induces an inflammatory response in the male genital tract and is associated with altered semen quality, Fert Ster *55(5):* 1017-1019

77.   Brostoff, J and Gamlin, L (1989) The Complete guide to Food Allergy and Intolerance, new York Crown Publisher Inc

78.   Buttram, H (1994) Controversal issues – 1 Candidiasis – The Phantom Illness, Unpublished paper

79.   Crook, W G (1983) The Yeast Connection, Professional Books

80.   Chaitow, L (1984) Candida Albicans Could Yeast Be Your Problem? Wellingborough, Thorsons

81.   Masefield, J (1988) Psychiatric illness caused or exacerbated by Food Allergies (Unpublished article)

82.   Eagle, R (1986) Eating and Allergy, Wellingborough, Thorsons

83.   Anon (1985) Microwaves The Invisible Danger to Expectant Mums, Healthy Living, 2 March

84.   Bithell, F J and Stewart, A M (1975) Prenatal irridation and childhood malignancy: a review of British data from the Oxford Survey, Br J Cancer 31: 271-287

85.   Sassenath, E N et al (1979) Reproduction in Rhesus Monkeys Chronically Exposed to Delta-9-THC Adv in the Biosciences, 22-23: 50 1-522

86.   Wertheimer, N and Leeper, E (1984) Adverse effects on foetal development associated with sources of exposure to 60 hz electric and magnetic fields (Abstract), 23rd Hanford Life Sciences Symposium Interaction of Biological Systems with Static and ELF Electric and Magnetic Fields, Richland, WA

87.   Wright, P (1988) Claims that power cables cause Cancer to be investigated, The Times, 18 March

88.   Cowdry, Q and Stokes, P (1989) Aluminium causes senility The Daily Telegraph, 13 January

89.   Freundlich, M et al (1985) Infant Formula as a Cause of Aluminium Toxicity in Neonatal Ureamia, Lancet ii: 527-529

90.   Ward, N I (1992) Environmental Aspects of Heavy Metals and Aluminium and the Effect on Human Health, Foresight Mid-Summer Newsletter, 26-38

91.   Chavez, G F et al (1989) Maternal cocaine use during pregnancy as a risk factor for congenital urogenital anomalies JAMA 262: 795-8

92.   Fantel, A G and Macphail, B J (1982) The teratogenicity of cocaine, Teratology 26: 17-19

93.   Mann, P (1985) Marijuana Alert, New York, McGraw-Hill

94.   Bingol, N et al (1987) Teratogenicy of cocaine in humans, J Pediatr 10(1): 93-96

95.   Smith, C G and Gilbean, PM (1985) Drug Abuse Effects on Reproductive Hormones In: J Thomas et al (eds) Endocrine Toxicology, New York, Raven Press

96.   Weber, LW D (1985) Benzodiazepines in pregnancy — academic debate or teratogenic risk? Biol Res in Preg, 64: 15 1-167

97.   Stenchever, M A et al (1974) Chromosome Breakages in Users of Marijuana, AmlObstetGynaecol, 118: 106-113

98.   Schelling, J L (1987) Which Drugs should not be Prescribed during Pregnancy, Ther Umsch Rev Ther 441: 48-53

99.   Rodriguez, A F et al (1986) Relationship between benzodiazepine ingestion during pregnancy and oral clefts in the newborn, a case-control study, Med Clin 87/18: 741-743

100. Robertson, W F (1962) Thalidomide (Distival) and vitamin B deficiency BMJ1: 792

101. Editorial (1964) The Drugged Sperm BMJ 1: 1063-1064

102. Consumers Association (1985) Drug and Therapeutics Bulletin, July 23:15

103. Blair, J H et al (1962) MAO inhibitors and sperm production, JAMA 181:192-193

104. Brazelton, T B (1970) Effect of Prenatal Drugs in the Behaviour of the

Neonate, Am J Psychiat 126: 1296-1303

105. Nutrition Search Inc (1979) Nutrition Almanac, New York, McGraw-Hill

106. Millstone, E & Abraham, I (1988) Additives A Guide for Everyone, Penguin

107. Hansen, J C et al (1980) Children with minimal brain dysfunction, Danish Bull 27(6): 259-262

108. Colgan, M (1982) Your Personal Vitamin Profile, London, Blond and Briggs

109. Schroeder, H and Mitchener, M (1971) Toxic Effects of Trace Elements on the Reproduction on Mice and Rats, Arch Envir Health 23; 102

110. Bryce-Smith, D (1981) Environmental Influences on Prenatal Development Thesssaloniki Conference, September

111. Spyker, J M Occupational Hazards and the Pregnant Worker, Behavioural Toxicology Overview, 470

112. Norwood, C (1980) At Highest Risk, New York, McGraw-Hill

113. Davies, S (1981) Lead, Beyond Nutrition, Summer 12-13

114. Clausen, J and Rastogi, S C (1977) Heavy metal pollution among autoworkers in Lead, Br J Ind Med 34: 208-2 15

115. El-Dakhakny, A and El-sadik, Y M (1972) Lead in hair among exposed workers, Am Ind Hygiene Assoc Journal 33

116. Kostial, K and Kello, D (1979) Bioavailability of lead in rats fed "human diets", Bull Environ Contam Toxic 21: 312-314

117. Bellinger, D et al (1987) Longitudinal analyses of prenatal and postnatal lead exposure and infant development in the first year, New Eng J Med 17: 1037-1043

118. Sohler, A et al (1977) Blood Lead Levels in Psychiatric Outpatients Reduced by Zinc and Vitamin C, J Orthomolecular Psychiat 6(3): 272-276

119. Bellinger, D et al (1978) Low level lead exposure and infant development in the first year, Neurobehavioural Toxic and Terat 8: 151-161

120. Mortimer, G R (1975) In the Beginning: Your Baby's Brain Before Birth, New York, New American Library

121. Lacranjan, 1(1975) Reproductive ability of workmen occupationally exr lead, Arch Envir Health 20: 396-401

122. Vitale, L F et al (1975) Blood lead - an inadequate measure of occupational exposure, J 0cc Med 17: 102-3

123. David, 0 J et al (1976) Lead and hyperactivity Behavioural response to chelation: a pilot study, Am J Psychiat 133(10): 1155-1158

124. Needleman, H L et al (1990) New Eng J Med 332: 83-88

125. Needleman, H L et al (1984) JAMA 25 1(22): 2956-9

126. Needleman, H L et al (1979) Deficits in psychologic and classroom performance of children with elevated dentine lead levels, New Eng J Med 300: 689-696

127. Blumer, W R T (1980) Leaded gasoline – a cause of cancer, Envir Int 3: 465-471

128. Moore, L S and Fleischman, A (1975) Subclinical Lead Toxicity, Orthomol Psychiatry 4(1): 6 1-70

129. Lester, M L et al (1986) Protective Effects of Zinc and Calcium Against Metal Impairment of Children's Cognitive Function, 145-161

130. Schwartz, J et al. (1986) Relationship between childhood blood lead levels and stature, Pediatrics 77(3): 281-283

131. Spivey, Fox M R (1975) New York Acad Science 258: 144

132. Kime, Z R (1980) Sunlight, Penryn, World Health Publications

133. Williams, R J (1973) Nutrition Against Disease, London, Bantam

134. Davis, A (1954) Let's Eat Right to Keep Fit, New York, New American Library

135. Pitkin, R M et al (1972) Maternal Nutrition, A Selective Review of Clinical Topics Obstet Gynaecol 40: 775

136. Gibbs, C E and Seitchik, J (1980) Nutrition in Pregnancy In: R S Goodhart and M Shils (eds) Modern Nutrition in Health and Disease, Philadephia, Lea and Febiger

137. Davis, A (1974) Let's have healthy children, Unwin Paperbacks

138. Hurley, L S et al (1976) Teratogenic effects of magnesium deficiency, J Nut 106: 1254-1260

139. Spatling, L and G (1988) Magnesium supplementation in pregnancy: a double-blind study, Br J Obstet Gynaecol 95: 111-116

140. Wynn M and Wynn A (1981) The Prevention of Handicap of Early Pregnancy Origin, London Foundation for Education and Research in Childbearing

141.   Wynn A and M (1986) Prevention of Handicap of Early Pregnancy Origin Today - Building Tomorrow International Conference on Physical Disabilities, Montreal, 4-6 June

142.   Schroeder, H A (1973) The Trace Elements and Man, Old Greenwich, Devin-Adair

143.   Hodges, R E and Adelman, R D (1980) Nutrition in Medical Practice, Philadelphia, W B Saunders

144.   Elam, D (1980) Building Better Babies Preconception Planning for Healthier Children, Milibare, Celestial Arts

145.   Ebrahim, O J (1979) The Problems of Undernutrition In: Ed: R J Jarrett Nutrition and Disease, Baltimore, University Park Press

146.   Crosby, W M et al (1977) Foetal Malnutrition: An Appraisal of Correlated Factors, Am J Obstet Gynaecol 128: 26

147.   Ballentine, R (1978) Diet and Nutrition, Honesdale, The Himalayan International Institute

148.   Kamen, B and S (1981)The Kamen Plan for Total Nutrition During Pregnancy, New York, Appleton-Century-Croft (This is an excellent book)

149.   Underwood, E J (1977) Trace Elements in Human and Animal Nutrition, New York, Academic Press

150.   Merz W: Clinical and Public Health Significance of Chromium In: Clinical, Biochemical, and Nurtritional Aspects of Trace Elements (Ed: AS Prasad) 315-323, Alan R Liss, Inc., New York, USA, 1982

151.   Anderson R A (1980) Chromium as a naturally occurring chemical in humans. Proceedings of Chromate Symposium, Industrial Health Foundation, Inc, Pittsburg, pp 332-345

152.   Doisy R J, Streeten DHP, Freiberg JM et al: chromium metabolism in man and biochemical effects. In: Trace Elements in Human Health and Disease (Ed:AS Prasad), Vol II, pp 79-104, New York Academy Press.

153.   Schroeder H A (1966) Chromium deficiency in rats: A syndrome simulating diabetes mellitus with retarded growth. J Nutr, 88:439-445

154.   Hambridge K M. Rodgerson D O, O'Brien D O (1968) The concentration of chromium in the hair of normal and children with diabetes mellitus. Diabetes. 17:517-519

155.   Nath R, Minocha J, Lyall V et al (1979) Assessment of chromium metabolism in maturity onset and juvenile diabetes using chromium 51 and therapeutic response of chromium administration on plasma lipids, glucose tolerance and insulin levels. In: Chromium in Nutrition and Metabolism

(Eds: D Shapcott and J Hubert) pp 213-222, Elsevier/North Holland

156. Morgan J M (1972) Hepatic chromium content in diabetic subjects. Metabolism 21:313-316

157. Schroeder H A (1965) Serum cholesterol levels in rats fed thirteen trace elements. J Nutr, 94:475-480

158. Schroeder H A (1970) Nason AP, Tipton IH: Chromium deficiency as a factor in atherosclerosis. J Chronic Dis, 23:123-142

159. Borel J S, Anderson R A (1984) Chromium. in: Biochemistry of the Essential Ultratrace Elements (Ed: E Frieden) Plenum Publishing Co.

160. Anderson R A and Polansky M M (1981) Dietary chromium sperm count and fertility in rats. Biol Trace Element Res, 3:1-5

161. Hambridge K M (1971) Newer Trace Elements in Nutrition. Eds: W Metrz and WE Cornatzer p.169, Dekker, New York

162. Hambridge K M (1974) Chromium nutrition in man. Am J Clin Nutr, 27:505-51

163. Tolonen M (1990) Vitamins and Minerals in Health and Nutrition. Ellis Horwood Ltd

164. Vallee, B (1965) Zinc In: Comar, C Land Bronner, C S (eds) Mineral Metabolism, Vol II B, London, Academic Press

165. Crews M G (1980) Taper U, Ritchey S I: Effects of oral contraceptive agents on copper and zinc balance in young women. Am J Clin Nutr, 33:1940

166. Carruthers M E (1966) Hobbs C B, Warren R L: Raised serum copper and .ceruloplasmin levels in subjects taking oral contraceptives. J Clin Pathol, 19:498-450

167. Bremmer I, Young B W, Mills C F (1976) Protective effects of zinc supplementation against copper toxicity in sheep. Br J Nutr, 36:551

168. Hall A C, Young B W, Bremmer I (1979) Intestinal metallothionin and the mutual antagonism between copper and zinc in the rat. J Inorg Biochem, 11:57

169. Bryce-Smith, D and Simpson, R I D (1984) Anorexia, Depression and Zinc Deficiency, Lancet, ii: 1162

170. Caldwell D F, Oberleas, D (1969) Effects of protein and zinc nutrition on behaviour in the rat. Perinatal factors affecting human development, 85: 2-8

171. Crawford, I Land Connor, J D (1975) Zinc and Hippocampal Function, J Orthomol Psych 4(1): 39-52

172. Hambidge, K M et al (1972) Low Levels of Zinc in Hair, Anorexia, Poor Growth,

241

and Hypogeusia in Children, Pediat Res, 6: 868-874

173. Sandstead, H H (1984) Zinc: Essentiality for Brain Development and Function, Nut Today November, December 26-30

174. Smith, I C et al (1973) Zinc: a trace element essential in vitamin A metabolism, Science, 181: 954-955

175. Smith, J C et al (1976) Alterations in vitamin A metabolism during zinc deficiency and food and growth restriction, J Nut 106: 569-574

176. Ward, N I (1995) Preconceptual care and pregnancy outcome, J of Nutritional & Environmental Medicine 5, 205-8

177. Pharoach, P 0 D Ct al (1971) Neurological damage to the foetus resulting from severe iodine deficiency during pregnancy Lancet i: 308-3 10

178. Lesser, M (1980) Nutrition and Vitamin Therapy, New York, Bantam

179. Pfeiffer C and laMola S (1985) Zinc and manganese in the schizophrenias. J Otrhomol Psychiartry, 12(3)215-234

180. Oberleas, D et al (1972) Trace Elements and Behaviour, Int Review Neurobiology Sup

181. National Research Council Committee on medical and Biological Effects of Environmental Pollutants. Manganese. Washington (1973) National Academy of Sciences, pp 1-191

182. Mervyn L (1985) The Dictionary of Minerals. Thorson Publishing Group

183. Tolonen M (1990) Vitamins and Minerals in Health and Nutrition, Ellis Horwood Series in Food Science and Technology

184. Erway L, Hurley LS and Fraser A (1966) neurological defect: Manganese in penocopy and prevention of a genetic abnormality of inner ear. Science 152:1766-68

185. Erway L, Hurley LS and Fraser AS 1970 Congenital ataxia and otolith defects due to manganese deficiency in mice. J Nutr, 100:643-654

186. Erway L, Fraser AS, Hurley LS (1971) Prevention of congenital otolith defects in pallid mutant mice by manganese supplementation. Genetics, 67:97-108

187. Ashton B (1980) Manganese and Man. J Orthomol Psychiatry, 9(4):237-249

188. Leach RM (1976) Metabolism and function of manganese. In: Trace Elements in Human Health and Disease. Vol:II, pp 235-47, Eds: Prasad AS and Oberleas DY, NY Academic Press, New York

189.   Everson GJ and Shrader RE: J.Nutr, 94:89, 1968 and Shrader RE and Everson GJ, p 296

190.   Doisy EA (1973) In: Proceedings of the University of Missouri's 6th Annual Conference on Trace Substances in Environmental Health, p. 193, Ed: DD Hemphill, Columbia, MO. University of Missouri Press

191.   Pfeiffer CC and Bacchi D (1975) Copper, zinc and manganese, niacin and pyridoxine in the schizophrenias. J Appl Nutr, 27:9-39

192.   Tanaka Y (1977) Low manganese level may trigger epilepsy. JAMA, 258: 1805

193.   Sohler A and Pfeiffer C C (1979) Direct method for the determination of manganese in whole blood, patients with seizure activity have low blood levels. J orthomol. Psychiatry, 8(4):275-80

194.   Kunin RA (1976) Manganese and niacin in the treatment of drug-induced dyskinesias. J Orthomol. Psychiatry, 5(1):4-27

195.   Doisy EA (1974) Trace Substances in Environmental health. Proceedings of the University of Missouri's 6th Annual Conference, p.193, 1972. In: Trace Element metabolism in Animals. Eds: WG Hoekstra, et al, Vol:2,p,664, Univer Park Press, Baltimore, Maryland

196.   Riopelle AJ and Hubbard DG: Prenatal manganese deprivation and early behaviour of primates. J Orthomol Psychiatry, 6(4)

197.   Gruden N (1979) Dietary variations and manganese transduodenal transport in rats. Periodicum Biologorum, 81:567-70

198.   Nielson, F H (1984a) Nickel In: Earl Frieden, (Ed) Biochemistry of the Essential Ultratrace Elements, Plenum Publishing

199.   Nielson, F H (1984b) Fluoride, Vanadium, Nickel, Arsenic, and Silicon in Total Parental Nutrition, Bull of the New York Academy of Med, 60(2), 177-195

200.   Anke M et al (undated) Nutritional Requirements of Nickel. Offprint available through Foresight.

201.   ASH, Oldfield J E, Shull L R, Cheeke P R (1979) Specific effect of selenium deficiency on rat sperm. Biol Reprod, 20:793

202.   Spears, J W S (1984) Effect of Dietary Nickel on Growth, Urease Activity, Blood Parameters and Tissue Mineral Concentrations in the Neonatal Pig, J Nut 114: 845-853

203.   McConnell K P, Burton R M (1981) Selenium in spermatogenesis. In: second International Symposium on Selenium in Biology and Medicine (Eds: JL Martin and JE Spallholz), Westport, Connecticut: AVI Publishing

204. Rayman MP (1997) Dietary selenium: time to act. Br Med J, 314:387-388

205. Jameson, S (1984) Zinc Status and Human Reproduction In; Zinc in Human Medicine Proceedings of a Symposium on the role of Zinc in Health and Disease, Isleworth, TIL Publications Ltd

206. Lazebik, N et al (1988) Zinc Status, Pregnancy Complications and labor Abnormalities, Am J Obstet Gynecol, 158: 161-166

207. Hurley, L (1969) Zinc Deficiency in the Developing Rat, Am J Clin Nut 22: 1332- 1339

CHAPTER 8

ELECTROMAGNETIC POLLUTION (OR ELECTROSMOG TO YOU AND ME)

In the excellent "Powerwatch Handbook", published in 2006, Alastair and Jean Phillips remind us that as early as the 1920s, the Marconi Company began its first speech transmissions from Chelmsford in the United Kingdom. What advances there have been in less than a century! From messages in Morse tapped from head-land to head-land, to television programmes on a mobile phone to "our foreign correspondent", now standing amid scenes of devastation and mayhem from every corner of the globe – live. (If there are ways we can help to alleviate or minimise such turmoil, one day, it may all have been worth it!)

However the point of this chapter is to talk about whether the actual *technology* involved, and the fallout from this, is affecting our health, our fertility and/or our future baby's health. Because sometimes it is.

Foresight started learning about electromagnetism rather late in the day, in the early 1990s. We met Alfred Riggs, possibly the most informed person on the planet on this subject. He told us of the dangers of becoming sensitised to electrosmog, (which you cannot see, smell, hear or feel in most cases) but which is now all around us as never before. "Minor" reactions to the bombardment include headaches, dizziness, sleeplessness, fatigue and depression, the ubiquitous "stress of modern life". More alarming consequences can include cancer, heart disease and leukaemia. There are questions over chromosomal damage in babies, and cot death, also infertility and miscarriage.

In the year 2000 an "expert group" was set up to study the effects of electromagnetic fields on human health.

We are grateful to Alistair and Jean for letting us know their conclusions:

"...that in making decisions about the siting of base stations, planning authorities should have the power to ensure that the radio frequency fields to which the public will be exposed will be kept to the lowest practical levels

that will be commensurate with the telecommunications operating effectively."

The six years that Judy and her husband had tried for a baby seemed like an eternity.

Two years after the wedding there was still no baby. Then in 2001 a referral for Judy and her husband at a hospital for an investigation came up. The examination revealed everything was perfectly fine except for some small cysts that were "too small for removal." IVF was organised and although there were plenty of embryos, there was no implantation in the first two IVF attempts.

A friend introduced them to Foresight and they started on the Programme. They also employed the help of a Foresight practitioner. However, following the lead of medically orientated friends, they felt a need to try for a 3rd IVF attempt with a private fertility specialist, although results of their hair mineral analysis were well below recommended levels for conception. Scans performed by the private clinic indicated 3 cysts on the left ovary (which previously were too small to remove) and adhesions in the uterus, all of which were then surgically removed. The implant failed. They decided to put the 4th IVF on hold in order to get Judy's body back to full fitness.

Foresight had suggested that perhaps a specialist in electromagnetic pollution, Roy Riggs, could identify a problem. Both were sceptical, but they decided to call him in. Roy found the whole house safe except for their bedroom where there was a problem exactly where their bed was located. They moved their bed into another room, continued with the Foresight Programme, and began to experience health. "Everything felt as if it was coming together. The combination was working well."

Late in December Judy was 4 days late. She was keenly aware of her cycle. They were about to attempt the 4th IVF but Gail decided to do a pregnancy test and as usual it proved negative. Two days later, urged by instinct, she did a second pregnancy test which proved positive! "Ah! I just sat there and couldn't believe it. My husband in surprise asked, "What does positive mean?" "It means we've *done* it!""

A little boy was conceived on Mummy's birthday and his birth was announced on Daddy's! Born 7lb 8oz by caesarean section. "He is a fantastic, lovely, laughing little boy and so happy."

Gail says "We changed our food to organic, threw out household chemicals such as air sprays, all our products are now eco friendly. I have kept up with the Foresight Programme all through breast feeding and found it so helpful."

Once again you spot the deliberate mistake, I am sure. The Expert is on the side of the commercial interest. Pollution must be kept as low as possible, but, this endeavour must not interfere with the ever rising need for telecommunication. Therefore the limit set will not in any way be linked to the health implications. It will be linked to the demand for – well, gadgets and wonder-toys that generate electrosmog. As their use proliferates, so this mobile "limit" will rise in line with commercial interests.

Once again, we do not want to wait for "the government", "the medics", or any other august body who rely on "the Expert" to protect us, or even warn us. We need to be looking out for ourselves, and most particularly for our future children.

There are in this country already in the region of 2 ½ million people suffering from a new and difficult-to-manage condition called EHS or electro-hypersensitivity. To put it in a nutshell, too much exposure to electro-magnetism has heightened their response to this, and each time they are exposed again, they become ill. For example, going near to mobile and cordless phones, to certain types of lighting, or to power lines or electrical appliances of all sorts affects them. People who have the condition very severely cannot be in a room with a mobile phone that is "live", for example. They can feel dizzy, sick, headachy or just tired to the point of being completely "wiped out".

To me, because my mind is always veering in one direction, this begs the question, "what does all this electrosmog do to the sperm, the ova, and the unborn child?"

What do we know so far? We know that carrying a mobile phone in the trouser pocket while it is on, means deformity and death to sperm. (I have recently heard of someone who did so all the time, who has had a tumour in the upper thigh.)

The police in recent years have been using a Tetra mast base station. This sends out a more powerful signal. Since then, they have found that carrying their phone in the trouser pocket caused prostate cancer, wearing it on their belt gave colon cancer, and wearing it in the breast pocket gave breast cancer. This latter is very unusual in men.

I think we can conclude that there is enough evidence that too much contact with these gadgets etc, could be more harmful than most people realise, or than the Powers-that-Be are willing to admit/allow themselves to realise, if intervention would interfere with a multi-million pound enterprise.

So What Do We Do?

It is possible to borrow, either from Foresight, or from Powerwatch, a small gadget called an Acousticom. This gadget makes a noise, anything from a low hum to a high-pitched scream, if it is placed near any electrical installation or appliance that is giving off an electromagnetic field. You can borrow this for a couple of days and go over your house/garden/place of work, and see what, if anything, is bugging you. Go around your skirting boards, plug sockets, around lamps while on, and around the Hoover, washing machine etc, (every piece of equipment you habitually use). If the buzz is not very bad, use it occasionally; the informed advice is, if possible keep well away from it while it is on. (Easier with a washing machine than with a Hoover!) If it is a lamp, for example, sit a bit further away from it. Arrange the room so you do not sit nearer to the television than you need to. Do not use a laptop on your lap! Test the VDU on and off. Throw away the DECT phone if you have one, they are one of the worst offenders! And so on. Inside the house it is all under your control. If your husband is reluctant to give up carrying a mobile phone in his trousers, explain to him that it kills and deforms his sperm and makes his testicles vulnerable to testicular cancer. This could mean they have to be removed. It is important that he knows this.

Outside your own house is more difficult. If it is a terraced house, there may be considerable debilitating and cancer-making fields coming through the wall from the back of a neighbour's television or VDU. It is possible to buy wallpaper with a sandwich effect – plain wallpaper on both sides of an aluminium foil lining. The rays cannot pass through aluminium. This can be put up and painted over, or wallpapered over again with one of your choice. There is also a carbon-based paint that is impenetrable. This is black, but can also be painted over. There are also silver mesh curtains that look just like ordinary net curtains, I am told, that can go up at the windows and will not let rays through. All/any of these may be helpful if circumstances are really difficult. www.powerwatch.org.uk is the relevant website. If the bed is vulnerable then it is important that the bedstead is wooden and the mattress has no metal springs, ie wool or latex etc. These can be obtained from Greenfibres in Totnes, or Healthy House in Ruscombe. See Useful Addresses.

Pylons, base stations, telephone wiring, mobile phone masts, also their boosters, and most especially Tetra masts, also TV broadcasting masts are all giving off at their various frequencies. In Germany, builders are not allowed to put up houses within 500m of a mast. Here, we can build right next door to them and furthermore, we plonk masts on the roofs of hospitals and schools. Again, if you stand around in your house, garden, patio, place of work, where ever, with an Acousticom, you can hear whether you are being zapped, and furthermore, by wandering around a bit, you can tell how badly, and by whom/what!

Do not blame your neighbour, he probably knows nothing about it, but help him to work out what is best for his family too. Maybe have an Acousticom Party and see how all of you can best protect your neighbourhood? We are all on the same side, and we all need to help each other as much as possible.

Sadly your local MP is unlikely to be helpful. (Please contact me immediately if you *are* an MP and intend to do something about this! Welcome on board!) The government line has been, *"you can complain on the grounds that they are unsightly, and we will take your complaint*

248

seriously, but you cannot complain on health grounds, as nothing is proven in that area." This is a crafty angle as it gives the industry the right/reason to hide the masts – in petrol station signs, in church steeples, in chimney stacks. *"The locals thought it was ugly, so we have to put it out of sight."* This is typical officialdom. What I call a "clever-clever" but not intelligent response.

Yes, they are hidden, people do not know they are there, so this solves the problem of coping with the *"fuss"*. Their friends in Telecom are happy – even gleeful. Probably punching the air over a glass of beer because the problem has been solved for them. Up go the masts.

The problems of the families where the breadwinner, or the young mother is dying of cancer, or where a precious child has been diagnosed with leukaemia, are not solved however.

Officialdom has yet to arrive at the stage of mental development where avoiding huge numbers of personal tragedies is more important than making huge amounts of money. We all need to come together over this, and push for their enlightenment.

The third problem is the electromagnetism from underground. This is where father and son Alfred and Roy Riggs have done such brilliant work. We will go over here to the chapter written for you by Gail Bradley, with additions to bring it up to date by Roy Riggs.

PHYSICAL HAZARDS IN THE WORKPLACE AND HOME

Information you need to check out at work and at home – is it safe for the unborn baby?

Some years ago if you opened a book on occupation health you would rarely find a mention of reproductive hazards. Now, with women of child-bearing age forming a large part of the workforce, and with recognition that occupational hazards can affect the male reproductive system, there are whole books on the subject, as well as large parts of others. The hazards are many, ranging from physical ones, such as radiation, VDUs, noise, light and heat, to chemical ones, such as formaldehyde and benzene.[1]

Here we consider radiation, which generates so much damage.

Ionising radiation

Rays of ionising radiation include alpha, beta and gamma rays, neutrons and X-rays. They are so powerful that they shatter atoms they touch, causing them to lose electrons, thereby developing an electric charge. These charged particles are called ions, hence the term 'ionising'. Because of their power they are extremely damaging to tissues in the body, and can cause death quickly or slowly. They penetrate the body without a person knowing. They hit atoms and molecules, breaking them up to form free radicals and oxidising agents. These two chemical groups may be quite damaging as they break up proteins, destroy chromosomes and change other chemicals. The results may be death of the cells, immediately or earlier than the usual lifespan, changes in the growth and division of the cell such that there may be no growth or uncontrolled growth (cancer), or prominent changes in the way the cell works.[2]

Man has always been exposed to some ionising radiation. However, Dr. Rosalie Bertell has pointed out that 'natural' levels have increased from an exposure of 60 millirem a year in 1940 to 100 in the 1950s to 200 millirems in the 1980s,[2] mainly due to weapons testing. No one disputes that more of us are exposed to more radiation than ever before.

Frequently we are reassured that low doses, such as that received in an X-ray, are safe. But the truth is that no level of radiation has been proved safe, and it is likely that any level is potentially harmful. A quick look through, for example, The Bulletin of the Atomic Scientist, reveals a number of studies which relate radiation dosages to malformations such as Down's syndrome, Patou's syndrome and Edward's syndrome, severe mental retardation, perinatal loss and neurological damage, to mention but a few.[3] Dr Bertell worries that scientists only ask about the risks of cancer from radiation exposure when it has other, more serious effects. She is especially concerned about the genetic pool: 'Children are now being born weakened by radioactivity, prone to enzyme disorders, allergies and asthma directly caused by cell mutations.' She talks of a weakened new generation less able to cope with an ever increasing dose of radiation in the environment. 'By the fifth generation of children born into the post-nuclear age the damage to the entire gene pool will be very clear indeed. She denounces the international 'safety' level that power stations work to: '...maximum 500 millirems a year to the public or plant workers, equivalent to 100 chest X-rays'[4]. Other researchers have also indicated that even increases in background radioactivity, within natural levels, may have damaging effects on the foetus and may be a reason for higher malformation rates.[5]

X-rays have been the subject of much research and concern, especially since Dr Alice Stewart showed that they could harm the foetus, causing a high risk of childhood leukemia.[6] Animal research confirms these adverse effects, in both males and females. When mature eggs of female mice were irradiated the offspring had a high incidence of cancer.[7] Where dominant mutations have been produced in male germ cells by X-rays, low birth weight results.[8]

Radiation Exposure in Hospitals & Clinics

X-rays: 0.6% of all cancers diagnosed in the UK are caused by medical X-rays. [700 of the 124,000 a year][9]

Mammograms: The dose from a single mammogram is about 7 times the dose rate of a single chest X-ray. [There is mixed debate whether the survival rate among women diagnosed by mammogram is any better than those who did not have a mammogram].

250

Ultrasound: UK survey showed that, for 1 in 200 babies where the pregnancy was terminated because the ultrasound showed major abnormalities, the diagnosis on post-mortem was less severe than predicted and the termination was probably unjustified. Research concluded some adverse effects: A summary of the safety of ultrasound in human studies published in May 2002 concluded that *'there may be a relation between prenatal ultrasound exposure and adverse outcome.'* Some of the reported effects are listed below:

- Growth restriction
- Delayed speech
- Dyslexia
- Non-right-handedness (Seen as marker of damage to developing brain)
- Damage to nerve myelin sheath
- Irreversible loss of brain cells

NB: Beverley Beech of The Association for Improvement in Maternity Services (AIMS) and myself have both sadly noted a number of occasions in which an early scan was given at 8 – 9 weeks, where the baby was seen to be kicking about and had a normal heartbeat. However, at the second scan a month or so later, they are told, "we are sorry to tell you, but your baby has died. He did not develop beyond 8 – 9 weeks. You must just have been lucky enough to catch a glimpse of him just before he died." It would be hard to expect the scanners to say that what they did may have been responsible, but I think it is time they took stock. This tragically happens far too often for the justification to be nothing but a strange co-incidence.

For those of you invited to go along for a scan, ask the reason. Is it just "routine"? Is it to help you "bond" with your baby? (You will do this anyway). Is there any really worrying medical reason? What is this?

Obtain all the details and then make your own mind up, in the light of all of the above. Your baby has to rely on you to protect him, when he needs this.

Cat Scans. These expose you to between 40 to a 100 times the dose of a conventional X-ray examination and represent the largest source of radiation exposure in both the UK and USA. The Health Protection Agency reported that in 1998, CAT scans constituted 4% of all medical examinations, contributing to 40% of the collective effective dose of X-rays.

MRI Scans: Use strong magnetic fields and radio frequency fields to build up a picture. Despite this they are probably the safest form of body imaging, and about a million MRI scans are performed each year in the UK.

NB: If you have to have one, consult a homeopath. There are homeopathic nosodes (remedies) to X-rays, that offer some protection from side effects. Alternatively, ring Ainsworths Homeopathic Chemists before you have the X-ray. You can take a nosode before and after.

Non-ionising radiation

Non-ionising rays, including ultra violet light, infra-red, lasers, microwaves, radar, radio -frequency waves and extra low frequency waves, are naturally produced by the sun and also created in the home, in industry and in military use. Although not powerful enough to create ions, no one should be fooled about their safety. The chief of research of non-ionising radiation at the National Institute of Environmental Health Sciences, North Carolina, Donald McCree, has said: *'In animal experiments, (the Russians) have found that this radiation causes changes in almost every system: behaviour, blood chemistry, the endocrine functions, reproductive organs, and the immune system. In studies of human workers exposed to microwave equipment for many years, they have reported abnormally slow heart beats, chest pains, and birth defects. And they've found a lot of more subjective effects, things like insomnia, irritability, headaches and loss of memory'.*[10]

Of major concern to us here are sunlight, ultra violet, microwaves, radar and radio frequency waves.

Sunlight

'Light is a primal element of life.[11] Indeed, without it we would not have life as we know it. We tend to talk about the benefits of 'fresh air' without being aware of the beneficial effects of natural light. Yet research has shown that natural light and artificial light have different physiological effects in animals, including human beings, which show in a variety of physical and mental conditions, such as tumours and hyperactivity.

Clearly, artificial lighting is an essential part of modern lifestyles. But it is possible to buy full-spectrum lighting, which is very similar to natural light and quite different from fluorescent, neon and other artificial forms. (See Appendix for addresses.) Full-spectrum lighting covers more specific wavelengths, especially the blue or ultra violet ones that are missing from artificial lighting. (See below.) If they are blocked out, an endocrine deficiency can arise.[12] Mice kept in artificial light conditions died prematurely or had very small litters, suggesting the need for further research.[13] Full-spectrum lighting has been shown to help alleviate seasonal affective depression.[14] Sunlight has been found to help with the elimination of toxic metals from the body, and the metabolism of desirable minerals.[15]

Ultra violet light

Ultra violet rays can be UV-A or UV-B type. The UV-B are the ones that give you sunburn, but although UV-A is weaker, one expert says it does the same damage, and may even be worse. To get brown, you need the same overall exposure, so with UV-A, it just means that you will have to sunbathe longer. However, UV-A penetrates deeper than UV-B, and may cause damage to collagen, blood vessels and elastic tissues. UV-B may therefore be safer, because the UV-A lulls you into a false sense of security. Also, once exposed to UV-A, the body is more susceptible to the aging and carcinogenic effects of UV-B radiation.[16]

There is now quite a scare about sunbathing and skin cancer. To induce skin cancer in animals, it is necessary to give a larger-than-normal dose of ultra violet light so that burning occurs.[17] There also seems to be a direct relationship between the amount of free radicals formed in the skin when it is exposed to sunlight and the tendency for that skin to burn. Stop the free radicals forming and you considerably reduce the sun burning. (Free radical formation can be inhibited by certain nutrients in the diet, such as Vitamins A, C and E.) Another factor that may be significant is cholesterol, which may be changed into a number of products when the ultra violet strikes the skin, one of which, cholesterol alphaoxide, can act as a free radical and cause cancer.[17] Oils and fats applied to the skin, or sunbathing creams may also stimulate cancer formation.[17]

So should you avoid ultra violet light? This is not the good idea that the advertisements would have us believe, since it means avoiding natural sunlight, or at least parts of it, and the ultra violet portion is the most biologically active. Ultraviolet wavelengths can kill bacteria, and infections are definitely to be avoided in pregnancy![17] Ultra violet treatments are provided by law to miners in Russia, as they have been found to help remove dust from the lungs.[17]

Visual display units — VDUs

VDUs were widely used in the workplace and home until a few years ago. There was considerable debate over their safety, especially for the pregnant woman, but few conclusions were drawn. Thankfully, computer technology has now marched ahead making VDU screens a thing of the past. These screens have now almost all been replaced by flat colour screens known as TFT or plasma screens which are only a few inches thick and give off almost zero magnetic fields. Laptop computers also give off very low electromagnetic fields but when run from the mains can radiate very high electric fields. If you use your laptop, make sure it is operated in battery mode. *It is better never to use it on your lap at all.* Be sure your VDU is a modern flat-screen one. This is really important.

Microwaves

Microwaves can penetrate deeply into the body, causing its temperature to rise. High intensity microwaves can lead to permanent damage. For example, the heat generated can cause the cell lining of the testicles to degenerate, therefore damaging them.[18] It is also suspected of causing breast cancer, especially where a microwave oven is placed at breast height.[19] The problem arises because the breast (and eyes) have poor blood supply so the heat is not dissipated. Microwaves may also cause genetic damage: one study has shown that more Down's syndrome children were fathered by men exposed to microwaves than by fathers not so exposed.[20] The highest concentration of microwaves in the home is emitted from DECT cordless phone, cordless baby monitors and wireless computer networks (WI-FI). To reduce your levels of microwave exposure in the home *replace your*

DECT cordless phones with land line phones. Buy baby alarm monitors of the type that route the signal through your house-hold electric circuit. Replace your WI-FI systems with a cable or ADSL modem/router.

Digital Cordless Baby Monitors. (by Roy Riggs)

Over the past five years, with the help of parents, I have measured a variety of baby monitors and the DECT pulsing ones seem to be far more disruptive to the infant's sleep and state of contentment (causing restlessness, irritability and crying). Wired ones and the plug-in ones (that use the electricity wiring to communicate between units) do not seem to cause the same problems. The older type of analogue ones/ that are still available from a number of brands, seem OK if kept at least one meter from the cot / bed. I have had various reports by parents that their babies did not sleep well and cried a lot when they used DECT monitors but were ok when no baby monitor was used. When they then tried a cheaper analogue monitor, the infant then slept as well as with no monitor.

Powerwatch UK strongly recommend that only low-band (35 to 50 MHz) analogue baby monitors are used. These use analogue frequency modulation (FM, Like VHP radio stations) that does not pulse at all. The analogue ones are often identifiable by their low number of channels (typically 2-4). You can hire or purchase suitable equipment (i.e. the A-COM and the Electrosmog Detector) from EMFields: www.emfields.org to check out the microwave environment from all sources that may surround your baby. It is preferable to check the place where the baby will be sleeping *before* he/she is born.

Most baby monitors are now advertised as using DECT phone technology which rims at 1890 MHz or 2400 MHz, which is 1.89 GHz or 2.4 GHz. 2.4 GHz is the microwave oven frequency. These are identifiable by the large number of claimed channels (usually at least 30 and often up to 120), which DECT automatically switches between. These emit sharply pulsing bursts of microwave radiation 100 times every second all the time they are turned on. **Avoid using these.**

With 'talk back' digital baby monitors, where parents can talk back to the baby, both units continuously emit pulsing radiation (on 2 different frequency channels - one for each way), not just when the baby is making a noise or the parent is talking to them. There are also some camera-based monitors which run at 2.4 GHz. Since these have to transmit video and sound, it is likely that they would have a higher power output. Also, the manufacturers note that these cannot be used in conjunction with computer wireless networks due to interference. **Avoid these also.**

The baby monitor mats that check temperature, heartbeat, breathing, etc/ should only be used if you have medical reasons to believe that your baby might be in danger of sudden infant death. When used with a wireless baby alarm they carry high levels of microwave radiation (up to 6 volts per meter) right into the cot and we believe that will not do your baby any good at all.

I do not recommend the use of wireless video baby monitors that allow you to see your baby on your TV or a portable TV monitor. If you really need that level of baby watching, then have a proper wired closed-circuit TV (CCTV) system installed - do not put a TV wireless transmitter in your child's bedroom and irradiate them unnecessarily.

Electricity

People living near high-voltage power lines have sometimes complained that their health was affected by them, though this has been dismissed as nonsense! However, in March 1988, the Chairman of the Central Electricity Generating Board launched a £500,000 study into the effects of high-voltage lines on health. At the launch, officials were still being dismissive of the likelihood of any link, though other countries accept the risks that the electromagnetic fields generated by them can damage health.[21] Russia limits the time a farm worker can spend near them to three hours, while the USA will not allow houses to be built near them.[22] The New York Power-Lines Project results showed that there was an increase in child cancers and significant behavioural and central nervous system effects: One group of researchers found an increase in all birth defects from conceptions that occurred during the time the father worked on high-voltage systems.[23] Men working in high-voltage switching yards were found to father more congenitally malformed children than would be expected.[24] A number of animal studies have reported health problems including foetal abnormailites.[18] Dr Nancy Wertheimer and her colleagues found an association between the use of electric blankets and infertility and birth defects. They hypothesised that strong electromagnetic fields may be generated by electric-blankets under certain circumstances. The seasonal variation of rates of birth and birth defects may agree with the time periods of peak electric blanket use. (Of course, they may also peak with many other factors, such as reduced sunlight or different food availability.) Dr Wertheimer has also undertaken a study, yet to be published, showing that women living in homes in which electric heating cables have been installed in the ceilings have higher rates of miscarriage.[18]

Heat

Extremes of heat and cold cause stress to the body, which can be disadvantageous in the preconception period. But as well as these general stress effects, there may be specific ones associated with heat.

In the man, heat can interfere with sperm production, since the testicles need to operate at a lower temperature than the rest of the body. Hours of sitting, such as happens with taxi and lorry drivers, travelling salesmen and business executives, may result in excess scrotal heat.[25] Skin-tight underwear or frequent hot baths can have a similar effect.[26]

In women, a high body temperature (hyperthermia) can cause damage to the foetus. Hyperthermia tends to stop the division of cells and very high temperatures may even kill cells.[26] In the foetus cell division is basic to growth so stopping it can have devastating consequences. Both brain size and function have been affected.

High temperatures may occur with infections and people have queried if problems arise as a result of the infection or the high temperature itself. Research suggests the latter alone can cause damage. One study of brain damaged children revealed that their healthy mothers had taken regular prolonged saunas. The researchers advise that prolonged saunas should be avoided during the first three to five months of pregnancy.[27] Short saunas, six to ten minutes long, such as are taken by the Fins, may be safe.

(NB However, as there is some doubt, I would avoid them).

EMFs and Pregnancy

Two epidemiology studies published in 2000 and 2002 suggest that a substantial proportion of miscarriages might be caused by maternal EMF exposure. They theorized that the added risk of miscarriage for a pregnant women exposed to EMF's may be 5 to 10 per cent. Overall, Dr De-Kun Li and his team for the 2002 study found that **women exposed to peak levels of 1.6 microtesla or greater were nearly twice as likely to miscarry as women not exposed to such strong fields.**[28]

Reducing your EMF and Microwave Exposure

- Keep at least one meter from the front of televisions.

- If you have an old type cathode-ray VDU monitor replace it with a TFT or Plasma display unit both at work and at home.

- Do not use a laptop on your lap.

- Minimise your use of electric appliances at worktop height in the kitchen.

- Move clock radios at least one meter away from your pillow.

- Reduce your use of electric household appliances such as vacuum cleaners, food mixers.

- If you have power lines over, or a substation next to, your garden, avoid sitting in the vicinity.

- Keep beds away from electric storage heaters, both sides of the wall.

- Don't hold a cordless phone or mobile phone near to your 'bump'. Preferably, don't use one at all.

- **Don't wear support bras that contain metal.** These can act as passive antennas near radio frequency sources such as mobile phones. For the same reason sprung mattresses should be replaced with one of the many non-sprung mattresses that are now on the market.

- Avoid standing or working near microwave oven, electric cooker or washing machine when switched on.

- Make little use of hairdryers and keep the unit well away from the growing foetus. Hand held hairdryers use high currents both to drive the motor and produce heat and are one of the highest sources of EMF exposure.

- Never keep any type of electric blanket turned on when you are in bed.

- Use a TFT or Plasma computer or TV monitor both at home and work.

- Do not use DECT cordless phones or baby alarms.

I am so grateful to Gail and Roy for all of the above.

As you will have gathered, the problems of underground radiation come mainly from either underground rivers, or from cracks in the substrata – especially where the substrata is granite, which is mainly the peninsula, Devon and Cornwall, or the very north of England and Scotland.

If you look at a geophysical map of the United Kingdom showing the areas of granite substrata, and also have a map of deformities in children, you will see they very largely coincide. I have pointed this out to people and the reply is usually, "Ah yes, but those are also the areas of highest poverty."

"Poverty" is always some sort of catch-all excuse. However, there may be a connection with a phenomena that makes people feel ill, dizzy, sick, sleep badly, be increasingly liable to cancer, and be generally under the weather, (quite apart from the elderly being more likely to develop mental infirmity and the babies more likely to be born deformed). This phenomena might, in very many cases, have a direct bearing on their ability to go out to work and earn a decent salary?

If anything is ever going to bring an end to "poverty" it is getting people *well*, and therefore better able to use their strength and their brains, and getting their babies born likewise.

So What Do We Do?

We suggest you call in Roy with his very precise instruments to go over the house, and see what and where, if at all, it is affected by electromagnetism.

He can then tell you exactly where the lines go. Where, if necessary, you need to move critical bits of furniture like the bed, and/or the favourite chair you sit in to eat, or to relax in the evening. It is also absolutely vital to know where to put the cot when the moment comes. Babies are known to be very magnetically sensitive, and to be unable to sleep in an electro-smog position.

257

They are also more liable to cot death, cancer and leukaemia, if exposed to large amount. Get him to check the type and position of the baby monitor.

Roy came to look at the house we are now living in before we bought it. He found a line that goes along inside the wall of two of the bedrooms, about a foot inside the wall. When he told us, the erstwhile owners of the house were very intrigued. He showed them how the line went across the pillow of their bed. The woman told us how she always woke up with a splitting headache and had tried all sorts of solutions from conventional and alternative medicine, and the man told us how he woke up with a pain in his neck every morning which he put down to an old rugby injury. In the weeks before the move took place, they moved the bed, and the pains ceased to happen.

It is a great shame that this is not part of the normal house survey when people move house, as so much pain and illness could be eliminated if people knew the best spots to put their furniture.

I am not an expert on this area of Foresight work, (but I know a man who is!) I would therefore suggest that:

a) You borrow our DVD of Alf Riggs (Roy's father, arguably the world authority on electromagnetism), giving his talk a few years ago. In this, he shows exactly what he does, and explains everything in a way that can be easily understood.

b) If you can, I would also try and hear a talk, read a book, or at least have a look at the website of Roger Coghill, MA (Cantab.) C. Biol. MI Biol. MA Environ Mgt, who is another highly intelligent radiesthesist. Roger is also very much into the harm being done to the bees, as he is convinced that the stress and confusion electrosmog is causing them lies behind this "mystery virus". He is also convinced it is causing sterility in the little song birds and other small wild animals by zapping their ovaries. If we all become more aware, it may be possible to find ways to minimise the hazards for them. I would look at Roger's website and see if there are things we can do to improve conditions for the wildlife as well as for ourselves. It is only fair. We do not have the right to destroy their environment and their fertility as well as our own.

c) Also, look at Powerwatch UK and read their excellent book "the Powerwatch Handbook" which will give you lots of useful pointers, in enormous detail, on how to keep your house safe. I would also borrow an Acousticom and nosy around with it. There are probably a million things that we do not yet know about electromagnetism because for most of us, we have only just become aware of it. But if we can make every effort to minimise the risks we *are* aware of, we will need to worry a lot less.

d) Make contact with Roger Muller of "Electricforester", a new organisation working in this field. Roger suffers himself very badly from EHS after working with electricity for many years. He gives meetings to explain the problem in simple terms to the lay person, and it is well worth attending one if you feel you need to become more informed.

e) If you have a fertility problem, have had a miscarriage or a Down's syndrome baby, or suffer from any of the symptoms described above, I would get Roy in and suss out the house, garden and workplace.

f) If you know anybody with cancer or leukaemia, or any of the symptoms described, let them know what can be done.

If you have masts on the top of your local school, hospital, nursery, or in the church tower, I would complain about it! For further advice on how to identify and deal with both electromagnetic and geopathic energies in the home and workplace, use Alf and Roy Riggs, Roger Coghill, Roger Muller, Dr Patrick Macmanaway and Powerwatch's websites to gather together the information you need. *Good luck!*

www.royriggs.co.uk
www.powerwatch.org.uk
www.cogreslab.co.uk
www.alfredriggs.com
www.electricforester.co.uk
www.westbank.org.uk

Discuss all of it with your neighbours, and help your community as much as you can. You can make a lot of difference to people's lives.

Onward!

References:

1. Franc, M.C., Meunier, A., et al., Archives du malades professionelles, du medicin du travail et due securite sociale. 1981, 42(3): 183-194

2. Bertell, Rosalie. In: Toynbee, Polly, 'Behind the Lines', *Guardian,* 15 December 1986, 12

3. Anon. *The Bulletin of the Atomic Commission.* 1992, 48(1)

4. Bertell, Rosalie, *No Immediate Danger.* 1988

5. Ferreira, Antonio J., *Prenatal Environmental,* Springfield, Ill, Charles C. Thomas 1969

6. Bithell, J.F., Stewart A.M., 'Prenatal irradiation and childhood malignancy: a review of British data from the Oxford Survey', *Br J Cancer,* 1975, 31, 271-287

7. Nomura, T., 'Parental exposure to X-Rays and chemicals induces heritable tumours and anomalies in mice', *Nature,* 1982, 296, 575-577

8. Kirk, K.M., Lyon, M.F., 'Induction of congenital malformations in the offspring of male mice treated with X-Rays at premeiotic and post-meiotic

stages', *Mutation Research,* 1984, 125, 75-85

8.   Herzog,P & Rieger,CT., Risk of Cancer from diagnostic X-rays, Lancet 2004 Jan 31: 363(9406):345-51, 2004

9.   McCree, Donald. In: Gold, Michael, 'Additional findings at low exposures have prompted serious second thoughts about US safeguards', *Science 80,* Premier Issue, 81

10.   Hollwich, Fritz, *The Influence of Ocular Light Perception on Metabolism in Man and Animals*, New York, Springer-Verlag, 1980, Preface

11.   Ott, John N., *Light Radiation and You,* Greenwich, CN, 1985, 78-139. These two chapters give some interesting examples

12.   Gabby, Samuel Lee, 'Observations on the effects of artificial light on the health and development of mice'. In: Ott, John N., *op. cit.,* 100

13.   Rosenthal, Norman E., et al., 'Antidepressant Effects of Light in Seasonal Effective Disorder', *Am J Psychiatr,* 1985, 2, 163-170

14.   Kime, Zane R., *Sunlight*, Penryn, World Health Publication, 1980, 199

15.   McCarthy, Paul, *Health,* February 1988, 32

16.   Kime, Zane R., *op. cit.,* 92

17.   Becker, Robert, *Cross Currents*, Bloomsbury, London, 1990, 276

18.   Schauss, Alexander G., 'Body Chemistry and Human Behaviour'. Course: Oxford, 18 November 1986

19.   Stellman, Jeanne, Daum, Susan M., *Work is Dangerous to your Health*, Vintage Books, 1979, 141

20.   Wright, Pearce, 'Claims that power cables cause Cancer to be investigated', *The Times,* 18 March 1988

21.   Anon, 'Power Lines Cancer Link', *Today,* 18 March 1988

22.   Nordstrom, S., et al., 'Reproductive hazards among workers at high-voltage systems', *Bioelectromagnetics,* 1981, 4, 91-101

23.   Nordstrom, S., et al., 'Genetic defects in offspring of power-frequency workers', *Bioelectromagnetics,* 1983, 4: 91

24.   Andrews, Lori, B., *New Conceptions,* New York, St Martin's Press, 1984, 23

25.   Teymor, Melvin L., *Infertility,* New York, Grune and Stratton Inc, 1978

26.   Smith, David W., *Mothering Your Unborn Baby,* Philadelphia, W.B. Saunders, 1979, 67

27.   Li,D.K. et.al, A population based prospective cohort study of personal exposure to magnetic fields during pregnancy and the risk of miscarriage,. Epidemiology, Jan: 13(1) :9-20, 2002

CHAPTER 9

CHEMICAL HAZARDS

"Nearly every chemical to which the pregnant woman is exposed will ultimately reach the foetus." So says Dr Joan Spyker, an eminent toxicologist. In 1984, Gail Bradley commented: *"we must also remember that the foetus does not have a mature system to detoxify all the poisons that may be passed on to it."*

In a study spearheaded by the Environmental Working Group (EWG) in collaboration with Commonweal, researchers at two major laboratories found an average of 200 industrial chemicals and pollutants in umbilical cord blood from 10 babies born in August and September of 2004 in U.S. hospitals. Tests revealed a total of 287 chemicals in the group. The umbilical cord blood of these 10 children, collected by Red Cross after the cord was cut, harbored pesticides, consumer product ingredients, and wastes from burning coal, gasoline, and garbage.

From: Environmental Working Group, July 14, 2005

Even in the UK, I am afraid we have to conclude that Our Hero is up against it!

Secondly, I think we now have to think on even further than Dr Spyker. The use of powerful medical drugs and hormones has become more and more common. We now know that when chemicals are voided (urinated or defecated) they enter the biosphere, and become cumulative until they can be found in measurable quantities in earth, water and so on. Of course this will be in minute quantities at present, and certainly not all the biosphere pollution has passed through people first! Much has come from smoke, pesticides, fluoride, industrial waste etc discharged into rivers direct from the factories, incinerators, and farmland. Poison such as is used to dip sheep, is dumped into rivers etc. (This is illegal, but it happens!)

At the same time we are told of the demise of the bees, butterflies and the small birds, to think of but a few "bio-tragedies". We need to become more thoughtful and a lot less gung ho with every type of chemical. We seem to have been the most destructive generation so far. This has gone on for long enough.

One health problem the establishment does seem to be becoming more aware of is obesity. Presumably because it is the most visible! Walking in any town in England now, you can spot the tendency!

The standard answer trotted out by the Establishment is "too much food/the wrong type of food, and too little exercise". Yes, well, this has to be factored in. But *how much* is down to these *simplistic* answers, and how much is down to exogenous hormones, statins, steroids, insulin, pig's thyroxin, tranquillisers and the like, urinated happily into the biosphere by the pill-taking public, and now coming from our tap water?

All these drugs are known to have "weight gain" listed among their side effects. Then what about the growth promoters, antibiotics etc given to livestock? (Firstly, is meat more fattening to *us* when the animals are reared on substances meant to be more fattening to *them*? Secondly, as their excrement seeps from the fields into the water-table, is this too laced with chemical "make-fatters"? Well?)

We cannot all be totally neurotic, but I think two at least partial solutions to all today's problems would be: (a) we do all we can to stay as healthy as possible, so we do not need to take medical drugs; (b) we use as few chemicals as possible, to keep the environment, and our own unborn children, as free from gunk as possible.

My grandmother lived to be 103 years old (compos mentis to the end) and never took a medical pill, even an aspirin, all her life. "I've watched what happens to my friends," she used to say, "when they start going to the doctor they get worse, not better. Your body knows what to do. Leave it alone and let it get on with it."

We can look at the problems we find commonest in our own lives, and the solutions:

CHECKLIST

1.   We can **eat organic food**, avoiding promoting further use of pesticides such as organophosphates and chemical fertilisers such as potassium, phosphorus, nitrates and "growth promoters" in the livestock. We could maybe even have a vegetable patch and grow our own, or hire an allotment.

2.   We can ask florists for organic flowers, (essential for maternity greetings and hospital gifts), and so discourage use of chemicals on flowers. (Using soapy water for greenfly on our own roses.)

3.   We can avoid inorganic "bug killers" in our own garden and kitchen. Common table salt discourages snails and slugs. So do coffee grounds. Picking things off food plants by hand is the easiest way. Feeding all plants with organic seaweed manure also seems to be a very good way of making plants strong enough to stand up to mould, blight, black spot etc. Pinch the hose into a small jet to knock the blackfly off dahlias etc. A line of flour will

deter ants from coming into the house, it sticks to their legs and they don't like it!

4.   If you eat mainly fresh food you will not come across additives much, but if you buy our booklet "FIND OUT", you can avoid any of the really unhelpful ones. It may also help the "General Cause" if you flourish it under the noses of the supermarket staff. Better still, give one to the Manager!

5.   Avoid toothpaste which contains fluoride. It is an endemic poison, used as a rat killer in the United States. All other European countries have given up putting it directly into the drinking water because of the health effects and the effects on the environment. Nevertheless, if we and 69 million other people spit it into the waste water twice a day, the cumulative effect must be horrendous. Think of the poor little fish wondering why they feel so queasy, and what the Dickens is happening to their genitalia? Apart from that, we know fluoride affects thyroid function. People keep telling me *"I'm on thyroxine....."* The thyroid is very near the inside of the mouth, if you think of facial geography. If the lining of the mouth is absorbing fluoride, then it must be reaching the thyroid. And then, how about the baby's thyroid? Remember Dr Spykes saying anything the mother is exposed to reaches Our Hero. Don't let's clobber his little thyroid. Fluoride free toothpastes are: Kingfisher, Tom of Maines', Nelson's Homeopathic, Euthymol, and Aloe Vera (I think the nicest).

6.   We needn't use the contraceptive pill or copper coil. Nobody needs an extra cancer risk. Wildlife doesn't need these. They have to drink the river water too. We can learn natural family planning – it is more thoughtful for the future fertility of all the species in the world.

7.   Well, I thought I would list for you all the noxious materials that seem to be put in a whole range of cosmetics, and what are loosely termed "bathroom products". However, when I came to consult our little booklet "WATCH IT", compiled in 2007 after Trojan work by Maria Griffiths, I found there were 67 such chemicals – all with chillingly long and complicated names! I realised you would never want to sit and read through them, any more than I wanted to copy them out! However, I noted that 39 of them were known to be carcinogenic (cancer–causing) and 12 were listed as causing miscarriage; 41 were skin and/or eye irritants; 16 were said to affect the central nervous system; 11 were said to cause "mild or serious insanity"(!?!); 10 to cause nausea and vomiting; 10 to cause asthma; and 9 were said to be teratogenic (baby damaging).

Reading through it, I realised we were once again sitting ducks for the pharmaceutical industry, as they pop little surprises into our face creams that cause eye irritation, asthma etc, and then benefit from the expensive little medicaments we use to try to get better.

So, the good news is there is this little booklet, "WATCH IT", and you can take it shopping. As with "FIND OUT", *flourish* it in the shops where you buy your cosmetics, so that worried shop owners can let manufacturers know that we are all switched on, and noseying around among their products!

The other bit of good news is that there are now 26 different firms making products they claim are free from noxious chemicals! You will have to check them out regarding what is available from where, and what the price is! We will list them all for you in the Useful Addresses Section. (They are also all in the back of "WATCH IT").

8.   Many household cleaners are also pretty suspect! Some are said to contain arsenic. EDTA (Ethylenediaminetetraacetic acid – you see what I *mean*?) is found in some bleaches, and causes headaches and skin rashes. Once in the river, it kills fish and shellfish. Hydrochloric acid is a severe irritant to the eyes and skin, and is found in toilet cleaners. Isopropyl is found in liquid cleaners and detergents. It is said to be a central nervous system depressant that can cause vomiting and coma.

Naphthalene in toilet cleaners etc and in pesticides is said to be poisonous to human beings, it irritates the skin and eyes, *and* is carcinogenic. Oxalic acid, also found in toilet cleaners, is another hazardous one that is also said to damage the liver and kidneys. Paradichloro benzene and also sodium bisulphate/biosulphide and two more chemicals in toilet cleaners and disinfectants, can trigger allergies.

Lots of different products in laundry powders and soaps are said to be carcinogenic.

So what do we do? There is good old hot water, table salt, and bicarbonate of soda. These have the merit of being cheap, as well as baby friendly, and not rough on the biosphere.

Furniture and Furnishings

"Hard" furniture, meaning mainly made from wood, is safe so long as it is genuine! It may be best bought second hand, so nothing "modern" has been done to it, like treating it in advance for woodworm etc. Some wood is treated with arsenic, to prevent mould and rotting. However, "old" furniture may also have been treated at some stage.

Always find out <u>exactly</u> what you are buying. If there are woodworm holes, leave it alone!

Even more, beware the fitted kitchen and bedroom furniture that is made from "chipboard". This is sawdust stuck together with noxious solvents and resins, which can out-gas benzene, nitrophenols, formaldehyde, and other volatile compounds which can be allergenic. Maybe stick to old family stuff or buy second hand and give it a lick and a promise, a coat of beeswax polish or a coat of eco-paint?

The good news is that it is now possible to buy carpets, curtain material and so on, *free* from chemicals. Blendworth, at Horndean, near Petersfield do this. They ask you if you would like it sprayed with moth proofing, fire retardant or Scotch guard or similar stain proofing? Just say no. If you are not asked this, find out if this has already been done. If so, ask for a length without any of it. This can come straight from the factory without anything added.

To my way of thinking, this *should* be cheaper, as they have not had to do anything with it? However, it will probably *not* be, but it certainly should not be *more* expensive!

There are places you can go to get mattresses and bedding that is organic, not treated, and in the case of mattresses, free from metal springs, (which can now be made "live" by the mobile phone masts! – frying tonight!) They are, Green Fibres, and Healthy House. (See Useful Addresses).

It is enormously important for Our Hero's cot mattress and bedding to be organic.

Non-organic mattresses can be full of wool from dipped sheep which can give off organophosphates. Although there is no "scientific proof" I have always been concerned that this might be a contributory factor to cot death. In New Zealand all babies' mattresses are put in waterproof covers, and there is said to be no cot death. (*Why has our Government not taken this on board?*)

Regarding getting a home together, there are bodies called the Ecological Design Association (EDA), who have a journal called "Ecodesign", (The British School, Slad Road, Stroud, Glos. Tel/Fax: 01453 765575), and the Building Research Establishment (www.bre.co.uk).

There is also the London Hazards Centre (www.lhc.org.uk) who can be quite informative on specific issues regarding chemicals.

Issues that are hopefully more under our control include private swimming pools – avoid the copper-containing algicides, and be somewhat sparing with the chlorine, consistent with keeping the water bug free.

I would be wary, for the moment, of the new "long life" light bulbs. They seem to be causing muscle aches, stiff necks, and headaches for people sitting under them for any length of time. Hopefully, this will be drawn to the attention of the industry and something will be done about it. Watch all relevant spaces. Meanwhile, I would buy up a little stock of old fashioned ones to tide you over!

Products such as household cleaners, washing-up machine tablets, washing powders and liquids can be bought from Ecover, who are the most ecologically sound source. Other products can cause allergies. This is often skin irritation, (which is hellish, but not life-threatening), but in some cases the products can cause asthma, (which can be).

Scraping off old paint – particularly that painted on in the 1960s or earlier - can produce lead dust, so it is as well to cover up with overalls, and wear rubber gloves and a face mask. Otherwise we can breathe in quite a lot of the dust, or absorb it through the skin – and it can take us months (working with hair charts and supplements) to get it down again!

If you are an artist, and you use lead based paint, then **do not lick your brushes**. This fills you with lead, and can give you cancer of the tongue and throat. It can also cause miscarriage, premature birth, stillbirth and birth defects.

Solvents such as Benzaldehyde can act as central nervous system depressants and cause generalised malaise and allergy as well as allergic irritation. Butyl cellosolve, can cause headaches, nausea, liver and kidney damage and birth defects. Ethanol in others can cause irritation of the eyes, throat and airways, and inhaling it could lead to lack of coordination and stupor. Ethylene glycol monobutyl acetate can damage internal organs and nerves through the skin, while Hydroxganisole is a skin and eye irritant and can cause cancer.

Toulene, used to remove wallpaper, can cause birth defects such as deformed ribs, which can prevent the baby from breathing properly, and cancer as well as the more usual allergic reactions.

From all of this, I am sure you have gathered that the Preconceptual period and pregnancy are not very good times for DIY and home decoration! This is very inconvenient, as I know so many of you move house at about this time, and set about decorating in a big way. But as you see, you have to pick your way, and be very, very careful what you use, as so much of what is out there can be hazardous.

Safe paints are Ecopaints, which has a good range of colours. They are at www.ecopaints.co.uk, or Ecopaints, Braintree Enterprise Centre, 46 Springwood Drive, Braintree, CM7 2YN, Tel: 0845 3457725. If you ring them, they will send a colour card straight away, and you get the paint within two or three days. So far as I know, at the time of going to press, these are the only truly non-toxic paints there are.

If you are doing anything other than just painting, check everything you use with our little booklet "WATCH IT", and if in doubt, consult the London Hazards Centre or the EHS.

Nappies. I am told there are substances such as bleach, in the paper (disposable) ones, that can shrink the genitalia of little boys, so Our Hero is not going to thank you for using *those*. Even if the makers managed to get round that one, there is the looming problem of literally *mountains* of undisposed of "disposables" growing until they literally take over whole huge sites of dumping ground..... and then what? One massive toxic Hero-Headache in 20 years time. He won't thank us for that either. Furthermore he will put it right down to lack of foresight. Well, wasn't it? They say there is a huge floating island of plastic waste out in the Atlantic Ocean...

So it looks as though the time has come now to go back to good old terry towelling. I used to put them on like a kilt for the first few weeks, while their legs were so very tiny.

I expect I will be executed, hung, drawn and chopped into pieces the size of sugar lumps, if I mention the potty? However, I will. In my day we used to sit them on the potty a few minutes after their feed. They do a wee then. Then they are put into a dry nappy that stays dry for a little longer. You do not expect them to be dry in between feeds, of course, or get ambitious about "potty training". However, many of them will wee every time they are put on the potty, and some of them, if encouraged, will poo into a potty most of the time, and I don't care what the experts tell you, it saves quite a lot of work, and I think the babies are a far more comfortable and less likely to get sore.

Obviously they wee in between times, and obviously they poo when they want to, and you may not be to hand, so tough! I suppose the "experts" current potty phobia was due to some baby being maltreated by an idiotic parent who expected too much. However, I do not feel *all* babies should be made to spend a lot more of their lives wet, or dirty, just because of this.

Many of the soap products etc can give babies rashes. Nappies that are just wet, I would simply wash in very hot water, and then hang them outside, location and weather permitting. On the whole, babies do not need lotions, powders etc etc, and just being washed with clean warm water will do.

If, however, very obvious nappy rash appears, (a) use a cream called Morhulin ointment, made with fish oils. It smells a bit fishy, but does the trick; (b) think about what you ate, if you are breast-feeding, sugar, citrus, wheat etc? Work out what it is he is not tolerating; (c) if he is also "eating" by now, what was it *he* was indulging in? Keep a food diary if you need to, and it will soon become clear what upsets him.

Very obvious People-Pollutants in adults are **mercury dental amalgams** and/or **fluoride**. Mercury amalgam fillings should now be a thing of the past.

Some areas are now putting fluoride in the water again. This is despite much opposition, since it has been found to cause upset stomachs, headaches and flu-like symptoms, also an increase in ovarian and women's cancers generally. One study in Florida found a *fourfold* increase in the birth of Down's syndrome babies, which reverted to the normal rate per year, after the addition of fluoride to the water was discontinued.

If your Water Board is adding fluoride to your water, I would (a) discontinue using toothpaste with fluoride in it; (b) drink bottled water, and; (c) have very quick showers rather than luxuriating in a bath tub, as it can be absorbed through the skin; (d) take plenty of selenium and vitamin E, as these fight fluoride; (e) discuss this with your Water Board. *They expect you to pay them money* for what they are supplying, right? You should have your say. Introduce them to the National Pure Water Association, and ask them to discuss things/arrange a meeting/take them the NPWA literature. Do what you can.

Ask your dentist if the white fillings you are having instead of amalgam ones are free from fluoride? Otherwise you rather go *"out of the frying pan into the fire."* Do not have a permanent source of fluoride put into your mouth. Many dentists are a bit in love with fluoride as they get a lot of propaganda directed their way. Take him/her the NPWA literature also. Remember, your mouth is your own.

AIMS, the Association for the Improvement in Maternity Services, has once again done some valuable research, and has linked the giving of **painkilling drugs in childbirth** with the child later going in for street drugs at adolescence.

While we are going to all this trouble to smooth his path for him all through the pregnancy, it seems a pity to put a stumbling block in his way the day he enters this world.

It is 45 years since I last gave birth, but nevertheless I have a pretty clear recollection of the whole event! Well, you definitely lie there thinking *"could there not have been another way of doing this; could we not have been fitted with zip fasteners....?"*

However, I gather nowadays there are Water Births, which people tell me is good news. There is reflexology. There is acupuncture. I am sure that homoeopathy will have something up its sleeve. People tell me of home births where they were walking about until the last half hour, and of warm hot water bottles, fore and aft...

Generally, I would say, it seems to be all much more human and friendly than it used to be, - and anyway, remember that it only goes on for so long. If you possibly can manage to keep him or her drug free you will probably have a much easier ride when they are teenagers, and believe me, that will be worth it! (Although I do understand that may not be *precisely* what is on your mind as you go into the second stage of labour!)

I remember Beverley Beech (director of AIMS) telling us about Queen Victoria being the first person to beg her physician to find something to make childbirth easier. You cannot really blame her, as she had to give birth in full view of the Prime Minister of the time, and others, so it was a particularly harassing situation.

But it is interesting that Edward VII was so louche and uncontrolled, so unlike his parents in every way. Despite all they did, they could not make any headway with him. Their anguish over his behaviour was probably a factor that contributed to his father's very early death.

Remember, every woman in the hereafter who has ever given birth is on your side, as you go through it – even if you are thinking, *"Eve, couldn't you have left that apple alone?"* at that moment in time.

See our website for the address of the Independent Midwives. I would be sure to contact them for a chat when you are making up your minds what best to do about the birth.

We have to factor in the prevalence of MRSA, C.difficile and so on in the hospitals while making the decision. If you do decide on a hospital birth, I would contact Ainsworths Homeopathic Chemists for nosodes for these infections.

The last of the major health hazards, one might say the Biggest of the Bugbears, is vaccination and immunisation.

Once again I will refer you on to those who have made a lifetime of study of this, and your decisions are your own. However, as it is pushed in some quarters as though the babies' lives depended on it, I will just point out where you can obtain a more balanced perspective:

Get the book *"Behavioural problems in childhood, the links to vaccination"* by Dr Viera Scheibner and her video. Also *"The Vaccination Bible"* by Lynn McTaggart, editor of "What Doctors Don't Tell You".

You can also get in touch with Magda Taylor, of The Informed Parent, P O Box 4481, Worthing, West Sussex, BN11 2WH, Telephone 01903 212969, www.informedparent.co.uk. She is a huge source of relevant information. She gives excellent talks. Ask for Foresight list of websites, also.

There is also an organisation called JABS, Telephone 01942 713565, www.jabs.org.uk. They have formed to get compensation for victim's families.

If you know anybody with an autistic child, I would ask if you can spend a day with them. See at first hand exactly what the issues are. First hand is always the best way to understand any problems.

Few of those who wholeheartedly advocate vaccination will have ever spent a day with an autistic child – let alone been in charge of him or her.

I would also contact a good homoeopath. We can help with this. Things that they can do to help:

    a) Give separate homoeopathic dilutions of measles, mumps and rubella that will prevent the illness from being severe, as the body will have been primed to deal with it.

    b) Once the child has caught the infection, they can give homoeopathic dilutions which will mean it is not severe and is over quite soon.

    c) Give homeopathic dilutions of the MMR vaccine to prime the immune system prior to receiving the vaccine, to lessen the impact if you insist on vaccination.

    d) Prior to the jab, the child needs to have plenty of zinc, so the immune system will be able to respond without badgering other organs, particularly the brain.

e) If the child has already been vaccinated and badly affected before you read this, a homeopath can give a dilution that will help him/her. (So will hair analysis and adjusting the mineral levels.)

Vitamins and minerals will also help.

The Department of Health has assured me that GP practices will be "disciplined" if they threaten to strike families off their register for not letting their children be given a vaccine. So be sure to tell the D of H if you are threatened. If possible, I would let your husband ring them. Officialdom is always more impressed by a male voice. This is galling, but true.

The way I see it is – over 2,000 families think their child became autistic after the MMR jab. This is presumably 4,000 parents and approximately 8,000 grandparents. This makes around 12,000 people. Are they *all* likely to be wrong? WHY? How is that NOT "scientific"? In the USA, the connection between the MMR jab and autism has at last been acknowledged. I expect the UK will be the last to get the message, as always.

As well as behavioural problems, Dr Schreibner has also linked vaccination to cot death. In Japan, they gave up vaccinating children under two years old, and *cot deaths virtually disappeared.* Why should we ignore all this evidence? *How dare they tell us to do so*?

So what do we do?

You get the general gist. We do not wish you to get too neurotic and jump at every shadow, but the modern world is not foeto-friendly or baby-friendly. However, we can make it much more so, without having to go completely bananas, or to break the bank. Just concentrate on your own home, and make it a place your body can truly relax in and feel safe. Make your own decisions on what goes on, with you and your baby.

Every little you can manage to get sorted out helps your own family, your long-suffering tax-paying country, the local wildlife and the rest of the world. Everything you do, makes you and your family that significantly little bit fitter. Feel joyful about this. Then what everybody else pollutes *you* with, it will not get to you so much!

Onward!

We are grateful to The Soil Association for allowing us to reproduce part of their recent literature on the whole subject of Genetic Modification in animal feed.

Brand New Types of "Scientific" Pollution!

<u>A FEW NOTES ON GENETIC MODIFICATION</u>

Do not be fooled by Government Statements. They cannot be trusted to give you the truth!

How to protect yourself and your family.

1. Grow as much of your own food ORGANICALLY as possible, and buy only organic.

2. Write to your MP and MEP if you do not want GM food, particularly UNLABELED GM food in this country.

3. Support groups fighting GM on your behalf, like ISIS and The Soil Association.

4. Look for the Soil Association logo on organic food when you buy it.

What is GM? Genetic Modification involves taking a gene from one organism (plant, animal, fungus, micro-organism) and inserting it into the genetic material of another. There are 5 main types.

Plant ↔ plant

Plant ↔ animal/micro-organism

Animal ↔ animal

Micro-organism ↔ animal

Micro-organism ↔ micro-organism

GM foods come from plants and animals whose DNA has been altered through the addition of genes from other organisms.

"It has become increasingly evident that GM technology is inherently hazardous and unreliable both in agriculture and in medicine."
Mae Wan Ho

Mae Wan Ho on Institute i-sis.org.uk

So claims an eminent scientist, whose career spans over 30 years with many years of research in the field of molecular genetics, as well as biochemistry, evolution and biophysics.

The simple answer. Quote from Dr Michael Antoniou, Gene Therapist, Guys Hospital.

"If the kind of detrimental effects seen in animals fed GM food were observed in a clinical setting, the use of the product would have been halted and further research instigated to determine the cause and find possible solutions. However, what we find repeatedly in the case of GM food is that both governments and industry plough on ahead with the development, endorsement, and marketing of GM foods despite the warnings of potential

ill health from animal feeding studies, as if nothing has happened. This is to the point where government and industry even seem to ignore the results of their own research! There is clearly a need more than ever before for independent research into the potential ill effects of GM food industry, most importantly with animal and human feeding trials".

Press Release from The Soil Association – 16th November 2007

(We are so grateful for their permission to reproduce this in this book.)

Nearly all the milk, dairy products and pork in UK supermarkets are being produced from animals fed on GM crops, and none of this is labelled, according to a Soil Association investigation. Tests of animal feed and a survey of company policies have revealed that all the supermarkets are widely allowing the use of GM feed. The report found that around 60% of the maize and 30% of the soya fed to dairy cattle and pigs is GM. [1] Most consumers are unwittingly eating food produced from GM crops everyday.

Supermarkets have been trumpeting their non-GM food policies, having removed all of their own-label foods made <u>directly</u> with GM ingredients by October 2002 in response to consumer concerns. However, unknown to most of the public, supermarkets did *not* prohibit the use of GM animal feed. Because of a legal loophole, there is no requirement to label food produced from GM-fed animals so shoppers will find it hard to avoid food produced from these. [2]

<u>Currently, the only food standard that guarantees the non-use of GM feed is organic</u>. The basic food industry mark, the 'Little Red Tractor', allows the use of GM feed. Even ethical labels like 'Freedom foods' allow animals to be fed GM crops. For non-organic food, Marks & Spencer offers the only refuge in offering all its milk and fresh meat from non-GM feed, but it does allow GM feed for its frozen and processed foods. All meat and dairy foods can and should be produced from non-GM feed. Unlike the dairy and pig sectors, the poultry sector has widely adopted non-GM feed policies, though around a third of eggs are from GM-fed hens. [3]

This GM stealth invasion of the UK food-chain is denying consumers their right to make fully informed choices. For years, the Food Standards Agency has been assuring consumers they would not be exposed to GM material by eating meat and dairy products from GM-fed animals. Scientific studies <u>have now found</u> small amounts of GM DNA in milk and animal tissues from GM-fed livestock. [4] And studies on GM-fed livestock are finding horrendous effects, including **lesions on the gut, toxic effects in body organs, unexplained deaths and stunted growth in their offspring**. [5] This raises concerns about the long-term health impacts on humans consuming products from GM-fed animals.

Patrick Holden, Soil Association director said: "This amounts to deception on a large-scale. This is not just accidental contamination, hundreds of thousands of tonnes of GM grain are being used to produce our food each year. Biotechnology companies have clearly used imported animal feed as a Trojan Horse to introduce GM into the UK food chain, despite the fact that the British public have voted overwhelmingly against GM.

"The research on the presence of GM DNA in food from GM-fed animals and the impacts on animals is alarming. We urge the public to only buy meat and dairy that are known to be produced from non-GM fed animals, and to write to the supermarkets and ask them to stop allowing the use of GM feed. While it is excellent that Marks & Spencer and the poultry industry have restricted GM feed already, all retailers and food sectors should follow their lead. We also call on the supermarkets to label these products so they are being honest with their customers."

A key concern is that future supplies of non-GM feed will be threatened unless there is wide-spread consumer awareness on this issue and pressure on the food industry to ensure that meat and dairy products come from livestock raised on non-GM feed. [6]

In the past, supermarkets have resisted direct demands for the use of non-GM feed, citing inadequate supplies of non-GM soya or excessive costs for farmers. The Soil Association has established that supplies are abundant and can expand to fit demand. The retail cost is minimal and should be paid for by the retailers, not farmers. The example of the poultry sector shows it can be done. [7]

Although food from GM-fed animals does not have to be labelled, animal feed *does* have to be labelled if it contains GM ingredients. Most feed (75%) is now labelled as 'GM', however, our survey found that most farmers (59%) did not know if their feed was GM. Soil Association tests also revealed a high level of breaches of the EU labelling laws - nearly 20% of feed contained GM soya above the 0.9% labelling threshold but bore no GM label. [8] The FSA are responsible for enforcing the legislation but are not conducting any tests to do so.

References:

[1] Silent Invasion - the hidden use of GM animal feed in the UK, Soil Association, November 2007. Full report available on request from The Soil Association.

The Soil Association tested 37 feed samples from dairy, pig and poultry farmers and surveyed supermarket and feed company sourcing policies. 73% of the feeds tested contained GM soya, with 27% containing soya that was over 70% GM. The company information showed that GM maize (used in the refined form, maize gluten, and so hard to identify in tests) is also widely used. The dairy sector is worst: in the tests, 51% of the soya was GM and it is widely using maize estimated to be around 60% GM. The pig sector is also a concern: the soya was 20% GM and soya makes up a larger proportion of the feed.

Based on our findings, we estimate that around 400,000 tonnes (290,000t of GM maize gluten and 146,000t of GM soya) are imported each year to produce manufactured feed for the dairy, pig and poultry sectors (out of a total of 467,000t of maize gluten and 1,123,000t of soya used in manufactured feed for these sectors). Note, the total amount of imported soya and maize gluten that *contains* GM is far higher. If imported grain used for 'home-mixing' of feed by farmers and the small amounts used for fattening beef and sheep (but not wholly grass-fed animals) are included, the total GM feed used would be higher.

[2] The Soil Association is calling on the Government and European Commission to introduce a legal requirement for GM labelling for foods produced from GM-fed animals. This is supported by the public:

An NOP survey in 2006 found that 87% of the UK public believe food from GM-fed animals should be labelled (up from a finding of 79% by the National Consumer Council in 2001).

A European-wide petition for such labelling collected a million signatures by February 2007.

NOP poll of 1000 UK adults carried out 9-11 June 2006 and weighted to be nationally representative.

"One million EU citizens call for labelling of GM foods", by Helena Spongenberg, 5 February 2007, EU Observer.

[3] In 2008, the only general sources of meat and dairy foods from non-GM-fed animals are:

For milk and pork: Marks & Spencer provides the only major source of non-organic milk and fresh pork produced from non-GM fed animals. In all other supermarkets, milk and pork is produced from GM-fed animals, *apart from organic food* and Sainsbury's 'Farm Promise' milk available in some stores.

For chicken: the British poultry industry is the one sector to have mostly excluded GM feed. Apart from Iceland, own-label fresh chicken and turkey in the major supermarkets and Lloyd Maunder poultrymeat, is all produced from non-GM feed. However, frozen chicken, processed chicken products (eg. chicken nuggets), chicken served in restaurants and take-aways are often not British but supplied by importers, and probably from GM fed animals.

For eggs: own-label eggs in the major supermarkets are produced with non-GM feed, except for Iceland. *All organic eggs* and the following egg brands are produced with non-GM feed: 'Woodland', 'Corn Gold', 'Columbus omega-3 rich', 'and 'Church and Manor' duck eggs. Nearly all 'free range' and 'barn' eggs are produced from GM feed. And there is no requirement for Lion Quality Eggs or 'free range' eggs to be produced from non-GM feed. This means non-organic eggs sold by independent retailers, including some 'free range' eggs, may, unless labelled otherwise, be from GM-fed chickens. About half of caged eggs, including probably most used in processing and catering, are produced with GM feed.

For frozen and processed meat and dairy foods: *organic is the only general option* for products such as yoghurt, cheese, cream, butter, ice cream, frozen meat, bacon, ham, sausages, meat pies, corned beef and ready meals.

M&S is well ahead of the other supermarkets. However, the Co-op, Sainsbury's and Waitrose offer a few non-organic meat and/or dairy items produced from non-GM feed, besides their own-label fresh chicken, turkey, eggs and farmed fish. Iceland offers no non-organic products from non-GM fed animals.

[4] Until 2005, studies which tried to detect GM DNA in milk, eggs and tissues from GM-fed animals had only detected *non-GM* DNA from the crops, indicating that GM DNA was also probably present in low quantities even if it had not been detected (Chowdhury *et al*, 2004; Phipps *et al*, 2003; Einspanier *et al*, 2001). On this basis, although it was not strictly supported by the science, the FSA and biotechnology industry claimed consumers would not be exposed to GM material by eating food from GM-fed animals. Now, however, TAKE NOTE: <u>four studies by different scientific teams have detected GM DNA in milk and pig and sheep tissues</u> from GM-fed animals (Sharma *et al*, 2006; Agodi *et al*, 2006, Mazza *et al*, 2005; reports by Ralf Einspanier, 20 October and 20 December 2000).

[5] The Soil Association report includes a review of GM feeding trials (12 animal and 1 human) that found <u>negative health effects</u> (all controlled against non-GM crops). Their report also describes some of the ways in which these findings were dismissed by the FSA / European Food Safety Authority and the biotechnology companies, and lists eleven scientific reasons why genetic engineering changes the biology of plants, posing risks to health.

1. Russian rat trial of GM soya: very high mortality and stunted growth in the offspring (Ermakova, 2005)

2. Italian mice trial of GM soya: metabolic effects on body organs (Malatesta *et al*, 2002 and 2003; Vecchio *et al*, 2004)

3. FSA-commissioned human trial of GM soya by Newcastle University: GM DNA transfers out of food into the body's gut bacteria (Netherwood *et al*, 2004)

4. Monsanto rat trial of GM maize: <u>changes in body organs indicating toxic effects</u> (report by Monsanto, 2002; review by Dr Pusztai, 2004; Séralini *et al*, 2007)

5. Aventis chicken trial of GM maize: <u>mortality doubled and significant change in composition of meat </u>(reports for the Chardon LL hearing, 2002; review in "Food safety – contaminants and toxins, CABI publishing, 2003)

6. Aventis rat trial of the novel protein of GM maize: <u>reduced body weight and metabolic effects</u> (same references as for Aventis chicken trial)

7. UK study on sheep: in a few minutes, <u>the genes in the GM maize move into the bacteria in the mouth, changing their characteristics</u> (Duggan *et al*, 2003)

8. Monsanto rat trials of GM oilseed rape: <u>reduction in body weight and increased liver weight</u> (significant as the liver is the organ of detoxification) (US FDA, 2002; Opinion of the Scientific Panel on Genetically Modified Organisms, 2004)

9. Australian mice trial of GM peas: <u>allergic reactions, including inflammation of lungs</u> (Prescott *et al*, 2005)

10. Calgene mice trials of GM tomatoes: <u>gut lesions and 7 of 40 died within two weeks</u> (review in "Food safety – contaminants and toxins, CABI publishing, 2003)

11. UK Government-commissioned rat trial of GM potatoes by Rowett Research Institute: <u>gut lesions</u> (Ewen and Pusztai, 1999)

NB: These studies were all designed to identify health impacts; the animal trials often referred to by the biotechnology companies are largely *irrelevant* as proof of safety, being mostly studies carried out for commercial purposes on the efficacy of the feed, rather than 'toxicological' studies involving tissue analysis.

[6] Due to promotion by the biotechnology companies, the area of GM soya is rapidly expanding in Brazil, the main global supplier of non-GM soya. GM soya now accounts for 45-50% of the total, up from 20-25% in 2005. The market for certified non-GM feed must be secured to ensure the current non-GM area remains and that the industry segregates the GM and non-GM crops.

[7] Based on calculations by the Royal College of Agriculture, the increase in costs of using non-GM feed at the retail end would be only 2-4p/kg for pork and bacon, and 0.4p/l for milk, if the non-GM soya premium is 7%.

[8] Since 18 April 2004, according to EU legislation, feed containing GM material or derivatives of GM crops must be labelled as GM. The only exception is if the feed producer uses a non-GM source but some EU approved GM material up to 0.9% is later found to be present due to contamination. 19% of the feed samples we tested (seven of the 37 samples) had no GM label, yet contained GM soya over 0.9% threshold. Remarkably, the soya in five of these samples was over 80% GM. Worse, two were pure soya feeds made of 100% GM soya.

Plant ↔ plant transfer between plant species

Transfer between cross-kingdom gene transfer

Transfer between plant – bacteria

"GM crops scrapped as mice made ill", Selina Mitchell and Leigh Dayton, The Australian, 18 November 2005:

Transgenic Expression of Bean -Amylase Inhibitor in Peas Results in Altered Structure and Immunogenicity

Vanessa E. Prescott, Peter M. Campbell, Andrew Moore, Joerg Mattes, Marc E. Rothenberg, Paul S. Foster, T. J. V. Higgins, and Simon P. Hogan

Identification of a Brazil-Nut Allergen in Transgenic Soybeans

Julie A. Nordlee, M.S., Steve L. Taylor, Ph.D., Jeffrey A. Townsend, B.S., Laurie A. Thomas, B.S., and Robert K. Bush, M.D.

(http://content.nejm.org/cgi/content/full/334/11/688)

To the more mundane, but in some ways equally depressing, subject of pesticide damage:

From Occupational and Environmental Medicine, Vol 51, 693-699

Time to pregnancy and occupational exposure to pesticides in fruit growers in The Netherlands

J de Cock, K Westveer, D Heederik, E te Velde and R van Kooij

Department of Epidemiology and Public Health, Wageningen Agricultural University, The Netherlands.

OBJECTIVES: Although pesticides are regularly used in agriculture, relatively little is known about possible adverse health effects, especially reproductive effects, due to occupational exposure. This explorative study investigates the relation between exposure of the fruit grower to pesticides and fecundability (probability of pregnancy) in a population of fruit growers.

METHODS: The analysis is based on self reported data and includes 91 pregnancies during 1978 - 1990 of 43 couples. Cox's proportional hazards model was used to analyse time to pregnancy after correction for gravidity and consultation with a physician for fertility problems.

RESULTS AND CONCLUSIONS: Application of pesticides solely by the owner was associated with a long time to pregnancy, resulting in a fecundability ratio of 0.46 (95% confidence interval (95% CI) 0.28-0.77). Similarly a low spraying velocity (< or = 1.5 hectares/h) resulted in a fecundability ratio of 0.47 (95% CI 0.29 - 0.76) and is associated with the use of older spraying techniques and tractors without a cabin. These factors were assumed to cause high exposure, which was confirmed by exposure measurements in the field. The effect of high exposure was mainly apparent if the couple had intended to become pregnant in the period from March-November (fecundability ratio 0.42, 95% CI 0.20-0.92). This is the period in which pesticides are applied. Out of the spraying season the effect of a high exposure was absent (fecundability ratio 0.82, 95% CI 0.33- 2.02). In the high exposure group 28% of the pregnancies had been preceded by consulting a physician because of fertility problems, compared with 8% in the low exposure group. These findings indicate that an adverse effect of exposure to pesticides on fecundability is likely.

NB: We need to be aware!

CHAPTER 10

ALTERNATIVE PRACTITIONERS

Herewith seven splendid articles by Foresight Practitioners, all of whom can give a lot of help in different situations with Foresight couples.

It is a good idea to postpone conception until the mineral balances are restored, but in some cases once the body is "ready to roll", some other therapy can just get things going. See what a lot of help is available out there.

Acupuncture – by Victoria Conran

Homeopathy – by Sue Saunders

Reflexology – by Stephanie Walker

Osteopathy – by Beate Guenther

Herbs for Fertility – by Cath Kay

Kinesiology – by Stella Broadbent

Endometriosis – by Dian Mills

Acupuncture and Pre Conceptual Care

Victoria Conran

Acupuncture has been used as a medical practice in China for over 2,000 years. By the end of the twentieth century, the practice of acupuncture is found not only in the Far East, but also Europe, USA and Australia. As part of a system of medicine called traditional Chinese medicine, its capacities are extensive and over time have proved to be an effective form of medicine in all areas of human health including gynaecology and fertility. Recent media from Europe and America has reported from research trials showing its effectiveness alongside IVF procedures.

In terms of human physiology, Chinese medicine is based upon theories of Qi (vital energetic capacity) and Blood as two important substances involved in health and disease. Pathology of either is understood to invoke disease. Diagnosis involves taking a case history to understand the causes of problems, and to aim treatment protocols towards correcting pathological imbalance. A Chinese saying translates as *'there are many diseases for one pattern and many patterns to one disease'* and means, for example, that scanty periods, lower back pain or migraine can correspond to one Chinese Medical pattern, and that several different patterns can correspond to one disease, for example, unexplained infertility. What is called Differential Diagnosis allows for problems in an area such as fertility or gynaecology to be interpreted and treated specifically to each individual case. A detailed case history will provide vital clues as to why and how conditions have arisen. This allows for a 'tailored approach' for each person which takes into account changes occurring with treatment. Observation of the pulse and tongue are added to accounts of symptoms reported by the client. The practitioner then constructs their treatment to guide energy and vitality towards appropriate functional health.

Treatment for fertility usually involves supporting and building up the substances necessary for conception to take place and pregnancy to proceed healthily. Causes of problems conceiving are understood as being a result of weak qi and blood, accumulation of pathogenic substances or lifestyle habits inhibiting or draining energetic resources within the body. If there are issues around sleep, relaxation, diet, overwork and other causes of exhaustion, these are discussed during consultation and during the examination of pulse and tongue. Unfortunately, Western lifestyle tends to minimise the time and resources needed to replenish the energies required by the body to make new life. Often rest and relaxation become less important than expending energy. The ability to relax can become a problem for many people without their realising it.

Acupuncturists use very fine, tiny needles which are inserted into specific places on the body. As a result of acute observation over centuries, the practitioners of ancient China were able to perceive a network of energy channels in the body, along which are found tiny points. These points are needled in acupuncture treatment in order to access specific physiological reactions. It is interesting that reported effects of acupuncture include amelioration of symptoms registered at both physical and mental levels.

As the idea of the body in Chinese Medicine encompasses complex ideas about interaction and interdependency of subtle energies, using needles to adjust imbalance is a delicate process that requires time. For example, the menstrual cycle is understood in Chinese Medicine to have five phases. Each phase can be interpreted according to signs on the pulse and tongue, as well as any symptoms reported. This understanding allows for imbalance in the menstrual cycle to be readily perceived and appropriate treatment given accordingly. Correcting the menstrual cycle is measured by a person's subjective experience, and results that are fed back inform the basis for future treatments. Treatment is therefore patient centred, and Chinese Medicine has the advantage of working with female energies as opposed to intervention through surgery or pharmacological drugs, which rarely deal with the cause of problems.

Although it has been shown to have good success when used alongside IVF, treating fertility will often take more than one or two sessions. Often people choose to use acupuncture to help with fertility difficulties when there is considerable depletion of physical and emotional resources. Time and commitment invested in acupuncture treatment is like attention and care taken in preparing a field so that when seeds are sown, the crop will thrive and be harvested.

Whilst the perceived pressures of time can cause concern, the pursuit of creating new life and bringing forth a child into this world perhaps deserves reflection. It may be worth considering the words of Lao Tzu, the wise Confucian sage who 2000 years ago wrote:

'Put things in order before they exist

A journey of one thousand miles

Begins with one step'

Homeopathy and Foresight

Sue Saunders RSHom

Homeopathy is a safe, effective and holistic system of medicine. It has been used for hundreds of years and is suitable for all the family. Homeopathy works by using minute doses of medicine to help stimulate the body's natural healing processes. It works very well for people using the Foresight programme.

A key element of the Foresight approach is to rid the body of toxic influences — to get you as clean and healthy as possible in preparation for conception. This is where homeopathy can come to your aid.

You can use homeopathic remedies in the home for minor first aid situations. Arnica is a remedy many people are familiar with and is used to help healing after any injury — whether you have fallen over or have experienced bruising after a blood test or tooth extraction. There are remedies you can use for coughs and colds, for headaches, for hay fever, for period pains to name just a few. These are all completely safe and will help avoid the use of other medications which could have unwanted side effects.

For more serious or long-standing complaints, it is important to consult a professional, qualified homeopath. Here you can investigate your health problems and hopefully reduce any medication you take. For instance, many people with asthma find that with good homeopathic treatment, their need for inhalers is dramatically reduced or even avoided. Your homeopath would work alongside your GP to manage safely any reduction in your medication.

Homeopathy works with issues with your mental, emotional and physical health. So for couples who have experienced the grief of repeated miscarriage for example, homeopathic remedies can help to address that grief and help to process it. The fear of history repeating itself can hold you back from conceiving again and homeopathy can help free you from that fear.

If you have genito-urinary infections homeopathy can be useful here too. Of course, your homeopath would advise investigation and treatment at your local genito-urinary medicines clinic. Homeopathic remedies can be used alongside orthodox medication, helping prevent any side - effects from medicines you may need to take if you have a genito-urinary infection. Many people who have thrush and / or recurrent cystitis find these conditions very efficiently treated homoeopathically.

Homeopathy is very effective in the treatment of polycystic ovaries and anovulation. Remedies help the body to return to its healthy state of balance and rhythm to get ovulation and menstruation re-established. It is always such a joy when someone who has been told she will never be able to have babies telephones to announce that she is pregnant!

Once you have conceived, homeopathic remedies can safely treat any problems you may have during pregnancy — morning sickness, piles, carpal tunnel syndrome all respond well — though we do notice that women on the Foresight programme tend to suffer less from these complaints.

Remedies assist too during the birth — if contractions fail to establish, if you are experiencing backache, if you are just getting exhausted. There are some great kits available now with an excellent selection of remedies you might need during and after the birth.

And of course, once your precious baby has finally arrived, homeopathy can safely help keep her healthy and happy. Colic, teething pains, constipation — all these and more are addressed easily with remedies. For babies, remedies can be given in tiny granules or can be diluted with a little water or milk — your homeopath will show you how.

Your homeopath will help you decide about vaccines too — you will be given unbiased advice on vaccination and your homeopath will help and support you in whatever decision you make.

From pre-conception through pregnancy and birth and throughout life, homeopathy can help keep you and your baby happy and healthy.

To find a homeopath in your area:

The Society of Homeopaths, 11 Brookfield, Duncan Close, Moulton Park, Northampton NN3 6WL. Tel 0845 450 6611

www.homeopathy-soh.org

Homeopathic pharmacies:

Helios, 89-97 Camden Rd, Tunbridge Wells, Kent TN1 2QR. 01892 537254
www.helios.co.uk

Ainsworths, 36 New Cavendish Street, London WIG 8UF. 020 7935 5330
www.ainsworths.com

Reflexology
By Stephanie Walker

Reflexology is a complementary medicine therapy, which concentrates on the feet and occasionally the hands. The body is represented in specific zones on the soles, sides and top areas of the feet. There are thousands of nerve endings (7,200, left and right, to be precise) in our feet and when stimulated with massage, along with finger and thumb pressure, a reaction is triggered in the corresponding system or organ.

The exact reason is still unclear but it is believed that reflexology removes blockages in the body's energy flow. As a therapy it is centuries old and there is evidence of it being used in China, India and Egypt circa 2500 BC. Papyrus scenes actually show medical practitioners treating patient's feet. Much of the credit for today's reflexology goes to an American woman named Eunice 0. lngham (1889-1974). In the 1930's she further developed the work of Dr. William Fitzgerald, an Ear, Nose and Throat specialist who, as far back as 1900, had studied "Zone Therapy" and noted that when pressure was applied on a reflex point, pain in another area was relieved.

My clients have typically tried for at least two years to become pregnant. They may be on an IVF programme and by the time Foresight clients get to me they have usually seen a nutritionist. The reflexology sessions are suggested to try and re-start ovulation by clearing blockages.

The first session begins with taking a detailed medical history. Unexplained infertility can have many causes and it is important to take time to build the whole picture, including the emotional side of things.

During a treatment only the feet are exposed and the therapy can be done with the client lying down or sitting up. I concentrate initially on the elimination and lymphatic systems. Experience and intuition enables me to spot or flag up potential problem areas. In 9 out of 10 cases, the corresponding pelvic region on the foot (below ankle bone and back of foot) is resistive, cold, or has a slightly different temperature. Sometimes there are areas which are either dead or hypersensitive to my touch.

Endocrine disorders manifest as an imbalance between the zones on each foot. A good example would be with the pituitary, the reflex point being in the middle of the big toe, on its underside. Visual clues such as broken veins suggest there may be fibroids, whilst in conditions like polycystic ovaries (PCOS) there may be other obvious physical signs like excessive facial hair or weight gain. The reflexology indicator for PCOS is to be found just under the anklebone. I usually find that in women with this illness, the area just under the ankle bone and slightly to the outside of the foot is pale by comparison with the colour of surrounding skin.

A reflexologist will have a range of special techniques to treat infertility. Each plan is tailor-made to deal with the problems of my client. If ovulation has failed I link the pituitary and ovaries, stimulating both points together. In cases of endometriosis, I first concentrate on the endocrine system to help normalise hormonal levels. The pelvic zone is then addressed in order to target lesions, followed by the spine, which helps to stimulate the nerves to the pelvic area and balance the nervous system, resulting in a more relaxed emotional state. Many people encountering fertility problems also complain of backache and these clients report an overall improvement after reflexology. It seems to be generally corrective.

As for men and infertility - they tend to wait until their wives have field-tested reflexology before agreeing to a session. The most common issues in men are a low sperm count or poor sperm motility i.e. not swimming forward properly. To improve total health, the session is similar to the women's but more attention to the zones across the top of the feet, just where the leg and foot meet. These are the points of the vasa deferentia, the tubes that carry mature sperm. In reflexology this corresponds to the same place as the fallopian tubes in women.

As to what the patients can expect to feel, most would say it is a thoroughly pleasant experience and very soothing. Occasionally I may locate tiny, hard crystals, or particles that feel a bit like bubble wrap. This suggests a blockage and I will pay more attention to these points. But to all intents and purposes there is minimal pain.

However, afterwards there may sometimes be what is termed a healing crisis - a good thing! It is important to drink lots of water, to clear any toxins released. There may be some tears, feelings of anger, a headache, more frequent trips to the loo or a tiredness. But all of these are normally expected to clear within a day or so. Reflexologists will always be on the end of the phone if things feel too uncomfortable, but clients are advised to stay positive during this time and to rest. Symptoms are a sure sign that things are moving!

The best results are obtained when reflexology is carried out for at least six weekly sessions, reducing to fortnightly and then monthly as a means to keep the body in balance and functioning optimally. I have had a number of instances where clients have become pregnant, but it is difficult to put a figure on success rates due to the differing circumstances involved in each case. I know from feedback that there is usually, at the very least, an improvement. Typically, menstrual cycles become more regular, endometriosis sufferers have less pain and breakthrough bleeding, and women who were not ovulating get a positive result when they check with test kits.

Osteopathy

By Beate Guenther

Osteopathy was developed by Andrew Taylor Still in the United States at the end of the 19th century. Nowadays it is a recognised system of diagnosis and treatment that lays its main emphasis on the structural integrity of the body. **If a body is structurally sound and correctly nourished it will function properly**. If, however, the body's structure is impaired it can cause a physiological malfunctioning that can lead to disease. In other words, mechanical problems can lead not only to aches and pains in joints and muscles, but also to disturbances in the internal organs including the reproductive system. When the body is balanced and efficient, just like a well tuned engine, it will function with the minimum of wear and tear, leaving more energy for living.

Many patients are aware that osteopathic treatment helps to improve the mobility of the spine and other joints, reduces irritation of nerves (e.g. sciatica) and improves muscle tensions. However, osteopathic techniques can also be employed to improve circulation of blood and lymph, to reduce congestion and improve nutrition for organs. This helps an organ work more effectively. It may be especially beneficial in patients with previous operations e.g. appendectomy, laparoscopy or adhesions following peritonitis as well as patients who suffer from chronic constipation and pelvic congestion.

Cranial Osteopathy

The body of techniques that is now called Cranial Osteopathy was originally conceived and developed by William Garner Sutherland from 1899. These techniques are very subtle and refined and use very gentle manipulative pressure to encourage the release of stresses throughout the body, including the head. It is often used in babies to help release birth strains but it can be equally used in adults and the elderly.

Cranial Osteopaths feel for a rhythmical shape change that is present in all body tissues - this is called involuntary motion. An injury anywhere in the body can affect this involuntary motion preventing healthy movement of the tissues from occurring and therefore can affect the physiological functioning.

Osteopathy in the treatment of Foresight patients

Osteopaths acknowledge that the body needs to be properly nourished in order to function effectively and the Foresight programme improves the chemical make-up by addressing nutritional input and deficiencies. However, osteopaths also place a great importance in the ability of the body to move. Movement after all means life. Using Osteopathy in conjunction with the Foresight programme means that the muscles, joints and organs will be of better health. Healthier couples will have a greater chance of conceiving and carrying a healthy pregnancy.

Gynaecological problems may be helped by improving the way the pelvis moves and the way the pelvic organs relate to the pelvis, its muscles, the blood vessels, nerves and lymph vessels. Such treatment may be useful in the treatment of adhesions, pelvic congestion, painful periods etc.

Osteopaths may work on the pelvic floor, a group of muscles at the bottom of the pelvis which act to support all the pelvic organs. In men this can be used in the treatment of chronic prostatitis or low sperm count. In women it helps to improve the stability of the pelvis and may also be used in women just before delivering a baby to reduce tensions and hopefully facilitate an easier birth.

The Osteopathic Consultation and Treatment

Before a treatment programme can be established a detailed case history and a thorough examination has to be done. Patients will be asked about their past medical history, current and past medication, illnesses, accidents, operations but also about their general health, digestion, breathing etc. and of course about gynaecological and urinary problems. The examination will evaluate a patient's posture, mobility, muscle tone and reflexes. Examining a patient's abdomen will provide information about the digestive tract, tensions in the uterus or surrounding structures. Together all of this information will allow the formation of a treatment programme. Such a treatment is patient centred, meaning that it is aimed at addressing the fundamental problems of that patient rather than trying to treat the symptoms. It also means that two patients with the same symptoms may therefore receive a different treatment.

As discussed above, osteopathy is a manual therapy that aims to improve the body's ability to function. An osteopath may use the following techniques:

- mobilisation or manipulation of spinal joints which can help and improve the functioning of the nervous system

- soft tissue techniques to relieve muscular tensions

- techniques applied directly to organs in order to improve blood supply to the organ or lymphatic drainage as well motility within an organ

- techniques to connective tissue and ligaments that support our organs

- techniques to release subtle strains and tensions in the head (these techniques are referred to as Cranial Osteopathy)

How to find an Osteopath

The osteopathic profession is regulated by the General Osteopathic Council and they publish a list of all registered osteopaths. To find an osteopath in your area, contact GOsC on 020 7357 6655 or see their website on www.osteopathy.org.uk, alternatively you may contact the British Osteopathic Association at www.osteopathy.org

Beate Guenther is a registered osteopath, naturopath and herbalist. She has been working with the Foresight programme for 10 years and has been treating patients with a wide variety of conditions by addressing their structural health as well as working with nutrition, herbs and lifestyle advice to improve well-being.

Herbs for Fertility

By Cath Kay

A common reason for seeking help from herbs, historically, is to do with fertility and childbearing. Certainly every country has a huge tradition of wise-woman remedies for this time. From the point of view of survival of the body, conception and reproduction is one of the last things necessary to the individual, and conditions have to be completely favourable for conception to take place. Most importantly, this means that the body must be properly nourished. Our bodies need hundreds of trace minerals and vitamins to ensure that all the delicately balanced processes within the body are able to happen. This is especially important where hormones are concerned – these are complex molecules. Herbs can provide these trace minerals and vitamins in carefully constructed packages, containing everything the body needs in easily assimilated form. Wild herbs in particular pick up trace minerals that simply aren't present any more in our over-farmed agricultural lands. Our bodies were designed to use a myriad of wild plants, and we simply don't get that diversity any more in our diets. So herbs can have subtle and profound effects on nutrition as well as harmonising and balancing the body. Conventional medicines tend to have one desired action and perhaps a few undesirable side-effects. Herbs work to encourage the body back into full health. The same herb can have totally different effects in different people – they tend to bring bodily processes back into balance.

In a herbal consultation, the herbalist works holistically, addressing diet and nutrition, stress and relaxation, exercise, lifestyle etc as well as addressing any underlying health problems. Both partners need to be in optimum health for conception to occur, and have a happy outcome. I much prefer to treat both partners – after all, it takes two, and too often the whole burden of fertility is put onto the woman, creating another level of stress. Even though most men are very supportive in principle, it tends to be hard for them to get involved in the treatment process (it involves talking, after all!) but it can be immensely liberating for them when they do participate. Therefore, the herbs I will talk about are safe and beneficial for both partners to take (and since they are aphrodisiac and increase male vitality, it shouldn't be too hard to convince the menfolk of the benefits!)

The herbs I am recommending here need to be taken as herbal infusions (strong teas). The active principles and especially the vitamins and minerals are extracted much better in water than in tincture(alcoholic extracts). Teas are nourishing and safe – tinctures are stronger, and besides, both partners should be avoiding alcohol. Still, everyone is different – it's best to try the herbs one at a time, mindfully, and be aware of how they affect your body.

RED CLOVER (Trifolium pratense)

THE herb for fertility according to the American herbalist and Wise Woman Susun Weed. It contains all the trace minerals necessary for health, in the right proportions to create optimum conditions for conception. It has especially high levels of magnesium and calcium which promote fertility and relax the nervous system. It has high levels of very high quality protein. Red Clover can help to restore and balance hormonal functions and tone the uterus. Lastly, it is alkaline and may help balance the acid/alkali balance in the vagina in favour of conception. I have had success with Red Clover in cases of high vaginal acidity, both taken internally and as a douche (in the latter case, combine with Scullcap). Alternatively, try adding the tea to a bath.

NETTLE (Urtica dioica)

This familiar stinging plant needs no description! It may not be the favourite of the gardener, but herbalists prize it greatly. It is an excellent food, containing just about every trace mineral and vitamin needed by the human body. Nettle has an especially high quantity of easily assimilated calcium, vital for fertility. It supports the kidneys and adrenals, important for dealing with the body's waste products. It is a superb tonic for the hormonal system and tones the uterus too. It nourishes both men and women, increasing fertility in both sexes.

Nettle's virtues don't stop there. I have used it in threatened miscarriage (1 cup of cold tea every 1-2 hours for 12 hours). It prevents cramps, and in later pregnancy reduces pain and the risk of haemorrhage. It also increases breastmilk – so one for the whole childbearing year.

RASPBERRY LEAF (Rubus ideaus)

Most people have heard of the benefits of raspberry leaf in the last trimester of pregnancy, preparing the uterus for labour. Less well known is its reputation for helping with sterility – but it has historically been prized for this. The main active constituent is fraganine, an effective uterine tonic that brings blood to the area and helps the smooth muscle of the uterus to work more efficiently. It works to tone all the muscles of the pelvis but most especially the uterus. The wild raspberry leaves contain far higher quantities of fraganine. Raspberry leaf also contains remarkably high levels of calcium (along with magnesium, thought to be the most important minerals for women preparing for conception). It contains significant amounts of iron, vitamins C and E and lesser but still useful amounts of vitamins A and B complex, phosphorus, potassium and other desirable trace minerals.

Traditionally this was a herb for all women, especially those having trouble conceiving, for threatened miscarriage or those with a history of miscarriage. It helps prevent haemorrhage and is a very effective cure for morning sickness - make the tea weak and freeze it into ice cubes. Suck the ice cube before getting up or whenever necessary. Recently there has been a trend towards warning women off raspberry leaf in the first two trimesters on the basis that it might 'over-tone' the uterus. I cannot find any evidence that this has been based on. Since women today tend to atonal rather than over-toned uteruses, I would suggest that there are very few women to whom this advice would apply – perhaps a very young woman with her first pregnancy, an athlete or dancer. However, since many women are in their thirties when they discover they are having trouble conceiving, and perhaps have a history of miscarriage, I think it unfair to prevent them using this useful herb that has been valued for centuries for these very conditions. I use it often in these cases, from pre-conception until the risk of miscarriage is past, and again in the last trimester alternating with nettle to prepare for labour. I find it very safe and useful *in low doses, as tea,* but as always consult a qualified practitioner for advice if you are in any doubt.

MINTS (mentha piperita or spicata or spp.)

Mints are traditionally esteemed for their ability to increase sexual desire and vigour. In Arabic countries, men believe that mint tea increases male virility (it is added to the feed of bulls and stallions to this day!). It is an aphrodisiac and increases fertility in both sexes, and what's more it adds flavour to the tea.

Any species of mint will work – garden mint, peppermint and spearmint are all fine. The more exotic types such as apple mint or chocolate mint are less effective but still fine.

FERTILITY BREW

Red Clover - 1 part
Nettle - 1 part
Raspberry leaf - ½ part
Mint - generous pinch to taste

Take 2 teaspoonfuls of the mix to each cup of boiling water (a cup is half a mug, like an old-fashioned teacup-full). Leave to infuse for 10-20 minutes, depending on the strength you like. Ideally, drink it straight but you can add honey or lemon to taste. Drink freely, at least 3 times a day.

The trick is to find a way that this fits into your life. Personally, I make a big potful, leave it to infuse then strain into a bottle (preferably glass, although plastic can be more convenient but may leach undesirables into the tea). Allow to cool and put in the fridge, where it will keep for up to 3 days. Then I fill a small bottle and carry that round with me, sipping the cold brew throughout the day. So many people carry water bottles these days that it is unremarkable, and it's an easy way to get the required dose. I also just prefer it cold! Other people relish the ritual of making the tea every day, and use the meditative space to think and dream about the desired outcome. Whatever works for you!

There are many other herbs, both as tea or tincture that can help with fertility. If there is an underlying or chronic condition, or if you try the fertility brew for 3 cycles and nothing happens, please please find a qualified practitioner that you like and trust, and work with her or him. Often this brew will work on quite difficult cases, and I always start with the mildest, most nutritious remedies before moving onto stronger ones. But conditions such as polycystic ovaries, endometriosis or pelvic inflammatory disease can be tricky to solve, and you will need help and support from someone who knows the herbs.

The National Institute of Medical Herbalists guarantees professional standards and can inform you about herbalists in your area (www.nimh.nih.gov)

BELLY OIL

This is a slightly different approach, which doesn't require taking anything (although it works better in conjunction with the tea), and smells gorgeous to boot!

Rose oil has been esteemed for centuries as the most luxurious, sensual experience possible. It increases fertility and desire, a potent aphrodisiac, a hormone balancer par excellence, a joy for women at every stage of life. Used for frigidity, impotence, depression, stress, nervous tension and headache, it covers all bases! It's an aphrodisiac for men too, great for potency and sperm mobility, so rub your belly against theirs if they're worried about smelling like a girl!

Rose oil is fearfully expensive. It takes a ton of petals to make a kilo of the oil. Buy the best you can afford – Neal's Yard Remedies sells Rose Absolute for £19.50 for 2.5ml. (Neal's Yard shops also sell it by the drop, take your own base oil or buy their excellent organic almond oil). Any cheaper than that and either the quality will be compromised, or it will have been diluted.

Buy the best base oil you can afford too – organic, cold-pressed. Almond oil is fine, grapeseed or olive are fine if you are on a budget, although you may find olive oil is a bit thick.

Organic cold pressed almond oil - 50ml

Rose absolute essential oil - 20 drops (this is a high dose, use less if the smell is overwhelming)

Rub on the belly daily, especially just before intercourse.

STRONGER HERBS FOR WOMEN

Again, I must stress that these herbs are safest and most effective when used under the supervision of a qualified herbalist. Each person is different, and these are powerful herbs. Please, please find someone to help, or read up very carefully as much as you can find before using these herbs. Since it is the alkaloid constituents that we are looking for, these herbs are best taken as tincture. (N.B. Tinctures contain alcohol – avoid this)

CHASTEBERRY *(Vitex agnus castus)*

Acts on the anterior pituitary to decrease progesterone and follicle stimulating hormone, while increasing oestrogen and luteinising hormone – although it acts to normalise the female hormonal system and may have different effects. This is one tricksy herb – it was used by monks to suppress desire, and was known as monk's pepper. It often causes water retention and bloating when used wrongly. However, it can help to regulate periods, and is especially useful in Polycystic Ovary Syndrome (PCOS). It takes at least 3 cycles to have an effect – take 2ml of standard (1:5) tincture when you get up in the morning.

(Nim Barnes' note: *I find it lowers levels of zinc, which is probably why it was so helpful to the monks. I would be wary of this one.*)

FALSE UNICORN ROOT *(Chamaelirium luteum)*

This herb is endangered, so please think carefully about using it, and find a reputable and sustainable source. It is a powerful uterine tonic, beneficial to the ovaries, uterus, kidneys and bladder. It has an alkalinizing effect on the system. Take 5-15 drops in the fertility brew.

CHINESE ANGELICA *(Angelica sinensis)*

Has a reputation as a menstrual regulator and fertility promoter. In my experience, especially useful in older women (40+) or those nearing the menopause, or in women with scanty and irregular periods. Best taken from ovulation (day 14) until start of period: NOT during the period or it may induce flooding (this is a risk anyway with this herb). Take a few drops of tincture in tea. (N.B. Again tinctures not recommended in pre-conception)

FOR MEN

GINSENG *(Panax spp)*

The author of the only male herbal I've found, James Green, says Ginseng is a 'tonic herb to help build a state of health and adaptation to stress necessary to produce adequate sperm count and *the libido to deliver it*' (my italics). Chinese Ginseng is the ultimate *yang* (male) tonic, increasing vitality, helps men deal with stress and increasing sperm count.

Buy the freshest, best quality product you can, as whole dried root. Capsules contain powdered ginseng which is often old and spent. If in doubt, open a capsule and taste it – it should taste powerfully bitter.

There is a Russian Ginseng, *Eleuthrococcus senticosus,* which increases endurance, stamina and resistance to infection. It is used by the Russian athletes and astronauts to improve performance.

Liquorice can be added, King of the adrenal tonics, BUT ONLY IF THERE IS NO HIGH BLOOD PRESSURE (ie not if you are taking blood pressure medication). If there is an issue with blood supply and circulation to the relevant area, add Hawthorn (*Crataegus oxyacanthoides*), Ginkgo (*Ginkgo biloba*) or Yarrow (*Achillea millefolium*)

DAMIANA(*Turnera diffusa*)

Damiana has a reputation for reversing infertility in both sexes. It increases adrenal energy, is tonic for the nerves, and has a strong affinity for the sexual organs. It can act as an aphrodisiac in situations where weariness, stress and pressure have acted to squash desire and sexual energy (in both partners).

SARSAPARILLA (*Smilax officinalis*)

Boosts low testosterone levels

BURDOCK (*Arctium lappa*)

Safe and effective deep-acting nourishing tonic. Improves gut and liver function (the liver both manufactures hormones and breaks them down, preventing build-up of stale hormones.)

Conclusion

Herbs have been used by humans throughout history. In their natural state, animals use herbs all the time. Tune in to these plants and their healing powers, and they will help. They demand respect, too, though – learn about each one individually, try them as simples (on their own) and listen to what your body tells you about them. Respect your individuality, and your knowledge of yourself and your cycles.

Share the herbs you find with your partner. Too often, conception becomes an obsession which divides people, rather than an amazing adventure to go on together. Try not to become fixed on the goal and forget the journey.

Biography

Cath Kay qualified as a Medical Herbalist from the Scottish School of Herbal Medicine in 2002, after a lifetime's interest in herbs and healing. She has 4 year-old twins, and used herbs throughout pregnancy and labour for a happy and healthy pregnancy.

References

1) Weed, Susun, 'Wise Woman Herbal for The Childbearing Year', 1986, Ash Tree Publishing, New York (available on amazon)

2) Gladstar, Rosemary

3) McIntyre, Annie

4) De Baracli Levy, Juliette, 'Natural Rearing of Children', 1970, Faber and Faber, London

5) Green, James, 'The Male Herbal', 1991, The Crossing Press, California.

Kinesiology and Pre-conceptual Care
By Stella Broadbent

With a background of Nursing, Midwifery and Health Visiting within the NHS, I found the following advert of interest: "Your Body can Heal Itself".

An evening's demonstration was to be held in Surbiton Library on a given date during 1986. This advert changed my way of thinking about health, and still offers amazing treatments often avoiding drugs and surgery.

Muscle Testing was demonstrated showing how parts of the body, when held, could correct weaknesses in other parts of the body. Kinesiology is pronounced (kin-easy-ology)

Kinesiology refers to the monitoring of muscle testing for imbalances, assessing energy levels, correcting imbalances and measuring the results. Testing muscles through a light pressure is not a test of strength but of using a bio-feedback mechanism. Originally used by Physiotherapists, it is now used widely by practitioners of Complimentary Therapies, Dentists, Doctors and Nurses.

Recent Government Legislation ruled that Complimentary Practitioners should be registered and be members of an organization. The Association of Systematic Kinesiology was one of the first Kinesiology Associations to be approved and registered with the National Occupational Standards (KNOS). To remain on the Register of Practitioners, annual training has to be maintained and recorded by the Association. Certificates of Registration are available on request from all members.

Kinesiology works as a circuit together with muscles, organs, meridians and the lymphatic system similar to the electrical circuit in a house. If there is a blown fuse in one area of a house it will affect other areas on that circuit. In the same way where an imbalance is found in the circuit of a client other parts of the body's systems will be affected. Imbalances may be due to a long standing problem or a sudden shock affecting one or more systems. Corrections to imbalances are made through a light touch to acupressure or lymphatic points. Treatments are used in a Priority Mode to ensure a systematic approach. Where supplements are needed muscle testing provides information about the correct supplement, dosage, strength and times of administration.

Before a treatment starts, energy levels may be discussed with the client using a count of 0-1000 and used as a measurement for the completed treatment.

Foresight advises couples about their aims and objectives and recommends a Hair Analysis from both partners to assess their vitamin and mineral levels. From these results a Programme of Care will be recommended. Dietary recommendations will also be discussed. The couple will be advised to avoid conception until the Programme of Care has been completed.

Foresight provides lists of Foresight Practitioners to their Clients who may wish to choose a Practitioner for further support. As a Foresight Practitioner, several clients have attended my Clinics.

<u>Case History of a Foresight Client:</u>

In an ideal situation, both partners attend for the first appointment when an in depth history is taken about their health, parents, siblings, place in family, type of work, stress levels, social life, fertility to date, menstrual cycle, environment they work and live in and duration of trying for a baby.

Mrs Sandy Jones (name changed)   Date first seen: June 2005   Age: 36 years
Occupation: Secretary
Relationship: Partner 10 years
Health Profile: Overweight, bloating, very stressed, frequent headaches, weepy.
Medication: No prescribed medication. Supplements from The Foresight Programme started in May, 2005
Placement in family: 4 of 5 children 2 sisters 2 brothers
Delivery: Spontaneous
Childhood illnesses: Coughs and colds.
Immunisations: Completed
Accidents: Broken arm following jump from a shed age 6 years
Illnesses: Suffered ear problems between ages 7 to 14 years
Menstrual Cycle: About 14 years, regular
Bowels: Frequently constipated
Sleep: Not very good
Diet: Regularly enjoys cereal for breakfast; midday salad or ham roll; evening meal with two vegetables.
Miscarriage: Following 8 week pregnancy - hospital care
Work: Stressful
Friends: Not very sociable
Hobbies: Reading
Partner: Work takes him away from home regularly
Partner's health: Good. Enjoys a pint

Kinesiology Assessment:

Before the assessment started, Sandy gave her Energy levels as 500. A muscle test response was 200 and on the low side. A further test would be given at the end of her treatment to establish if any improvement had been made.

The practice of Kinesiology was described and demonstrated to Sandy.

The first test was to ensure Sandy was not dehydrated. This test is a slight tug on a strand of hair near the front of the ear. A weak muscle challenge indicated water was needed and the assessment continued.

All 36 muscles were tested. A correction was needed to the Psoas (Kidney) Neuro-Lymphatic Point using a light massage on the back at T12 and L1.

294

Muscles were rechecked and responded with strength. A further test was made through the Alarm Point System to ensure these points were also in strength. The Triple Warmer Point was found to be weak and a correction to the over energy Acupressure holding points were made. The Alarm Points were re tested for completion of the treatment.

The latter treatment is usually used to correct a Thyroid Imbalance, which may be why Sandy was tearful as mentioned in her medical history.

Priority treatments were given for her headaches using Emotional Stress Release. This treatment is with a light pressure over the frontal points above eyebrows and the back of the head where the neck and head meet releasing tension and clearing unwanted thoughts.

Testing wheat for her bloating gave an insight to Sandy's nutrition. Reducing wheat and replacing it with wheat free breads available from many supermarkets was advised. Rotating food every 3 days, increase fruit and vegetables and to drink more water to help disperse toxins. Food sensitivities may be temporary and need reviewing regularly.

On completion of Sandy's treatment, a review of her Energy Levels, originally 200, were now tested at 800 and Sandy was smiling. When energy levels are low the mind plays tricks with our thoughts which are usually negative. With synchronization of the body's systems, changes are felt and wellbeing greatly improved.

Sandy was given information about how she may feel after her treatment and advised to keep a couple of bottles of water in the fridge to ensure she increases her water intake during the next few days. Bottles in the fridge confirm the amount taken or not!

"Follow Up" treatments were continued on a monthly basis when Sandy reported she had more energy, was enjoying work, crying had stopped and felt that relationships were improving as was her sleep pattern.

Treatments continued with success, Foresight gave the "Go Ahead" for conception some six months later when Vitamins and Minerals had been replenished for both partners.

Following this news, a full muscle balance was given requiring a treatment for an emotional problem which was resolved using Emotional Stress Release.

The Facia Latta (large intestine) was corrected through the Peroneus / bladder meridian points known as the Glabella neuro lymphatic points. These points are close to the centre and above the eyebrows and top of the nose. This is another example of how all parts of the body are connected.

Muscle testing responded well, she was hydrated and drinking more water. Energy levels checked as 900.

February 06

- Conception achieved.
- Supplements from Foresight taken as advised.
- Partner now having his Pint!! - having abstained for several months.
- A GP appointment made.
- Sandy is feeling confident and happy.
- Throughout pregnancy Sandy maintained her health apart from feeling tired at times.
- Maintenance Kinesiology treatments continued

October 06

- The expected date of delivery now in a couple of weeks.
- Pregnancy has been a happy event with good support from family and friends.
- It was at this stage that Sandy was having Irritable Leg Syndrome. A muscle test with fruit juice revealed a sensitivity thought to be due to the amount of sugar it contained. After reducing sugar sweetened food and drinks the syndrome cleared up.
- Maternity leave gave Sandy time to prepare a room for the baby.
- Labour & Delivery of baby discussed.
- Management of Breast Feeding and options advised.
- Post Natal Care and how to avoid Baby blues discussed.

November 06

- Sandy had a spontaneous delivery of a daughter 7lb 5oz.
- Breast feeding established and continued until weaning introduced.
- Sandy needed to return to work and Child Minding arrangements were made.

At six weeks baby Jane had a complete balance using Mother as her Surrogate. Imbalances corrected for the Abdominal Muscle holding points at L5. Jane's skin is clear and with a good colour, feeding established and appeared very contented

Kinesiology is used for a wide variety of treatments, is painless, drug free and can establish instant results at the time of treatments. Practitioners can always find a treatment to ease mental, physical and chemical traumas.

Further information about Kinesiology from: www.systematic-kinesiology.co.uk

Endometriosis

by Dian Shepperson Mills

The prevalence of endometriosis in the female population is said to be "8- 10 % of women in reproductive years and 20-50% of women with infertility".[1] Endometriosis is an endocrine and auto-immune disease which affects women of every nation on earth. This is a disease that may be asymptomatic in some, whereas other women have massive debilitating pains, fatigue and sadness as their quality of life is drastically reduced. The profound loss of the ability to live a normal life can have a devastating effect on confidence and sense of self. The distress of sub-fertility can be exhausting month after month, and severe abdominal pain at ovulation is a double whammy. The causes of endometriosis are as yet unknown, so the cure is elusive.

Signs and symptoms.

Endometriosis is multi -factorial so look for all the symptoms, which affect the body. The principle accepted symptoms of endometriosis would be

1. chronic/acute period pains
2. ovulation pain
3. pain on intercourse
4. sub-fertility

Other reported symptoms are abdominal bloating, bladder pressure, extreme fatigue, ovary pains, chronic bowel symptoms, rectal bleeding, low body temperature, recurrent infections, immune system failures, hormonal imbalances and pains at all times of the month to varying degrees.

Every woman's endometriosis will be growing in a different place. Many women have small specks of endometriosis and enormous pain, whilst others have huge lumps of endometriosis and yet have never had any pain at all. It is a conundrum. One in four women operated on for abdominal problems are found to have endometriosis. The youngest reported diagnosed case is 9 years and the oldest woman was 73 years of age. Rarely it may grow on other organs such as the lung, gums, kidneys, diaphragm, stomach, liver. The first diagnosed case in 1860 was in a woman who bled from her eye at every period.

What causes endometriosis?

The inside lining of the womb, the endometrium, sheds as a menstrual period in a cycle every 28 days or so. From day 1 to day 14/15 it is rebuilding itself ready for conception around day 15 when women ovulate; an egg should be released from the ovary. The endometrium builds up in response to oestrogen and this tissue becomes nutrient rich – ready to support the embryo should a sperm and egg collide and form the embryo or blastocyst. The blastocyst rolls around the endometrium inside the womb looking for a nutrient rich spot to attach to and form its placenta. This process takes around 10 days, so those nutrients are crucial.

What happens in endometriosis is that this normal endometrium tissue begins to grow on other organs of the body. It can invade the healthy tissue on the outside of the womb, or on the ovaries, bowel, bladder or abdominal wall. Why it starts to do this is unknown. Normal endometrium, inside the womb, breaks down to liquid and sheds from the body via the vagina, and women lose this blood at their period if no pregnancy has begun. At this point a woman should lose some red healthy blood with mild or no pain for 4-5 days. With endometriosis this blood filled rogue tissue sheds into the inside of the abdominal cavity, so the blood is trapped inside the tummy area where the bowels, bladder and kidneys reside – and basically it may create hell. When the blood has no-where to escape to it floods into the peritoneal fluid and it sets off an inflammatory response by the body. The immune cells are just reacting to this bloody debris, which really has no right to be trapped inside the abdomen at all. Research reports that as that many as half of all menstruating women are affected by period pain and of these 10% have severe pain, which limits activities for one to three days each month.[2] In fact, 25% of all absences from work are reported in the UK are women with period pain. This costs the nation dear, but few take heed of the plight of women with endometriosis, not even when their fertility is threatened.

Peritoneal fluid naturally bathes all the abdominal organs allowing them to slip and slide over each other with no friction. The white blood cells of the immune system are present to clear out debris, like dead cells, which are meant to be mopped up. When all this extra blood is present it causes mayhem. Histamines are released and prostaglandin PGE2 is produced and they trigger an inflammatory response and the excruciating pain ensues. Crippling period or ovary pains and heavy brown sludgy menstrual blood may suggest endometriosis is present and this needs to be diagnosed by laparoscopy. Sometimes women have brown spotting at ovulation if ovarian cysts are present. When cysts rupture the pain is indescribable. Women who have given birth describe the pain as far worse than labour... It is like peritonitis pain. This inflammatory response may have an effect on the reproductive areas of the body, the ova, the incoming sperm and the true endometrium inside the womb, as chemicals, which should not be present in peritoneal fluid are bathing the organs. In effect it could be harming fertility.

As sticky blood hardens inside the abdomen it can form adhesions, which may stick vital organs together. This can also have a detrimental effect on fertility if the womb and ovaries are stuck to the bowel wall, or if an ovary is stuck behind the womb or appendix. The Fallopian tubes are meant to be floating suspended above each ovary to suck up the egg or ova, if they are pulled out of their true position this may not happen. All in all endometriosis is insidious.

Oestrogen Dominance

In the 1990's the Endometriosis Association in the USA found that 79% of a group of monkeys developed endometriosis after having been exposed to dioxins in their food during a research study several years earlier. The severity of endometriosis found in the monkeys was directly related to the amount of TCDD (2,3,7,8-tetrachlorodibenzo-*p*-dioxin – the most toxic type of dioxin) to which they had been exposed. In addition, the dioxin-exposed monkeys showed immune abnormalities similar to those observed in women with endometriosis. Such man-made chemicals stay in the body for years and are passed to babies through breast milk. They have an oestrogenic effect in the body. . ' In Belgium Koninckx et al (1994) noted that the incidence of endometriosis in women presenting at clinics with infertility is 60-80 per cent and TCDD concentrations in the breast milk are among the highest in the world (WHO environmental series (1992)'. The association, between human endometriosis and PCB's was first suggested by Gerhard and Runnebaum in 1992. Other research has shown that more infertile women with endometriosis had detectable high TCDD levels in serum than the fertile women tested without the disease. Meanwhile avoidance of fatty foods that may be high in PCB and dioxins should therefore be taken by women with endometriosis in order to reduce their exposure.[3]

As endometriosis is seemingly starting to be found in younger and younger women and girls it may be that a toxic burden in younger people is growing due to food contamination from excess use of pesticides. The fertility of future generations is being compromised. Mankind's fertility and survival is compromised due to these insidious chemicals which are used in farming. Unless you use organic food you will be eating them in plant and animal foods, they adhere to fat molecules. They are changing some animals from male to female as they are oestrogenic.

In such places as the St.Laurence Seaway in Canada, and around Spitzburgen in the Arctic, hermaphrodite whales and fish are found. In Florida, where water is polluted, male alligators have small genitals. This pollution is happening worldwide.

To protect yourself you need to reduce your intake of dairy foods and red meats, all highly fatty foods. Try to eat organic foods when possible. Choose to eat fish which is from the deep sea – never farmed; buy organic fruits and vegetables and use only a little organic butter and extra-virgin cold pressed olive oil. Eat wild game and nuts, seeds and berries, fruits and vegetables. Turn into a hunter-gatherer. When it is feasible grow your own in the garden, window boxes or on an allotment. You can have boxes of organic foods delivered to your door, look at the Soil Association website.

Getting a diagnosis - tests to request from your GP

As each person is unique there is no certain test other than laparoscopy, where a small camera is inserted into the abdomen to look for visible signs. Endometriosis can only be diagnosed by a laparoscopy. No blood tests or scans can reveal it is present when only small spots are present. Scans may show the presence of large cysts on the ovaries (known as endometriomas). It is felt to exist in several forms, microscopic, deep infiltrating, endometriomas /ovarian cysts, or when it distorts organs with adhesions. The Chinese recognize 11 forms of the disease.

The All Party Parliamentary Group at the House of Commons in 2005 in an on-line questionnaire, which was answered by 7500 women with surgically diagnosed endometriosis, showed that on average it took 5.11 years before a GP referred a woman to a specialist gynaecologist, and 9.11 years from reporting pain to her GP to get to a complete diagnosis. This is bad news. Obviously the sooner endometriosis is found and treated the less harm it can do. Not everyone with mild endometriosis develops severe endometriosis; it is not progressive in all cases. If you have mild endometriosis it may well stay mild.

Large lumps of endometriosis and large ovarian cysts and adhesions probably require an operation to remove them. Left alone large cysts may rupture – causing extremes of pain; adhesions may damage other organs like the bowel, bladder, kidney and urethra, so it is imperative that the GP refers you <u>to a gynaecologist who specializes in treating endometriosis</u>. Many Health Authorities now have <u>specialist endometriosis clinics – request to be sent to the lead one in your area</u>. The gynaecologist you see needs to be able to recognize endometriosis in all its forms, from clear blisters to yellow, orange, red active petichial patches and brown or black powder burns, and time the operation to remove all the offending patches, rather than leave some behind to treat with drugs. A bowel prep should be done if the intestines are involved. Other specialists should be on call during the operation if the bowel or bladder are involved, i.e. a colorectal surgeon or urologist.

Various tests may be helpful according to individual needs. You may look for heavy metals using hair mineral analysis or sweat tests; vitamin B and D level tests; thyroid function tests; female hormone profile tests; liver enzyme function; anemia; and a food intolerance test if an exclusion diet was inconclusive.

Medical Management of Endometriosis

Often at first hysterectomy with or without ovary removal was just accepted as one of the main treatments for women with endometriosis. If you did not respond to the drug treatments, surgery was the only option. The endometriosis would be just cut or burnt out as implants kept returning; alternately drugs like Danazol or the oral contraceptive pill were the only other option. Nowadays surgery takes a more gentle approach, trying to excise only the spots of endometriosis that are found and conserve the rest of the organs. Laser laparoscopies via the navel are done instead of laparotomies. In the skilled hands of an endometriosis specialist gynaecologist laser surgery can remove the deeper implants and cysts on the ovaries. However, too many women are undergoing "Look-See" assessment laparoscopes instead of having adequate treatment there and then. They then have to wait 6 months or more in pain to have their implants or cysts removed.

We have to find out what is triggering the endometrium to transfer to other organs of the body and grow there before we are able to 'cure' it. At present drug treatments are offered to many women, they are either are put onto the oral contraceptive pill continuously to mimic a pregnancy, or are fitted with a Mirena coil for five years progesterone treatment. Others are placed onto pseudo-menopausal drugs such as Zoladex GnRH analogues, for 6 months to simulate menopause. It is felt that during pregnancy and menopause, the rogue endometriosis implants 'die-back' due to lower oestrogen production, and therefore simulation of these processes may cause the endometriosis to go away. This is not always the case. Large cysts over 6cm may have to be removed by surgery, as may adhesions, which can distort organs and block the bowel or urethra. Of course, if you are trying to get pregnant a mimicked pregnancy or pseudo-menopause for 6 months is unwanted, as it delays a pregnancy. If the endometriosis implants are left in situ after an operation, the doctor may suggest drugs treatment to 'dry-out' the remaining patches. Preferably at operations all the endometriosis should be removed, but that takes time, and often operations are curtailed if the theatre has not been booked for long enough.

IVF treatments may make endometriosis worse, due to the way the drugs work in the body, and yet this is a path many women use in order to become pregnant when they are desperate. Informed choice should always be given to each patient, according to their needs so that they can assess whether that path of action is right for them. Trying to become healthy is the first step and a natural drug-free pregnancy is the optimum first choice. Three months on a healthy diet, for both partners, will make sure that the egg and sperm are better quality. You cannot expect a healthy baby to be produced if the egg and/or sperm are poor quality.

Case History

Mary's periods began when she was 12 years old; they were always heavy and painful, so bad that at night she had to sleep on towels. She was eventually diagnosed with polycystic ovaries at 25 years of age. By then she was plagued by severe back pains at periods and was unable to sleep. Two years later another laparoscopy was done but it showed nothing. The pain was so bad she was unable to work. She sought a second opinion. A year later another operation showed a large lump of endometriosis inside the bowel. She was placed on pseudo-menopause drugs for 6 months to stop periods and shrink the lump. After 6 months it was still there so a bowel operation was undertaken to remove it. Two years later the symptoms returned with bleeding from the bowel, so another bowel operation was done to remove a section of the bowel and the endometriosis lump which was now the size of a golf ball. After the operation she was so ill she could not get out of bed and a third bowel operation was done with a blood transfusion.

She and her husband wanted to have a family but the doctors said that this was unlikely from the state of the endometriosis and her bowel. Mary was very ill and could not work or do much in a day. She read my book and came to see me. We obviously had to work on the GI tract first so we looked for yeast overgrowth and food intolerances. We used all the anti-inflammatory omega 3 oils and probiotics. We excluded dairy foods from the diet. Hair mineral analysis showed high copper levels so we used zinc to chelate the mineral. We used anti-oxidants to reduce the inflammation and improved diet to include cooked vegetables as raw ones caused problems. Stewed fruits and fish were accepted. Slowly but surely the bowel began to function normally again and we were able to introduce more foods. After a few months Mary fell pregnant and gave birth to a baby girl. Two years later I worked with her again and she has just given birth to a baby boy. Now Mary is very careful with her diet. Her periods are fine unless she eats the wrong foods.

The Endometriosis and Fertility Clinic

We use the Measure Yourself Medical Outcome Profile Clinical Audit Questionnaire (MYMOP) with all the patients so that we have firm fact based research data to present at conferences around the world. Dian Shepperson Mills is an invited speaker at the main gynaecology meetings in the EU and USA. From a recent EFC research trial the selected participants who reported sub-fertility had a 52.5% success rate in falling pregnant.

Many gynaecologist's all over the world support the research and many have read the book and recommend it to their patients and refer them for treatment. Dian attends courses several times each year at major conferences all over the world to keep up to date with changes in research and put forward the EFC research.

Nutritional Management of Endometriosis

a) Pain

Pain is an important alarm signal. It tells us when all is not well with one of our body systems and has been described as the guardian of health. However, when pain becomes intense and recurring, it can erode every part of one's normal life. Pain is defined in the Oxford American Dictionary as "an unpleasant feeling caused by injury or disease of the body". Endometriosis pain is stunning, leaving you unable to breathe. Often diseases shown to be the result of vitamin deficiency are associated with unspecific pains. Changes in the central nervous system, mucus membranes and skin inflammation are often highlighted in these conditions. One piece of research does show that women with severe pain, infertility, and endometriosis had raised levels of PG Series 2 (from arachidonic acid) in their peritoneal fluid, and this could be the trigger for the inflammation.[4]

Various nutrients are known to play a role in relieving pain, chiefly these are the essential fatty acids from fats and natural cold pressed oils, vitamin C, E, K, and some of the B vitamins, DLPA, zinc, selenium and magnesium. Only the natural horseshoe shape cis-form of linoleic and alpha-linolenic fatty acids is able to contribute to the formation of anti-inflammatory prostaglandins.[5]

Research done looking at the effects of fish oils on endometrial implants showed positive results in that the sites of endometrial tissue shrank when fish oils were fed to rabbits with surgically induced endometriosis.[6] Proinflammatory prostaglandins in the peritoneal fluid were significantly lower in the fish oil group versus the controls. Total endometriotic implants diameter eight weeks after the induction was significantly smaller in the experimental group versus the controls. Studies, looking at the use of omega 3 fish oils in subjects with severe menstrual pain showed that they were effective at reducing pain.[7]

Severe vitamin C deficiency causes scurvy, which involves bleeding gums and considerable pain in the joints. Vitamin C can combat inflammation and pain by inhibiting the secretion (of pro-inflammatory) prostaglandins, which contribute to the symptoms.[8] Vitamin C may inhibit dopamine binding to membranes and inhibit prostaglandin levels, it has the property of natural anti-histamine and it reduces the severity of histamine attacks from internal inflammation, and may be able to detoxify excess histamine produced when the body is under stress.[9] Animal model trials looked at histamine induced wheals in the peritoneal cavity, when given vitamin C with bioflavinoids and digestive enzymes they reduced the effect of the histamine. It was felt that this was due to the nutrients strengthening cells against agents, which were causing the inflammation.[10]

Vitamin B6 (pyrodixine) has analgesic effects. If B6 is deficient the amount of serotonin in the brain decreases and this can lead to depression. B6 helps to relieve the pain associated with premenstrual syndrome. It should always be taken along with other B complex vitamins as they work in synergy. Vitamin B12 was shown in three independent trials to have an analgesic effect when injected intramuscularly.[11] When vitamin B12 is taken with vitamin B1 and B6, they can together produce significant dose-dependent pain relief and inhibition of inflammation, comparable to the action of standard treatments in orthodox medicine, but without the side effects.[12] It is known from research that high doses of thiamine (B1) can suppress pain transmission. There appears to be some relationship between thiamine and morphine.[13] The use of B vitamins seems to be crucial for women with endometriosis.

Vitamin E has an analgesic effect because it is able to inhibit pro-inflammatory prostaglandin production. Research has shown that 300iu per day reduced muscle cramps and pains in the lower back.[14] Studies suggest that vitamin E has anti-inflammatory action as it protects lysosome membranes (inside cell particles which produce enzymes) from histamine and serotonin damage. It acts slowly to limit inflammation so it needs to be taken regularly.[15] Vitamin E seems to help with adhesion pain. Care needs to be taken with vitamin E, only take it in a natural form at low doses (200-300iu). It can accumulate in the liver at high doses (800iu) when taken for a long time.

Vitamin K seems to strengthen these effects; it has anti-inflammatory and analgesic effect in animal models. In a trial it was shown to produce a significant inhibition of inflammation and pain when administered at a level of 4mg/kg body weight orally in animals.[16]

Magnesium relaxes smooth muscle. It works to produce ATP (adenosine triphosphate), which produces energy in each cell. Without magnesium we would be plagued with cramps, spasms and convulsions. Magnesium plays a vital role in synthesizing myelin around nerves and without it they become sensitive to pain. Magnesium has an anaesthetizing effect on the central nervous system. Adequate magnesium is an important preventative against miscarriage and painful contractions of the uterus muscle.[17]

Zinc is known from research to have anti-inflammatory effects. "In a twelve week double blind trial using a placebo, patients taking zinc sulphate showed significant improvement for joint swelling, morning stiffness, and their personal impressions of their overall condition was high. Zinc is known to inhibit the immunologically induced histamine and leukotrine release from mast cells. Thus it can dampen down inflammation".[18]

Selenium may have useful anti-inflammatory effects, and may enhance immune response. Little research has so far, been carried out on the use of selenium in the management of inflammatory conditions and where immunological status is poor.[19,20]

Supplementation with a good multi-vitamin-mineral may be helpful. A vitamin and mineral level check to look at status can tell you where there is a deficiency.

b) Fertility

First you get married and then you have a baby.

[21] It is expected, it is hoped for, it may just feel like a dream, but many women expect to have a baby at some point in their life. When nothing happens month after month life becomes bleak, a grey hollow world. It is difficult to move forward. Sub-fertility is being seen more and more in Western culture and we want to know why? In the sixties and seventies women were desperately trying NOT to get pregnant, hence the advent of the OCP. It freed you from constraint. Various reasons have been put forward for the present high infertility rate – stress, poor diet, lack of exercise, pesticide pollution, excess alcohol and smoking. It is a mixture of all these things, different for each woman, no doubt, but mega stressful. That is it – catch 22, can't get pregnant equals even more stress, and so it spirals on. The stress hormones upset the balance of oestrogen and progesterone, so staying as calm and relaxed as possible is a must. Be positive, you are trying all the right things.

A healthy immune system is supposed to recognize cells growing in the wrong place, like cancer and endometriosis, and the white blood cells home in on it and remove the offending cells. If the immune system is not working properly the white blood cells leave the rogue cells alone and so they proliferate. If harmful chemicals are in the peritoneal fluid of women with endometriosis, this may be setting up an immune response against the sperm or blastocyst.

Cellular immunity in the endometriotic tissue of women with endometriosis is decreased.[22] These women have lower NK cell activity in both plasma and peritoneal fluid, which correlates with disease severity. However, it is unclear whether this phenomenon is a cause or an effect of endometriosis. Endometrial cells from women with endometriosis also have higher concentrations of P450 aromatase, interleukins 6 and 11,[23] heat shock protein 27, and angeogenesis factors which are important modulators of cell growth and neo-angiogenesis.[24] When applied to reproduction, an exaggerated or abnormal immune response has been implicated in recurrent pregnancy loss, preterm birth, foetal growth restriction, and pre-eclampsia. In women with endometriosis cytokines were found in significantly greater amounts than in controls.[25]

It is well known that various vitamin and mineral deficiencies can cause health problems and deformities in the foetus. Twenty percent of first trimester pregnancy losses are characterized by hypocomplementemia. Complement activation is required for the recurrent foetal loss associated with antiphospholipid antibodies. Natural killer cells secrete complement. (Alternate pathway).[26] Macrophages secrete interleukin 1 from stroma cells. The endometrial implants are also secreting their own oestrodial which acts as an immune suppressant. All of this creates an exaggerated immune response. IgG and complement deposits are in eutopic endometrium. Severe forms of endometriosis are more immune deficient in NK cells. There may be implantation failure when excess immune cells are around. Cytokines sit between the blastocyst and the endometrium. There is a question as to whether sperm activate the immune system in women with endometriosis. What we do not know is why women with endometriosis develop these rogue implants and why other women do not. Research is ongoing to look for differences between normal endometrium and the endometriotic implants. Clearly the rogue endometrium is creating problems for fertility in some women.

Nutrient quality is especially important shortly before conception and during pregnancy and breast-feeding, with vitamin B12, folate, vitamin D, iodine, selenium and omega 3 fatty acids being of particular concern. [27] Research at the University of Leeds suggests that women taking a multi-vitamin capsule every day may double their chance of getting pregnant, as it is felt that better quality ova are produced by the ovary. [28] Research shows that when women were taking zinc at 25mg per day from the nineteen week of their pregnancy, their babies had a greater birth weight and head circumference.[29]

The genetic trait that confers gluten sensitivity, it does interfere with reproduction. There is a high prevalence of infertility regardless of which spouse has disease. The mother is more likely to experience recurring miscarriage, premature births, and low birth weight.

[30] Oestrogen's do acutely inhibit the rate of hormone release from the thyroid in adults, but any effect appears to be transient.[31] This maybe so, in healthy individuals, but in those who are ill with hormonal imbalances and endocrine dysfunction may have problems balancing hormones correctly. This area requires more research into the way it may affect endometriosis and be creating sub-fertility. The thyroid hormone and oestrogen hormone are antagonistic. If the oestrogen goes up – which happens when women don't have enough of the B vitamins and protein and have too much sugar – the thyroid hormone goes down. The woman may end up with dry skin, constipation, colds and fatigue. She may feel chilled when other people are not and need more clothing than other people, considering the temperature. High or normal thyroid hormone is protective against cancer, low thyroid hormone invites it. High oestrogen invites cancer; normal oestrogen discourages it.

[32] Hormone levels need to be checked in women with endometriosis as many of the drug treatments do have profound effects on normal pituitary and ovarian hormone levels. which do take some time to correct after the pharmaceutical drug course is completed.

Autoimmune diseases, such as those involving the thyroid , are thought to be involved in infertility, indeed, thyroid autoantibodies are used to predict women at risk for miscarriage.[33] Fourteen per cent of women with disease were found to have thyroid disorders.[34] The relationship between thyroid function , endometriosis and sub-fertility and the use of oestrogenic hormones is intriguing. There appears to be a link between hormone balance of the thyroid and adrenal endocrine glands and the symptoms of endometriosis. Rare diseases of the ovaries cause thyroid to be over-stimulated.[35] Some research on thyroid auto-antibodies has shown that the use of selenium at 200mcg per day, for three months, had significantly reduced the concentrations of antibodies in women with thyroid autoimmune disease.[36]

Pregnancy rates for women with advanced endometriosis were significantly lower with respect to women with mild disease...the chances of success of IVF in women with endometriosis are to some extent reduced.[37]

Facts to Enhance Fertility.

1. Relax, fertility hormone levels are not helped if adrenaline and cortisol are high. Do things you enjoy and that help to relax you.
2. Eat the freshest food you can, fruits, vegetables, nuts, seeds berries,

wild fish. More variety means you absorb a variety of nutrients.

3. Correct your digestion if you have any problems.
4. Sleep well, take a magnesium supplement if sleep is poor.
5. Avoid all the bad stimulant foods caffeine, alcohol, cigarettes, and refined sugars.
6. Exercise gently, walk, swim, yoga, Pilates etc. Get your BMI between 21 and 25 which is best for fertility.
7. Surround yourself with loving family and friends, hugs are important.
8. Try acupuncture and herbs or homeopathy if you feel they will help you.
9. Enjoy life, do things you both enjoy doing – together.
10. Reduce stress, make a list of all the things you find stressful – which stressors can you do something about? Do it now.

Dietary advice

Eating a hunter-gatherer diet has been shown to be beneficial. Your diet must be rich in nutrients if it is to aid the function of the reproductive /endocrine system. Some women are ill prepared to change their eating habits even after tests show that they should avoid a food due to allergies or intolerances, and others do not want to take nutritional supplements but would rather use diet to correct their problems. Nutritional therapy requires you do both in order to speed up healing and may well improve reproductive health. A few doctors are skeptical and feel that only drugs and surgery can correct the balance of body biochemistry, but enlightened doctors with an interest in integrated medicine feel that diet has to have a profound impact on reproductive health as it is only logical that the nutrients and phytochemicals that you input into your body on a daily basis can have profound effects on all aspects of your health.

Dian's Rules for a Healthy Diet!

1. **Eat 2 fresh fruits and 4 fresh vegetables daily.** Green leafy vegetables are rich in the B vitamins and magnesium that are needed by the reproductive system daily. Red-orange vegetables and fruits are rich in vitamin A. Dried apricots are a good source of iron. Snack on fruits.

2. **Eat wholegrain cereals and unrefined foods**. Include a variety of cereals in your diet, and if wheat triggers fatigue and/or bloating avoid it. Use oats, rye, barley, millet, rice, corn, quinoa, tapioca, or buckwheat instead. Nuts and seeds are rich in vitamins and minerals, as well as important cis-vegetable oils, eat a handful every day. Use fresh unprocessed organic foods as a basis for your meals, eg. lean meat, poultry, fish, and game. Oily fish such as herrings, fresh tuna, mackerel, sardines, wild salmon, pilchards, wild non-GM trout and Pacific halibut contain essential oils. Calcium is found in nuts and seeds, rhubarb, cereals like oats and fresh green leafy vegetables.

3. **Drink at least half a pint of fresh water daily.** Try diluting unsweetened fruit juices or use various herb teas. Chamomile helps sleep, lime blossom aids relaxation, mint, ginger and fennel aid digestion. Carrot juice also helps digestion. V8 vegetable and lemon juice help to cleanse the liver.

4. **Use only cold pressed vegetable oils.** Our bodies require essential oils to strengthen cell walls and to build hormones and the anti-inflammatory prostaglandins of series one from vegetable oils and series three from fish oils. Use unprocessed vegetable oils that have not been chemically or heat treated eg- unrefined, unhydrogenated, cold pressed extra virgin olive oils. Evening primrose oil is a good source of omega 6 oils. Edible food grade linseed oil from a health food shop is omega 3 but has an oestrogenic effect in excess. Organic Guernsey Butter may be used in moderation.

5. **Half your diet should consist of alkaline forming foods** such as vegetables, fruits, sprouted seeds, live soya*-ewes-goats milk yoghurts, almonds, pecan, pistachio, millet or buckwheat. The remaining half should be acid forming foods such as rye, corn, rice, peas, beans, lentils, nuts, seeds, eggs, cheese, fish, and poultry. This helps to balance your digestive enzymes.

6. **Reduce your intake of sugary foods.** Avoid all refined-sugar consumption as it can cause fluid retention and may prevent other vital nutrients from being absorbed. Sugar also thickens blood and stops immune cells from working efficiently for 4 hours after intake. Avoid chocolate, sweets, biscuits, cakes, puddings, ice-cream, sugary fizzy drinks, sweet tea or coffee, jams. Eat carob bars or fruit and nut bars. Avoid artificial sweeteners eg. aspartame.

7. **Avoid excess salt intake.** Too much salt causes fluid retention and some PMT symptoms. Reduce the amount of salt added to cooked foods and avoid eating salty crisps, nuts, etc. Use herbs, spices, lemon juice or root ginger to impart flavour instead. Your body only requires 3gm salt per day and most diets give up to 10gm. If you suffer from low blood pressure then a little salt is fine; it is a danger with high blood pressure.

8. **Cut down your intake of tea, and avoid coffee, alcohol, and tobacco.** Caffeine is felt from research to impair ovarian and testes function and may effect fertility, as may excess alcohol. Tobacco and alcohol can aggravate some PMT symptoms. Use herb teas or dilute juices. Coffee and alcohol are diuretics – preventing mineral absorption.

    *N.B. only organic soya. Some can be G.M.

9. **Avoid excess animal fats** eg. beef, lamb, pork. Red meat and dairy foods supply of series two prostaglandins - the pro-inflammatory ones, so should be eaten in moderation. Wild game is a less fatty meat. Use organic white meat and fish, with occasional New Zealand lamb. Use

cold pressed olive oil and organic butter to stir-fry. Eat a sensible amount of organic dairy foods unless you are lactose or casein intolerant. Jersey and Guernsey milk are the best source.

10. **Regularly exercise.** Gentle exercise and exposure to fresh air and sunshine are vital in maintaining health. Take walks, go swimming or cycling if you are able. Gentle exercise helps the body produce endorphins - natural painkillers and stimulates the digestive tract. In order for your ovaries to get the right hormonal message from your pituitary gland you need at least 20 minutes of natural daylight on the retina of your eyes every day. If you work in an office under fluorescent lights go for a walk every lunchtime around the block.

11. **High fibre diet.** We all need to include more fibre in our diet to ensure the stools are well formed and that waste can pass through us at an even rate, avoiding the build up of harmful toxins in the intestines. Fibre of the type provided by FOS fructoolligosacchardes also helps to maintain the good bifdobacteria gut flora that produces the B vitamins needed by the liver enzymes. The presence of fibre also stimulates peristalsis and binds to cholesterols and oestrogens to escort them from the body. Fibre can be from wholegrain cereals, nuts, seeds or from fruits and vegetables, at least 30gms is needed each day.

12. **Candida Albicans.** If you think you have a yeast overgrowth, or allergy or sensitivity to the yeast candida albicans in your digestive tract and suffer abdominal bloating after meals or thrush, then remove the foods which are 'feeding' the yeast: refined sugars, yeasts, wheat, fermented foods, dried fruits, dairy foods – for at least 2 or 3 months. The following foods have anti-yeast properties and should be used frequently; garlic, onions, cabbage, broccoli, brussel sprouts, kale, watercress, mustard cress, cauliflower, turnips, cinnamon, olive oil, aloe vera juice, Pau d'arco tea. Do not try to get pregnant whilst you are eliminating the yeast overgrowth as toxins will be present in the blood stream. Rather wait for two months whilst the balance is corrected and then begin the try for a pregnancy once your system is cleared.

Suggestions for Weekly Menu Plans

	Breakfast	Lunch	Tea/Dinner
1.	Prune Juice Corncakes & Hummus Mint tea	Potato & Leek soup Oatcakes &Apple Figs	Turkey breast Rice, Broccoli, Carrots
2.	Sheep's yogurt with ground almonds, oatbran berries. Cranberry Juice. Fennel Tea	Mackerel Mixed Salads Baked potato Dates	Chestnut pâté Pumpernickel rye bread Tomato & Celery Apple
3.	Corn & Buckwheat pancakes Blueberries Mint tea	Chicken with lemon & olives Boiled rice Broccoli, Carrots Fig	Carrot & almond soup Corn Tacos Apple
4.	Rye bread & poached egg Tomato Juice & Herb tea	Grilled chicken Green beans, carrots Jacket potato Dates	Veg & lentil soup Rye crackers Pineapple
5.	Potato cakes Sugar free baked beans Mint Tea	Stuffed Aubergne (Eggplant) Baked tomato, green salad Pear	Turkey breast Boiled potato Green beans, beetroot
6.	Sheep's Greek Yoghurt with peaches, oatbran, Flaked almonds Herb tea	Frittata Green salad Soya yoghurt + mint, cucumber	Salmon pate & ricecakes Tomato, Celery Apple
7.	Oatcakes & hummus Apple juice Fennel tea	Chickpea & spinach curry Lentil Dhal, rice Potato	Green leafy salads Crab pate and Cornbread Pear & figs

Suggestions for Week 2 Menu Plans

	Breakfast	Lunch	Tea/Dinner
1.	Scrambled egg Rice cakes Herb tea	Watercress soup Apple Beverage	Lamb and olive casserole Rice Rhubarb Fool
2.	Soya yogurt with dates, ground almonds, bananas Tea	Chicken Salad Jacket potato Fig	Avocado pate & rice cakes Salad
3.	Rye bread and hummus Herb tea	Nut Loaf Boiled new potatoes Broccoli, Carrots Banana	Asparagus soup Oatcakes Apple
4.	Rye crackers & poached egg Herb tea	Poached Halibut Green beans, sweetcorn Jacket potato Melon	Lentil & apricot soup Ryvita Dates
5.	Potato cakes Baked beans Tea	Chicken breasts with ginger & leeks Red cabbage Grilled tomato, peas Pear	Mushroom & pea stroganoff Chickpea pasta Kiwi
6.	Provamel Soya Yoghurt* with banana Herb tea	Vegetable and bean stir fry St Helen's Goat's milk yoghurt with mint, cucumber	Tuna pate & rye crackers Tomato, Celery Apple
7.	Oat crackers & nut butter herb tea	New Zealand lamb Shepherds pie Broccoli, carrots Melon	North African rice salad Tomato salad Pear

*N.B. only organic soya.

Snacks between meals;

Nuts
Sunflower seeds
Date & fig bars
Raisins & sultanas
Savoury popcorn
Hazelnut butter on crispbreads
Replace cow's milk with soya milk in recipes.

Nutrition Research

In one study, serum retinol levels were found to be significantly lower in 71 women with menorrhagia than in healthy controls. After 40 of these were given 25,000iu of vitamin A daily for 15 days, blood loss returned to normal in 23 and was reduced in a further 14. i.e. 92.5 per cent of these women had either complete relief or significant improvement".[38] However, vitamin A above 2000iu is not recommended for women who are trying to become pregnant, eat red/orange vegetables every day, food form vitamins will help. Capillary fragility is believed to play a role in many cases of menorraghia. Supplementation with vitamin C (200mg t.i.d.) and bioflavinoids has been shown to reduce menorrahgia in 14 out of 16 patients."[39]

Research on endometriosis showed that when women eliminated caffeine and supplemented with essential fatty acids there was an anti-inflammatory effect and a significant decrease in symptoms was recorded.[40]

Although the symptom of fatigue is related to iron deficiency anaemia, evidence is lacking for any association between iron deficiency and tiredness in the absence of anaemia. Iron deficiency associated with increased fatigue was, however, shown in recent longitudinal study on women's health, in a European study, that about 20% of women of childbearing age had serum ferritin concentration less than 15ug/l, and only 4% of these women had iron deficiency anaemia.[41]

Descriptions of the disease (endometriosis) are found in 17th and 18th century texts.[42] The need for a cure grows ever keener as younger and younger women are being diagnosed, we are now in the twenty-first century and we should be trying to find the cure rather than just suppress it. We need more pure science research to look at what is happening on a cellular level.

Nutritional Supplements

The judicious use of nutritional supplements whilst the diet is being corrected can improve reproductive health. Due to the methods of farming with depleted soils and overuse of pesticides (which have an oestrogenic effect on the body and may cause endometriosis to proliferate); Harvard University and the American Dietetics Association both advise that a multi-vitamin-mineral should be taken each day.[43]

There are a few rules to remember when taking supplements:

1. Choosing supplements on these occasions requires trained advice from a nutritional therapist. All the supplements you buy should be hypoallergenic, yeast, wheat gluten, lactose, sugar and dairy-free.*

2. Always consult a doctor before you try to get pregnant or if you are planning to lose weight. Ask for various tests to be done like thyroid and alergy tests.

3. Vitamin E should only be taken at 100iu dose if you have high blood pressure. It should not be taken with magnesium as they are antagonistic and cancel one another out. (Similarly never take zinc and iron together).

4. Always take folic acid alongside zinc; take a B vitamin complex with a single B vitamin - otherwise the one taken singly stays high whilst the

* Don't worry. All the Foresight ones are!

others are knocked down low; vitamin C taken with iron helps its absorption; calcium uptake is improved when evening primrose oil is taken; likewise boron improves calcium uptake.

5. Evening primrose oil should not be taken by anyone prone to epilepsy.

6. Most supplements are designed to be taken with food.

7. Prebiotics and probiotics and digestive enzymes should be taken with a cold drink. If your digestion is out of sorts you must correct that first – take a slippery elm and acidophilus for 2 months.

Summary

Make the changes and give your new 'diet' 3 months to help your body renew itself and to stimulate the cells to work efficiently at producing hormones, enzymes and prostaglandin's. If you suspect one or two foods are upsetting you exclude them for one month. If it makes a difference to the way you feel you are halfway there, and the second half of the journey gets much easier. Once you begin to taste that feeling of wellness there is no going back.

Variety is the spice of life! Eat as many different foods each day as you can, the more different foods eaten the more nutrients you absorb. What is the end point? To have a healthy baby, who will grow to be a healthy adult – hopefully living to a ripe old age. Burke et al, looked at mothers who had eaten good/excellent diets, they gave birth to babies judged to be in good/superior health 94% of the time. Contrasted with mother's whose diets were classified as poor and whose infants had good health only 8% of the time.[44] A perfectly good reason to eat well.

"Endometriosis: a key to healing and fertility" Dian Shepperson Mills and Michael Vernon, Thorsons ISBN 0-00-713310-3. Women all over the world email to say how much they have been helped. Dian holds consultations at The Hale Clinic in London 0207 631 0156 and works with gynaecologists the world over. dian@endometriosis.co.uk

References

1. Eskenazi B, Warner ML, 'Epidemiology of endometriosis.' *Obstet Gynecol Clin North Am* 1997;24(2):235-258

2. Galeao R, 'La Dysmenorrhea, syndrome multiforme.' *Gynecologie* 1974;25:125 (in French)

3. Rier S et al. 2001. 'Serum levels of TCDD and dioxin-like Chemicals in Rhesus Monkeys Chronically Exposed to Dioxin: Correlation of Increased Serum PCB Levels with Endometriosis'. *Toxiological Sciences 59*, 147-159

4. Halme JK, 'Role of peritoneal inflammation in endometriosis associated with infertility. Endometriosis Today: advances in research and practice' – *The Proceedings of the Vth World Congress on Endometriosis, Yokahama, Japan* Oct 1996 pp 132-135. Parthenon Publishing.

5. Kassis V. 'The Prostaglandin system in human skin'. *Danish Medical*

Bulletin 1983:320-342

6. Covens A, et al. 'The effect of dietary supplementation with fish oils fatty acids on surgically induced endomteriosis in the rabbit'. *Fertility and Sterility* 1988 49:698-703.

7. Deutch B, 'Menstrual pain in Danish Women correlated with low N3 polyunsaturated fatty acid intake'. *Euro J Clin Nutri* 1995;49:508-516

8. Kronhauser E, et al. *'Formula for Life.'* Published by William Morrow & Co. New York, 1989:95

9. Hanck A, et al.'Analgesic and anti-inflammatory properties in vitamins'. *Int J Vit and Nutri Res* 1985;27:189-206

10. Taraye JP, et al. 'Advantages of a combination of proteolytic enzymes, flavenoids and ascorbic acid in comparison with non-steroidal inflammatory drugs'. *Ameim Forsch* 1977; (1): 1144-1149

11. Hieber H. Die Behandlung vertebragener Schmerzen und Sebsibliatsstorungen mit Hochdosiertem Hydroxoxcobalamin. *Med Onoatsschr* 1974;28:545-548

12. Greenwood J, "Optimum vitamin C intake as a factor in the preservation of disc integrity" in Med Ann DC. 33:274, 1964

13. Misra AL. Et al.'Differential effects of opiates on the incorporation of (14C) thiamine in the central nervous system of the rat'. *Experimentia* 33:372-374. 1977

14. Cathcart RF, et al. Leg cramps and vitamin E. *J Am Med Assoc* 1972;219:216-217

15. Kammura M, 'Anti-inflammatory effects of vitamin E' J Vitaminol 1972;18:204-209

16. Wiser H, Kormann AW. 'Biopotency of vitamin K1; Antihaemorrhagic properties of structural analogues of phylloquinone as determined by curative prothrombin time tests.' *Int J Nutri Res* 53; 143-15. 1983

17. Muller P, *First international symposium on magnesium deficit in human physiology..* 1971

18. Marone G, et al. 'Physiological concentrations of zinc inhibit the release of histamine from human basophils and lung mast cells.' *Agents Action.* 1986;18-103-106

19. Roberts ME (1963) 'Anti-inflammatory studies 1 & 11 Anti-inflammatory properties of Selenium.' *Toxicology and Applied Pharmacology* 5; 485-499.

20. Spallholz et al. 'Immunological responses of mice fed diets supplemented with selenite selenium.' *Proceedings Society Experimental Biology & Medicine* 143;685-689, 1973a, b, 1974.

21. Martinez-Jover, C.' I want to have a child: whatever it takes.' *Impresora Apolo*, Mexico. 2004.

22. Ishimura T, Masuzaki H, 'Peritoneal endometriosis; endometrial tissue implantation as its primary etio-logic mechanism.' *Am J Obstet Gynaecol*

1991; 165:210-14

23. Noble LS, et al, 'Aromatase expression in endometriosis.' *J Clin Endocrinol Metab* 1996;81:174-9.

24. Hii LL, Rogers PA, 'Endometrial vascular and glandular expression of integrin alpha (v) beta(3) in women with and without endometriosis'. *Human Reprod* 1998;13:1030-5

25. ElovitzM, Toll-like receptors polymorphisms and reproductive outcome. "Innate immunity in the reproductive tract. C11. *ARSM PG Program*. 2005:104 Montreal, CA.

26. Molina H, 'The Complement System During Pregnancy. "Innate immunity in the reproductive tract.' C11. ARSM PG Program. 2005:104 Montreal, CA.

27. Walsh S, '*Plant Based Nutrition and Health*.' The Vegan Society. 2003; 136

28. Crzeizel, A. 1996.'The effect of preconceptual multivitamin supplementation on fertility'. *International Journal of Vitamin and Nutrition Research* 66, 55-58.

29. Goldenburg. 'The effects of zinc supplementation on pregnancy outcome'. J Am Med Assoc, vol.274, no.6;4635. 1995

30. Braley, J. Hoggan R. '*Dangerous Grains*.', New York. Avery 2002, pp28-29.

31. Gambert SR.' Factors that control thyroid function:Environmental effects and physiologic variables.' In LE Braverman & Utiger RD (Eds.). *The Thyroid Gland* (pp347-357). Philadelphia. JB Lippincott. 1991.

32. Fredericks C' Guide to Women's Nutrition: dietary advice for women of all ages'. Perigree Books, 1989.pp53

33. Sungh A, Dantes ZN. Stone SC, et al. 'Presence of thyroid autoantibodies in early reproductive failure: biochemical versus clinical pregnancies'. *Fertility and Steril*. 63(2):277-81.1995

34. Councell L, Trenew N. 'Probiotics'. *Thorsens*, London pp70-71. 1990

35. Ditcoff BA. Gerfo PL. 'The Thyroid Guide'. *Harper Collins*. 2000. pp28

36. Gartner R, Gasnier BC, 2003, 'Selenium in the treatment of autoimmune thyroiditis.' *Biofactors*,19;3-4,165-170.

37. Somigliana E, et al, 'Should endometriomas be treated before IVF-ICSI cycles?' *Hum Reprod Update* 2006;12:57-64

38. Lithgow D, Politzer W, 'Vitamin A in the treatment of menorrhagia.' *S.Africa Med J* 1977: 51:191-193

39. Cohne JD, Rubin HW, 'Functional menorrhagia treatment with bioflavinoids and vitamin C.' Curr Ther Res. 1960; 2:539-542

40. Mathais J, et al, 1998 'Relation of endometriosis and neuromascular disease of the gastro-intestinal tract, new insights'. *Fertility and ~Sterility*, 70:81-87

41. Galan P et al, 'Determining factors in the iron status of adult women in the SUVIMAX study'. *Euro J Clin Nutri* 1. 1998:52;383-8

42. Knapp VJ, 'How old is endometriosis? Late 17th and 18th century European descriptions of the disease.' *Fertility and Sterility.* Vol 72. No.1, July 1999

43. Willett WC , Stampfer MJ, 'Rebuilding the Food Pyramid' *Scientific American reports: Special Edition on Diet and Health*, Vol 16; number 4, pp13..2006

44. Burke BS, Harding W, Stuart HC. 'Nutrition studies during pregnancy'. *J Paediatrics.* 1943 Vol 23:506-515

CHAPTER 11

Talking To The Powers-That-Be On What Could Be Done To Help

> *"Must the citizen even for a moment, or in the least degree, resign his conscience to the legislation? Why has every man a conscience, then? I think that we should be men first, and subjects afterward. It is not desirable to cultivate a respect for the law, so much as for the right. The only obligation which I have a right to assume is to do at any time what I think right. Law never made men a whit more just; and, by means of their respect for it, even the well-disposed are daily made the agents of injustice."*
>
> *Henry David Thoreau, from Civil Disobedience. 1849*

In the penultimate chapter I have decided to list all the steps I can think of that the Government could take that would make our lives one whole lot easier, while we fight to get our country (and our Planet) back to health and sanity – and thus back to fertility and normal family happiness.

1.   They could take more interest in promoting organic growing, and thus healthier soil and food:

a) By taxing agricultural chemicals such as artificial fertilizers and pesticides more heavily to discourage use.

b) By giving much bigger subsidies to *organic* farmers and market gardeners.

c) By seeing that built-up areas have land set aside for allotments, especially where people are in high-rise apartment blocks.

d) By encouraging *future* town planners to give each house enough garden to have a patch for vegetables, and possibly a few fruit trees, and/or space for a few hens.

e) By banning outright genetically modified foods or animal feed, as many dangers and no benefits have been identified.

f) By encouraging the growing of organic fruit and vegetables on school premises wherever possible. Learning about organic growing should become part of the curriculum.

g) By encouraging and, if *necessary funding*, agricultural colleges to teach organic farming.

317

h) By encouraging the growing of organic flowers for hospital and maternity greetings, as organophosphate contamination is not helpful in these circumstances.

i) By presenting a prestigious award for the supermarket providing the highest percentage of organic food. This might help - if made sufficiently "high profile".

j) By avoiding GM foods. The Soil Association will be able to help with advice on avoiding bringing in GM foods, including animal foodstuffs. Dr Mae Wong Ho is also a brilliant scientist in this area. This is extremely important. The portents are dire.

2.   **The Government could promote a *"National Loaf"*** as in World War II, with an approximately 85-90% extraction rate, fortified with powdered Brewer's Yeast. They could juggle with the recipe until they managed to approximate natural, organic whole-wheat. This would help people who do not like the taste of "brown" bread and flour, or whose children refuse to eat it!

3.   **The Government should ban all the food additives** known to cause health problems, most of which are already banned in other European countries, Canada, Australia and so on. On this issue, they should recognise the fact that the "research" they are shown is worthless. The way this is conducted, the "experts" dose small rodents with huge, poisonous doses of a substance until half of them die. They then pronounce that one fiftieth of this dose is safe! *There is no evidence to support this*, and all the more informed health professionals know that with some people (especially children) even a homeopathic dose of a toxic substance can set up a reaction in the body.

Most people know by now that the reason these substances continue to be produced is because the same pharmaceutical companies that make them also make the medicaments that have to be taken to alleviate the illnesses that they cause, e.g. they make tartrazine, known to cause hyperactivity, then they make the Ritalin. This way they manufacture the illness, and then the cure/masking medicine, and get paid handsomely for both! This is very lucrative. Those doing the suspect "research" will also be involved in the pharmaceutical industry.

Politicians making decisions on these issues on behalf of the hapless sufferers and sufferers' parents, need to remember that these parents are also the taxpayers who have to pay for the medicaments down both nostrils, *and* they are the Voting Public. They are becoming more beady eyed than they used to be.

It would not be a hugely big deal just to say that all the dangerous additives are not to be used in food manufacture in 6 months' time (giving time to reform recipes), and all to be off the shelves in 18 months' time, with leniency over time scale to be *withdrawn* if there is resistance. The safe list has every type of additive they need. Those alone can suffice.

4.   **The Government needs to become equally informed regarding pesticides.** The organophosphate pesticides are still present on many of the foods we eat. Christopher Robbins in his book "*Poisoned Harvest*" published in 1991, maintained that only 13% of the substances used at the time were really necessary. We gather that since this time pesticide use has dropped to 47%. Good. But there is another 34% to go! Advice should be taken from the particularly successful organic farmers, from the Pesticide Action Network (PAN), the Soil Association, Friends of the Earth, Garden Organic and the Good Gardeners' Association – and NOT from the manufacturers of the pesticides! The more that poisonous and nerve damaging pesticides can be eliminated, the less "mental illness", "behavioural problems", epilepsy, multiple sclerosis, motor neuron disease, and Alzheimer's etc, there will be. (The trace element manganese carries oxygen to the mitochondria of the brain cell. The organophosphate pesticides prevent the uptake of manganese from the gut into the blood making the blood short of manganese, and so the cells short of oxygen. Thus, over time, reducing the ability of the brain cells to function.)

In addition the Government should ensure all carpets, furnishing materials, pillows, duvets, mattresses etc are free from pesticides used for moth-proofing and fire retardant and other chemicals. This is particularly important with cot and pram mattresses and bedding, also pen mats, children's car seats and pushchairs.

Veterinary use of "flea killer" drops on the necks of cats and dogs should be discontinued. These are organophosphates and can give the pets epilepsy. Also they can affect children who cuddle and stroke them, as they get contaminated. The same applies with "flea collars". They need to be banned.

How to reduce the amount of pesticides to be discussed with PAN (Pesticides Action Network), The Soil Association and Friends of the Earth, with a view to withdrawing "time scale lenience" unless cooperation is forthcoming, in the same way as with additives.

5.   **The Government should ban the importing of GM human and animal food** until much more research is available regarding genetic modification (GM), . Dr Mae Wan Ho is a brilliant scientist in this area. She and the Soil Association will be able to advise.

The growing of GM foodstuffs in this country should be discontinued. The repercussions may be irreparable and unstoppable. It may be contributing to the demise of the bees, butterflies and song birds. Please study the evidence.

6.   **Cigarettes** should be labelled "Smoking can reduce fertility, cause miscarriage, premature birth and malformation." The ban on smoking in public places is excellent and should be retained despite opposition from tobacco addicts!

7.   **Alcohol** should not be sold to pregnant women, as well as children. There should be notices in pubs, and in the liquor aisles in supermarkets, saying "Alcohol can reduce fertility, cause miscarriage and can damage the unborn child both mentally and physically." School children should be educated about this and also told that alcohol causes depression, and impedes mental functioning, and can cause mental illness and violence.

Pubs should close at 11 p.m. as formerly. Drinks such as Alcopops should be made significantly more expensive. 3 pence will achieve nothing – £1 per bottle might help. If they have been made containing colourings, aspartame etc that are known to be addictive, these should be removed.

Teenagers should be taught about Foetal Alcohol Syndrome in school, and examined on their knowledge.

8.   **Coffee** should be labelled: "Research has revealed that drinking coffee can contribute to miscarriage. Pregnant women are advised to avoid it. It has also been found to cause crying and sleeplessness in the breast-feeding baby."

9.   **Education on the effects of street drugs** on mental health, fertility and on the unborn child should also be given in all secondary schools (www.talkingaboutcannabis.com).

10.   **The use of Seroxat and Prozac** should be reviewed with the medical profession in the light of the increase in deeper depression and suicide amongst users. All mood altering drugs have severe side-effects.

11.   The Department of Health should acknowledge the **harmful effects of exogenous hormones**, both psychologically and physically – the contraceptive pill, Stilbistrol, fertility drugs such as Clomid, and HRT. More publicity should be given to psychological consequences, thrombosis, heart disease, cancer risks etc, so women could take control of their own destinies, and not be used as money spinners for the drug companies.

Dr Ellen Grant's organisation DASH, Doctors Against Steroid Hormones, should be consulted. The Pill should not be available on the internet. All FPCs also to publicise health problems associated with Pill use, including later fertility problems directly due to the Pill. Young girls should not be encouraged to use the pill as this can lead to infertility later in life.

Natural Family Planning (NFP) to be promoted as the method of choice at all Family Planning Centres. To be used with barriers in the Fertile Phase if preferred. Natural Family Planning (fertility awareness), should also be taught as part of biology in all secondary schools. Advice should be sought from Mrs Colleen Norman (www.fertilityet.org.uk).

12.   Genito-Urinary Medicine needs to be given more publicity. Clinics should be advertised in Yellow Pages. Notices, with easily remembered helpline phone numbers, should be put up in prominent places - bus stops,

stations, toilets, libraries, underground stations etc, as in World War II. Nothing lurid. Just how to contact and website addresses. The internet should then list all the symptoms, as well as effects on future fertility for both men and women, and the links to problems in pregnancy.

13.   **Medical Schools** should be asked to give more attention to nutrition and illness caused by deficiencies, and by high levels of toxic metals. Also to allergic illnesses, candida, intestinal parasites and exogenous hormones as mentioned in 11. All these areas are germane to most modern illnesses, but appear to be largely missing from basic medical training, and too few doctors specialise in them. The Government should set up a Think Tank composed of people from Alternative Medicine to advise them. They should not be intimidated by the out-dated prejudices of the medics, which are largely fuelled by ignorance of the methods and the achievements of those working in the Alternative field.

The antagonism is keeping a lot of very useful work from helping the large majority of the general public whose illnesses are caused by contemporary environmental hazards, not to mention by the side effects of the medical drugs themselves. Co-operation between the two groups, and exchange of information should be encouraged by the Department of Health consulting with both.

14.   **The NHS should set up its own laboratories for hair mineral analysis**, and to analyse water, dust and other environmental factors relevant to the intake of trace minerals and heavy metals.

15.   **The Government should ban adding fluoride** to the water supplies. This has been discontinued all over Europe after the experiment failed. The contribution to stomach problems, thyroid problems, osteoporosis, women's cancers and the increase in Down's syndrome babies should be recognized. Efforts should be made to find ways of chelating it out of people/children who start to show signs of dental fluorosis or other adverse reactions.

Adding fluoride to toothpastes should be discontinued, owing to the link to thyroid dysfunction.

Fluoride being added to white filling material for teeth should be discontinued, as it will be slowly released into the saliva for many years, and could also affect thyroid function.

Massive amounts of research on the harm done by fluoride can be obtained from NPWA, the National Pure Water Association, and from the internet. It should be forbidden outright that any more of this endemic poison is put into our water supplies. (It is a waste product of the pesticide industry, so as we use less pesticides, disposing of it will not be such a problem!)

16.   **The Government should ban the use of mercury dental repair amalgams**, as they have been found to cause mental problems and infertility especially in women dentists and dental nurses and their children.

This will also be the case with some patients. By now there are plenty of alternatives available. (More attention paid to diet will greatly reduce the number of cavities in any case!)

The Association for Mercury Free Dentistry should be the body to give official advice and should replace the BDA who are stuck in a time warp. There are plenty of types of white filling available. However, these should be fluoride-free or the poor patient goes out of the frying pan into the fire!

In addition, tuna fish should be tested for mercury contamination before being tinned.

17.   **The Government should become aware of** the contribution made by **electromagnetic pollution** to cancer, leukaemia and infertility, and the malformation of babies. Also sleeplessness, leading to depression and mental illness, should be acknowledged. In Germany, mobile phone masts are sited away from dwellings, as are pylons. The UK should study the findings from other countries, and apply them.

DECT (cordless) telephones need to be discontinued, and all computers need to have flat screens.

18.   **The proposed ban on street lighting all nigh**t should be pursued. Most people would welcome darkness from midnight to 6am. To have no glaring street lights in the middle of the night would make urban dwellers' sleep patterns much more normal.   Probably millions of prescriptions for sleeping pills could be saved. This would also save fuel and help reduce global warming, and save billions of pounds of rate-payers' money.

Towns should be informed at least a month before. It should be introduced thoughtfully, with people told well in advance, explaining all the advantages, both health wise and financial. Also, suggesting that people review their home security, maybe investing in torches, courtesy lights, window bars, bolts on doors etc, where necessary. This will also be popular with security firms – suggest they advise people and stock up!

Also, better security could mean an end to public buildings being lit all night long. In summer, there would probably be no need for street lights at all. The savings of both energy and rate payer's money would be awesome. The negative effect on global warming would be significant. The financial savings should be passed back to the rate-payer!

19.   **The Government should upgrade the role of the Surveyors' house surveys to include a Geopathic Survey**. Acousticom and other scanning should be carried out for electromagnetic pollution, from cracks in granite substrata and from underground rivers, as well as man-made hazards, such as pylons, mobile phone masts, electrical substations etc. Experts should be called in to give training in the use of the instruments.

In semi-detached or terraced housing or blocks of flats, the intrusion of

322

electromagnetism from adjoining dwellings should be investigated. Instructions/grants for reinforcing the defence of a property by insulating wallpaper, carbon paints, or silver mesh curtains, etc should be mandatory.

20.   **Surveyors should also be required to test the water supply** of the house for lead and copper contamination, also aluminium. The two former are present in excess in the hair of approximately 10-15% of the couples who we see. This is usually from the tap water due to a corroding joint, where either a lead connecting pipe is joined to a copper one, or where two copper pipes have been joined with a lead-containing solder. This can cause corrosion and contamination of the water, so needs to be removed.

Lead over 0.01ppm, or copper over 0.2ppm should not be allowed. Corroding pipes should be replaced possibly with ABS plastic (kite mark BS7291) if the water is acidic, or possibly glass if this new technology is sufficiently developed.

21.   **The Government should make sure all water connecting pipes** from the mains to the boundary stopcocks of private properties **are no longer lead**. In some areas where the water is acidic, ABS plastic or glass may be the material of choice for piping, rather than copper. Algaecide for swimming pools should not be allowed to contain copper.

22.   **The aluminium contamination of water** can be from aluminium gel used in the reservoir for collecting peaty particles.. The effluent from this needs to be monitored more efficiently.

23.   **The Government needs to ban the addition of aluminium** to deodorants. It can be absorbed into the body, and will ultimately affect brain function and be a contributory cause of Alzheimer's. We regularly find high levels of it in the head hair of those who use the deodorants, showing it is circulating in the blood. It will therefore reach the brain.

24.   **The Government should ensure that if artists' paints contain lead, they should be labelled** as such, and the risks of cancer of the mouth and throat emphasised if they lick the brushes. If possible, lead in oil paint should be banned altogether.

25.   **The Government should make a study of permanent hair dyes** regarding substances that have been found to cause bladder cancer in hairdressers. Hair dyes which contain lead should be banned. Pomades which contain lead should be banned. Braids for use in making plaits in African hair need to be made free from lead and cadmium. Lipsticks should not be allowed to contain lead.

26.   **The Government should forbid the use of aluminium in antacids**. It is a stomach irritant and is present to increase sales. The Government should forbid the addition of copper or aluminium to epilepsy medication as it will increase the likelihood of fits. A biochemically trained branch of the police needs to be set up to monitor the formulae for

medicaments to be sure they do not contain substances designed to perpetuate the condition, and thus increase the sales of the drug. The NHS drug bill is said to be costing the taxpayers over £8billion a year, so it is more than time this was investigated.

27.   **The giving of aspirin in pregnancy** should be reviewed by an independent body. The links with maternal post partum haemorrhage, HDMB (Haemorrhagic Disease of the Newborn), and bleeding into the eyes and sub-dermal bleeding in the babies needs studying, as do strokes in young mothers following labour. All of these problems seem to have come to light comparatively recently, since the fashion for large doses of aspirin throughout the first six months of pregnancy, and this is receiving insufficient attention.

28.   **The Vaccination Question** needs to be studied again. WDDTY (What Doctors Don't Tell You) have written "The Vaccination Bible". Dr Viera Scheibner has written "Behavioural Problems in Childhood, the links with vaccination". There is a magazine, "The Informed Parent" that comes out thrice yearly. There is also an organisation called JABS (Justice, Awareness and Basic Support for vaccine damaged children). It is known from their parents, that in this country 2,000 children every year become autistic after the MMR vaccine. This means that over 80 years, 160,000 children would be so afflicted. How would the country cope with this huge population needing constant care? How many of the so-called disaffected or difficult teenagers are "sub clinically autistic" but never diagnosed? Although they are possibly sectioned or imprisoned at a later date. Dr Scheibner who has studied the evidence in detail over a lifetime, also believes the cascade of allergic illness – irritable bowel syndrome, eczema, asthma, and conditions such as dyslexia and ADHD – all followed the cascade of immunisations that started in the 1950s. Certainly, the timings are coincidental, and no other explanation is so convincing. If so, we are losing 2,000 children to autism, 2,000 children to asthma and approximately 400 to cot death every year. 2,000 lose their sanity, and 2,400 lose their lives, to save about 10 deaths from measles? Is this intelligent? (Deaths from measles would be much less likely, possibly non-existant, if nutrients and homeopathy were used as part of normal child health care.) Every MP making a decision on this should spend a day with an autistic child, and a day with a little mite screaming with itching eczema, and spend time with a tiny child fighting an asthma attack – made worse by the crying with terror that makes it even more severe. Nobody should ever legislate about things they have never seen or experienced, or even talked about with someone who has. **The Government should talk more to parents** and less to so-called "experts" who are financially involved, and emotionally detatched.

29.   The Government should be less dismissive of people running the **Voluntary Organisations** and **Charities** for health problems. We have our fingers on the pulse of the nation. We are in touch with all the groups

who are suffering from any number of disadvantages. We know the day-to-day problems and we know the causes.

Much of the suffering (which, quite apart from the personal angle, is disabling and very expensive to the nation) could be avoided altogether if we were listened to, and our recommendations acted upon. We are in many ways far more representative of the nation than are "scientists" or other so-called "experts", who are not necessarily honest, disinterested, experienced in the practical aspects of a problem, or well informed.

Most "experts" are paid to have a certain point of view. "Qualifications" do not necessarily mean that people are intelligent, independent or right. They are just powerful. Commonsense coupled to years of experience of coping with the problem in "real life" situations, will provide a more practical and effective solutions in most cases. It would be a better idea to embrace these than the view of an "expert" totally divorced from his subject. Please consider this viewpoint.

If Government co-operated with the relevant Voluntary Organisations, they could tap into a wealth of concentrated, hands-on experience with each particular problem. If they took advantage of this, so *much* could be achieved so *quickly*. The volunteers have no axe to grind. They have a much more in-depth grasp of the problems in their specialised area than any other body.

The Government is using too much "paper knowledge" – Quangos and think-tanks' reports – and having too little conversation with the people on the ground. If the Government seeks advice from the people who do research, the only answer they will *ever* get is: "*It needs more research.*" This is how these people make their livelihood. There will <u>never</u> be a conclusion, as this would inhibit their income. Surely this is self-explanatory?

In many areas, the Government needs to take action, the problems are not hard to grasp. The research is all done and all out there, including on the internet. The Government needs to be less limp and more executive.

CHAPTER 12

ONWARDS!

Therefore, openly before the churches, show them the proof of your love and of our reason for boasting about you. 2 Corinthians 8:24

So we are nearing the end of what has been quite a Marathon for all of us – but I hope a joyful one. Let's just *recap* about exactly what there is to do:

Optimise the diet

Firstly, the food! To build up the sperm and the ova with living nutrients so they feel enormously energetic and joyful and like springing towards each other to create a new life!

Fresh, raw, organic natural food, as near to straight out of the ground as you can manage! The old McCarrison Society mantra of "Nothing added, nothing taken away," is a good rough guide. No GM. As few additives as you can manage. Use and flourish "FIND OUT" as you shop. Don't be shy; show it to the supermarket personnel, as you go round. Preferably, show it to the manager!

If, for example, you find a product that could cause asthma, or cancer, *tell them so.* If several thousand of you introduce them to this book, who knows what we might achieve? *"The customers are saying....."* can be a powerful phrase to the hard-pressed rep whose mortgage depends on his commission. There are safe alternatives to all the unsafe additives. Change is possible tell him, this is just a wake-up call not a death knell to his producers.

Anyway, most of what *you* choose will not have had any additives near it, and if you are growing your own, a lot of it will not have even seen a supermarket!

Start together to leave the dead stuff in the tins and the packets on the shelves, and bring home real food and cook it yourselves, with élan!

Voluntary Social Poisons

Alcohol, tobacco, cannabis etc, caffeine, tranquilisers, anti-depressants, sleeping pills, over-the-counter medical drugs.

Well, the more we get rid of the first four poisons, the less we need the rest of them! So it is more or less a self-solving puzzle with the solution built in.

Alcohol in relatively small quantities can enhance the fun of a social

327

gathering, but an excess inevitably means for the next few days you are less organised, less even-tempered, and much less efficient than you need be! You will feel more put upon, and find other people more exasperating than at other times. Observe yourself more closely, and see if I am right! For these reasons alone it does not enhance job satisfaction or family life!

Tobacco is a similar story. Any substance that changes mood, either dramatically or marginally, will kick-back proportionally in the opposite direction when the immediate effect wears off.

So, if something appears to "relax" or "enliven" you – wait for it –the directly converse mood will appear in due course! This means you will crave the substance yet again and the very worst scenario means that addiction can set in, then gradually you become a less worth-while person at home and at work, BUT an excellent money spinner for the alcohol, tobacco or pharmaceutical industry.

The tranquilisers, the sleeping pills, the anti-depressants (please put me into a better mood – please help me to find oblivion) are the inevitable follow-on to the "social drugs" that produced the agitation, sleeplessness, misery and gloom in the first place.

It has to be said, however, that the person seeking the medication may not *always* be the one using the suspect substances! They may just be on the receiving end of the petulance, gloom and paranoia from a relative, colleague or an employer. Whatever, factor these issues into your decisions/reactions, and don't be the one who is driven to medication!

Street drugs are on the same band-wagon, but the effects are more easily recognised, so they are more universally condemned. See Mary Brett's chapter regarding street drugs, and her report on our website. (There should be a Mary Brett clone in every school.)

Chocolate, coffee and tea all contain caffeine, but in small quantities these are not a major problem for most "non-baby-making" people. However, caffeine, even in quite reasonable amounts, does affect the poor little foetus, and so has been linked to miscarriage. So, under present circumstances we suggest giving them a miss in favour of organic smoothies and fruit juices and water, and the occasional herb tea, Marmite, Bovril (beef or chicken), milk shakes, vegetable juices (carrot or beetroot etc) and Rice Dream, Oatley, Provomil, Horlicks etc. Anything that is known to cause miscarriage will inevitably take its toll on the developing sperm and ova, and these are the two we are all intensely interested in, as you are reading this page. You know what to do as well as I do!

Contraception

Whatever happens, we want to get away from the pill, which has proved such a disaster for women's health, both physically (thrombosis, cancer, PMT) and mentally (masculinisation, lack of natural maternal instinct, lack of libido, frank mental illness, violence and suicides). It has also been linked to lowered zinc, and thus to many malformations, and epilepsy, hyperactivity, dyslexia, asthma, eczema, diarrhoea and so on in the children.

Time to throw it away.

So, just for the interim, to give time for all the health benefits to kick in, (and for your organic vegetables to grow!), we suggest natural family planning (NFP). Finding out exactly when you ovulate so that this knowledge can be harnessed, so you can do precisely what you would want to do.

While you are cosseting and feeding up the relevant little ova and sperm, you can avoid unprotected intercourse for the crucial few days coming up to ovulation itself, and thus avoid a conception before you want it, or before your body is quite ready to roll.

If, during the fertile stage, you decide to use barrier methods, at least it keeps this to a minimum. If you do, I would use liquid honey rather than a spermicidal gel. It seems to work as well, is less likely to set up a reaction, it also has an anti candida action which is always useful, and I do feel if must be nicer for the sperm! (By this stage we are all feeling quite maternal towards them, even the hundreds of millions who are just the supporting cast!) It will also be jollier for the wildlife.

The easiest form of barrier, if you don't like condoms, is the diaphragm. They can provide and fit these at your local Family Planning Clinic.

Once the mineral levels are optimised, and, as far as we can manage, all traces of poisons gone from the body etc, then, as you will know the most propitious date to try, it will be all the easier, and hopefully quicker, to conceive once you are ready to do so!

Colleen Norman at the Fertility Trust, who I have known for about thirty years, is absolutely ACE at teaching NFP, so I suggest that your first stop is 218 Heathwood Road, Heath, Cardiff, CF14 4BS, Tel: 029 2075 4628. Write to her, or give her a ring and ask where your nearest NFP teacher is. It will be useful to have learned the technique for the rest of your life. It will mean you never have to go back to hazardous pills and devices. This will lessen your risk of cancer, depression, thrombosis, migraine, and also of any more infertility in the future.

Genito-Urinary Infections

Get these checked out and sorted. If any bugs are on board, these can cause a miscarriage, or can prevent conception in the first place. No point in keeping them, as this will stimulate the immune system, and this will use up zinc, which is often in short supply.

No problems, as the check up can be obtained on the NHS, *free!*

To find out where your local GUM clinic is, you only have to ring your nearest big hospital and ask if they have a GUM clinic and if so, to put you through to them. If not, ask where the nearest one is. They are also very easy to find using the internet.

The doctors in the GUM clinics are some of the nicest people I know, and are surprised by nothing!

If you have a positive result, one option is to take the anti-biotic they give you, (plus taking extra B-complex vitamins, an extra Forebiotic capsule and eating lots of yoghurt).

Alternatively, we could give you the name and address of a homeopath in your locality who can give you a homeopathic remedy. We find these are just as effective and less likely to upset your digestion. Alternatively, again, the homeopathic chemists Ainsworths at 36 New Cavendish Street, London, W1G 8UF, Tel: 020 7935 5330, will be able to let you have a remedy for almost any of them. Just ring them up, tell them what you have, and you can pay by card and they will send it to you. All homeopathic remedies are very reasonably priced and completely safe. However, most homeopaths would say that you would be better consulting one of them on your "whole body state of health" – and having a "constitutional remedy" also. Most homeopaths are very knowledgeable and careful and this is likely to be helpful in re-establishing your general health.

Whatever you do, recheck at the GUM clinic afterwards to make sure you are clear of the specific infection.

Allergies, Malabsorption and Parasites

Allergies are very common, and very easily solved in most cases, by manipulating the diet or making adjustments to the environment. It may just be as simple as some noxious food additive, (study "FIND OUT"). Or, it may be very commonly eaten foods like grains or milk. Whatever, see if you can puzzle it/them out and avoid. Then, not only are you more likely to conceive, but also the baby will be much less likely to be born with allergies of his or her own. It will also usually mean a much pleasanter pregnancy with less sickness and fatigue.

Parasites are a major source of tummy cramps, itching anus, malabsorption, diarrhoea, bloating – all the things you really DO NOT WANT in pregnancy. If in doubt, find a local nutritionist – we can probably find you one - and check it out with a stool sample. He or she will arrange for this to be sent to a laboratory and they will be able to put a name to it/them. Again, as with GUI, your homeopath can give you a remedy, or Ainsworths may turn up trumps again, or your nutritionist/herbalist will know of some useful herbal products. Always recheck a few weeks after the treatment to make sure all is now sorted. Sometimes they appear to die down, and then a few weeks later the survivors have reproduced again. Seek advice on timing of medication, if so. Don't be embarrassed, lots of people have them!

An alternative approach to detection is being pioneered by nutritionist Lynn Alford-Burow. I have no experience of this, so can only be helpful in this limited way, but it is worth looking at her website or giving her a ring and telling her your symptoms. Lynn Alford-Burow, Cinnamon Health, Worton Gardens, Isleworth, tel: 020 8568 4797, or www.cinnamonhealth.co.uk.

All parasites *can* be got rid of, and you will be amazed how much better and more energetic you feel once they are dealt with.

Hair Mineral Analysis

If you have not done so already, I would get this done ASAP. The benefits are twofold:

If the beneficial minerals are all well up where they are meant to be – i.e. into the Recommended Range on your chart - then this eliminates a whole tranche of hazards. From physical and mental problems in the future baby, to exhaustion and depression in the mother, to lactation failure and early weaning, with all the misery of a screaming baby with colic and diarrhoea.... You name it, the mother's body working as it should, will safeguard against it.

The other side of the coin is the elimination of the destructive substances aluminium, cadmium, mercury and lead; and the reduction of over-high copper. Similarly, getting rid of the body-burden of unwanted metals can also guard against disaster with the foetus, and anguish for the mother. The details about the problems caused by low trace minerals and high toxic metals are given in the Hair Mineral Analysis chapter.

For people who want to study the research on mineral metabolism in even more detail, we will be getting the relevant research papers out onto our website.

The better we can get the hair levels, and thus the levels throughout the body, the easier it will be to conceive, and the smoother the course of the pregnancy and the breastfeeding, and the healthier and more intelligent the future child will be. It is worth sticking with it.

Electromagnetism

Again, this can be a vital element in success, although one where it is harder to judge what needs to be done, when, where?

The hazards are growing – tetra masts, mobile phones, DECT phones - and microwave ovens, we are told, can leak. Even vacuum cleaners, hair dryers and VDUs, although innocuous to the average adult, can become hazardous to the unborn and tiny babies.

There are ancient hazards known about in the Middle Ages, but comparatively recently brought to our attention again, such as underground rivers, and cracks in the substrata, particularly granite substrata, that send up rogue electricity.....

I am told that in the olden days, people used to build their cottage "where the cows lie down" as there, "the ground as peaceful". If only we were all as bright as the cows!

Sadly not, as this is all rather outside my intellectual range, but experience and research has taught us that where these hazards are found, they can have bearing on miscarriage, malformations and illnesses such as leukaemia and cancer. I therefore asked some very informed people to write some of the chapter on this subject for us.

We are also putting a section on the website. Study these, and if in doubt, I would call in one of our experts. If you have suffered more than one miscarriage, or if you have had the sadness of a damaged baby – especially if it was due to a chromosomal break (such as Down's, Edward's or Paton's Syndrome) I would enlist this particular area of help without delay.

You would be amazed at how much difference it can make. One of our North Country couples had been struggling for over a year, but the husband had a sperm count of only 15m. He was, however, resistant to the idea of a house check-over, until Roy was going up to the borders anyway, and so the fares would be a lot less to pay! After the visit I heard from the wife that the chair he constantly sat on was directly over the edge of an underground river. The friction of the water against the rock always sends up an electrical charge in these cases, and Roy can always pick this up – both by dowsing (at which he is brilliant) and also with his instruments which are very expensive and accurate!.

For a few months I heard no more, then the wife rang me: *Guess what, Nim, Val* (our redoubtable Branch Secretary) *came over a few months ago. She asked Robert if he had moved his chair yet. "No", he replied. He doesn't go much for that sort of thing. "Well come on now", she said, and she caught hold of the chair. Rob had to go and help her, she's only a little bit of a thing. "Where will we put it then?" asked Rob. "Over here" said Val. "There's a table there", Rob said. "Yes, well we'll move the table then, it's not going to cost you anything Robert, you know." replied Val. So they moved the whole room around. That was a couple of months ago. Today he went for another sperm count, and would you believe it, there were 63m! It's like a miracle, isn't it?" (A mercifully cheap miracle, for once!) God bless Val.*

Anovulation, as well as low sperm counts, can be due to electromagnetism. Sometimes just moving the bed or a much used chair can work wonders with a woman's cycle. If you wake up in the mornings with a particular ache or pain always in the same place, this can be a reason. Somebody we were helping woke up with a headache every day. Roy Riggs found a ley-line going through her pillow. He knew this would go through the pituitary gland, causing it to malfunction and this could be preventing ovulation. Within a month or so of moving her bed, she conceived – twin boys! Another person had a constantly stiff neck – the line went across the bottom of the pillow. He had been putting it down to an old rugger injury, but moving the bed solved it completely.

332

For this reason also, remember to ask Roy to check the place where you are planning to put the cot. Babies are very sensitive to electromagnetism, and it may be one of several contributing causes of cot death.

If you have seen Roy and had a positive finding, then you need to move the furniture as he suggested, and possibly replace a metal sprung mattress. There are many well thought through solutions now available. You may or may not need (according to the findings) – silver mesh net curtains, foil sandwich wall paper, carbon containing paint, metal-free mattresses, a new invention of Roy's that earths you while you sleep, and so on. But anyway, if you do, it is all there for you.

Remember not to carry a mobile phone while it is "live" and not to have a cordless (DECT) phone at home. A mobile in the trouser pocket microwaves the testicles. Be aware!

New Hazards, and New Solutions

The answer is to keep one jump ahead of the game! Sometimes we feel like hyperactive kangaroos!

Hair Dyes.

Hair dyes turn out to be hazardous. They are absorbed through the scalp into the bloodstream, and have been linked to kidney damage and bladder cancer. The wash-in, wash-out ones, however, are said to be OK. These are obtainable from chemists and health stores. Seek them out *"because you're worth it!"*

Dental Amalgams

Avoid any *more* mercury fillings, even if you are sticking with the ones you have, for the time being. It appears that the jury is still out on whether removing the existing fillings – which can create a lot of mercury dust etc as it is done – is the best thing to do. My feelings are that it is probably dependent on (a) how much mercury is leaking from the existing filling and (b) how experienced/conscientious the dentist is who is removing them!

We are lucky that an Association for Mercury Free Dentistry has been formed. These are the people to contact, for an expert opinion (www. mercuryfreedentistry.org.uk, The British Society for Mercury Free Dentistry, The Weathervane, 22a Moorend Park Road, Cheltenham, Glos, GL5 0JY, Tel: 01242 226918.)

Cosmetics

Buy our new little booklet "WATCH IT" and see what can lurk in cosmetics, household cleaners, furnishings, decorator's materials, and the like. What a minefield it all is – but it is navigable. Just a bit of extra awareness pays off.

So, when we've made all this amazing effort – what are we going to see in the way of tangible results?

Well, hopefully, first and foremost a conception – the conception of a really beautiful baby with everything he/she needs to be perfectly formed, equipped with a good working brain, and a strong immune system. We hope he will be conceived in most cases with a surge of living love (not a clattering of test-tubes) and the springing up of a happy and lively little soul!

Hopefully also his/her mum and dad will feel strong and blissfully happy and well able to cope. Above all, they will have a sense of humour about the ups and downs, something that seems abysmally lacking in the "experts" who have proliferated recently! This will mean he/she will be reared by maternal instinct – demand feeding and lots of lovely milk, and mum well able to stand up to any officious advice that would have them separated, harassed by conflicting theories, or put on schedules that are not their own!

Mothers who have plenty of the particularly helpful nutrients, (vitamins, Omega-3s, zinc and manganese), bond well and lactate abundantly! Plenty of breast milk given when wanted, and no unnecessary crying will mean much joy, and much less chance of eczema, asthma, hyperactivity etc. Good breast milk is made by good food, plenty of fresh water, and the sheer joy of love between mother and baby. It is not a medical matter, it is a natural happening. Every mouse in the skirting board, every fox in its lair, every rabbit in the burrow, every sow in the stye knows what to do, and (as long as hazards from their environment are not running them ragged,) so do women. Why does this surprise anyone?

If babies are left with their mothers and the mothers are allowed to handle them as they wish (and as the babies wish!), this will hugely reduce the amount of crying, and this will be a great relief to both mother and baby.

The baby will grow into a much calmer and happier child which will make learning an easier and jollier process. It will make such a happy mother-baby relationship, that leaving the baby to "go out to work" would be an agonising choice, and I feel very many fewer mothers will do this. This will make for a generation of much happier babies and children, and mothers – and even fathers!

Although I worked in one, and adored the babies, my gut feeling is that nurseries are not natural places. Homes are. For life in general, it seems to me, the money angle has got blown out of all proportion. Greedy estate agents push house prices higher and higher. Rents rise commensurately. "A roof over our heads" is beginning to use up half of everybody's lives and all the family intimacy, fun and happiness.

Women were not meant to be computer-fodder. *We are a different sex.* A survey by the National Council of Women in 1994 found that 94% of working women with children felt "stressed" and exhausted. Most would have preferred not to go out to work. <u>It does not seem sensible or kind to ignore these findings</u>. If you are one of the 94% you do not have to be browbeaten! Our babies need us. In many cases we don't have to leave them with strangers. Some of the strangers do not love them. There could *never be enough* extra-loving, extra-maternal strangers to go round, so that all children could be removed from their own mothers (who love them) and given to another woman who is capable of replacing that love. It would be a pretty ridiculous situation to expect this and, whatever, she would still only be there for a short time and then be replaced. (Babies need *permanent* love and continuity.)

At best, they will be occupied and amused with affection and without cruelty. At worst, if the staff are unsuitable, as is often the case, they will be lonely and bored and feeling abandoned while miserably waiting for Mummy's return. Occasionally, we hear of abuse.

What is the point of all this? Who gains in the long term? Not the mothers and not the babies.

Does it mean we are better off financially? As taxpayers, we have to pay for all the very expensive nurseries, nurses and supporting staff. We could do with this money to help us run *our own* homes. Why is it taken in ever increasing taxes from the pockets of women to make them do something that *94% of them do not want to do?*

There is usually some pressure at school from childless (virgin?) headmistresses for "career women" to be valued above home-makers and mothers. Getting girls to university is a feather in their cap, and a source of satisfaction. These girls are their "success symbols". They are "meeting targets."

I suspect there can also be the same relentless angst from other career women and women MPs – or from MPs whose wives who have chosen the career path. You can always feel the tension in these women. They have fought down their own instincts, but they cannot subdue them entirely, and this makes them want to bully the instinctive mother. Suppressing nature has been quite painful for them, there is a thrust of primitive jealousy the men cannot understand, and often they do not understand themselves. They tend to lecture the home-making mother with aggressive vibes, talking about abstract theories such as "supporting the Economy".

Many of them have probably been biochemically confused by the testosterone in the pill, and by their lack of zinc, (due also to copper water pipes) and lack of manganese (due also to organophosphate pesticides). Both these deficiencies are instinct quellers and gender-confusers par excellence.

I don't believe working mothers benefit "The Economy" much anyway. Once we have paid for the upkeep of the Nurseries - the buildings, the furnishings, the equipment, the food? What is the cost of the training of the nurses? Then it is not only *their* wages, but those of the cleaners, the cooks, the handyman, the laundry people?

I have worked in a nursery – way back at the end of World War II. As far as I remember, we had 24 staff all told, for 93 babies and children. We couldn't have managed with less. All this, presumably, had to be funded by the tax payer? We were paid very little, compared with what people have to be paid now.

Some august "Think Tank" has just come up with the fact that the "Sure Start" programme has cost billions and benefitted nobody. Whoever thought it would do otherwise?

Do not ever be bullied. Keep yourself on top! Do your own thinking, your own nurturing and your own loving. It is your life and your child.

OK, I hear you say, it would be lovely to stay with the baby all day, but we need the money. Well, I do know the feeling, but there are possible nice little earners that can be done from home, in little snippets of flexitime, maybe while he has his nap?

Do you sew? Dressmaking, soft furnishings (but mind the pins) embroidery, knitting, crochet, lampshades?

Do you type? Could you take in typing, website design, and transcribing books? Better still, write your own stories? Think of JK Rowling! Cookbooks – think of Jamie or Nigella. Simpler stuff? Help hard-pressed offices with mail outs?

Are you an outdoor type? How about growing *organic* fruit or veg, or flowers? (especially for maternity hospitals)? Keeping hens if circumstances permit? Keeping bees? Thoughts of "River Cottage for Ever", and "The Good Life" seep into the mind...?

Are you artistic? Painting pictures, taking photos, making designs for book covers, greetings cards, wall papers, table maps, paper napkins? Dream it up!

Are you musical? Could you write music, pop songs, ballads, opera!?! I am told this is very difficult to break into, but, hey! Who knows?

Have more innovative ideas for flexi-time home-working and send them into us for our website? We could start a page for it in the Newsletter? *You* could lead the way! (It does not mean you have to be alone all day, you can form little groups, and the children will also make little friends.....)

Also, I have often wondered if, when the children go to school, there could be some job sharing arrangements, such as young-at-heart pensioners working to fill in the school holidays? Possibly in an ideal world, the one who had just retired from the job in question? Would she like to come back for about 14 weeks in each year to augment her pension, while our Mum takes unpaid leave?

Alternatively, could you find a student who would like to work off a bit of the student debt problem by working Monday to Friday through the school holidays? Have a bit of "work experience" on the job, rather than spending the days idle and bored?

It all depends on the type of work, the expertise necessary, and the whole situation, but these are just ideas to toss around? An advert in the local paper might bring amazing results!

Whatever, I know you Foresight mums do wonderfully well! We get such heartening feedback about our Foresight children. As with plants that are properly fed, they blossom! We hear of them getting scholarships, playing in orchestras, playing in chess tournaments, being in teams, getting into their choice of university and so on....

We can all do the world a very good turn, producing some outstanding people – we can also save the taxpayer (*us*) a vast fortune in SCBU time, Special Needs Schools, Hospital time, and later Mental Hospital time and Prison time!

I suspect that as our glorious undamaged children grow to maturity, they will produce better music, poetry, fiction writing, plays, TV programmes, dancing, singing, furniture, clothes – whatever! - than we have at present, and some will be playing in orchestras (some are already.) They will go in for beautiful architecture, gardens, parks and open spaces, maybe just window boxes, hanging baskets, courtyards, allotments. Who knows, they may make Britain a flowering paradise!

Benefits to a struggling planet

Contact with the earth brings tremendous rewards. Tiny children are thrilled as "their" seeds come up out of the soil. Organic gardening makes this possible to share as they can handle the soil without fear of damage from chemicals. Every spark of joy can become a flame.

Domestic animals will benefit from an organic environment with much less illness. Children love pets and benefit from animals in the house where this is possible. With a mother based at home, a much more expanded home environment *is* possible.

Small children also love watching birds come to a bird-table. (I remember buying a bird-bath when one of my sons was about five, and him asking me, *"Can we watch them – what is their bath-time?"* We *have* to keep the birds!

As human contamination of earth and water lessens, wildlife will also benefit. This is really important. At the moment sparrows and other little songbirds are disappearing rapidly. This may be partly because of pesticides, GM crops, and voided medicines, but it is also likely to be due to radiation from tetra masts etc. The poisons and the electromagnetic pollution may be making the birds' eggs, if any, sterile. It may compromise the immune system in the bees. We cannot do without bees. They pollinate everything. There will be no fruit, only some vegetables, no flowers. If we have no bees, *we* may also disappear, as food production will be very, very difficult. Although at the moment, any intelligent protest will be greeted with screams of *"You cannot stop progress!"* This will be followed by, a decade later, *"If only we had realised at the time."* So, we must ignore this, and press on resolutely!

It has been said that the homing pigeons can no longer navigate by instinct (vibrations). It has been noticed they are using sight and going by the road systems. This is a drastic adaptation they have had to make. Other birds may not be so resourceful or adaptable.

Maybe the bees can't manage this, or are finding it totally exhausting/depressing/terrifying. Is this progress? So we need to reduce the use of pesticides to nil, and reduce our dependency on mobile phones etc. We need to reduce the amount of medical drugs, exogenous hormones, alcohol, tobacco, heavy metals, effluent etc we are urinating into the biosphere!

We do need to follow through on this one. If the songbirds all go, they will *never come back.* Apart from their beauty, we need them desperately to control the insect population. We could lose all our glorious butterflies. How will future populations feel about us? They will say: "They had a world full of beautiful birds, butterflies and flowers. They created mobile phones that destroyed their fertility. It was just so they could chat to one another from the train, *"Hello, how are you? All right? See you soon, I'll be home in a mo, bye."*

Was it worth it?

I remember in the 1970s when the Pill first came out, all the men in London started growing huge bosoms. It was from the extra female hormones in the pill finding their way into the women's urine, and hence into the sewage and down to the water tables. This was a somewhat dramatic demonstration that, in the end, a whole population drinks what is in the rest of the population's urine! *Think on.* More and more people are being put on to medical substances. I read the other day that in studies of the *cord blood* of a sample of American babies, **287 different toxic chemicals were identified**. This means *at least this amount* was in the mother's body. We need to wonder where they came from? Was it food additives, pesticides, medicines, fluoride, lead, mercury, aluminium, tobacco, alcohol, street drugs, disinfectants, hormones, insulin, thyroxin, statins, steroids, hormones, Benzodiazepam, Prozac, Seroxat? How much is in the water now? *What were they all?* From the drinking water? From bathing in it? From breathing in polluted air? From the food? From cosmetics?

Have we a right to inflict this on our own and each other's babies? On each other? On all the animals and livestock on the farms? On wildlife? It will all be in the tiny birds' eggs, in the bee hives, in the frog spawn and so on.

We need to take stock very fast over this. We are the custodians of the natural world – and we also depend on it. We haven't got much time left to get it right! We need to love money a lot less, and people and animals and the whole of the natural world a whole lot more.

The Foresight programme is what we can do for you as a *starting point*. Take all the pieces and do your own jigsaw. Talk to us and let us know what *you* can do. We are there for you, and we will help all we can.

338

It is becoming clear that we need to breed a generation very much brighter than the one we have at present! We are working on that one. But we cannot leave it all to our babies, even if they are little geniuses! We/us/you, the Foresight parents need to lead the way.

I am sure that when you have read all of this, you will have seen how limited and inadequate the approach of the "Establishment" is to health matters.

They do not look at the whole jigsaw puzzle of life, and see how it all fits together. My MP cries out, *"No, no, I can only talk about one thing, we only have 15 minutes"*. The doctor says, *"We cannot look at anything* unless there has been a *"Double-blind, Randomised, Controlled, Cross Over Trial"*, (which of course, could not be done with babies, or with a lot of other conditions for that matter.) Also, it means only *one* factor can be isolated and studied. The results therefore will be "inconclusive", as the problem stems from a whole series of interacting factors. So nothing will be done.

Even very obvious reforms such as the banning of noxious food additives, pesticides, fluoride, mercury dental amalgams, the pill, GM foods, vaccines and so on, many of which are banned in other countries, will not take place in the foreseeable future.

To understand why, you have to look at the mindsets. The present day MPs are very wedded to the "bottom line". Their background is mainly from small businesses, their own, or a friend's or relative's. They are imbued with the feelings of having to scoop up enough profit to stay in business, pay the mortgage, feed the family, and so on.

They find it hard to take a view beyond this. Instinctively, they identify with manufacturers. This is a very blinkered view.

Britain needs more women who have brought up a family – more farming people – more organic growers – more alternative practitioners, *going into Parliament*. People with a wider perspective. If you are in a position of selecting a candidate for election, study their background very carefully. Remember, habitual patterns of thought die hard.

Meanwhile, we can all take charge of our *own* lives - eat good organic food, drink pure water, avoid all the drugs, bugs, plugs and fugs that we can, and do our bit for our own families.

All the modern agonies - the alcoholism, the drug taking, are mainly the result of biochemically induced brain malfunction. This leads people down the wrong path. This is the background contributing to drug dealing, knife crime, etc. It needs to be tackled in a different way.

My late husband, who was the Deputy Director of Public Prosecutions at one time, used to say that the prison population was made up of around 92% inadequates and perverts, and about 8% master criminals who manipulated them.

If this is so, attention to preconceptual health could maybe rescue the 92%, and there might only be 8% of criminal masterminds to put behind bars! What a saving that would be!

It would certainly more than cover the cost of free preconceptual care for everyone!

Talking of covering the costs – I have read recently (in the Daily Mail of 29th June 2008) that the numbers of drug addicts and alcoholics on benefits in the UK is 17,000. Ex-cannabis smokers suffering from psychosis have topped 148,000.

Many of these could respond to our stop-alcohol programme – supplements, oils, homeopathy and the elimination of allergens.

The number of claimants with back pain is said to be 123,000. People suffering from back pain usually need osteopathy, also zinc and manganese to prevent the cartilage in the discs from swelling, and magnesium and selenium to strengthen the muscles. Why don't the doctors try it?

The number of children born deaf has trebled in the last 10 years. This is tragic, and is almost certainly due to lack of Vitamin A before birth, due to the culpable mistake by the Department of Health in advising mothers not to take any.

Learning difficulties are due to all the factors we have mentioned elsewhere. This also has risen in the last 10 years from 182,000 to 282,000. We were not told in the Daily Mail's article how many are disabled by epilepsy, MS, ME, arthritis etc.

Many more struggle to work with diabetes, migraine, asthma, skin problems, IBS, etc. Most of this could have been fully pre-empted by a pristine pregnancy and a good beginning.

So what do we do?

If Preconceptual care were there for every baby, so that they did not suffer with Foetal Alcohol Syndrome, Foetal Tobacco Syndrome, and they were not zinc deficient, nor gender confused by extraneous hormones, nor polluted by heavy metal, nor ill with chlamydia, nor kept awake all night by electrosmog, and if they were then breast-fed, and not vaccinated – well, we might have normal brain power all round and a virtually crime-free world!

So lets turn things around for the next generation. Also, let's get all the rest of it out on the web, so that even those who have these health problems, but are *not* planning a pregnancy, can all have a crack at getting well again, anyway.

In this book I have tried to tell you all how I think and feel, and everything I know.

I want you to take it on board, to take up the baton and run. As St Paul wrote to St Timothy: *"Stir up the gift of God that is within you"* (II Timothy, 1.6).

You and your children are the Custodians of the Future. It is all quite simple really. Let your body be healthy, let your God-given instincts guide you. Have a welcoming womb inside a beautiful body, inside a happy home, within a wonderful world.

Much happiness and courage to you all. May your God go with you, whatever road you take.

Onward!

So let us not grow weary in doing what is right, for we will reap at harvest time, if we do not give up. Galations 6:9

Appendix 1

The Contraceptive Pill
by Dr Ellen Grant

It is probably true that no other medication has received so much attention as the oral contraceptive pill (the Pill) - a progesterone with or without oestrogen. It is probably also true that the general public and much of the medical profession have never been so mislead about the dangers of taking these hormones.

Even to the lay person there have long been obvious discrepancies. Women older than 35 are told they have more risk of clotting if they take the Pill but older menopausal women are given HRT which is also progesterone and oestrogen. Both the Pill and combined HRT act mostly like progesterone and activate progesterone receptors in cells.

How does the Pill work?

The Pill mimics pregnancy when high progesterone levels prevent further ovulation by stopping the production of brain and pituitary hormones which stimulate the ovary to develop and release an egg.

Natural and Synthetic progesterones

Many regarded the development of the Pill as a great medical breakthrough. It involved the manufacture of synthetic forms of progesterone which could prevent ovulation when given as pills. Synthetic hormones are usually cheaper to make than "natural" hormones but the main actions are the same. Unfortunately, for those who claim natural hormones are safe to take, both synthetic progestogens and natural progesterones work the same way by attaching to Progesterone Receptors (PRs) in the cells.

Why is the Pill so dangerous?

Progesterone receptors activate thousands of genes. Four times more genes are up or down regulated by progesterone than oestrogen. Taking progesterones causes 3-4 times more breast cancer than taking oestrogens by stimulating breast growth, instant blood vessel development and by altering immunity.

Highest level carcinogens

The result has been very large increases in breast cancer and other illnesses in countries using hormones. Many studies have shown Pill and HRT

343

hormones cause cancer including breast, cervical, endometrial, ovarian, liver and brain cancers and skin melanomas. Eventually in 2004 the International Agency for Cancer Research of the World Health Organization listed progestogens and oestrogens, whether given as the Pill or HRT, as highest level (Group 1) carcinogens. By 2007 the advice to stop HRT resulted in large falls in deaths from breast cancer. Unbelievably teenagers are still being told to start taking the progesterone in the most dangerous long-acting types of progesterone-only pills because ever more underage girls have unplanned pregnancies since the Pill was introduced in the 1960s.

Basic research ignored

Although animal research in the 1930s proved that progesterones and oestrogen cause a range of hormone dependent cancers including breast, ovary, womb and pituitary cancers, the Pill has been marketed worldwide since the 1960s. Basic research has continued to be ignored and millions of women and their families have suffered dire consequences.

My own research for the Family Planning Association in London during the 1960s found it was impossible to produce a safe Pill, however doses or balances were changed. The detailed results were published in papers in the Lancet and British Medical Journal. The propaganda after this was that newer Pills would be safer, but all contraceptive Pills must have enough progesterone power to prevent ovulation and erratic bleeding, and therefore they will also cause serious dangers to health.

Progesterone induces the crypts (glands) in the lining of the womb (endometrium) to make secretion in a normal cycle. In a contraceptive progesterone dominant cycle, the glands shrivel, and the lining thins, but the blood vessels can dilate and overgrow especially in women with side-effects. Women with headaches and increased risk of stroke or heart attacks have more overdeveloped small arteries (arterioles) while those with sore legs or sore breasts have very large dilated veins (sinusoids). Activities of enzymes increase or decrease, which can alter women's reactions to food or can cause mental symptoms. Progesterone increases or decreases the activities of thousands of genes - four times more than oestrogens and it also causes four times more breast cancer than oestrogens do. Progesterone increases monoamine oxidase levels (a mood changing enzyme) and can induce depression and loss of libido when oestrogen levels are low. Higher doses of oestrogens increase the risk of thrombosis.

The unwelcome fact was that my research proved that however the doses and balances of progesterones and oestrogens were altered, too many side-effects would result sooner or later. The average length of overall use reported in 54 Pill studies and in 51 HRT studies, in two Collaborative re-analyses, were only 3 years and 2 years (Lancet 1996 and Lancet 1997). Durations of total hormone use, including fertility medications, were not revealed.

Oestrogen doses were lowered in Pills which were misleadingly labeled "Low Dose" and claimed to be safer. However newer synthetic progestogens were evolved to be more powerful than the originals. "Third" generation Pills surprised by causing twice as much thrombosis as older higher dose (but less powerful) Pills.

For decades the well documented large increases in cancers and vascular diseases among young and middle-aged women were ignored, because of epidemiological studies which were deeply flawed for numerous reasons, including falsely regarding women as non-Pill users even though they were using hormones with the same actions as HRT.

Eventually, in 2004, double blind controlled randomized international trials of HRT were stopped prematurely, to prevent even more cancers and vascular diseases being recorded. There have been no such DBCT Pill trials because placebos cannot be used for contraception. Whereas women were warned to only take HRT for the shortest time and in the lowest possible dose, no such warning went out to Pill takers.

Teenagers and the Pill

The health of teenagers is not apparently worthy of even such imperfect care. On the contrary, more teenagers are being implanted with powerful long-acting progestogens with names like Implanon, Depot-Provera or Noristat. Mirena is a coil or IUD containing levonorgestrel which is effective for 5 years.

The idea is that teen-age pregnancy must be prevented in an era when sexual contact is actively encouraged by the "pop culture". Adolescents using implants have more risk of progesterone-induced osteoporosis, but an implant cannot be forgotten like a daily Pill. Adverse effects of Pills and progestogen-only implants include headaches, migraine, sore breasts, vaginal bleeding, fluid retention and weight gain. These cannot be easily stopped. Progesterone or synthetic progestogens can accumulate in fat stores. The large increase in obesity in young women is being blamed as a cause of cancer. However, thin premenopausal women on the Pill or HRT get breast cancer perhaps because the dose taken is relatively greater for their weight. Side effects can last for up to a year or more, although the contraceptive effect of a single injection wears off by 3 months.

There have been no double blind randomized control Pill trials as inert placebos cannot be used for contraception. Pill trials have attempted to compare the effect of different Pills (as we did in the London trials in the 1960s) or else tried to compare takers with non-takers who were using a different method of contraception. From 1968 to 1972 in the "Royal College of General Practitioners Contraceptive Pill Trial", over 60 conditions were increased in Pill takers compared with non users. The press report was "The Pill gets the All Clear".

Significant increases in breast, cervical, and liver cancers, and in vascular diseases, both in incidence and mortality, were found in later follow-ups. By 2004 the RCGP study found 7 times more deaths from brain and pituitary tumours in Pill takers. Pituitary tumours are more likely to develop when girls have been given the Pill because of irregular periods when menstruation starts. This may be because of the suppression at the start of their biological fertility clock. A nonsensical result of "no increase in breast cancer deaths" was claimed. This was because the women who took the Pill in their 20s and died from breast cancer in their 50s were likely to be taking a second dose of hormones again as HRT, but no records of this were ever kept.

Women were then warned to use lowest doses of HRT for the shortest possible time and only to suppress menopausal symptoms. (This is absurd advice. Why should women with symptoms that are due to nutritional deficiencies and allergies take a carcinogen?)

In some studies all those developing breast cancer under age 36 had taken the Pill. The risk of fatal breast cancer increases the younger the Pill is taken.

How can the main cause of modern-day cancer epidemics be thought of as a medical breakthrough?

Natural and Synthetic Progesterones

Progesterone up or down regulates 4 times more genes than oestrogen and also using progesterones causes 3-4 times more breast cancer than taking oestrogens alone.

By 2007 the immediate resulting falls in breast cancer incidences and mortality due to millions of women stopping taking hormones (HRT) could no longer be denied. Unfortunately the message still seems to be take the Pill and HRT unless you are part of a DBRCT and someone is recording the disasters.

What is the Pill?

All hormonal contraceptives act predominantly like progesterone. Hormones acting like progesterone are known as progestogens, progestogens or progestins and are given as pills, skin creams or implants. Cheaper, but more powerful, synthetic hormones are used in the Pill

Usually contraceptive pills also contain a small amount of oestrogen to prevent irregular bleeding, vaginal dryness and depression.

How do the Pill and hormonal contraceptives work?

A high blood level of progesterone during pregnancy prevents further ovulations by blocking ovarian stimulating hormones from the brain (hypothalamus and pituitary gland). The Pill uses this action to trick a woman's brain into pregnancy mode. One unfortunate result of this has been a seven times increase in previously rare brain tumours of the hypothalamic region and the pituitary (prolactinomas). There is also some evidence that progesterones and oestrogens increase the risk of other brain tumours (meningiomas).

Progesterone up and down regulates thousands of genes to maintain and support a pregnancy. Progesterone activates four times more genes than does oestrogen, causing extensive biochemical changes. Any inherent weaknesses in the body's cells can become compromised causing numerous illnesses. Confusingly, because progesterone and oestrogen are immune suppressing steroids, some women can be fooled into taking hormones because they feel better.

Although it was discovered that Pill takers had higher copper and lower zinc levels in the 1960s, mineral analyses are still not in general use 50 years later. Women with nutritional deficiencies or imbalances are less able to cope with hormone-induced changes in every cell in their body. Taking hormones causes cancer, vascular, mental illnesses and immune disorders. Warning symptoms include headaches, migraine, mood changes, bleeding and weight gain. Risk of serious illness is reduced by stopping the Pill.

Probably because progesterone activates four times more genes than oestrogen, progesterone-dominant hormonal contraceptives, or HRT, cause 3 to 4 times more breast cancer than oestogen. Why then is the Pill (and progesterone cream), still being recommended by doctors, family planners, nutritionists and various "health gurus" and allowed to be sold without prescription, and promoted worldwide on the internet?

Animal studies in the 1930s proved that progesterone and oestrogen caused breast, ovarian, womb and liver cancers. Japanese women had a low incidence of breast cancer, not because they ate soy, but because the Pill was not allowed in Japan until 1996. Also because for decades numerous flawed epidemiological studies claimed spurious health benefits from hormone taking while grossly underestimating the increased risk of potentially fatal illnesses. Eventually, by 2004, the "US Women's Health Investigators (WHI) Study" proved to the world that taking hormones was too dangerous. The WHI trails were randomized controlled double-blind trials which are only suitable for HRT and not the Pill. Women needing contraception cannot be randomized to take an inactive placebo.

Taking HRT increased breast and endometrial cancers, strokes, thrombosis, heart attacks and dementia. The WHI trials, and several other international trials, were stopped immediately and prematurely before the intended duration. Trials of hormones in women with breast cancer were also stopped early when the risk of a second cancer increased about 6 times. Hormone use is still acceptable provided no one is recording the disasters it seems.

Even the WHI study underestimated the risks. Most women had already taken hormones who were being randomized to use or not to use hormones. It was demonstrated that risks increase with longer use and since then women have been told to take the smallest doses of HRT for the shortest possible time. This is still wrong because some adverse reactions, including breast cancer, can happen within weeks. Menopausal symptoms are usually due to allergies, smoking, drinking alcohol and nutritional deficiencies, or to infections especially with gut candida. Therefore, there is no indication to "treat" them with symptom-suppressing, carcinogenic progesterones and oestrogens.

The Pill contains powerful synthetic progesterones and oestrogens. There is no warning cautioning for teenage girls. On the contrary, children as young as 13 are being given the pill, often by an unfortunate school/clinic collaboration. Apparently clinics do not need to inform either parents or GPs that their daughter or patient is now taking hormones and is at increased risk of numerous illnesses. It is illegal to have sex with a girl under age 16 so secrecy may not only be covering up child abuse or pedophilia, but also preventing the disclosure of medical or familial contraindications to Pill use. Because the pill causes headaches, migraine, vomiting, sore breasts, weight gain and mood changes, many girls stop taking the Pill.

Sexual health clinics are desperate to reduce the number of teenage pregnancies, which have increased yearly as Pill use has increased. Girls are now being told that they have no risk of thrombosis if they only take long-acting forms of progesterones deposited or implanted as rods under the skin. This is frightening as the adverse hormonal effects cannot be quickly stopped. Progesterone accumulates in fat stores and the effects can last for as long as 9 months. So-called bio-identical progesterone is much less powerful by mouth than synthetic progestogens and is not used for contraception. The Pill breakthrough was to make cheap "low dose" pills which prevented ovulation. Progesterone cream, progesterone vaginal suppositories or progesterone injections can cause vaginal dryness, weight gain, depression, irregular bleeding, and immune disorders with risk of more infections.

References

Breast cancer and hormone replacement therapy: collaborative reanalysis of data from 51 epidemiological studies of 52,705 women with breast cancer and 108,411 women without breast cancer. Collaborative Group on Hormonal Factors in Breast Cancer. Lancet. 1997 Oct 11;350(9084):1047-59. Erratum in: Lancet 1997 Nov 15;350(9089):1484. PMID:10213546 [PubMed – indexed for MEDLINE]

Breast cancer and hormonal contraceptives; collaborative reanalysis of individual data on 53,297 women with breast cancer and 100,239 women without breast cancer from 54 epidemiological studies. Collaborative Group on Hormonal Factors in Breast Cancer. Lancet. 1996 Jun22:347(9017):1713-27. PMIT:8656904[PubMed-indexed for MEDLINE]

Appendix 2

Excerpts from The Adverse Effects of Alcohol on Reproduction, by Tuula E Tuormaa

It was not until 1967, in France, that Lemoine and his team first described in scientific terms a group of children affected by maternal alcohol abuse, which included defective intra-uterine and post-partum growth, unusual facial features, congenital malformations, such as cardiac defects, cleft palate etc. combined with mental sub-normality.[5]

These findings in France and, five years later, independent observations by Dr Jones and his colleagues from the United States, led finally to a recognition of a distinct dysmorphic condition associated with maternal gestational alcoholism named as Foetal Alcohol Syndrome (FAS), which has since become a clearly established clinical entity.[6-36]

FOETAL ALCOHOL SYNDROME (FAS):

The most common characteristics of children born with FAS are as follows:

Growth abnormalities: Prenatal growth deficiency can be significant and includes all three of the following parameters of growth, weight, length and head circumference.[2,20-24]

Frequently the growth deficiencies are so severe that the newborn has to be hospitalised because of obvious failure to thrive.[20] Postnatal growth and weight retardation is also significant and this continues for life despite the infant being reared in an ideal nutritional and social environment.[21]

Craniofacial abnormalities: The eyes of the affected children are often small with exaggerated inner epicanthic folds, and squints are common in later years.[21] The nasal bridge is usually poorly formed, giving the nose a small 'retrousse' appearance. The vertical groove running from the nose down to the upper lip tends to be shallow or absent, and the upper lip itself is often narrow. The ears tend to be large and somewhat simple in form.[2, 20-24] Cleft palate may also be present.[21]

Musculoskeletal abnormalities: Variable musculoskeletal and limb defects are found in approximately 40% of cases, ranging in severity from minor problems such as contractures of the finger joints to more severe lesions, such as congenital hip dislocations and thoracic cage abnormalities.[24]

349

Genital abnormalities are also frequent, such as undescended testes and malformations of the lower wall of the urethra in males and hypoplastic labia in females. Minor kidney abnormalities have also been detected.[21]

Cardiac abnormalities: Congenital heart disease is found in 29-50% of reported cases.[26] They are commonly atrical or ventricular septal defects, but also complex and sometimes lethal cardiac abnormalities can occur.[2,20-26]

Nervous system abnormalities: When first delivered, the affected infants may show clear evidence of alcohol withdrawal. They are often fretful, tremulous, have a weak grasp, poor eye-hand coordination and frequently a great difficulty with sucking and feeding. Cerebellar damage is also common, resulting later on in excessive clumsiness and even in recurrent seizures.[21]

Neuro-developmental delay or mental deficiency: The average IQ in children born with FAS is around 65, indicating moderate mental handicap. Mental retardation also occurs frequently in varying degrees.[21,28-30] In fact FAS is now recognised as the leading known cause of mental retardation, surpassing Down's syndrome and spina bifida.[2,31,32] Around 70% of children with FAS are severely hyperactive, frequently engaging in body rocking, head banging or head rolling.[22,33-36] Without exception all children with FAS suffer from severe developmental disabilities. With the onset of school, these severe IQ and attention deficits, combined with various behavioural problems, emerge as serious intellectual and learning disabilities.[22,28-30,33-39]

Adolescents/Adults with FAS: The natural history of FAS has now been traced into adulthood.[39-41] The short stature and microcephaly seem to be permanent. The average academic functioning of these adolescents and adults does not ever seem to develop beyond early school grade level, even though in one sample of 61 studied, 42% had IQ levels above 70 and all had received constant remedial help at school. A particular deficit was found in arithmetic skills and extreme difficulties with abstractions like time and space, cause and effect, as well generalising from one situation to another. The most noticeable behaviour problems were found to be with comprehension, judgement and attention skills, causing these adults born with FAS to experience major psychosocial and adjustment problems for the rest of their lives.[41]

The effects can induce foetal malformations both at the earliest, as well as at the lowest level of intake, its effectiveness spreading differentially over the whole spectrum of reproduction, affecting the developing foetus in varying degrees, in both extent and severity, depending on the dosage and timing.

This explains also why maternal alcohol consumption can affect the offspring through all gradations of teratogenesis, ranging from moderately affected right up to the full blown Foetal Alcohol Syndrome.

Alcohol is quite capable of crossing the placental barrier and entering the foetus, causing the level of alcohol in the foetus to be approximate to that of the mother.[48] In the first 21 days of the foetal development the preliminary cell organisation of the embryo begins to take place. If an excessive amount of alcohol is consumed before the blastocyst is embedded in the uterus, the impact can be so severe that the foetus is miscarried.[45] By the end of the 36th day, often long before the woman even realises that she is pregnant, the neural tube is clearly present and open, and, most of the rudimentary organs have already been formed, such as limbs, heart, brain, eyes, mouth, digestive tract etc.

It is therefore obvious that if a teratogenic substance such as alcohol is consumed during critical days this can result in various forms of malformation in the newborn, such as defective heart, musculoskeletal abnormalities, mental handicap etc., without any specific outward signs of FAS.

Even though it is considered that the first three months of gestation is the most critical period for alcohol-induced malformations to occur, both human and animal experiments have been able to demonstrate that the teratogenic effects of alcohol continues throughout the whole gestational period, affecting at the later stage particularly the brain development and function.[20,42,45]

FOETAL ALCOHOL EFFECTS:

The teratogenic effects of alcohol spreads differentially over the whole spectrum of reproduction, varying only in the extent and degree. At one end of the spectrum are the children warranting a firm diagnosis of FAS, and at the other end of the spectrum are the children who lack the common physical characteristics of FAS but who, nevertheless, have some subtle or marked physical and/or mental deficiencies by being exposed to varying amounts of alcohol in utero.

It is now widely accepted that the classical diagnosis of FAS is totally inadequate as for every child born with FAS there are thousands of others whose lives are partially handicapped, or limited, by being exposed to alcohol during gestational development. These children, without sufficient physical stigmata for firm diagnosis of FAS, are now identified as suffering from Foetal Alcohol Effects (FAE).[33]

On the second day of life they had a longer latency to begin sucking and had a weaker suck as measured on a pressure transducer with non-nutritive nipple.[74,75] They also suffered from disrupted sleep patterns[76-78] ,low level of arousal, unusual body orientation, abnormal reflexes, hypotonia and excessive mouthing.[48]

By eight months, and then onwards, these infants seemed to continue suffering from disrupted sleep-wake patterns, poorer balance and motor control, longer latency to respond, poorer attention, visual recognition and memory, decrements in mental development, spoken language and verbal comprehension, including lower IQ scores.[36,79-86] As references indicate, these findings have also been confirmed independently by other workers.

The conclusion of this study was that two maternal alcohol use patterns have now been identified as being particularly detrimental to the offspring i.e. two or more drinks on average per day during pregnancy, and "binge-pattern" of alcohol consumption, e.g. five or more drinks on any occasion, particularly when consumed in the month before pregnancy recognition, as both can lead to marked behaviour and learning disabilities in school-age children.

It was also concluded that these alcohol-related behaviour and attention decrements seem to have been already clearly observable from an early infancy, long before academic learning had even occurred.

This wide pattern of performance deficits uniformly occurred despite the presence of average IQ, suggesting that maternal alcohol induced behaviour decrements in the offspring seem to be a more sensitive indicator of central nervous system damage than the IQ scale itself. The study concluded that maternal social drinking seemed to result in the offspring having similar, but less severe consequences than those seen in children born with FAS, indicating in both cases, *the clear occurrence of alcohol-induced permanent central nervous system damage* during critical stages of foetal development. FAE in adolescents and adults: As with children born with FAS, population based studies carried out on the offspring born to socially drinking mothers have shown that, on maturation, these children can still show subtle and permanent alcohol-related neurobehavioral deficits, IQ and achievement decrements, combined with various attention, memory and learning problems.[36,39]

ALCOHOL AND MALE REPRODUCTION:

Alcohol is a direct testicular toxin.[90] It causes atrophy of semeniferous tubules, loss of sperm cells, and an increase in abnormal sperms.[91] Alcohol is also known to be a strong Leydig cell toxin [92], and it can have an adverse effect on the synthesis and secretion of testosterone.[93,94] Alcohol can cause significant deterioration in sperm concentration, sperm output and motility. [95,96] Semen samples of men consuming excessive amounts of alcohol have shown distinct morphological abnormalities.[97,98] It has been also established that approximately 80% of chronic alcoholic men are sterile[99] and, furthermore, that alcohol is one of the most common causes of male impotence.[100]

SUMMARY:

There is now an ever-increasing recognition that alcohol is the most common chemical teratogen presently causing malformations and mental deficiency in the human offspring.[20]

In 1977 the following statement was made by Dr Ernest Noble, Director of the National Institute of Alcohol Abuse and Alcoholism of the. United States: "The Foetal Alcohol Syndrome is the third leading cause of mental retardation and neurological problems in infants, ranking after Down's syndrome and spina bifida".[31] Several other investigators have also recognised maternal alcohol abuse as being one of the leading causes for the occurrence of mental

352

retardation in children in the Western world.[6,33,42,66,120-122]

In addition, it has been estimated that maternal alcoholism may be responsible for at least 10% of all infant congenital malformations.

As stated previously, alcohol is a poison at all levels, and therefore no totally safe level of alcohol use during pregnancy can be established. Alcohol-related damage to the foetus has been linked with every form of drinking pattern, from heavy drinking to intermittent as well as moderate social drinking i.e. one or two drinks daily most days during pregnancy; and from very infrequent, but relatively heavy, drinking to one single drinking binge prior to pregnancy recognition.

The teratogenic effects of maternal "social drinking" is considered less detrimental to the foetus than that of abusive drinking, but it can still nevertheless affect the infant, maybe in a less serious but much more subtle manner.

The infant may be born with lighter weight, suffer from difficulties with habituation, feeding, and disrupted sleep-wake patterns. By eight months onwards to young school age, the children born to social drinkers seem to show poorer balance, motor control, attention, visual recognition, memory, sleep patterns and mental development than infants born to non-drinking mothers. When at school, the academic performance and IQ of these children seem to be generally below average. In addition, overall classroom behaviour of these children have been found to be negatively related to: co-operation, retention of information, comprehension of words, memory, impulsiveness, tactfulness, word recall, organisation, as well as attention skills, all indicating increased risk in learning abilities.

On maturation and as adults, these children born to social drinkers showed still subtle, but permanent, alcohol-related neurobehavioral deficits, including IQ and achievement decrements, as well as attention, memory and learning difficulties.

In summary, it now seems to be evident that maternal social drinking results in the offspring having similar, but less severe consequences, than those seen in children born with Foetal Alcohol Syndrome. This finding is not unexpected, as the toxic effect of alcohol can damage the foetus permanently and irreversibly through all gradations of teratogenesis.

During the 1990 Betty Ford Lecture Dr Streissguth stated: "In summary, every community should know the following about alcohol and pregnancy: There is no known safe level of alcohol consumption during pregnancy. Pregnant women should be advised to abstain from drinking during pregnancy and when they are planning a pregnancy

The most salient point that can be made about alcohol induced foetal damage is that it is totally preventable, and by informing both prospective parents of the potential dangers of alcohol consumption before conception,

353

and particularly all women during pregnancy, we can hope to control the problem. It is frightening to' realize how long the knowledge has been there that alcohol indeed damages the unborn child, without anyone seemingly worrying about it.

REFERENCES:

1. Judges 13:7
2. Lewis DD: Alcohol & pregnancy outcome. Midwives Chronicle & Nursing Notes, 420-423, Dec. 1983
3. Library, The Royal College of Physicians, 1725
4. Report from the Select Committee on "Inquiry into Drunkenness", House of Commons Library, 5 August, 1834
5. Lemoine P. Harousseau H, Borteyru J-P, Menuet J-C: Les enfants de parents alcoholiques: anomalies observees a propos de 127 cas. Quest Medical, 25:476-482, 1968
6. Jones KL, Smith DW, Ulleland CN, Streissguth AP: Pattern of malformation in offspring of chronic alcoholic mothers The Lancet, 1:1267-1271, 1973
7. Ferrier FE, Nicod I, Ferrier S: Foetal Alcohol Syndrome The Lancet, 2:1496, 1973
8. Jones KL, Smith DW, Streissguth AP et al: Incidence of Foetal Alcohol Syndrome in offspring of chronically alcoholic women. Pediatr Res, 8:440-466, 1974
9. Jones KL, Smith DW, Streissguth AP, Myrianthoupolis NC: Outcome in offspring of chronic alcoholic women. The Lancet, 1076-1078, 1974
10. Jones KL and Smith DW: The Foetal Alcohol Syndrome Teratology, 12:1 1975
11. Tenbrinck MS and Buchirt SY: Foetal Alcohol Syndrome: Report of a case. JAMA, 232(11):1144, 1975
12. Jones KL, Smith DW, Hanson JW: The Foetal Alcohol Syndrome: Clinical delineation. Ann N.Y. Acad Sci, 273:130 1976
13. Mulvihill JJ and Yeager AM: Foetal Alcohol Syndrome. Teratology, 13:345 1976
14. Mulvihill JJ, Klimas JT, Stokes DC, Risemberg HM: Foetal Alcohol Syndrome: Seven new cases. Am J Obstet Gynecol, 125(7):937 1976
15. Quelette EM and Rosett HL: A pilot prospective study of the Foetal Alcohol Syndrome at the Boston City Hospital: Part II, The infants. Ann N.Y. Acad Sci, 273:123-129, 1976
16. Smith DW, Jones KL, Hanson JW: Perspectives on the cause and frequency of Foetal Alcohol Syndrome. Ann N.Y. Acad Sci, 173:138 1976
17. Martin JM: The Foetal Alcohol Syndrome: Recent findings. Alc Health and Res World, 1(3):8 1977
18. Streissguth AP: Foetal Alcohol Syndrome: An epidemiological perspective. Am J Epidemiol, 107(6):467-478, 1978
19. Schenker S. Becker HC, Randall CL, Henderson GI: Foetal Alcohol Syndrome; Current status and pathogenesis. Alc Clin Exp Res, 14:635-647, 1990
20. Alcohol and the Unborn Child -The Foetal Alcohol Syndrome The National

Council of Women Working Party on Alcohol Problems, 36. Lower Sloane Street, London SW1D 8BP,1980

21. Beattie J: Foetal Alcohol Syndrome - The incurable hangover. Health Visitor, 54:468-469, November, 1981

22. Streissguth AP: Foetal Alcohol Syndrome: Early and long-term consequences. In: Problems with Drug Dependence: Proceedings of the 53rd Annual Scientific Meeting (NIDA Research Monograph No:119) Ed, L Harris, Rockville, MD, U.S. Department of Health and Human Services. 1991

23. Jones KL and Smith DW: Recognition of Foetal Alcohol Syndrome in early infancy. The Lancet 2:999-1001, 1973

24. Hanson JW, Jones KL, Smith DW: Foetal Alcohol Syndrome: Experience with 41 patients. JAMA, 235:1458-1460, 1976

25. Noonan JA: Congenital heart disease in Foetal Alcohol Syndrome. Am J Cardiol, 37:160 1976

26. Sandor GCS, Smith DF, MacLeod PM: Cardiac malformations in the Foetal Alcohol Syndrome. J Pediatr, 98(5):771-773, 1981

27. Pieroq S, Chandauasu 0, Wexler I: Withdrawal symptoms in infants with the Foetal Alcohol Syndrome. J Pediatr, 90(4):630 1977

28. Streissguth AP: Psychologic handicaps in children with Foetal Alcohol Syndrome. Ann N.Y. Acad Sci, 273:140 1976

29. Streissguth AP, Herman CS, Smith DW: Intelligence, behaviour and dysmorphogenesis in Foetal Alcohol Syndrome: A report on 20 patients. J Pediatr, 92:363-367, 1978

30. Streissguth AP, Herman CS, Smith DW: Stability of intelligence in Foetal Alcohol Syndrome. Alc Clin Exp Res, 2:165-170, 1978

31. Noble EF: Foetal Alcohol Syndrome. Drug Survival News, 6:3, Nov-Dec[1] 1977

32. Abel EL, Sokol RJ: Incidence of Foetal Alcohol Syndrome and economic impact of FAS-related anomalies. Drug Alcohol Depend, 19:51-70, 1987

33. Clarren SK and Smith DW: The Foetal Alcohol Syndrome. New Engl J Med, 298:1063-1067, 1978

34. Forbes R: Alcohol-related birth defects. Publ Health, London, 98:238-241, 1984

35. Streissguth AP, Aase JM, Clarren SK, Jones KL: Natural history of the Foetal Alcohol Syndrome: A ten-year follow up of 11 patients. The Lancet, 2:85-92, 1985

36. Streissguth AP: The behavioural teratology of alcohol; performance, behavioural, and intellectual deficits in prenatally exposed children. In: Alcohol and brain development, Ed: JR West pp 3-44, New York, Oxford University Press, 1986

37. Spohr HL, Steinhausen HC: Follow-up studies of children with Foetal Alcohol Syndrome. Neuropediatrics, 18:13-17, 1987

38. Streissguth AP, LaDue RA: Foetal Alcohol Syndrome and Foetal Alcohol Effects: Teratogenic causes of mental retardation and developmental disabilities. In: Toxic substances and mental retardation, Ed, SR Schroeder. Washington DC, American Association on Mental Deficiency, 1-32, 1987

39. Streissguth AP, Sampson PS, Barr HM: Neurobehavioral dose-response effects of prenatal alcohol exposure in humans from infancy to adulthood. In: Prenatal Abuse of Licit and illicit Drugs, Ed, DE Hutchings, New York Academy of Sciences, 562:145-158, 1989

40.   Gray JK, Streissguth A?: Memory deficits and life adjustment in adults
        with Foetal Alcohol Syndrome: a case-control study. Alc Clin Exp Res,
        14:294 1990
41.   Streissguth AP, Aase JM, Sterling MD, Clarren K et al: Foetal Alcohol
        Syndrome in adolescents and adults. JAMA, 265(15):1961-1967, 1991
42.   Woollam OHM: Alcohol and the safety of the unborn child. R.S.H. 6:241-
        244, 1981
43.   Smith DW: Alcohol effects in foetus. In: Foetal Drug Syndrome; Effects of
        Ethanol and Hydantoins. Pediatrics in Review 1, American Academy of
        Pediatrics, 1979
44.   Tittmar H-G: Some effects of alcohol in reproduction. Br J Alcohol and
        Alcoholism, 13:3 1978
45.   Smith DW: Mothering your Unborn Baby. W.B. Saunders Co, Philadelphia,
        1979
46.   Alcohol and Brain Development. West JR, Ed. New York, Oxford University
        Press, 1986
47.   Vorhees CV, Mollnow E: Behavioural teratogertesis; Long term influences
        on behaviour from early exposure to environmental agents. In: Handbook
        on infant development, 2nd edition, Ed:JD Osofsky, pp 913-971, New York,
        Wiley, 1987
48.   Streissguth AP, Barr HM, Sampson PD, Bookstein FL, Darby BL:
        Neurobehavioral effects of prenatal alcohol; Part I, Research Strategy.
        (Review of the literature) Neurotoxicolgy and Teratology, 11;461-476, 1989
49.   Clarren SK, Alvord EC, Sumi SM, Streissguth AP, Smith DW: Brain
        malformations related to prenatal exposure to ethanol. J Pediatr, 92(1):64,
        1978
50.   Streissguth AP: Prenatal alcohol-induced brain damage and long term
        postnatal consequences. Alc Clin Exp Res, 14(5):648-649, 1990
51.   Barnes DE and Walker DW: Prenatal ethanol exposure permanently
        reduces the number .of pyramidal neurons in right hippocampus. Dev Brain
        Res, 1:333-340, 1981
52.   West JR, Dewey SL, Pierce DR, Black AC: Prenatal and early postnatal
        exposure to ethanol permanently alters the rat hippocampus. In:
        Mechanisms of alcohol damage in utero. CIBA Foundation Symposium, 105.
        London, Pitman, 1984
53.   Riley EP, Barron S, Hannigan JP: Response inhibition deficits following
        prenatal alcohol exposure: A comparison to the effects of hippocampal lesion
        in rats. In: Alcohol and Brain Development, J.R. West, Ed., London, Oxford
        University Press, 1986
54.   Kelly SJ, Black AC, West JR: Changes in the muscarinic: Cholinergic
        receptors in the hippocampus of rats exposed to ethyl alcohol during the
        brain growth spurt. J Pharm Exp Ther, 249:798-804, 1989
55.   Havlicek V, Childiaeva R, Chernick V: EEC frequency spectrum
        characteristics of sleep states in infants of alcoholic mothers.
        Neuropadiatrie, 8:360-373, 1977
56.   Chernick V, Childiaeva R, Ioffe S: Maternal alcohol intake and smoking on
        neonatal electroencephalogram and anthropometric measurements. Am J
        Obstet Gynecol, 146(1):41-47, 1983
57.   Ioffe S. Childiaeva R, Chernick V: Prolonged effects of maternal alcohol
        ingestion on the neonatal electroencephalogram. Pediatrics, 74:330-335,
        1984

58. Olegard R, Sabel KG, Aronson M, Sandin B, et al.: Effects on the child of alcohol abuse during pregnancy. Acta Paediatr Scand Suppl, 275:112-121, 1979

59. Pettigrew AG, Hutchinson I: Effects of alcohol on functional development of the auditory pathway in the brainstem of infants and chick embryos. In: Mechanism of alcohol damage in utero. Eds: M O'Connor and J Whelan, pp 26-46, Ciba Foundation Symposium 105, London, Pitman Publishing, 1984

60. Blanchard BA, Riley EP, Hannigan JH: Deficits on a spatial navigation task following prenatal exposure to ethanol. Neurotoxiol Teratol. 9:253-258, 1987

61. Goodlett CR, Kelly SJ, West JR: Early postnatal alcohol exposure that produces high blood alcohol levels impairs development of spatial navigation learning. Psychobiology, 15:64-74, 1987

62. Clarren SK: Neuropathology in the Foetal Alcohol Syndrome. In: Alcohol and brain development. Ed: JR West, pp 158-166, New York, Oxford University Press, 1986

63. Streissguth AP, Martin DC, Martin JC, Barr HM: The Seattle longitudial prospective study on alcohol and pregnancy. Neurobehav Toxicol Teratol, 3:223-233, 1981

64. Streissguth AP, Barr HM, Sampson PD: Moderate prenatal alcohol exposure; Effects on child IQ and learning problems at age 7½ years. Alc Clin Exp Res, 14(5):66269, 1990

65. Little RE: Moderate alcohol use during pregnancy and decreased infant birth weight. Am J Pubi Health, 67(12):1154-1156, 1977

66. Quelette EM, Rosett HL, Rosman NP, Weiner L: Adverse effects on offspring of maternal alcohol abuse during pregnancy. N Engl J Med, 297(10):528-530, 1977

67. Hanson JW, Streissguth AP, Smith DW: The effects of moderate alcohol consumption during pregnancy on foetal growth and morphogenesis. J Pediatr, 92:457-460, 1978

68. Wright JT, Waterson EJ, Barrison IG et al.: Alcohol consumption, pregnancy and low birth weight. The Lancet, 663-665, March 26, 1983

69. Coles CD, Smith MPH, Fernhoff PM, Falek A: Neonatal ethanol withdrawal: characteristics in clinically normal, nondysmorphic neonates. J Pediatr, 105(3):445-451, 1984

70. Martin JC, Martin DC, Lund CA, Streissguth AP: Maternal alcohol ingestion and cigarette smoking and their effects on newborn conditioning. Alc Clin Exp Res, 1:234-247, 1977

71. Landesman-Dwyer S. Keller L, Streissguth AP: Naturalistic observations of newborns; effects of maternal alcohol intake. Alc Clin Exp Res, 2:171-177, 1978

72. Rosett HL, Snyder P, Sander LW, Lee A et al.: Effects of maternal drinking on neonatal state regulation. Dev Med Child Neurol, 21(4):464-473, 1979

73. Streissguth AP, Barr HM, Martin DC: Maternal alcohol use and neonatal habituation assessed with the Brazelton Scale. Child Development, 54:1109-1118, 1983

74. Martin DC, Martin JC, Streissguth A?, Lund CA: Sucking frequency and amplitude in newborns as a function of maternal drinking and smoking. In: Currents in Alcoholism, Vol,5. Ed: M Galanter pp 359-366, New York, Grune & Stratton, 1979

75. Stock DL, Streissguth AP, Martin DC: Neonatal sucking as an outcome variable: Comparison of quantitive and clinical assessments. Early Human Development, 10:273-278, 1985
76. Sander LW, Snyder P. Rosett HL et al.: Effects of alcohol intake during pregnancy on newborn state regulation; A progress report. Alc Clin Exp Res, 1(3):233-241, 1977
77. Rosett HL, Snyder P, Sander LW et al.: Effects of maternal drinking on neonate state regulation. Dev Med Child Neurol, 21 (4):464-473, 1979
78. Landesman-Dwyer S, Sackett GP, Meltzoff A: Perinatal nicotine and alcohol exposure and sleep-wake patterns in infants. Paper presented at Society for Research in Child Development, Detroit, MI, April, 1983
79. Streissguth AP, Barr HM, Martin DC, Herman CS: Effects of maternal alcohol, nicotine and caffeine use during pregnancy on infant mental and motor development at 8 months. Alc Clin Exp Res, 4(2):152-164, 1980
80. Gusella JL, Fried PA: Effects of maternal social drinking and smoking on offspring at 13 months. Neurobehav Toxicol Teratol, 6:13-17, 1984
81. O'Connor MJ, Brill NJ, Sigman M: Alcohol use in primiparous women older than 30 years of age; Relation to infant development. Pediatrics, 78(3):444-450, 1986
82. Landesman-Dwyer S, Ragozin AS, Little RE: Behavioural correlates of prenatal alcohol exposure; A four-year follow-up study. Neurobehav Toxicol Teratol, 3:187-193, 1981
83. Streissguth AP, Barr HM, Martin DC: Alcohol exposure in utero and functional deficits in children during the first four years of life. In: Mechanism of alcohol damage in utero, Eds: R Porter, M O'Connor, J Whelan, Ciba Foundation Symposium 105, London, Pitman Publishing, 1984
84. Streissguth AP, Martin DC, Barr HM, Sandman BM et al. Intrauterine alcohol and nicotine exposure; Attention and reaction in 4-year-old children. Dev Psychol, 20:533-541, 1984
85. Streissguth AP, Barr HM, Sampson PD, Darby BL, Martin DC: IQ at age four in relation to maternal alcohol use and smoking during pregnancy. Dev Psychol, 25(1):3-11, 1989
86. Barr HM, Streissguth AP, Darby BL, Sampson PD: Prenatal exposure to alcohol, caffeine, tobacco and aspirin; Effects on fine and gross motor performance in 4-year-old children. Develop Psychol, 26:339-348, 1990
87. Streissguth AP, Barr HM, Sampson PD, Parrish-Johnson J et al: Attention, distraction and reaction time at age 7 years and prenatal alcohol exposure. Neurobehav Toxicol Teratol, 8(6):717-725, 1986
88. Sampson PD, Streissguth AP, Barr HM, Bookstein FL: Neurobehavioral effects of prenatal alcohol; Part II, Partial least squares analysis. Neurotoxicology and Teratology, 11:477-491, 1987
89. Streissguth AP, Bookstein FL, Sampson PD, Barr HM: Neurobehavioral effects of prenatal alcohol; Part III, PLS analyses of neuropsychologic tests. Neurotoxicology and Teratology, 11:493-507, 1989
90. van Thiel OH, Gavaler JS, Lester R, Goodman MD: Alcohol induced testicular atrophy: An experimental model for hypogonadism occurring in chronic alcoholic man. Gastroenterology, 69:326- 332, 1975
91. Bennet HS, Baggenstgors AH, Butt HR: The testes, breast and prostate in men who die of cirrhosis of liver. Am J Clin Pathol, 20:814-828, 1950
92. Lipsett MB: Physiology and pathology of the Leydig cell. In: MC Bleich,

MJN Moore, Eds. Seminars in Medicine, Engi J Med, 85:682-688, 1980

93.   Ylikahri R, Huttunen M, Harkonen M, Adlercreutz H: Hangover and testosterone. Br Med J, 2:445   1974

94.   Mendelson JM, Ellingboe J, Mello NK, Kuehnli J: Effects of alcohol on plasma testosterone and luteinizing hormone levels. Alc Clin Exp Res, 2:255-258, 1978

95.   Kucheria K, Saxena R, Mohan D: Semen analysis in alcohol dependence syndrome. Andrologia, 17:558-563, 1985

96.   Brzek A: Alcohol and male fertility (Preliminary report) Andrologia, 19:32-36, 1987

97.   Dixit VP, Agarwal M, Lohiya NK: Effects of a single ethanol injection into the vas deferens on the testicular function in rats. Endokrinologie, 67:8-13, 1983

98.   Wichman L: The value of semen analysis in predicting pregnancy. Acta Universitatis Tamperensis, ser A Vol 346, p5, 1992

99.   van Thiel DM, Lester R, Sherins RJ: Hypogonadism in alcoholic liver disease: Evidence for a double defect. Gastroenterology, 67:1188-1199, 1974

100.   Masters WH and Johnson VE: Human Sexual Inadequacy. Boston, Little, Brown and Company, 1970

101.   Papara-Nicholson D, Telford IR: Effects of alcohol in reproduction and foetal development in guinea pig. Anat Rec, 127:438-439, 1957

102.   Sandor S, Elias S: The influence of acetyl-alcohol on the development of the chick embryo. Rev Roum Embryol Cytol (Ser Embryol) 5:51-76, 1968

103.   Chernoff G: A mouse model of the Foetal Alcohol Syndrome. Teratology, 11:14A, 1975

104.   Tze WJ and Lee M: Adverse effects of maternal alcohol consumption on pregnancy and foetal growth in rats. Nature, 257:479-480, 1975

105.   Branchey L and Friedhoff AJ: Biochemical and behavioural changes in rats exposed to alcohol in utero. Ann NY Acad Sci, 273:328-330, 1976

106.   Ellis FW and Pick JR: Beagle model of the Foetal Alcohol Syndrome. Pharmalogist, 18:190 1976

107.   Kronick JB: Teratogenic effects of ethyl alcohol administered to pregnant mice. Am J Obstet Gynecol, 124:676-680, 1976

108.   Chernoff GF: The Foetal Alcohol Syndrome in mice: An animal model. Teratology, 15:223 1977

109.   Randall CM, Taylor WJ, Walker DW: Ethanol-induced malformations in mice. Alc Clin Exp Res, 1:219-223, 1977

110.   Randall CM, Taylor WJ, Walker DW: Teratogenic effects of in utero ethanol exposure, Alcohol and Opiates; In: Neurochemical and Behavioural Mechanisms K Blum, Bard DL, MG Hamilton, Eds. New York Academy Press, pp. 91-017, 1977

111.   Weinberg J: Effects of ethanol and maternal nutrition status on foetal development. Alc Clin Exp Res, 9:49-55, 1985

112.   Vallee BL, Wacker WE, Bartholonay AF, Robin ED: Zinc metabolism in hepatic dysfunction; serum Zinc concentrations in Laenne's cirrhosis and their validation by sequential analysis New Engl J Med, 135:403-408, 1956

113.   Sullivan JF and Lankford HG: Urinary excretion of zinc in alcoholic and post-alcoholic cirrhosis. Am J Clin Nutr, 10:153-157, 1962

114.   Helwig HI, Hoffer EM, Thulen WC et al: Urinary excretion of zinc in chronic alcoholism. Am J Clin Pathol, 45:156-159, 1966

115.   Flynn A, Miller SI, Marther SS, Golden NL, Sokol RJ, Del Villano BC: Zinc

status of pregnant alcoholic women: A determination of foetal outcome. The Lancet, 572-575, March 14, 1981

116.   Jameson S: Effects of Zinc deficiency in human reproduction. Acta Med Scand, 593 (suppl);1-89, 1976

117.   Davies S: Zinc, nutrition and health. 1984-85 Yearbook of Nutritional Medicine, pp. 113-152, Keats Publishing, New Canaan, Connecticut.

118.   Ward NI, Watson R, Bryce-Smith D: Placental element levels in relation to foetal development for obstetrically "normal" births: A study of 37 elements. Evidence for effects of cadmium, lead and zinc on foetal growth, and smoking as a source of cadmium. Int J Biosocial Res, 9(1):63-81, 1987

119.   Laurence KM, James N. Miller MH, Tennant HB, Campbell H: Double-blind randomized controlled trial of folate treatment before conception to prevent recurrence of neural-tube defects. Brit Med J, 282:1509-1511, 1981

120.   Spohr H-L, Wilims J, Steinhausen H-C: Prenatal alcohol exposure and long-term developmental consequences. The Lancet, 341:908-910, 1993

121.   Majewski F, Bierich JR, Loser H, Michaelis R, et al: Zur Klinik und Pathogenese der Alkoholemybryopathie uber 68 Falle. Munch Med Wochensch. 118:1635-1642, 1976

122.   Dehaene F, Samaille-Villette P. Crepin G, et al: Le syndrome d'alcoolisme foetal dans le nord de la France. Rev L'alcoolisme, 145-148, 1977

123.   Abel EL: Foetal alcohol syndrome and foetal alcohol effects. New York, Plenum Press, 1983

124.   Streissguth AP: The 1990 Betty Ford Lecture: What every community should know about drinking during pregnancy and the lifelong consequences for society. Substance Abuse, 12(3):114-127, 1991

Appendix 3

A Further Survey of Foresight Results over the period of 1997-1999

<u>Circumstances of Survey.</u>

This was an exceptionally difficult period for Foresight as many of you may remember. The University was not able to continue doing the hair analysis for us, and it was with much difficulty that we got our own Laboratory together and found Michael Cain, who ran it. We had an interim period of 7 months when we had to beg the University to cover for us, which they did, during vacations only. During the long gaps, quite understandably, couples got tired of waiting and left us to try other therapies, etc. For this and other reasons, not everybody completed their supplementation programme etc. The results are therefore not quite as good as those in our first Survey, but still compare very favourably with results nationwide.

We are now getting a greater ratio of couples with fertility problems than before, as this seems to be the aspect of our work that is now receiving the most media attention.

Outcomes

The most noteworthy figures are:

Out of 1,076 couples, (1,061 had previous fertility or miscarriage problems), 729 couples conceived - 67.75%. These couples have given birth to 779 babies. If we counted each baby as a success (as with the HFEA), this would give us a 72.4% overall success rate! Among the couples there were 67 who were pregnant when the survey ended (all of these gave birth successfully.) Added in, this would make 78.4% success rate.

Among the 1,076 participating couples, there were 393 who had previously suffered miscarriage. From this group we had, sadly, 28 miscarriages. From those who had not miscarried previously, there were no miscarriages. There were therefore 28 miscarriages all told.

From the 779 conceptions, the expected rate of miscarriage nationally would be 218.5, (25%). From the particular 393 group of women who had previously miscarried, the national average rate would have been 131 (In percentage terms, 33% of 393 would be expected). In place of 25% we had 3.2%. For those who had previously miscarried, in place of 33% we had 7.1%. So 28, although a sad loss, was a big improvement on what might have been.

Malformations and Terminations

One couple terminated twins on being told there was twin-to-twin transfusion. One lady, who had only been on the programme a short while prior to starting the pregnancy, had a Downs Syndrome baby. One little foetus was terminated due to multiple deformity, but his parents did live on a landfill site. One other little boy was born with an adhesion of the intestine, but went home at 3 weeks old, with no further problems (4 problems in 846 pregnancies (0.47% problems). NHS rate is I in 17 (6%).

Stillbirths

Tragically there were 3 stillbirths. In one case, the mother and previous Foresight baby aged 20 months, were attacked by a dog and the mother was bitten while rescuing the child. Her baby was born that night, prematurely and dead. She had been 28 weeks pregnant.

In another case, the mother was admitted to hospital in the late evening and given a strong sedative to stop labour. Her beautiful 8lb baby boy was born dead in the morning.

I have not got the exact circumstances of the 3rd but know the parents concerned did not complete the full programme.

One in 282 (0.35%) National rate is 1 in 73, (1,37%).

Birth Weights

Our average birth weight for single babies was 7lb 11 oz, (despite including quite a few elective Caesarians with our older mothers). Our average birth weights with multiples, was 5lb 12oz. Twin births, all except for one set of triplets.

The number of babies born below 5lb 8oz (official figure for low birth weight). Percentage of babies from 779 was 4.6% (National rate is 9%, so just about half). Of these babies, 20 were from multiple births. Of the 36 small birth weight babies, 9 were born between 30 and 36 weeks. One was born at 29 weeks (mother was found to have an infection). The triplets were born by Caesarian at 34 weeks.

High-Tech Births

Some couples went in for the Foresight programme plus high-tech and the results were as follows:

Couples using lUl	44.6% success rate
Couples using IVF	47.1% success rate
Couples using ICSI	43.1% success rate
Couples using donors	33.3% success rate

All told, results using all the different artificial methods: success rate = 43.5%

National average for IVF is 22.6%

I am glad to see we have more than doubled this at 47.1%

Conclusions

From this we see that from the basic Foresight programme (even when working under difficulties) it is possible to:

More than double the success rate of IVF (22.6% to 47.1%)

Raise the success rate of infertile couples overall from 22.6% to 72.4%

Drop the miscarriage rate from 33% to 7.1% with those who had previously miscarried.

Drop the miscarriage rate to 0 with those who have not previously miscarried.

Drop the stillbirth rate from 1.37% to 0.35%

Drop the malformation rate from 6% to 0.47%

Drop the low birth-weight rate from 9% to 4.6%

Beautiful Babies

Appendix 4

From The Journal of Nutritional & Environmental Medicine (1995) 5, 205-208

Letters to the Editor

PRECONCEPTIONAL CARE AND PREGNANCY OUTCOME

Sirs: We would like to report the pregnancy outcomes achieved by 367 couples, average ages 34^{22-45} for females and 36^{25-59} for males, who had been enrolled on a Foresight (The Association for the Promotion of Preconception Care)[1] preconception programme during 1990-92. Foresight clinicians completed investigations of both partners which included health questionnaires, analysis of essential nutrient status in blood, hair and / or sweat, and semen analysis. Common, but often symptomless, genito-urinary infections were sought by testing endocervical swabs, urine and post-prostatic massage secretions while blood was tested for chlamydial antibodies to diagnose active pelvic inflammatory disease.[2,3]

Previous Histories

Data evaluation showed that 90% of males and 60% of females regularly drank alcohol while 45% of the men but 57% of the women smoked.

Among the 367 couples, 217 (59%) had a previous history of reproductive problems; 136 (37%) had suffered from infertility (for <1 to >10 years) and 139 (38%) had histories of from one to five previous miscarriages; 11 (3%) had given birth to a stillborn child, 40 of these babies were small-for-dates and 15 were of low birthweight (<2500g); 7 were malformed and 3 infants died of sudden infant death syndrome. A total of 86 females reported more than one of these problems. Of the male partners, 154 (42%) had a semen analysis because of infertility and most had a reduction in sperm quality. Commonest complaints among prospective parents were fatigue, headaches/migraine, cold feet, back pain, abdominal bloating and constipation.

Follw-ups after Foresight programme

Written and telephone follow-ups carried out in 1993 revealed that 327 (89%) of the women had become pregnant and 327 children had been born since enrolment. There were no multiple pregnancies. In remarkable contrast to the couples' previous experience, all their babies (137 males and

190 females) were born healthy and were well developed at birth which occurred from 36 to 41 weeks (mean 38.5 weeks). Average birth weight was 3265g (2368 - 4145). None were malformed and none were transferred to special baby care units. Among 204 couples with infertility problems, 175 (86%) had achieved healthy pregnancies.

NEIL WARD PhD

Director of Research, Department of Chemistry, University of Surrey, Guildford, GU2 5XH

With acknowledgements to the following doctors who participated in the study:

Dr Marilyn Glenville BEd MA PhD Dip EHP NLP

Dr Ellen Grant MB ChB DObst RCOG

Dr Jonathan Hardy MA BM MF HOM

Dr Tom Heyes MA MB BC HIR DR COG MRCGP

Dr Patrick Kingsley MB BS MRCS LRCP DObst RCOG

Dr J. Meldrum MB ChB DCH DA DObst RCOG MRCGP HTD

Dr Jenny Nevison MN BS

Dr M. Nightingale MB BS MRCGP FFDRCS MRCS LRCP

Dr Patricia Sankey MB ChB MRCGP DObst RCOG

Dr C. Scott-Moncrieff MB ChB MFH OM

Dr Pamela Tatham MB BS (London)

Dr K. Thorley MA MB BChir MRC GP DRCOG .

REFERENCES:-

[1] Barnes B, Grant E, Mumby K et al. Nutrition and pre-conception care. Lancet 1985; i: 1297.

[2] Barnes B, Bradley SG. Planning for a Healthy Baby. London: Ebury Press, 1990.

[3] Grant ECG. Sexual Chemistry. London: Cedar, Reed Books, 1994.

Appendix 5

Article by Jean Philips from Powerwatch.org.uk

Are electromagnetic fields (EMFs) affecting your ability to have the family you want?

What on earth are electromagnetic fields (EMFs), you might ask, and what do they have to do with conceiving a child and bringing him or her to birth?

To answer these questions, we include a little information to put them into context.

We have evolved with a background level of natural EMFs generated by the earth herself. This had remained unchanged for millennia. Since the beginning of the 20th century all that changed.

We added powerfrequency fields from electricity generating power stations, powerlines that cross our country to supply electricity to consumers in cities, towns, villages and in rural areas. The number of electrical appliances we use at home and at work has grown enormously. We then added radiofrequency fields from radio, radar, television, mobile phones and their masts, wireless computers giving access to the internet at home and on the move, we give wireless games to the children and introduce wireless into their classrooms with interactive whiteboards and WiFi systems. All our transport is flooded with electromagnetic fields, as are our hospitals, shops and leisure venues.

We are so used to the benefits that undeniably accompany all of these innovations, that we rarely consider whether they may have disadvantages.

It was the military that first began to find occupational exposure to EMFs made some of their personnel very ill indeed. In the 1970s childhood leukaemia was linked to residential electricity supply (Wertheimer & Leeper 1979) and 'microwave sickness' was described (Silverman 1973) after people had been exposed to radiofrequency (RF) radiation. Since then there have been an ever increasing number of studies looking at the potential health effects experienced by people as a result of exposure to both powerfrequency (PF) and radiofrequency (RF) fields.

The research

The research has looked intensively at childhood leukaemia and there is international agreement that this illness is linked to PF electromagnetic fields, though the mechanisms of causation are not agreed on. In the course of the research, other illnesses have been looked at and there seems to be a growing body of evidence that illnesses other than childhood cancer may be implicated, and health effects other than those that lead to illness.

There has been a phenomenal growth in the use of equipment using RF technology. The scientists began to wonder whether this, too, might have the sort of effects on the general population as those suggested by Charlotte Silverman.

Many of you may have seen the debate in the media about whether mobile phones cause brain tumours. This is very concerning indeed, as there seems to be ever increasing evidence that these two are firmly linked.

However, that is not the focus of this article, and it is here that we look at the research that has investigated whether there are any links between PF or RF fields and reproductive problems.

The following research information is a 'snapshot in time' as research is ongoing; new papers are being published frequently and the science is still as new as our exposures.

Occupational exposure

Many studies look at occupational effects as employers have an obligation to provide safe working environments for their employees, and to minimise known risks.

Two studies (Møllerløkken 2008, Baste 2008) investigating reproductive effects in the Norwegian Navy found that exposure to RF fields produced an increased risk of infertility, and the higher the exposure, the greater the risk. Where children were born, there seemed to be a greater number of girls than boys. Occupational exposure is frequently at higher levels than those allowed for the general population, as it is assumed that workers are healthier and less vulnerable to ill health effects as a result of exposure to environmental toxins.

A study by De-Kun Li, which he presented in June 2008 to the annual meeting of the Society for Epidemiologic Research in Chicago, found that men who are exposed to levels of magnetic fields of only $0.16\mu T$ for six or more hours a day were four times as likely to have substandard sperm.

Kim (2008) found cell apoptosis (cell death) in mouse testicular germ cells from exposure to $14\mu T$ 60 Hz magnetic fields. This is a long way above typical chronic background exposure, but is also considerably below International Commission on Non-Ionizing Radiation Protection (ICNIRP) guidance levels.

Physiotherapists can be exposed to RF radiation by some of the equipment they use therapeutically. A study of pregnant physiotherapists (Ouellet-Hellstrom & Stewart 1993) found that being exposed to RF radiation increased the risk of miscarriage and the higher the exposure the greater the risk. The levels they were exposed to were not very high, similar to those which will be found in many places near mobile phone base stations and in homes and workplaces with digital DECT cordless phones and wireless Local Area Network (wLAN) systems.

Other studies have looked at residential rather than occupational exposure, or exposure as a result of lifestyle choices (e.g. mobile phone use, travel by train, etc.)

Powerfrequency fields

Powerfrequency fields occur as a result of our use of electricity. Some research is based on human exposure, some is done in laboratories or using animals. It is not always easy to say whether animal and cell studies provide information which will apply to people, but many of the experimental procedures cannot be done on people, so we are stuck with it, and the accompanying uncertainty.

The California report (Neutra 2002), which reviewed the available research studies, concluded that there was a link between miscarriage and powerfrequency magnetic fields, and two surveys carried out by local residents in Stoke on Trent, UK, found highly significant links between proximity to high-voltage powerlines and the incidence of miscarriage.

Li (2002) and Lee (2002) found that exposure to EMFs during pregnancy was linked to an increased risk of miscarriage. Lee's study found that the link was especially strong where there were high 'transient' fields, that is, where field levels changed rapidly in a short period of time. This type of exposure can happen in e.g. electric train travel; working near or passing through anti-theft pillars in shops, etc.

Experiments with mice by Hong (2003) and Cao (2006) found that low frequency EMF exposure had some adverse effects on reproduction, including miscarriage, foetal loss and malformation and developmental delay in the offspring.

Radiofrequency fields

Radiofrequency fields are produced round wireless transmitters of various types, many of which were mentioned in the introductory paragraphs. Distance from these sources is not an easy guide to determine at what point the levels are 'low' as it is not always clear how 'high' they were in the first place. Different types of transmitters give off different types of radiation (e.g. pulsed or continuous) and it is believed that different signals may have different health effects, like the 'transients' mentioned above. Whether animals and cells respond in the same ways as humans is also not known.

Dr de Pomerai found changes in growth rate and maturation in the reproductive stage of nematode worms, when the larvae were exposed to weak microwave fields (2002). In an experiment on flies, Dr Reba Goodman

(Blank & Goodman 1997) of Colombia University found that 2 hours mobile phone exposure for 10 days caused significant changes in reproductive genes and cell division.

It is advisable that men should not carry a phone in their front trouser pockets, because of the potential effect this may have on their reproductive ability. A study at the University of Western Australia, published by the Royal Society in June 2005, and others (Fejes 2005, Erogul 2006, Yan 2007, Agarwal 2008) concluded that usage of mobile phones, exposure to mobile phone signals, or storage of a mobile phone close to the testes affected sperm counts, motility, viability and morphology. *"In addition to these acute adverse effects of electromagnetic radiation (EMR) on sperm motility, long-term EMR exposure may lead to behavioural or structural changes of the male germ cell. These effects may be observed later in life, and they are to be investigated more seriously."* This should be borne in mind by young men using a mobile phone to send text messages while holding the phone on their lap.

The graph below shows that it takes the body some time to start producing viable sperm after RF exposure.

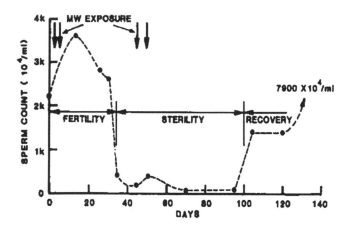

C K Chou (from article in Chinese)

At the annual meeting of the American Society for Reproductive Medicine in October 2006 in New Orleans, US researchers in Cleveland and New Orleans and doctors in Mumbai, India reported that the more that men used a mobile phone, the worse their sperm count and the poorer the quality of their sperm would be, see also Agarwal (2008). Using the phone for more than 4 hours a day caused a 25% drop in the number of sperm produced and only 20% of these looked normal. Sperm counts in UK men have fallen by 29% in the last decade. The researchers said that *"many in the lowest group for sperm count would be below normal as defined by the World Health Organisation."*

However, the research does not always find evidence of effects, and this could reflect sensitivity to different frequencies (Ribeiro 2007, Panagopoulos 2007).

It may be that RF radiation affects semen quality in general, or maybe sperm are affected differently as to whether they contain the XX chromosome or the XY chromosome. Where girls are born more often, perhaps there is DNA damage to the Y chromosome that makes the conception of boys less likely.

A paper (Vorobtsova 2008) looking at the history of radiobiological investigations in Russia, found that there is a possibility that the germ cells of irradiated parents may transmit genomic instability to their children, thus increasing risk of their getting cancer. This transgenerational effect has been well documented by Herbst in the 1970s who reported that diethylstilboestrol (DES), prescribed for newly pregnant women to prevent abortion, miscarriage and premature labour, resulted in a small number of cases of a rare cancer, vaginal clear-cell adenocarcinoma, in the daughters who were born as a result of the pregnancy concerned.

This was not a result of EMF exposure, but it shows the complexity of investigating the causes of reproductive problems. Individual susceptibility and exposure to other environmental pollutants further complicate the picture. For example, Cherry (2008) showed that painters and decorators, exposed to glycol solvents, were 2½ times more likely to produce fewer 'normal' sperm. RF radiation has been shown to alter the effects of relatively common drugs such as valium, anti-histamines, steroids, anti-cancer drugs such as tamoxifen, and to interact with other environmental stimuli.

Scassellati Sforzolini (2004) concluded *"The possibility that ELF-MF might interfere with the genotoxic activity of xenobiotics has important implications, since human populations are likely to be exposed to a variety of genotoxic agents concomitantly with exposure to this type of physical agent."* Koyama (2005) also found that EMF exposure just before or after X-ray irradiation increased mutation and altered the spectrum of mutations.

So, why are the concerns not better known about? Here we turn to politics.

The politics

Despite the increasing evidence that there are all sorts of physiological effects associated with exposure to EMFs, both high- and low-frequency, there is very little political will to make changes. Most political decisions have to be made as a result of a cost-benefit risk analysis consideration. As a lot of the research has been into relatively rare illnesses, it is considered that the cost of change would be too expensive for the amount of lives saved (family traumatisation is not included in cost benefit analysis). Pharmaceutical companies do not fund research into EMFs as any link may reduce the need for medication and thus reduce their profits.

Companies involved in the telecommunications industry provide tax income in the billions annually to government coffers, from the sale of mobile phones, calls and infrastructure development. The government would find it hard to replace this revenue. In fact, MacMillan, in the 1950s acknowledged the ill health effects from smoking, but it was not government policy to promote this, because of the income received from the tobacco industry.

Many studies partly funded by the government have put health effects down as psychosomatic (all in the mind). This absolves them from the necessity to take precautionary action.

What you can do

If you are wondering whether you, or your partner, may be affected by EMFs, that they may be playing a part in your difficulties in having the family you would like, you might decide to measure the levels of EMFs at home, as you travel, and in the workplace. There are easy to use instruments available to hire from www.emfields.org which can help you find out. If you feel you then want to take some protective measures, there are also ways of reducing your exposure, such as replacing your digital cordless phone with a landline or low emission phone; accessing broadband using a wired system rather than a wireless one; reducing the use of your mobile phone and charging it away from the bedroom. There are plenty of other possibilities that are easy and cheap to implement, as well as the more expensive ones which may not always offer the protection they claim.

Remember that electromagnetic fields are everywhere and have a lot of advantages, reasonable precautions to limit exposure are wise if you are having problems conceiving or carrying a baby to term, but worry increases tension and reduces wellbeing. Laugh a lot, do the things you enjoy, walk in nature, and eat well.

References

Agarwal A et al – 2008, *Effect of cell phone usage on semen analysis in men attending infertility clinic: an observational study* Fertil Steril 89(1):124-8

Baste V et al – 2008, *Radiofrequency electric fields; male infertility and sex ratio of offspring* Eur J Epidemiol 23(5):369-77

Blank M and Goodman R – 1997, *Do electromagnetic fields interact directly with DNA?* Bioelectromagnetics 18: 111-115

Cao YN et al – 2006, *Effects of exposure to extremely low frequency electromagnetic fields on reproduction of female mice and development of offsprings* Zhonghua Lao Dong Wei Sheng Zhi Ye Bing Za Zhi 24(8):468-70

Cherry N et al – 2008, *Occupation and male infertility: glycol ethers and other exposures* Occup Environ Med 65(10):708-14

De Pomerai D et al – 2002, *Growth and maturation of the nemaotode c. elegans* *following exposure to weak microwave fields,* Enzyme and Microbial Technology 30; pp 73-79

Erogul O et al – 2006, *Effects of electromagnetic radiation from a cellular phone on human sperm motility: an in vitro study,* Arch Med Research 2006 Oct;37(7):840-3.

Fejes I et al – 2005, *Is there a relationship between cell phone use and semen quality?* Arch Androl 51(5): 385-93

Herbst AL et al – 1971, *Adenocarcinoma of the vagina: Association of maternal stilbestrol therapy with tumor appearance in young women* N Engl J Med 284(15):878-881

Hong R et al - 2003, *[Effects of extremely low frequency electromagnetic fields on male reproduction in mice* - article in Chinese] Zhonghua Lao Dong Wei Sheng Zhi Ye Bing Za Zhi 21(5): 342-5

Kim YW et al - 2008, *Effects of 60 Hz 14 microT magnetic field on the apoptosis of testicular germ cell in mice* Bioelectromagnetics Oct 6 [Epub ahead of print]

Koyama S et al – 2005, *Combined exposure of ELF magnetic fields and x-rays increased mutant yields compared with x-rays alone in pTN89 plasmids* J Radiat Res (Tokyo) 46(2):257-64

Lee GM et al – 2002, *A nested case-control study of residential and personal magnetic field measures and miscarriages* Epidemiology 13(1):21-31

Li D-K et al – 2002, *A population-based prospective cohort study of personal exposure to magnetic fields during pregnancy and the risk of miscarriage* Epidemiology 13(1):9-20

Møllerløkken OJ & BE Moen – 2008, *Is fertility reduced among men exposed to radiofrequency fields in the Norwegian Navy?* Bioelectromagnetics 29(5):345-52

Neutra RR et al – 2002, *An Evaluation of the Possible Risks From Electric and Magnetic Fields (EMFs) From Power Lines, Internal Wiring, Electrical Occupations and Appliances.* California EMF Program, California Department of Health and Human Services. http://www.ehib.org/emf/

Ouellet-Hellstrom R & WF Stewart – 1993, *Miscarriages among female physical therapists who report using radio- and microwave-frequency electromagnetic radiation* Am J Epidemiol 138(10):775-86

Panagopoulos DJ et al – 2007, *Comparison of bioactivity between GSM 900 MHz and DCS 1800 MHz mobile telephony radiation* Electromagn Biol Med 26(1):33-44

Ribeiro EP et al – 2007, *Effects of subchronic exposure to radio frequency from a conventional cellular telephone on testicular function in adult rats* J Urol 177(1):395-9

Scassellati Sforzolini et al – 2004, *[Evaluation of genotoxic and/or co-genotoxic effects in cells exposed in vitro to extremely-low frequency electromagnetic fields]* Ann Ig 16(1-2):321-40

Silverman C – 1973, *Nervous and behavioural effects of microwave radiation in humans* Am J Epidemiol 97(4):219-24

Vorobtsova IE – 2008, *Transgenerational transmission of radiation-induced genomic instability and predisposition to carcinogenesis* Vopr Onkol 54(4):490-3

Wertheimer N & E Leeper – 1979, *Electrical wiring configurations and childhood cancer* Am J Epidemiol 109(3):273-84

Yan JG et al – 2007, *Effects of cellular phone emissions on sperm motility in rats* Fertil Steril 88(4):957-64

Appendix *6*

Facsimile reproduction of the University of Surrey Research Paper results in 1993 by Dr Neil I Ward

<u>FORESIGHT QUESTIONNAIRE RESEARCH PROJECT</u>

<u>PART I : INTRODUCTION</u>

The following Foresight research project was established to evaluate the Foresight Preconceptual approach using specialised Foresight clinicians. A series of questionnaires (Appendix 1) were prepared for completion of both the female and male patients at the time of approaching the Foresight clinician. These documents provided a confidential database of the individuals history including previous reproductive problems (infertility, miscarriage, therapeutic termination, stillbirths, SIDS, premature birth, etc), gravida status, medical history (including data on 59 possible allergic deficiency conditions or health problems), environmental history (including heavy metal, electrical, and chemical pollution), alcohol and smoking history, dietary status, gynaecological information (including contraception, disorders, etc), and a clinicians assessment of cytomegalovirus, rubella, or toxoplasmosis status. For male patients a special "fertility" check was undertaken, with special attention to sperm count, motility and condition. The completion of the female and male patient questionnaires was undertaken with the assistance of the Foresight clinician.

A second questionnaire (Number 2: 6 Month Follow-up) and 18 month follow-up letter were also provided where necessary. The final document related to the Baby Follow-up questionnaire which provided specific details about the Foresight baby, including baby's condition at birth (gestational age, weight, and any problems, such as, jaundice, malformation, skin condition, colic, diarrhoea, etc).

RESEARCH POPULATION

The research database consists of 367 Foresight couples. At least 418 sets of questionnaires had been returned but unfortunately in some cases information was absent. The population statistics are summarised in Table 1.

Table 1.   Foresight Research Project Population Statistics

	Female		Male	
	mean	range	mean	range
Age (years)	34	22 - 45	36	25 - 59
Height (cm)	165	152 - 183	182	158 - 225
Weight (kg)	59	40 - 93	75	56 - 101
% Ethnic Origin				
Caucasian	92		91	
Black	2		2	
Asian	6		7	

The Female Foresight population were classified according to the following information:

(F1)   Previous Reproductive Problems

According to the questions 3.1 to 3.13 in the Female Foresight Questionnaire 1., Table 2 summarises the percentage of cases relating to no history or the types of previous reproductive problems.

Table 2.   Percentage (%) of Female Cases with No History or With Types of Previous Reproductive Problems

Reproductive problems	%	Specific details
No history	41	-
Infertility	37	Period: 11% ≤ 1y, 36% ≤ 2y, 33% ≥ 5 yr, 7% ≥ 10 yr
Miscarriage	38	Number: 63% only 1, 14% only 2, 16% only 3, 3% only 4 or 5
Therapeutic abortions	11	Number: 89% only 1, 11% only 2
Stillbirths	3	-
SIDS	1	-
Small-for-date/low birth weight (<2300g)	15	11% small-for-date
Malformations	2	Spina bifida

(F2)   Gravida Status

Seventy percent (70%) of the Female Foresight population were primagravida, with the remaining 30% being multi gravide, having 1 to 3 children. Table 3 shows the trace element hair status of female prima or multigravida cases; which in summary shows no significant differences between the two groups.

(F3)   Medical History

According to questions 4.4, Table 4 summarises the percentage allergic/deficiency conditions or health problems for the Female Foresight population.

Table 3. Female Foresight Trace Element Hair Status of Prima or Multigravida Classification

Function/Element	Mean Trace Element (μg/g) content		Difference*
	Prima	Multi	
Age (yrs)	33.4	35.7	
Height (cm)	165	164	
Weight (kg)	60	58	
Ca	407	402	
Mg	39	42	
P	148	144	
Na	147	167	*
K	75	71	
Fe	26	26	
Cu	28	27	
Zn	171	163	*
Cr	0.72	0.75	
Mn	1.55	1.45	
Se	1.8	1.8	
Ni	0.65	0.63	
Co	0.23	0.20	
Pb	3.9	3.7	
Hg	0.43	0.42	
Cd	0.19	0.16	
As	0.14	0.11	
Al	1.5	1.4	

* No significant differences

Table 4.   Medical History

Condition	%	Condition	%
Acne	8	Hair loss	8
Anorexia	1	Halitosis (bad breath)	14
Asthma	5	Headaches/migraines	39
Back pain	32	High blood pressure	<1
Bleeding gums	26	High raised palate	<1
Bloated after meals	30	Hives	3
Blood shot eyes		Hostility (no cause)	6
Body odour (severe)	<1	Hyperactivity	3
Bowel cramps	18	Insomnia	11
Brittle nails	20	Irritable bowel	13
Bruising (no cause)	6	Joint pain	16
Burning feet	5	Kidney disorders	1
Catarrh	29	Memory loss	9
Coelia disease	<1	Mouth ulcers	19
Cold feet	48	Multiple sclerosis	1
Cold hands	30	Nervousness	15
Colitus	3	Palpitations	9
Constipation	28	Panic attacks	6
Cystitus	9	R. Arthritis	1
Dandruff	25	Sciatica/lumbago	6
Dental decay	15	Sensitivity to noise	13
Depression	21	Stretch marks	23
Diarrhoea	14	Sweating (heavy)	3
Dizzy spells	10	Swollen feet	6
Dyslexia	1	Tinnitus	7
Ear infections	5	Urticaria	6
Eczema	9	Varicose veins	15
Enlarged glands	5	Weight problems (low)	2
Epilepsy	<1	(high)	15
Fatigue/lethergy	41	White spots on nails	27
Urinating frequency	17		
Griping after meals	4		
Grooved tongue	3		

(F4)   Common Social Habits

Table 5 reports the alcohol and smoking history of the Female Foresight population.

Table 5.   Female Alcohol and Smoking History

Social habit		Percentage
Alcohol		
Never		8
Previously		32
Drink		60
	Occasionally	51
	Regularly	9
Smoking		
Never		15
Previously		28
Smoke		57
	Occasionally	12
	Regularly	45

(F5)   Form of Contraception

Table 6 lists the forms of contraception that the Foresight couples (as related to the Female) had been using and whether they reported suffering from any side effects.

Table 6.   Contraception History

Type	Percentage	(%) Reported problems
Pill	18	12
Coil	12	-
Diaphragm	5	-
Cap	-	-
Sheath	52	5
Sponge	-	-
Natural planning	13	-

(F6)   Female Foresight Population Trace Element Hair Status

Table 7 reports the mean and range of Biolab Medical Unit Hair Mineral Test results for the Female Foresight Population. Values are compared with the reference range (in parts per million) provided by Biolab.

Table 7.   Female Foresight Population Biolab Trace Element Hair Status

Element	Female Foresight Population				Biolab Ref. Range		
	Mean	Min	-	Max	Min	-	Max
Ca	405	246	-	722	200	-	600
Mg	40	15	-	175	30	-	95
P	147	75	-	193	100	-	210
Na	154	44	-	496	90	-	340
K	74	13	-	317	50	-	120
Fe	26	19	-	50	20	-	60
Cu	28	17	-	47	10	-	40
Zn	168	125	-	263	150	-	240
Cr	0.73	0.41	-	0.90	0.60	-	1.50
Mn	1.5	0.8	-	2.1	1.0	-	2.6
Se	1.8	0.4	-	2.4	1.5	-	4.0
Ni	0.64	0.34	-	0.94	0.40	-	1.40
Co	0.22	0.11	-	0.56	0.10	-	0.70
					Accept		
Pb	3.80	0.2	-	10.7	< 15.0		
Hg	0.42	0.24	-	0.89	<2.0		
Cd	0.18	0.11	-	0.49	< 0.5		
As	0.13	0.05	-	1.10	<2.0		
Al	1.5	0.9	-	5.4	<10.0		

(F7) Female Foresight Population Trace Element Blood Status

Table 8 gives the mean and range of St Luke's Hospital Blood Test results for the limited number of Female Foresight Cases. Values are compared with reference range (in μmol/l or mmol/l) provided by St. Luke's Hospital.

Table 8. Female Foresight Population St. Luke's Trace Element Blood

Element (units)	Female Foresight Population			Def. Range		
	Mean	Min	- Max	Min	-	Max
Cu (μmol/l)	16	12	- 23	11	-	20
Zn (μmol/l)	12	7	- 18	11	-	24
Pb (μmol/l)	0.2	<0.1	- 0.8		<1.4	
Mg (mmol/l)	0.9	0.5	- 1.2	0.65	-	1.00

The Male Foresight population were sub-divided into similar groupings. However, details on medical history and allergic/deficiency conditions (questionnaire section 4.4) had only a limited number of responses. For this report only three areas will be reviewed in any detail:

(M1) Common Social Habits

Table 9 reports the alcohol and smoking history of the Male Foresight population. Approximately 2% admitted to using drugs, namely cannabis.

Table 9.   Male Alcohol and Smoking History

Social habit		Percentage	
Alcohol			
Never			6
Previously			4
Drink			90
	Light	56	
	Heavy	34	
Smoking			
Never			34
Previously			21
Smoke			45
	Light	27	
	Heavy	18	

(M2)   "Fertility" Status

Section 8 of the Male Foresight Questionnaire asked 16 questions about "fertility" status, including suffering from thrush (candida albicans), herpes, and sperm count, motility and condition. In most cases only a limited number of comments were recorded; the majority of these relating to mumps. However, the Foresight clinicians did refer to sections 8.12 (sperm test?) and 8.13 to 8.16 (sperm factors). Table 10 gives the percentage of reported males who had a sperm test and the results relating to sperm factors (antibodies, low sperm count, poor motility, malformed condition).

Table 10. Foresight Male "Fertility" Status

"Fertility"	Percentage reported
Sperm test	42
Antibodies	12
Low sperm count	30
Poor motility	35
Malformed sperm	5

In some cases a seminal fluid test was carried out by JSPS and MetPath (CLS), Harley St. Data is provided on pH, count, motility and abnormal forms (Table 11).

Table 11. Seminal Fluid Tests (JSPS and MetPath)

Conditions	Test mean and range		Ref. value
Volume (mL)	5.0	2.4 - 6.8	-
pH	7.8	7.6 - 8.2	-
Count (million/ml)	121	45 - 350	50 - 200
Motility			
Active (%)	60	42 - 85	
Sluggish (%)	20	5 - 35	
Non-motile (%)	30	20 - 48	
Abnormal forms (%)	<15	-	up to 40

(M3)   Male Foresight Population Trace Element Hair Status

Table 12 provides the mean and range of Biolab Medical Unit Hair Mineral Test results for the Male Foresight Population. Values are compared with the reference range (in parts per million) provided by Biolab.

Table 12. Male Foresight Population Biolab Trace Element Hair Status

Element	Male Foresight Population			Biolab Ref. Range		
	Mean	Min -	Max	Min -		Max
Ca	410	229 -	690	200	-	600
Mg	39	17 -	128	30	-	95
P	160	126 -	210	100	-	210
Na	149	92 -	325	90	-	340
K	69	23 -	293	50	-	120
Fe	37	19 -	67	20	-	60
Cu	18	14 -	36	10	-	40
Zn	172	119 -	239	150	-	240
Cr	0.60	0.40 -	0.83	0.60	-	1.50
Mn	1.3	1.0 -	1.9	1.0	-	2.6
Se	2.0	1.1 -	2.7	1.5	-	4.0
Ni	0.64	0.42 -	0.92	0.40	-	1.40
Co	0.21	0.17 -	0.38	0.10	-	0.70
				Accept		
Pb	4.50	0.8 -	12.9	<15.0		
Hg	0.39	0.21 -	0.82	<2.0		
Cd	0.23	0.13 -	0.62	<0.5		
As	0.12	0.08 -	0.74	<0.2		
Al	1.7	0.9 -	6.9	<10.0		

PART 2 : PRECONCEPTUAL CARE FORESIGHT RESEARCH PROJECT

The following results summarise the research database of 367 Foresight couples using the information provided on the various Foresight Questionnaires. This report presents the results and at this stage does not attempt to provide a detailed interpretation of the values. That information will be included in subsequent scientific publications.

2.1 Foresight Research Project Pregnancy Outcome Statistics

Table 2.1 shows that 89% of the Foresight couples involved in this research project had mono-birth children; 42% of which were male and 58% female. Only 11% of the Foresight couples (females) failed within the time period of the project to become pregnant. All Foresight children had a mean birth weight (3265g) and mean gestational age (38.5 weeks). Femalel babies were in general 60g less in birth weight than male babies. Figure 2.1 shows the relationship between birth weight and gestational age for the Foresight pregnancies.

Table 2.1 Foresight Research Project Outcome Statistics

Pregnancy/Non-pregnancy*		Birth weight (g)		Gestational age (wks)	
		mean	range	mean	range
Pregnancy	89%	3265	2368 - 4145	38.5	36 - 41
Males[+]	42%	3299	2484 - 4145	38.5	36 - 40
Females[+]	58%	3240	2368 - 4089	38.5	36 - 41
Non-pregnancy	11%	-	-	-	-

*   expressed as percentage of total Foresight Research number of cases

[+]   expressed as percentage of pregnancy cases.

Whilst there is a slight spread in the data, a good correlation exists for both birth parameters.

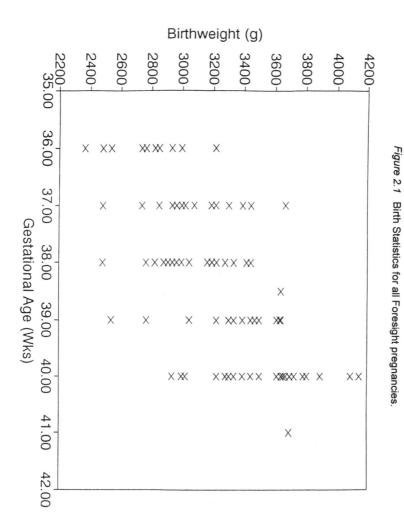

Figure 2.1 Birth Statistics for all Foresight pregnancies.

Fig. 2.1 Birth statistics for all Foresight pregnancies

2.2   Influence of Previous Reproductive Problem History on Pregnancy Outcome

Table 2.2 shows the percentage of Foresight pregnant and non-pregnant cases as a function of their previous history of reproductive problems. Couples with no history of such problems subdivides into 96% who became pregnant and 4% non-pregnant. Couples who had reported histories of reproductive problems, such as infertility, miscarriage, therapeutic terminations or stillbirths in general had 73 to 83% success in having a Foresight baby, whilst 17 to 27% were non-pregnant. The very small number of SID's cases (n=3) were all non-pregnant. However, couples who were reporting histories of small-for-date (low birth weight) or malformations (spina bifida) had a 100% success rate for a Foresight pregnancy.

Table 2.2 Percentage of Foresight Pregnant and Non-pregnancy Cases Related to Previous Reproductive Problems

Previous history	% Foresight pregnant	% Non-pregnant
No history	96	4
Infertility	81	19
Miscarriage	83	17
Therapeutic Term.	73	27
Stillbirths	80	20
SIDS		100
Small-for-dates (low birth weights)	100	0
Malformations	100	0

For those Foresight couples who successfully had a pregnancy Table 2.3 reports the influence of their previous reproductive problems (or non-problem) history on their Foresight pregnancy outcome (birth weight and gestational age). Whilst there is no significant difference in mean gestational age (weeks) between the groups, all previous reproductive problem groups had lower birth weights than for couples with no history of previous problems. Stillbirths and malformation groups had the lowest birth weight (grams), approximately 400g lower than for the no history group.

2.3   Mineral Female (Hair) Analysis for Assessing the Influence of Previous Reproductive Problems

Table 2.4 reports the age (years) and mineral hair analysis for Ca, Mg, P, Na, K, Fe, Cu, Zn, Cr, Mn, Se, Ni, Co, Pb, Hg, Cd, As, and Al for the females in terms of previous reproductive problem (or non-problem, NH) history; infertility (INF), miscarriage (MIS), therapeutic terminations (THTE), stillbirths (STIL), small-for-dates or low birth weights (SFD), and malformation (MAL). Those elements showing significant differences between the various groups are shown in Figures 2.2 to2.8 respectively (Cd, Cu, Fe, Hg, Mn, Pb, and Zn). In general the malformation and possibly stillbirth group show high levels of toxic effects and low levels of essential elements. The highest zinc levels are for the no history (NH) group; with all the other groups reporting previous reproductive problems having lower Zn values.

Table 2.3 Influence of Previous Reproductive Problems on Foresight Pregnancy Outcome* (birthweight and gestational age)

Previous History	Sex* (%)		Mean birthweight (g)	Mean gestational age (wks)
	Male	Female		
No history	37	63	3384	39
Infertility	44	56	3166	38
Miscarriage	52	48	3138	38
Therapeutic Therm.	36	64	3143	38
Stillbirths	0	100	3017	38
Small-for-dates (low-for-weight)	50	50	3060	38
Malformations	33	67	2887	37

*   expressed as a percentage of pregnancy outcome for that group

Table 2.4 Influence of Previous Reproductive Problems (mean female hair value, ug/g)

Function/Element	No History	Infertility	Miscarriage	Therap. Term.	Stillbirths	SIDS	Small for date	Malform
Age (y)	34	35	35	36	36	36	37	36
Ca	420	389	407	394	418	0	388	411
Mg	38	40	40	59	48	0	52	28
P	151	144	147	147	138	0	147	130
Na	175	133	143	160	181	0	157	167
K	92	61	61	54	70	0	71	40
Fe	26	26	26	27	27	0	27	26
Cu	28	28	28	30	23	0	27	19
Zn	170	159	169	169	163	0	151	141
Cr	0.73	0.71	0.72	0.69	0.81	0	0.76	0.8
Mn	1.56	1.52	1.46	1.4	1.7	0	1.25	1.2
Sc	1.85	1.77	1.78	1.77	1.95	0	1.75	1.7
Ni	0.66	0.66	0.61	0.64	0.66	0	0.64	0.6
Co	0.24	0.21	0.2	0.22	0.26	0	0.21	0.2
Pb	3.8	3.5	3.8	3.8	4.3	0	3.5	6.9
Hg	0.43	0.41	0.42	0.43	0.32	0	0.39	0.48
Cd	0.19	0.18	0.17	0.21	0.15	0	0.16	0.38
As	0.12	0.15	0.12	0.12	0.1	0	0.11	0.11
Al	1.7	1.4	1.3	1.4	1.2	0	1.3	1.2

Fig. 2.2

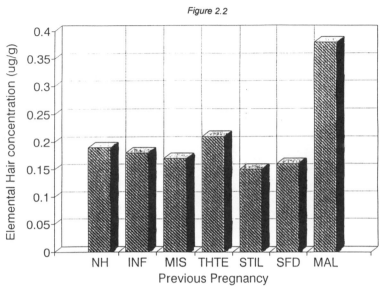

Hair Cd content and previous pregnancy history

Figure 2.2

Fig. 2.3

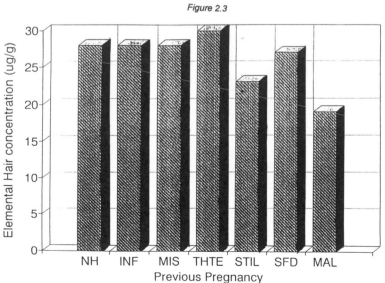

Hair Cu content and previous pregnancy history

Figure 2.3

Fig. 2.4

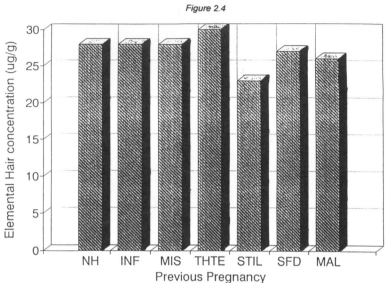

Hair Fe content and previous
pregnancy history

Figure 2.4

Fig. 2.5

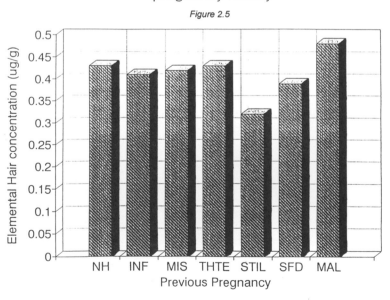

Hair Hg content and previous
pregnancy history

Figure 2.5

Fig. 2.6

Hair Mn content and previous pregnancy history

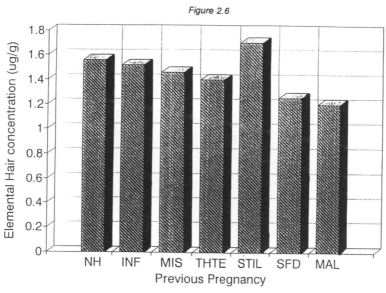

Figure 2.6

Fig. 2.7

Hair Pb content and previous pregnancy history

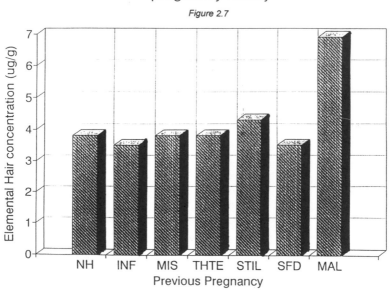

Figure 2.7

Fig. 2.8

Hair Zn content and previous pregnancy history

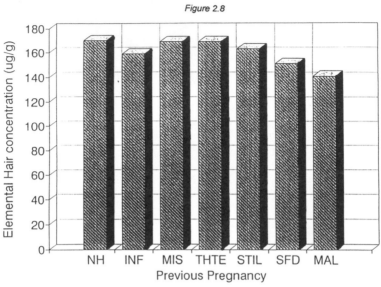

Figure 2.8

Fig. 3.1

Male Fertility Status and Hair Element (Iron) Content (ug/g)

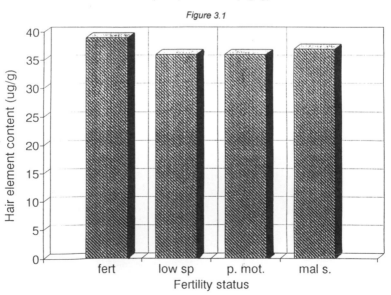

Figure 3.1

2.4   Mineral Female (Hair) Analysis for Assessing the Influence of Previous Reproductive
       Problems on the Outcome of Foresight Pregnancy or Non-Pregnancy Cases

The above results (Table 2.4, Figures 2.2 to 2.8) relate to all Female Foresight cases whether

or not they successfully became pregnant. Table 2.5 reports the mineral female hair data for

those females who were pregnant or non-pregnant as a function of their previous reproductive

problem (or non-problem) history.   Data is only provided for No History, Infertility,

Miscarriage and Therapeutic Termination groups.

3.1   Foresight Research Project - Male Statistics

Section 2.1 onwards have summarised the Foresight Research Project Pregnancy Outcome

Statistics with data relating predominantly to the baby or the female partner. In section 3.1

onwards the limited amount of data relating to the Foresight male partners will be reviewed.

Table 3.1(a) and (b) shows the male "fertility" status and the mineral hair element content (μ

g/g). The four fertility groups relate to (1) no obvious infertility, (2) low sperm count, (3)

poor motility, and (4) malformed sperm. Table3.1 (a) reports means and range values for Fe,

Cu, Zn, Se, Pb and Pb; whilst Table 3.1(b) covers Ca, Mg, Na, and K (electrolytes). This data

is graphically shown in Figs. 3.1 to 3.10. Both Fe and Cu show no significant changes

between the four groups. All three sperm problem ("infertility") groups show lower levels of

Zn and possibly Se (especially for malformed sperm), and elevated levels of the toxic elements

Pb and Cd. For the electrolytes there is a general trend to have reduced levels for the three

sperm problem groups. Low levels of Ca, Mg, and K exist for the poor mobility group when

compared with the no obvious infertility cases group.

3.2   Male Foresight Hair Element Content and Smoking Activity

Smoking activity is well known to be a source of cadmium. Table 3.2 gives the Fe and Cd hair

date for male non smoking, light and heavy smokers, and those who reported to have

previously smoked. The same data is graphically presented in Figures 2.9 to 2.11. There is

clear evidence of raised Cd and lower Zn and Fe as a function of smoking activity (heavy >

light > non). Those Foresight males who previously smoked also have the same pattern but

continued on last page of Appendix

Table 2.5 Influence of Previous Reproductive Problem on Foresight Pregnancy or Non-Pregnancy cases (mean hair value, ug/g)

Function/Element	No History		Infertility		Miscarriage		Therapeutic Term.	
	For. Preg.	Non Preg.	For. Preg.	Non Preg.	For. Preg.	Non Preg.	For. Preg.	Non Preg.
Age (y)	34	35	34	37	34	37	36	37
Ca	409	463	392	358	408	407	380	476
Mg	43	24	41	27	43	26	65	25
P	151	143	144	140	149	137	148	147
Na	172	126	130	139	144	98	168	110
K	86	101	62	50	61	38	58	35
Fe	26	27	26	24	26	25	27	29
Cu	29	30	28	29	27	33	29	31
Zn	173	147	160	149	171	170	163	206
Cr	0.74	0.66	0.72	0.66	0.72	0.65	0.69	0.65
Mn	1.55	1.5	1.51	1.55	1.5	1.15	1.48	0.9
Se	1.85	1.7	1.79	1.63	1.76	2	1.68	2.3
Ni	0.65	0.62	0.65	0.68	0.6	0.65	0.62	0.73
Co	0.24	0.18	0.21	0.22	0.2	0.21	0.22	0.25
Pb	3.8	4.1	3.5	3.9	3.8	3.5	3.9	3.7
Hg	0.42	0.51	0.41	0.44	0.43	0.41	0.43	0.41
Cd	0.19	0.15	0.17	0.21	0.18	0.17	0.21	0.15
As	0.12	0.12	0.16	0.12	0.12	0.1	0.12	0.1
Al	1.7	1.6	1.4	1.6	1.3	1.5	1.4	1.3

Fig. 3.2

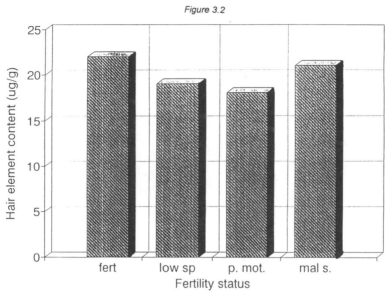

Male Fertility Status and Hair Element
(Copper) Content (ug/g)

Fig. 3.3

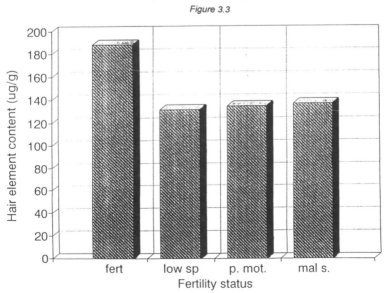

Male Fertility Status and Hair Element
(Zinc) Content (ug/g)

Fig. 3.4

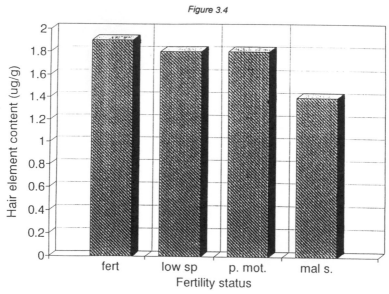

Male Fertility Status and Hair Element
(Selenium) Content (ug/g)

Figure 3.4

Fig. 3.5

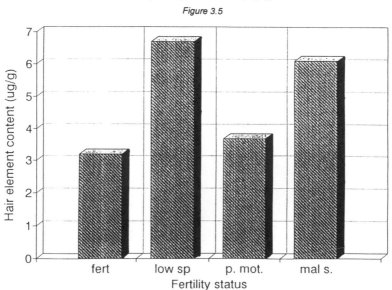

Male Fertility Status and Hair Element
(Lead) Content (ug/g)

Figure 3.5

Fig. 3.6

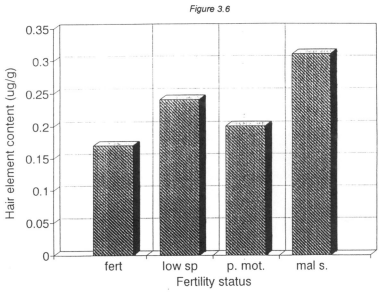

Male Fertility Status and Hair Element
(Cadmium) Content (ug/g)

Figure 3.6

Fig. 3.7

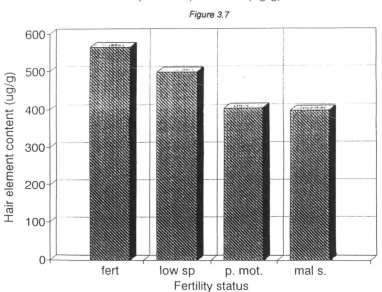

Male Fertility Status and Hair Element
(Calcium) Content (ug/g)

Figure 3.7

Fig. 3.8

Male Fertility Status and Hair Element
(Magnesium) Content (ug/g)

Figure 3.8

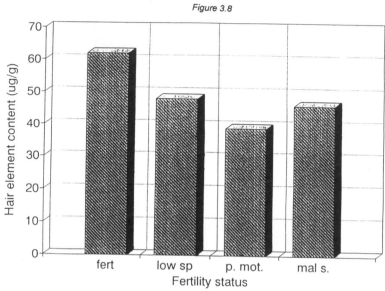

Fig. 3.9

Male Fertility Status and Hair Element
(Sodium) Content (ug/g)

Figure 3.9

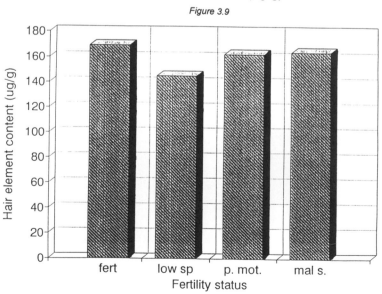

Fig. 3.10

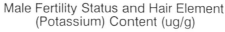

Male Fertility Status and Hair Element (Potassium) Content (ug/g)

Figure 3.10

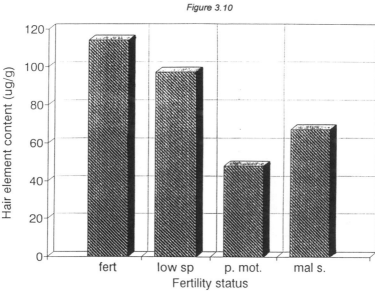

Fig. 2.9

Hair Cd concentration and smoking activity

Figure 2.9

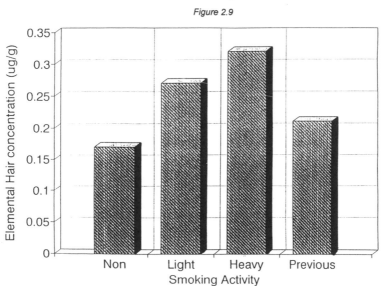

Beautiful Babies

Fig. 2.10

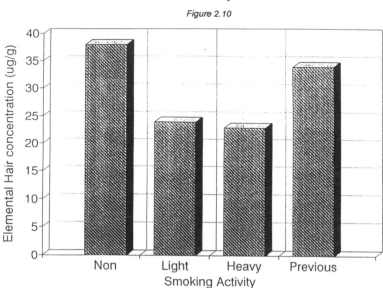

Hair Iron concentration and smoking activity

Figure 2.10

Fig. 2.11

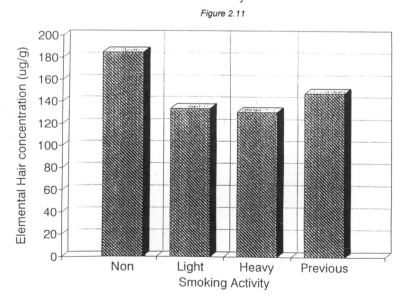

Hair Zinc concentration and smoking activity

Figure 2.11

402

Fig. 2.12

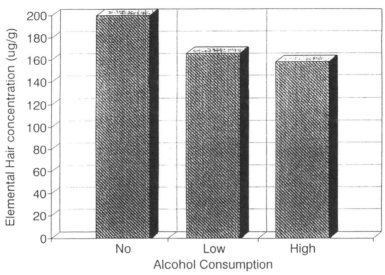

Male Hair Zn concentration and alcohol consumption

Figure 2.12

Fig. 2.13

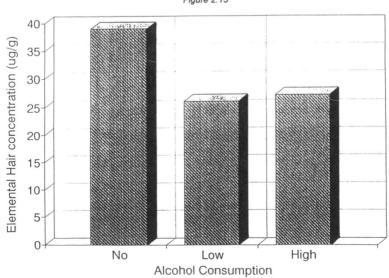

Hair Fe concentration and alcohol consumption

Figure 2.13

with a reduced impact when compared with active smokers. The relationship between smoking activity, hair mineral status, and fertility status is still to be assessed.

3.3   Male Foresight Hair Element Content and Alcohol Consumption

Alcohol consumption is known to influence male zinc status and thereby be a possible problem for fertility status. Table 3.3 shows the male Fe and Zn hair data for those individuals who reported to consume no alcohol or who were light or low (occasional glass of wine or pint of beer per day) and heavy or high (more than 5 pints of beer for 1 bottle of wine per day) alcohol consumers. The same data is graphically represented in Figures 2.12 and 2.13. The Foresight male data clearly supports the inverse relationship between alcohol consumption and male hair Zn and Fe status. The impact on fertility status is still to be assessed.

3.4   Male Foresight Hair Element Content and Pregnancy Outcome

The mean hair elemental content ($\mu g/g$) of Foresight Males subdivided into either non-pregnant or Foresight pregnant case groups is shown in Table 3.4. In general the Foresight Males relating to non-pregnant outcome cases had lower levels of Ca, K, Z, Cr, and possibly Fe and Mn. Conversely, they had raised levels of Pb, Cd, Al, and possibly Hg.

Suggested Reading

Pregnancy and Childhood

- A Child is Born. Lars Neilsson. Faber Paperbacks. 1977
- At Highest Risk. Christopher Norwood. McGraw-Hill. 1980
- Building Better Babies. Daniel Elam. Celestial Arts. 1980
- The First Nine Months of Life. Geraldine Lux Flanagan. Simon and Schuster. 1962
- The Poisoned Womb. John Elkington. Viking. 1985
- The Prevention of Handicap and the Health of Women. Margaret and Arthur Wynn. Routledge and Kegan Paul. 1979
- The Prevention of Handicap of Perinatal Origin. M and A Wynn.
- Foundation for Education and Research in Child Bearing. 1976
- The Unborn Child. Roy Ridgway. Karnac Books. 1-85575-420-7
- What Every Pregnant Woman Should Know. The Truth about Diets and Drugs and Pregnancy. G S and T Brewer. Penguin. 1977

Nutrition

- Additives. A Guide for Everyone. Erik Millstone and John Abraham. Penguin. 1988
- Diet and Disease. E. Cheraskin, M.D, D.M.D. W.M Ringsdorf, Jnr., D.M.D. J.W Clark, D.D.S Keats Publishing. 0-87983-666-0
- FIND OUT. Foresight. 1986, updated 2004
- Good Food Before Birth. Catherine Lewis. Unwin Paperbacks. 1984
- Growing Up with Good Food. Catherine Lewis. Unwin Paperbacks. 1982
- Let's Eat Right to Keep Fit. Adelle Davis. Signet Books. 1970
- Male Infertility – Fighting Back. Belinda Barnes. 2003
- Mental and Elemental Nutrients. Carl C Pfeiffer. Keats. 1975
- Metabolic Toxaemia of Late Pregnancy. A Disease of Malnutrition. T S Brewer. Keats Publishing. 1982
- Nutrition and Health. Sir Robert McCarrison. The McCarrison Society. 1981
- Nutrition and Physical Degeneration. Weston A Price. Price-Pottenger Nutrition Foundation. 1945
- Nutrition for Learning. Jan Katzen-Luchenta, AMI Emunah Publishing Co. 2007
- Nutritional Medicine. Stephen Davis and Alan Stewart. Pan. 1987
- Pottenger's Cats. A Study in Nutrition. F M Pottenger Nutrition Foundation. 1983
- Prescription for Nutritional Healing. Phyllis A Balch., CNC James F Balch,MD. Penguin Putnam Inc 1-58333-077-1
- Raw Energy. Leslie and Susannah Kenton. Century. 1984

- The Food Factor. Barbara Griggs. Penguin. 1988
- The Foresight Wholefood Cookbook. Norman and Ruth Jervis. Autumn Press. 1986
- The Green Home How to Make Your Home a Better Place 1995 Karen Christensen. Judy Piatkus 0-7499-1460-2
- The Healing Nutrients Within. Eric R Bravermann, with Carl Pfeiffer. Keats. 1987
- The Politics of Food 1987 Geoffrey Cannon. Century Hutchinson Australia Pty Ltd 0-7126-1210-60
- The Proof of The Pudding. Sally Bunday, 2008
- The Trace Elements and Man. Henry A Schoeder M.D. Devin-Adair Co. 0-8159-6907-4
- The Yeast Conncetion and the Woman 1995 William G Crook. Professional Books 0-933478-22-4
- The Yeast Connection Handbook 1999. William G Crook. Professional Books 0-933478-24-0
- Trace Elements in Human and Animal Nutrition. Eric J Underwood. Academic Press. 1977
- Trace Elements, Hair Analysis and Nutrition. Richard A Passwater and Elmer Cranton. Keats. 1983
- WATCH IT. Foresight. 2007.
- We Want Real Food. Graham Harvey. Constable 1-84529-267-7
- Zinc and Other Micro-nutrients. Carl C Pfeiffer. Keats. 1987

Birth Control

- The Bitter Pill. Ellen Grant. Corgi. 1985
- The Manual of Natural Family Planning. Anna Flynn and Melissa Brooks. Unwin Paperbacks. 1984
- Sexual Chemistry, Understanding Your Hormones, The Pill and HRT. Dr Ellen Grant. Cedar. 1994

Environmental Factors

- C for Chemicals. Chemical Hazards and How to Avoid Them 1989 Michael Birkin & Brian Price. Green Print 1-85425-027-2
- Earth Radiation. The Startling Discoveries of a Dowser. Kathe Bachler. Wordmasters Ltd. 0951415107
- Chemical Children: How to Protect Your Family from Harmful Pollutants. Dr Peter Mansfield & Dr Jean Monro. Century Hutchinson Ltd 0-7126-1729-9
- Daylight Robbery. Damien Downing. Century. 1988
- Light, Radiation and You. John Ott. Devin-Adair Pub.1985
- Poisoned Harvest - A Consumer's Guide to Pesticide Use and Abuse. Christopher Robbins. 1992
- Silent Spring. Rachel Carson

Soil, Food and Health

- Behavioural Problems in Childhood. The Link to Vaccination. Viera Scheibner. 0-9578007-0-3
- Brave New Seeds. Robert Ali Brac La Perriere. Zed Books 1-85649-900-6
- Eat Your Genes. Stephen Nottingham. Zed Books. 1-84277-347-X
- Gardening Without Chemicals. Jack Temple. Thorsons. 1986
- Genescapes The Ecology of Genetic Engineering. Stephen Nottingham. Zed Books. 1-84277-037-3
- Living Soil. E B Balfour and Walter Yellowlees. McCarrison Society.
- P for Pesticides. Dr Tim Lang and Dr C Clutterbuck.
- Redesigning Life? The Worldwide Challenge. Brian Tokar. Zed Books. 1-85649-835-2
- Stolen Harvest. Vandana Shiva. Zed Books 1-84277-025-X
- The Living Soil and The Haughley Experiment. E B Balfour.
- The Pesticide Detox Jules Pretty Earthscan 1-84407-142-1
- The Suffering Gene. Roy Burdon. Zed Books 1-84277-285-6

Health Problems

- Allergies Breakthrough to Health 2004. Gwynne H Davies. Capall Bann 186163230-4
- Allergies in the Under Fives 2004 Ellen Rothera. Environmental
- Assistance Nunsthorpe 0-9541031-1-4
- Allergies Your Hidden Enemy 1980 Theron G Randolph. Turnstone Press Ltd 0-85500-151-8. 1981.
- Allergy: Think About Food 1984 . Susan Lewis. Wisebuy 0-9509751-1-7
- Chemical Victims. Richard MacKarness. Pan. 1980
- Chronic Fatigue Syndrome & the Yeast Connection. William G Crook. Professional Books 0-933478-20-8
- Detecting Your Hidden Allergies 1988 . William G Crook. Professional Books 0-933478-15-1
- Encyclopedia of Allergy & Environmental Illness 1991 Ellen Rothera. David & Charles Plc 0-7153-9954-3
- Perhaps it's an Allergy: A Guide to Self Survival in a Chemical Age 1988 Ellen Rothera. W Foulsham & Co Ltd 0-572-01459-7
- Skewed 2003 Martin J Walker. Slingshot Publications 0-09519646-4X
- Stop the 21ˢᵗ Century Killing You 2005 Dr Paula Baillie-Hamilton Vermillion 009189467-0
- The Allergy Connection 1985 Barbara Paterson. Thorsons 0-7225-0984-7
- The Allergy Problem: Why People Suffer and What Should be Done. Vicky Rippere. Thorson. 1983

- The Allergy Relief Programm 1985 Alan Scott Levin & Merla Zellerbach. Gateway Books 0-946551-15-4
- The Allergy Survival Guide 1993 Jane Houlton. Vermillion 0-09-177505-1
- The Complete Guide to Food Allergy and Intolerance. Dr Brostoff and Gamlin.
- The Cure All Diseases Hulda Regehr Clark, Ph.D.,N.D New Century Press 1-890035-01-7
- The E.I. Syndrome An Rx for Environmental Illness Sherry A Rogers, MD 0-9618-821-0-7
- The Food Allergy Plan 1985 Keith Mumby. Unwin Paperbacks 0-04-641047-3
- The Hyperactive Child, What The Family Can Do. Bunday & Barnes.
- The Sanctity of Human Blood : Vaccination is Not Immunization Tim O'Shea 1929487088
- These Can Make You Ill: Not All In The Mind. 1976 Dr Richard Mackarness. Pan Books
- What Really Goes Into The Food On Your Plate NOT ON THE LABEL Felicity Lawrence Penguin Books 0-141-01566-7

Useful Addresses

Abel and Cole Organic Box Delivery, 8-15 MGI Estate, Milkwood Road, London, SW24 OJF, Telephone: 08452 626364 www.abelandcole.co.uk

Action Against Allergy, PO Box 278, Twickenham, Middlesex, TW1 4QQ Telephone: 0208 892 2711 www.actionagainstallergy.co.uk

Active Birth Movement, The Active Birth Centre, 25 Bickerton Road, London, N19 5JT, Telephone: 0207 281 6760 www.activebirthcenre.com

AIMS, Association for the Improvement of Maternity Services, 5 Ann's Court, Grove Road, Surbiton, Surrey, KT6 4BE Telephone: 08707 651453 www.aims.co.uk

Ainsworths Homeopathic Chemists, 36 New Cavendish Street, London, W1M 7LH, Telephone: 0207 935 5330 www.ainsworth.com

Angus Horticulture (Rock Dust), Polmood, Guthrie, By Forfar, DD8 2TW www.angus-horticulture.co.uk

ARM, Association of Radical Midwives, 16 Wytham Street, Oxford, Oxon, OX1 4SU Telephone: 01865 248159 www.midwifery.org.uk

Association for Breastfeeding Mothers, PO Box 207, Bridgewater, Somerset, TA6 7YT, Telephone: 08444 122949 www.abm.me.uk

Association for Mercury Free Dentists, The Weathervane, 22a Moorend Park Road, Cheltenham, GL53 0JY, Telephone: 01242 226918), www.HolisticDentalCentre.co.uk

Biodynamic Agricultural Association, Painswick Inn Project, Gloucester Street, Stroud, Gloucestershire, GL5 1QG Telephone: 01453 759501 www.biodynamic.org.uk

Biolab Medical Unit, The Stone House, 9 Weymouth Street, London, W1W 6DB, Telephone: 0207 636 5959 www.biolab.co.uk

Breastfeeding Helpline (NCT), 0870 444 8708

Brett, Mary, 6 Pines Close, Amersham, Bucks, HP6 5QW Telephone: 01494 726958

British College of Osteopathy and Naturopathy, 6 Nethershall Gardens, London, SW3 5RP, Telephone: 0207 435 7830 www.bcom.ac.uk

British Homeopathic Association, Hahnemann House, 29 Park Street West, Luton, Bedfordshire, LU1 3BE Telephone: 08704 443950 www.trusthomeopathy.org

British Institute for Allergy and Environmental Therapy, Llangwyryfon, Aberystwyth,Ceredigion, SY23 4EY Telephone: 01974 241 1376 www.allergy.org.uk

British Society for Allergy, Environmental and Nutritional Medicine, PO Box 7, Knighton, Powys, LD7 1WT, Telephone: 09063 020010 (information) 01547 550380 (contact) www.bsaenm.org.uk

Penny Brohn Cancer Help Centre, Chapel Pill Lane, Pill, Bristol, BS20 0HH Telephone: 01275 370100 www.pennybrohncancercare.org

Centre for Complimentary Health Studies, Exeter University, Exeter, Devon, EX2 4NT Telephone: 01392 424989 www.pms.ac.uk/compmed

Cerebra Centre for Brain Injured Children, Second Floor Offices, The Lyric Building, King Street, Carmarthen, SA31 1BD Telephone: 01267 244200 www.cerebra.org.uk

Coeliac Society Helpline: 0870 444 8804, www.coeliac.org.uk

Coghill, Roger, Coghill Research Laboratory, Lower Race, Pontypool, South Wales NP4 5UH www.cogreslab.co.uk

Compassion in World Farming, River Court, Mill Lane, Godalming, Surrey, GU7 1EZ. Telephone: 01483 521950 www.ciwf.org

Compost, The Compost Centre, Organic compost delivered in SE England, Telephone: 01483 472423. www.thecompostcentre.co.uk

Consumers For Health Choice, Abbey House, 4 Abbey Orchard Street, London, SW1P 2JJ. Telephone: 0207 222 8182 www.consumersforhealthchoice.com

Cryshame (Vaccine damage), Wilton House, Southbank Road, Kenilworth, Warwickshire, CV8 1LA www.cryshame.co.uk

DASH Doctors Against Steroid Hormones, Dr Ellen Grant, 20 Coombe Ridings, Kingston Upon Thames, Surrey, KT2 7JU Telephone: 0208 564 9482

Dental Nurses with Mercury Damage, Mrs Rebecca Dutton, Mistletoe Barn, Smithfield Road, Bearley, Stratford-on-Avon, CV37 0EX Telephone: 01789 730330 www.mercurymadness.org

Down's Syndrome Association, The Langdon Down's Centre, 2a Langdon Park, Teddington, Middlesex, TW11 9PS, Telephone: 08452 300362 www.downs-syndrome.org.uk

Eco Paints, Unit 34, Heysham Business Park, Middleton Road, Heysham, Lancs, LA3 3PP, Telephone: 01524 852371 www.ecospaints.com

Ecover, 165 Main Street, New Greenham Park, Newbury, Berks, RG19 6HM, Telephone: 0845 1302230 www.ecover.com

Electric Forrester, Unit 2, 1 Rona Court, Weybridge, Surrey, KT13 0DW, Telephone: 0845 3451892, Fax: 0845 3451893 www.electricforrester.co.uk

Endometriosis Society, (Dian Shepperson Mills, MA), 56 London Road, Hailsham, East Sussex, BN27 3DD Telephone: 01323 846888 www.endometriosis.co.uk

Endometriosis Lazar Treatment, Dr Davies, Stobhill Hospital, Glasgow

The Environment Agency, (Government body for pollution control), Telephone: 0845 933 3111 www.environment-agency.gov.uk

Ecology Building Society, 7 Belton Road, Silsden, Keighley, West Yorkshire, BD20 0EE, Telephone: 0845 674 5566 www.ecology.co.uk

Ewe-Too Spinners, Organic Wool, Silver Street, Hordle, Hants, SO41 0FN Telephone: 01425 616203

Full Spectrum Lighting (FSL) Ltd, Unit 48, Marlowe Road, Stokenchurch, High Wycombe, Bucks, HP14 3QJ Telephone: 01494 484852

Fertility Thermometers, Burkton-Dickenson, Omiss, Ontario, L5J 2M8, CANADA

Flint, Professor Caroline, Midwifery Services. 34 Elm Quay Court, Nine Elms Lane, London, SW8 5DE. Telephone: 0207 498 2322 caroline@birthcentre.com

Food Commission, 94 White Lion Street, London, N1 9PF. Telephone: 0207 837 2250 www.foodcomm.org.uk

Foresight The Association for the Promotion of Preconceptual Care, 178 Hawthorn Road, Bognor Regis, West Sussex, PO21 2UY. Telephone: 01243 868001 www.foresight-preconception.org.uk

Foresight Laboratory, Unit 6, Brocklands Farm, West Meon, Hampshire, GU32 1JN. Telephone: 01730 829861

Foresight Resource Centre, Telephone: 01483 869944

Freshwater Filters, Carlton House, Aylmer Road, Leytonstone, London, E11 3AD. Telephone: 0208 558 7495   www.freshwaterfilter.com

Friends of the Earth, 26-28 Underwood Street, London, N1 7JQ. Telephone: 0207 490 1555 www.foe.co.uk

G and G, Vitality House, 2-3 Imberhorne Way, East Grinstead, West Sussex, RH19 1RL. Telephone: 01342 312811 www.gandgvitamins.com   www.gandginfo.com

Garden Organic, Wolston Lane, Ryton-on-Dunsmore, Coventry, Warwickshire, CV8 3LG. Telephone: 02476 303517 www.gardenorganic.org.uk

Green People Ltd, Pondtail Farm, Coolham Road, West Grinstead, West Sussex, RH13 8LN Telephone: 01403 740 350 www.greenpeople.co.uk

Garthenor Organic Wool, Llanlo Road, Tregaron, Ceredigion, SY25 6UR Telephone: 01570 493347 www.organicpurewool.co.uk

The Good Gardeners' Association, 4 Lisle Place, Wooton Under Edge, Gloucestershire, GL12 7AZ Telephone: 01453 520322 www.goodgardeners.org.uk

The Green Party HQ, 1a Waterloo Road, London, N19 5NJ Telephone: 0207 272 4474 www.greenparty.org.uk

Greenfibres (Organic Cot Mattresses), 11-13 Fore Street, Totnes, Devon, TQ9 6ND Telephone: 01803 868001 www.greenfibres.com

Greenlink, Mrs Vera Chavey, 9 Clairmont Road, Colchester, Essex 01206 504486

Greenpeace, Canonbury Villas, London, N1 2PN, Telephone: 0207 865 8100 www.greenpeace.org.uk

Healthy House Ltd, The Old Co-op, Lower Street, Ruscombe, Stroud, Glos, GL6 6BU Telephone: 01453 752216 www.healthy-house.co.uk

Harrison, Donald, Homeopathic Remedies, Telephone: 01974 241376

HFEA, Human Fertility and Embryology Authority, 21 Bloomsbury Street, London, WC1B 3HF Telephone: 0207 291 8200 www.hfea.gov.uk

HER Clinic (Minimal drug use in IVF), Dr Geeta Nargund, FRCOG., St George's House Clinic, 3-5 Pepys Road, Raynes Park, London, SW20 8NJ Telephone: 0208 947 9600 www.createhealth.org

High Barn Oils, Nunthan House Farm, Barns Green, Horsham, Sussex. RH13 0NH. Telephone: 01403 730326 www.highbarnoils.co.uk

Holland and Barrett Headquarters, Samuel Ryder House, Townsend Drive, Nuneaton, Warwickshire, CV11 6XW www.hollandandbarrett.com

Hyperactive Children's Support Group, Mrs Sally Bunday, 71 Whyke Lane, Chichester, West Sussex, PO19 7PD, Telephone: 01243 539966 www.hacsg.org.uk

The Informed Parent (Vaccination Information), Ms Magda Taylor, PO Box 4481, Worthing, West Sussex, BN11 2WH, Telephone: 01903 212969 www.informedparent.co.uk

Institute of Optimum Nutrition, Avalon House, 72 Lower Mortlake Road, Richmond, Surrey, TW9 2JY Telephone: 0870 9791122 www.ion.ac.uk

The International Federation of Reflexologists, 8-9 Talbot Court, London, EC3V 0BP, Telephone: 0870 879 3562 www.intfedreflexologists.org

JABS (information on vaccine damage and compensation), Telephone: 01942 713565, www.jabs.org.uk

Just Organic Box Scheme, Freepost, Just Organic, www.justorganic.org.uk

Katzen-Luchenta, Jan, (Foresight American Branch Secretary), 51-31 North 18th Street, Phoenix, Arizona 85016, USA, Telephone (Mobile): 602 370 4036, (Home): 602 954 9540

La Leche League GB, PO Box 29, West Bridgford, Nottingham, NG2 7NP, Helpline: 0845 1202918, www.laleche.org.uk

The Life Centre, Yew Tree Lane, West Derby, Liverpool, L12 9HH, Telephone: 0151 228 0353, www.zoesplaceliverpool.org

The London Hazards Centre Trust Ltd, Hampstead Town Hall, 213 Haverstock Hill, London, SW3 4QP, Telephone: 0207 749 5999 www.lhc.org.uk

MacManaway, Dr Patrick, (Electromagnetism Surveyor), Westbank Natural Health Centre, Strathmilgo. Fife, KY14 7QP. Telephone: 01233 750253 www.geomancy.org.uk

The McCarrison Society, c/o The Institute of Brain Chemistry, and Human Nutrition, London Metropolitan University, 166-222 Holloway Road, London, N7 8BD. Telephone: 0207 133 2446 (afternoons only)

The National Association of Health Stores, Telephone: 0114 235 3478 Email: info@nahs.co.uk

The National Childbirth Trust (NCT), Alexandra House, Oldham Terrace, Acton, London, W3 6NH. Telephone: 0300 330 0771

National Pure Water Association, Mrs E McConagh, Melton Brand Farm, Melton Brand, Doncaster, DN5 7EB. Telephone: 01302 785542 www.tpa-uk.org.uk

The National Society for Research into Allergy (NSRA), PO Box 45, Hinckley, Leicestershire, LE10 1JY. Telephone: 01455 250175 www.patient.co.uk

Natural Family Planning (Fertility Education Trust), Mrs Colleen Norman, 218 Heathwood Road, Heath, Cardiff, Telephone: 02920 754628 www.fertilityet.org.uk

Nutri-Link Ltd, Parasite Information, Unit 24, Milber Trading Estate, Newton Abbot, Devon TW12 4SG Telephone: 0870 4054002 www.nutri-linkltd.co.uk

Organic Meat, Carole Hockley, Newton Farm, Fordingbridge, Nr Ringwood, Hampshire. Telephone: 01425 652542

Organic Farmers and Growers Association, The Old Estate Yard, Albrighton, Shrewsbury, Shropshire, SY4 3AG. Telephone: 0845 330 5122 / 01939 291800 www.organicfarmers.org.uk

The Organic Flower Company, 28 Mount Street, Shrewsbury, Shropshire, SY3 8QH. Telephone: 01743 358856 www.theorganicflowercompany.co.uk

OrganicAssistant, Compass House, Le Petit Val, Alderny, GY9 3UU. www.organicassistant.com

Passion For The Planet Radio, Zeal House, Deer Park Road, Wimbledon, London, SW19 3GY. www.passionfortheplanet.com

Pesticides Action Network, Development House, 56-64 Leonard Street, London, EC2A 4LT. Telephone: 0207 065 0905 www.pan-uk.org

Plastic Pipes, British Plastics Association, Chestwood, 3 Kneeton Park, Middleton Tyas, Richmond, DL10 6SB, Telephone: 01325 339184, www.plasticpipesgroup.com

Powerwatch, Alasdair and Jean Phillips, 2 Tower Road, Sutton, Ely, Cambridgeshire, CB6 2QA. Telephone: 01353 778814 www.powerwatch.co.uk www.enfields.org

Price Pottenger Foundation, Le Mesa, 4200 Wisconsin Avenue, NW380, Washington DC,

20016, USA . Telephone: 619 462 7600. www.westonaprice.org

Raworth College of Nutrition, 20-26 South Street, Dorking, Surrey, RH4 7HQ. Telephone: 01306 740150. www.raworth.com

Reeves, John (Mycorrhiza), Eastleigh, Greenfield Close, Joys Green, Lydbrook, Gloucestershire. GL17 9QU

Reflexologists, The International Federation of, 76-78 Edridge Road, Croydon, Surrey, CR0 1EF Telephone: 0870 8793562 www.intfedreflexologists.org

Riggs, Alfred (Electromagnetic and Geopathic Energy Surveyor), 52 St John's Fogge, Ashford, Kent, TN23 3GA Telephone: 01233 620036 www.alfredriggs.com

Riggs, Roy (Electromagnetic and Geopathic Energy Surveyor), 25 Coleridge Street, Poet's Corner, Hove, Sussex, BN3 5AB. Telephone: 01273 732523 Roy.riggs@ntlworld.com

Right From The Start, Sarah Woodhouse, Chief Executive, Welcome Cottage, Wiveton, Nr Holt, Norfolk NR25 7TH Telephone: 01263 740935 email: sarah@rightfromthestart.fsnet.co.uk

Riverford Organic Vegetables, Wash Barn, Buckfastleigh, Devon. TQ11 0LD www.riverford.co.uk

Royal College of Midwives, 15 Mansfield Street, London, W1, Telephone: 0207 580 3535 www.rcm.org.uk

SAFTA (Support after Termination for Abnormalities), 73 Charlotte Street, London, W1 1LB Telephone: 0207 439 6124

Scheibner, Dr Viera, 178 Govett's Leap Road, Blackheath, New South Wales, Australia. Telephone: 0061 24787 8203

The Scottish Institute of Reflexology, www.scottishreflexology.org

The Soil Association, South Plaza, Marlborough Street, Bristol, BS1 3NX, Telephone: 0117 314 500 (main), 0117 914 24444 (information), www.soilassociation.org

Special Foods, (Gluten-free root flours), 9207 Shotgun Court, Springfield, VA 22153, USA Telephone: 001 703 644 0991 www.specialfoods.com

Tom's of Maine, Tom's of Maine Professional Advocacy, 302 Lafayette Center, Kennebunk, ME 04043. www.tomsofmaine.com

"Ultrasound Unsound", Shane Ridley, Manor Barn, Thurloxton ,Taunton, Somerset, TA2 8RH

The University of Surrey, Department of Chemistry, Guildford, Surrey, GU2 7HX. Telephone: 01483 300800 www.surrey.ac.uk

The Vegetarian Society, Parkdale Dunham Road, Altringham, Cheshire, WA14 4QG. Telephone: 0161 925 2000 www.vegsoc.org

Vitacare Ltd (Dried Goat's Milk), Utopia Village Unit 1, 7 Shalcot Road, Primrose Hill, London, NW1 8LH. Telephone: 0800 328 5826 www.vitacare.co.uk

Weleda, Heanor Road, Ilkeston, Derbyshire, DE7 8BR. Telephone: 0115 944 8222 www.weleda.co.uk

What Doctors Don't Tell You, Satellite House, 2 Salisbury Road, London, SW19 4EZ. Telephone: 0870 444 9886, 0800 146054 www.wddty.co.uk

Wholistic Research Company, Unit 1 Fiver House Farm, Sandon Road, Therfield, Royston, Hertfordshire, SG8 9RE. Telephone: 0845 430 3100 www.wholistic research.com

WISH, Westminster City Council Drug and Alcohol Foundation, 18 Dartmouth Street, London, SW1H 9BL. Telephone: 0207 233 0400 www.daf-london.org.uk

Women's Environmental Network (WEN), 4 Pinchin Street, London, E1. Telephone: 0207 481 9004 www.wen.org.uk

Working Weekends on Organic Farms (WWOOF), PO Box 2154, Winslow, Buckingham, MK18 3WS. www.wwoof.org

The World Federation of Doctors who Respect Human Life, PO Box 17317, London, SW3 4WJ. Telephone: 0207 730 3059 www.doctorsfed.org.uk

Zed Books (Environment), 7 Cynthia Street, London, N1 9JF. Telephone: 020 7837 4014 www.zedbooks.co.uk

Zinc Bangles. Perfect Pillow, Unit A, Lantsbury Drive, Liverton North Industrial Estate, Liverton Mines, Nr Loftus, Cleveland, TS13 4QZ. Telephone: 01287 644444 or 01287 643333 www.aromarelief.co.uk

INDEX